SAVAGE EYE

Sa

MELVILLE

EDITED

THE KENT STATE

KENT, OHIO, AND

vage Eye

AND THE VISUAL ARTS

BY CHRISTOPHER STEN

UNIVERSITY PRESS

LONDON, ENGLAND

© 1991 by The Kent State University Press, Kent, Ohio 44242
ALL RIGHTS RESERVED
Library of Congress Catalog Card Number 91-9994
ISBN 0-87338-444-X
Manufactured in the United States of America

Library of Congress Cataloging-in-Publication Data

Savage eye : Melville and the visual arts / edited by Christopher
Sten.
    p. cm.
  Includes bibliographical references and index.
  ISBN 0-87338-444-X (cloth : alk.) ∞
  1. Melville, Herman, 1819–1891—Knowledge—Art. 2. Art and
literature—United States—History—19th Century. I. Sten,
Christopher, 1944– .
PS2388.A75S38 1991
813′.3—dc20   91-9994

British Library Cataloging-in-Publication data are available.

All authors have their muses.
Mine are named Jan, Caroline, and Elizabeth.
This book is dedicated to them.

Contents

Illustrations

"Long exile from Christendom and civilization inevitably restores a man to that condition in which God placed him, *i.e.* what is called savagery. . . . I myself am a savage. . . ."

—Chapter 57, *Moby-Dick*

Preface

This collection had its origin in an invitation to arrange the program for the 1986 meeting of the Melville Society in New York, an event scheduled to coincide with the annual convention of the Modern Language Association. Coincidentally, the society had been asked to celebrate the opening of the Herman Melville Study Center at the newly reconstructed South Street Seaport in lower Manhattan, an architecturally distinctive section of the city with which Melville had long been familiar. When I realized the society had never before featured a program on Melville's relation to the arts, I jumped at the chance to arrange a series of talks on the subject. Almost immediately it became clear there were many Americanists concentrating on the relatively more circumscribed field of "Melville and the *visual* arts" (there were, and are, so far as I know, just a few working on Melville and music or on Melville and dance). But it wasn't until the December 1986 meeting of the Melville Society itself that I first began fully to appreciate how much critical interest there is in the subject, or to sense that a collection of essays by various experts, on Melville and the visual arts, would help to fill a sizable gap, not just in Melville scholarship, but in the study of American life and literature of the nineteenth century. This collection is the result of an effort to capture some of that critical interest and to make it readily available to those having similar or related interests in nineteenth-century American literature and culture. My hope is that they will find, as I have, that their reading of Melville, and of American literary culture of the previous century, has been permanently altered, and enriched, by the discoveries presented here.

In bringing together the essays for this volume, I have been guided by the same principles that guided me in choosing the papers for the Melville Society program. As in that case, so here, I wanted the contributions to be fresh discussions based on original research, and I thought they would be most useful if they addressed one or both of the following questions: What did Melville know about the visual arts (here broadly defined to include not only painting, graphics, and sculpture but architecture as well)? and how is that knowledge manifested in his writings? The essays could focus on a single visual artist or on several, on a particular work of art or a whole genre. But they had to make, or try to make, an evidentiary connection with Melville's own work—not necessarily the kind that would hold up in a court of law, but at least the kind that reasonable people, accustomed to dealing with the slippery issue of sources, would find illuminating and useful and possibly even be willing to give their assent to. Above all, they had to try to make the kind of connection that would in some way extend our understanding of Melville and his writing.

It should be said that the collection as a whole does not attempt to provide a comprehensive overview of the whole question of Melville's relation to the visual arts. That would have resulted in a very different project from this one. In fact, a considerable amount of scholarly work has already been accomplished in this area, as the bibliography of secondary studies in Appendix B attests. A comprehensive overview, therefore, would have resulted in a good deal of duplication of existing scholarship. What this collection attempts to do is to supplement those several, scattered previous studies, to fill in some of the major gaps still remaining in our understanding of Melville's knowledge of the subject, and to make a general case for the importance of the visual arts as a significant (and still widely overlooked) source and shaping influence in Melville's writings. At the same time, this collection attempts to bring together in a single volume some of the very best work by some of the most talented interdisciplinary scholars currently working on Melville. In a relatively abbreviated way, my introduction does attempt to provide the kind of overview the subject demands, first by placing the essays in this collection in relation to the whole history of scholarship on the subject, and second by offering a complete survey of the whole history of Melville's engagement with the visual arts. While experts in the field are likely to be familiar with much, even most of what I have to say in the introduction, it does, I hope, serve a useful purpose in bringing virtually all of this diverse material together for the first time.

In a project such as this, an editor accumulates a great Heidelberg Tun full of debts, and I am happy to have the opportunity to acknowledge at least the largest ones here. This collection has, in fact, necessarily been a collaborative effort from the very start, and that has made it, for me at least, a joyful and enriching experience beyond compare. A scholar's life is often lonely, sometimes blessedly so, but the chance to work with a group of people who share a powerful interest, and to gain new friends in the process, is the chance of a lifetime. The bounty of wisdom and friendship I have received from this particular group of people is much more than I can ever repay. My apologies to all of them for not finishing the project sooner; my thanks to each of them for their good counsel, their unflagging support, and their patience beyond measure. To Don Yannella, then secretary-treasurer of the Melville Society, who gave the idea all the encouragement it needed at a time when it was little more than a hunch, and provided much valuable practical assistance in the weeks leading up to the 1986 program in New York City; to Bob Wallace, Gail Coffler, Dennis Berthold, and Allan Emery, who breathed life into the subject and stirred me to sense its still greater promise; to Sandy Marovitz, who believed in the project from the very beginning; to Doug Robillard, who gave much useful advice and support in the early stages, and in the end agreed to write not just one but two essays for the volume; to John Bryant, who by his formidable example, and friendly goading, challenged me to be a smarter editor than I knew how to be; to Hennig Cohen, who graciously agreed to read the introduction and took the time to make it better; and to Bob Wallace (once again) and to my students, Nancy Gwinn and Etsuko Taketani, who did the same. Thanks are due, too, to the George Washington University Committee on Research, which provided funds to secure use of most of the illustrations for this volume, and to Dean Robert Kenny of the Columbian College of Arts and Sciences, who made sure I had some of the time, if not all the "Strength, Cash, and Patience!" that the editor of a project like this requires. To the editorial staff at The Kent State University Press—John Hubbell, Julia Morton, and Linda Cuckovich—as well as Jeanne West, I am most grateful for practical assistance of another kind at every stage. No editor ever received more encouragement and support from his publisher, or was ever treated with greater attentiveness and kindness. Last of all, thanks to my wife and daughters, who helped in ways that I have tried to explain in the dedication.

SAVAGE EYE

Melville and the Visual Arts:
An Overview

CHRISTOPHER STEN

*J*n the introduction to his 1857–58 lecture on Roman statuary, Melville spoke with modesty about his claim to expertise, saying he was "neither critic nor connoisseur" and could admit "no pretension" to the kind of cultivation found in the people who might usually be heard to talk on such topics. "I shall speak of the impressions," he told his audience, "produced upon my mind as one who looks upon a work of art as he would upon a violet or a cloud, and admires or condemns as he finds an answering sentiment awakened in his soul. My object is to paint the appearance of Roman statuary objectively and afterward to speculate upon the emotions and pleasure that appearance is apt to excite in the human breast" (*Melville as Lecturer* 129–30).[1] Though it understates Melville's attainments, this rare self-assessment contains an important kernel of truth about one of America's most extraordinary writers. Melville approached the subject of art as an American *naif* or "savage," with no formal training and few preconceptions, but a powerful imagination and an easy self-assurance. In this lecture, repeated many times over the course of several months, and in his dealings with artistic matters generally, his interest was personal and subjective, not technical or social, and only marginally historical. As in this lecture, he was concerned simply to capture his own response to the works of art under consideration, to report his impressions, without much concern for how they might be taken.

This is not to say that Melville was ignorant or innocent about his subject. When he started on his lecture tour late in 1857, he had just

1

returned from an extensive European trip, which included several weeks in Rome (and other Italian cities containing sculpture important to his lecture), where he visited not only the galleries and museums, the public squares and courtyards, but also the studios of several practicing sculptors. What is even more important, this exploration of the world of art and artists is hardly an isolated incident in Melville's remarkably diverse career. From his youth on, he demonstrated a keen or "savage" eye— avid, eager, grasping—for the kind of experience and self-knowledge that the visual arts can provide. Untutored, even "uncultivated" or lacking systematic education though he might have been, Melville spoke, and wrote, out of a lifelong interest in the visual arts, one which deepened in his later decades to the point of becoming a passion. If not an expert, he was at least a true *amateur,* a lover of the arts, one of the least recognized ones in the nineteenth century, and one of the most fascinating.

Although it is not always readily apparent, one can see considerable evidence of Melville's passion for the arts in almost any of his writings, and in a moment I will turn to an overview of this subject. But for a brief, dramatic demonstration, one has only to visit the Herman Melville Memorial Room in the Berkshire Athenaeum, where it is possible to see in an instant several of the many paintings, prints, and other works of art which Melville collected in his later years. There one can instantly appreciate how important the visual arts were to him, and sense how instrumental they must have been, and were, in the shaping of his life and writing. Included in this varied collection are watercolors inspired by Melville's own writings, such as the one of Rock Rodondo, from "The Encantadas," given to him by the American artist, Peter Toft; a haunting illustration of Satan, by John Martin, for *Paradise Lost;* engravings of pastoral scenes and classical landscapes by Nicholas Poussin, Copley Fielding, and J. M. W. Turner; an engraving of one of George Romney's many portraits of Lady Hamilton; a seascape by Charles Herbert Woodbury; a lithograph of an American whaler by Nathaniel Currier; and a substantial collection of objets d'art.

These provide just a hint of the many artistic works once owned by Melville and now available at the Athenaeum, however. Robert K. Wallace ("Melville's Prints") has recently catalogued what amounts to a sizable collection of Melville's acquisitions in the pictorial arts, and thanks to his work and the labors of a growing number of other scholars over the last forty years, we are beginning to get a clearer understanding of the extent of Melville's experience with this copious, many-faceted subject—the work of artists he is known to have seen, referred to, and commented upon, in his fiction, poetry, and miscellaneous writings, as well as what he is known to have owned. In both instances, the range of materials is remarkable. Melville, a man of modest means, managed to acquire nearly three hundred prints and engravings, several original paintings, and at least a few pieces of sculpture; and his own writings—particularly his journals and the fiction and poetry from *Moby-Dick* on—are studded with an even more various number of references to artists, classical and modern, across the whole range of the visual arts, including architecture, sculpture, painting, engraving, and even caricature or cartoons.[2] All of this suggests the need to reassess not only the whole question of Melville's "sources," which even most specialists continue to think of in strictly literary terms, but also the larger question of Melville's relationship (and, indirectly, the relationship of other American writers of the previous century), to the arts in America, Europe, the Mediterranean, and other parts of the world, as we learn more and more about what was available to him and his contemporaries in Boston, New York, Albany, and elsewhere, or what he sought out on his travels, particularly his trips abroad. Beyond the simple if impressive matter of the range of Melville's interests in the arts, there is the question of influence, indebtedness, or appropriation—the question of Melville's use of the other arts in his own work. Because the author is one of America's most compelling and closely studied literary figures, we are naturally interested in these questions, for as the essays in this collection demonstrate, they can lead to a richer understanding of Melville's writings and a fuller comprehension of the man—of his work and vision.

What can be known about Melville's early engagement with the arts, particularly before he began his career as a writer, is relatively sketchy; Melville's biographers are all but silent on the subject. They have sometimes had a bit more to say about Melville's engagement with the arts in his later years, in the late 1850s and after, but the matter has generally been overlooked, and much underestimated. The little we do know about the subject in his formative years suggests a more than modestly cultivated, enriching family background and an unusually hungry if not yet well-formed natural inclination toward art, which from the start was closely integrated with an early love of books and fascination with travel. Thus Melville's interest was the product of a combination of early exposure to a range of classical and modern European works and a natural bent or inclination—a strong visual sensibility and a powerful visual memory. In *Redburn*, the quasi-autobiographical novel which treats the author's childhood and adolescent years, Melville recalls with fondness "several oil paintings and rare old engravings of my father's," which hung in the dining room of his mother's Hudson River village home, and "two large green French portfolios of colored prints," including pictures of

Versailles and various rural scenes, which he and his siblings would spread on the floor and gaze at "with neverfailing delight" (6; see also Gilman, *Melville's Early Life* 35); and there is the enchanting little glass ship, which may or may not have had a counterpart in Melville's own life. While these may be embroidered memories, there is reason to take them as *representative* of Melville's own early experience, even if not precisely true in every detail. Also, from *Pierre* and other, more exacting biographical and autobiographical sources—Raymond Weaver, Eleanor Melville Metcalf, and Jay Leyda—we know there were portraits of his parents and grandparents available to him, including a Gilbert Stuart rendering of his maternal grandfather, Peter Gansevoort, the Revolutionary War hero; from these portraits Melville would have gained exposure to the painting of personalities. But otherwise we have to reconstruct what Melville knew about the arts, in his childhood and adult years, from the artistic allusions in his imaginative writings; from the brief references to or discussions of artists in his journals and miscellaneous works; and, in his later years, from the markings in the books on art and artists which he is known to have borrowed or collected, and from the many prints and engravings he assembled over the same period.

From the start of his career, Melville showed that he was at least modestly conversant with the arts and capable of developing his subject by using analogies to arts other than literature, though, ironically, his first references to the arts almost certainly derived from his reading of other works of literature, particularly Byron's *Childe Harold's Pilgrimage* (see Star 38–39). Perhaps most importantly, he showed a habit of mind that by the time of *Moby-Dick* (1851) he had developed into a high art in itself. In his juvenilia, "Fragments from a Writing Desk," he reveals a basic knowledge of some of the standard classical works of sculpture (*Apollo, Jupiter,* the *Venus of Medici*), of the best known architectural orders (Doric, Ionian, and Corinthian), and of some of the most important artists of classical antiquity (the sculptor Phidias and the painter Apelles, in particular), though he does so in the very rudimentary way one might if he had only read about ancient art in a schoolbook or popular history. *Typee, Omoo,* and *Mardi,* the first of Melville's more mature works, do not lend themselves particularly well, because of their exotic Polynesian subject matter, to the display of a rich knowledge of Western artistic culture. But in fact these works do contain several brief references to the arts: the description in *Typee* of the native taboo-figure, Marnoo, as a "Polynesian Apollo" (135) and an aside on the Gothic imps in Teniers's portraits of saints (211); an allusion in *Omoo* to a print in Hogarth's *The Rake's Progress* (310); and a mention in *Mardi* of Phidias's *Jupiter,* the *Dying Gladiator* or "Dying Gaul," the Elgin

Marbles, and Sir Edwin Landseer, whose paintings of animals had made him famous. In one particularly memorable instance, the "Time and Temples" chapter in *Mardi,* there is an epic display of learning regarding the history of architecture. In this, the first of many indications that the image of the temple was of special importance to him, Melville pulls together references to more than a score of remarkable old structures, ranging from Nero's House of Gold to the Alhambra, the Parthenon, and the Strasbourg Cathedral, to emphasize the idea that "great towers take time to construct. And so of all else" (228–29). *Mardi* in particular, like *Moby-Dick* and *Pierre,* also contains evidence, as Morris Star has pointed out, of Melville's use of Flaxman's illustrations for a well-known edition of Dante's *Divine Comedy.*[3] What is just as significant, these early works show a sharp pictorial sense, and more than a passing interest in native versions of the visual arts of various South Sea island populations—the wood-carving, the shrines and ancient Druid-like monuments, the tattooing and face-painting, the tapa-making, and the colorful tapa-decoration.

By the time of *Redburn* (1849) and *White-Jacket* (1850) Melville's techniques of allusion had become more sophisticated, and his firsthand experience of the arts seems to have become more sharply focused. At the same time, there is a noticeable shift from the early bookish preoccupation with classical sculpture and architecture to the work of some of the notable painters and printmakers of more recent times, even some verging on his own era. Now we find, in *Redburn,* for example, not just allusions to the Gobelin tapestry, the Laocoön statue, Caryatides, and the temple of Aphrodite in Corinth, but references to an "old quarto" Hogarth (143), "the dark, moody hand" of Salvator Rosa (275)—one of Melville's favorite artists, called "Savage Rosa" in the eighteenth century—the beggar-boys of Murillo (247), the "ever youthful Apollo" of Guido Reni (228), as well as pastoral scenes of Claude Lorrain or possibly one of the many painters from the Dutch School (6),[4] and allusions to St. Paul's Cathedral in London and to Lord Nelson's statue and a series of buildings in Liverpool, where the young hero attempts to retrace his father's footsteps with the help of illustrations from an outdated guidebook. And in *White-Jacket,* we encounter not just casual references to the *Dying Gladiator,* the Parthenon, the Alhambra, St. Peter's and St. Paul's, York Minster, and the Bunker Hill Monument, we find also descriptions of a specific print of Hogarth's, with borrowings from others (377)—identified by Morris Star (153–56) as belonging to the series, *Industry and Idleness*—and knowledgeable allusions to the signature work of Wilkie and Cruikshank as well as Teniers (387). Douglas Robillard, in a ground-breaking essay on "The Visual Arts in

Melville's *Redburn*," makes the point also that Melville came to use the "art analogy" in a way that is not simply decorative but structural, so that "the imagery of art" reveals "at the level of language what is concealed at the level of narrative." Robillard demonstrates this to be the case particularly in *Redburn,* in the scene of the eponymous hero's visit with his young friend Harry Bolton to a house of promiscuity known as Aladdin's Palace, a scene which relies on a series of seemingly learned but ultimately false or fictional references to the arts to create its effect of decadence and corruption.[5]

What accounts for this dramatic new display of Melville's knowledge of art is hard to say, for the biographical record for these years is still quite slim. Remarkably, it occurred before Melville had made the 1849–50 trip to England and the Continent that provided his first opportunity to see the art of Europe in any extensive way. His earlier trip to Liverpool, as a youth of 19, at best offered him the opportunity to view the work at the famous Liverpool Athenaeum; but there is no evidence that he ever visited that institution. Whatever the precise cause, this growing sophistication clearly had as much to do with his marriage to Elizabeth Shaw, daughter of the prominent Judge Lemuel Shaw of Boston, where Melville made several visits before and after his wedding in the summer of 1847, as it did with his move, that same summer, from Lansingburg to New York City. There he had access to several museums and reading rooms, and to the libraries of a circle of new friends centering on Evert and George Duyckinck. The museums in New York then flourishing included the National Academy of Design (established in 1826), the American Art-Union (originally established in 1838 as the Apollo Association), the New York Gallery of the Fine Arts (established in 1846), and, somewhat later, the Düsseldorf Gallery (established in 1849) and the International Art Union (established in 1849), the latter two specializing in European art. On October 6, 1847, Melville was the guest of Evert Duyckinck at the opening of the Art-Union's new quarters on Broadway, where he met the American painter William S. Mount and saw paintings by Thomas Cole, William Page, Regis Gignoux, Thomas Hicks, and Thomas Sully, in particular one featuring "bathing nymphs" which, according to Duyckinck, "suggested Fayaway."[6] Still other evidence suggests that his gallery-going was more frequent than this incident alone might suggest, and that it included museums where European art was regularly on display. In a significant recent find, John Gretchko unearthed the fact that, earlier in this same year, Melville paid the one-dollar lifetime membership fee giving him unlimited access to the holdings of the New York Gallery of the Fine Arts, which was then known for its paintings by American artists but included also several works by old masters.

Boston, early considered "the Athens of America," remained for most of the century the chief repository of European art in the United States. Thanks to the New England Museum, the waterfront gallery at Faneuil Hall, and in particular the Boston Athenaeum, which opened its gallery in 1826 (later forming the nucleus of the Museum of Fine Arts), Boston afforded Melville several unusual opportunities to see both American and European painting and sculpture, including copies of an extensive array of famous classical works. During the mid-1800s, however, New York was quickly becoming the center of museum art in America, and although it was much stronger in American than European art in the early decades, it also provided venues where Melville could have seen and learned about European art, ancient as well as modern. Melville's residence in New York also made it relatively easy for him to see or purchase copies of engravings, the most popular form of visual art in America at the time, such as those issued by the American Art-Union, among other sources, and to borrow or purchase books relating to the arts. He is known, for example, to have bought "Cary's Dante," in an edition which probably included several of Flaxman's illustrations of the *Divine Comedy*.[7] This is just one of more than fifty titles on the visual arts that Melville owned or borrowed in his lifetime (see Appendix A). The personal library of his friend, Evert Duyckinck, was especially rich in illustrated literary works and in engravings, though unfortunately these have not been catalogued.

However, it was Melville's new relationship with the Shaws in Boston that left the clearest trail of evidence of his growing interest in the visual arts. Thanks to the connections of Judge Shaw, a founding proprietor of the Boston Athenaeum, Melville was able to borrow books on art, as well as other subjects, from that institution.[8] He is believed to have done so at least three times in 1848: Roger de Piles's *The Art of Painting, with the Lives and Characters of above 300 of the Most Eminent Painters . . . to which is Added, An Essay towards an English School* (London, [1754?]), Charles Eastlake's *Materials for a History of Oil Painting* (London, 1847), and Ruskin's *Modern Painters,* volume 2 (London, 1846). And in early 1849 he is believed to have borrowed Eastlake's *Contributions to the Literature of the Fine Arts* (London, 1848) and John Burnet's *A Treatise on Painting* (London, 1834–37). Much of what a relative neophyte would want to know about the history of European art, at mid-century, can be found in these few volumes.

With his extended visit to London and the Continent at the end of 1849, Melville's exposure to the European tradition of the visual arts deepened dramatically. There, in the course of two months, he took in a considerable number of the sights of London, Paris, and Cologne, and of several other towns or cities along his way. Fortunately, he kept a journal, so we know quite precisely, in most cases, just what he took time to examine. It is fair to say, moreover, that insofar as this journal reflects his movements over the months of November and December 1849, this was a trip devoted almost exclusively to absorbing the art and the architecture of the European tradition, and to a lesser extent of ancient Mediterranean culture. The search for a London publisher of *White-Jacket* was what prompted Melville to take the journey at this time, but it had been his plan all along to make a six-month tour through the Continent, reaching all the way to Rome. Not until he met with difficulty finding a publisher did he decide to confine his tour to Northern Europe. As might be expected, Melville saw a great many paintings, but he mentions seeing also several works of statuary: the Nineveh sculptures at the British Museum; a bust of Lord Nelson at Windsor Castle and Nollekins' bust of Dr. Johnson at a Fleet Street tavern; an "[a]dmirable collection of antique statuary" at the Louvre ("Beats the British Museum" [54]); and other pieces in Paris and its environs. And he remarks on seeing several notable works of architecture as well, including Canterbury Cathedral; Notre Dame Cathedral; the Hôtel de Cluny, which surmounts the vaulted ruins of the Roman palace of Thermes (referred to in the "Moby Dick" chapter of Melville's epic [161]); the unfinished cathedral at Cologne (cited in *Moby-Dick* as an analogue to Ishmael's unfinished cetological "system" [127]); the medieval fortress, Ehrenbreitstein, near Coblenz; and "the old Cathedral & the townhouse" at Aix-la-Chapelle (67).

Melville saw more paintings than anything else on this European sojourn, but it is worth noting that many of them inspired only a phrase or two, at most, in his journal. Indeed, most of the works he viewed in Paris and Cologne, on the second and third legs of his journey, merited hardly a mention; in many cases, not even the names of the artists have been recorded. Of the collection at the Hôtel des Invalides, for example, Melville says only, "Gallery of paintings." Clearly this is a Melville "on holiday," one who—like Americans of every generation—was quickly trying to take in more sights than he could absorb, and he seems to have grown a bit tired of the process by the time he left London for Paris. Practically the only works on the Continent he mentions by name are some "plates of Albert Durer, & Holbein" which he saw at the Bibliotheque Royale in Paris (57) and what he called "the celebrated *Descent from the Cross* by Rubens" at St. Peter's Church in Cologne (62). By contrast, in London, on the initial leg of his trip, Melville typically recorded at least some basic details, and sometimes something of his own impressions, of the paintings he saw there.

The range of paintings Melville commented on is hardly extraordinary, but it is important to notice just what he witnessed, if only because it constitutes a part of the larger picture of his engagement with the arts. From the Italian Renaissance, he mentions seeing Titians at Hampton Court and Dulwich Gallery; "The Cartoons" of Mantegna (or, perhaps, the more famous ones of Raphael), also at Hampton Court; and at least one Taddeo Gaddi at the National Gallery. From the Northern Renaissance, he saw Rembrandts, or the work of his pupils, again at Hampton Court and the National Gallery (including an unidentified "Jew" attributed to Rembrandt); a few other works, which he claimed to have looked at for an hour (74); and the "mottled horse of Wouvermans" (34) at Dulwich. From the Italian Baroque period, he records seeing Guido Renis at the National Gallery and Hampton Court. And from the Northern Baroque, Lelys and Van Dycks at Hampton Court and the one Rubens in Cologne. Also "gems" by some of his favorite artists—Murillo, Claude, and Salvator Rosa—at Dulwich, and several sea-pieces, including possibly Turner's *Battle of Trafalgar* (see Wallace, "New Evidence" [8]); portraits of naval heroes; and a "fine painting" of St. Paul, by Benjamin West, at Greenwich Hospital.

The fates, however, saved the best for last. Shortly after Melville returned to London from the Continent, he received an invitation for breakfast at the home of Samuel Rogers, a well-known wit and man of letters who owned one of the finest art collections in London at the time. In his journal, Melville commented only on the "Superb paintings" (77) he saw on display in Rogers's apartments on the occasion of the first of two breakfasts he shared with him on December 20 and 23, 1849. However, as Wallace has demonstrated in a series of illuminating essays on Melville and J. M. W. Turner, this proved for Melville to be a momentous encounter personally—an important step in his own education in the arts—and one which was soon to affect his own work, from the writing of *Moby-Dick* until the end of his career. According to Wallace, who quotes from Murray's 1849 *Handbook for London,* Rogers's well-known collection included at least one representative work by each of the following old and more recent masters: Claude, Giorgione, Guido, Paul Veronese, Poussin, Raphael, Tintoretto, Titian, Velasquez, Michelangelo, Rembrandt, Rubens, Gainsborough, Richard Wilson, and Sir Joshua Reynolds. Most importantly, it also included several Turners—an oil, a watercolor, a sketch, and a large number of engravings. Though none of these included the four late works on whaling themes, which became so important to the construction and the aesthetic philosophy of *Moby-Dick,* Wallace builds a masterful case for Melville's having learned a great deal *about* these works from Rogers and from a combination of written sources and conversations with several other contemporary authorities on Turner. Among the latter were Peter Cunningham, author of Murray's 1849 *Handbook for London,* and the American painter Charles R. Leslie, who had access to Turner's private studio; Melville met and dined with both men and other Turner connoisseurs during the last days of his 1849 trip in London. Rogers was the most important of the personal contacts Melville made in the final days of his journey; he provided an occasion for Melville to see several Turners all at once and to hear a learned collector discourse on the wonders of England's greatest painter. Thackeray, Wallace argues, was the most important of the literary sources; his 1845 review, in *Fraser's Magazine,* of Turner's *The Whale Ship* and *Whalers,* from the Royal Academy Exhibition of that year, provided a written version of the process of perceiving Turner's whale that served as the model for Melville's rendering of Ishmael's encounter with the mesmerizing painting of a whale in the "Spouter-Inn" chapter of *Moby-Dick* (12). To be sure, there are other evidences of Melville's indebtedness to Turner in *Moby-Dick,* not the least of which is to be found in that pivotally important Spouter-Inn painting itself, as Wallace and others, particularly Richard S. Moore (127–36), have shown.[9] It is a story to which Wallace adds a new chapter in this collection of essays, in his discussion of the mysterious Bulkington, a figure through whom Wallace sees Melville paying secret homage to Turner, who was then dying in London.

No other pictorial artist, it now seems certain, can be said to have had so profound an effect on Melville's *Moby-Dick* as Turner; the impact of this visual artist ranks with the impact of literary artists like Shakespeare, Hawthorne, or the authors of the Bible in the shaping of Melville's book. As Wallace argues, Turner in effect opened Melville's eyes to the art of abstraction. But the works of other artists, it has long been known, do enter into Melville's magnum opus, either substantially or, as is more often the case, incidentally in the form of allusions. Examples of the latter include references to works on mythological subjects: "Cellini's cast Perseus" in connection with Ahab (110; see note in Hendricks House ed. 670); "Phidias's marble Jove" (291; see note in Hendricks House ed. 774: 'The Greek sculptor . . . probably did no work in marble'; see also *Mardi* 254); and Michelangelo's portrayal of God (315) in connection with various descriptions of the great whale. Allusions to artists also include references to contemporary works of public sculpture, such as those of Napoleon, George Washington, and Lord Nelson in Paris, Baltimore, and London, respectively, or in connection with the practice of masthead standing (136). In some instances, however, Melville made very substantial use of artistic subjects, as in the discussion of several seascapes and whaling scenes by particular painters and engravers in chapters 55–57. These are important chapters in *Moby-Dick,* for they bring into focus one of Ishmael's chief preoccupations—the difficulty, or impossibility, that even the most dedicated artist faces, of ever capturing a true, undistorted likeness of the living whale.

Stuart M. Frank, in a handsomely illustrated study entitled *Herman Melville's Picture Gallery: Sources and Types of the "Pictorial" Chapters of* Moby-Dick, has carefully examined the visual sources and many of their analogues in these chapters, and though much of his effort was anticipated in a ground-breaking dissertation by Sumner W. D. Scott in 1950, a good deal of what Frank offers is new and valuable. He looks first at the "Monstrous Pictures of Whales" in chapter 55, what Melville calls "those pictorial delusions": Guido Reni's Perseus rescuing Andromeda from the sea-monster; William Hogarth's *Perseus Descending* (see notes in Hendricks House ed. 746–47); and the many representations of the whale found in more recent scientific literature. According to Ishmael, it is important to add that all of these seem to have their origin in the "oldest Hindoo, Egyptian, and Grecian sculptures" (225). Frank also looks closely at "Of the Less Erroneous Pictures of Whales, and the True Pictures of Whaling Scenes," in Melville's next chapter, those found in the principal literary sources of *Moby-Dick,* namely, Thomas Beale, J. Ross Browne, and William Scoresby, Jr. Most of the works examined in connection with this chapter are engravings by William John Huggins, William James Linton, John Halpin, and W. and D. Lizars, and Melville dismisses all except a few of those in Beale as untrue. Only the engravings of oils by the French painter Ambroise Louis Garneray and those of an engraver whom Melville identified only as "H. Durand" (identified by Frank as Jean-Baptiste-Henri Durand-Brager), in addition to the few in Beale, earn any praise from Melville, for the simple reason that they alone bear some resemblance to the real thing—a living whale, as he is known by the men who hunt him. Melville's subject in chapter 57 would at first seem inappropriate to this discussion, because it treats handicraft rather than fine arts representations of whales "In Paint; In Teeth; In Wood; In Sheet-Iron; In Stone; In Mountains; In Stars." But just the opposite is true. For in fact, Melville argues here for a theory of primitivism in art according to which the artist who is closest to Nature is the one whose work is most likely to be true. This is not to say that Melville was calling for a populist or primitive art, such as one might find only in the anonymous makers of scrimshaw whales and corset stays, but that he was insisting on a sense of immediacy and honesty in the creation of any work of art—a feeling of liveliness, or of something beyond what the eye can see, as well as accuracy of representation. What was required was a "barbaric spirit and suggestive-ness" such as Ishmael says he found in the Hawaiian savage who can be seen patiently fashioning a warclub, or in "the prints of that fine old German savage, Albert Durer" (232).[10]

Even more than *Moby-Dick*, *Pierre* shows Melville's ever-deepening interest in the visual arts, in the range of allusions and in the way the visual arts are integrated into the book's plot and theme. Here we find references to the architectural ruins of ancient Palmyra; the Egyptian colossus of Memnon; the massive sepulcher in honor of Mausolus (one of the seven wonders of the ancient world, sculpture Melville is likely to have seen at the British Museum); the Laocoön statue; and the leaden Titan, or *Bassin d'Encelade*, of Balthazar Marsy, which Melville had seen in his 1849 visit to Versailles. We also find mention and extensive use of the Cenci of Guido Reni (or a copy), which provided an important precedent for treating the themes of incest and parricide found in *Pierre;* the landscapes of Thomas Gainsborough which figure in a discussion of the differences between the "picturesque" and the "povertiresque" (276–78); John Flaxman's illustrations of Homer and Dante; and the master-works (or, more particularly, obvious fakes) of Rubens, Raphael, Michelangelo, Domenichino, and da Vinci. Few of these references are incidental. The figure of Marsy's Titan, for example, is important to Melville's working out of the Enceladus theme, and to the young Pierre's fate, in the latter portion of book 25, and provides another occasion for him to speak, as he had in *Moby-Dick*, of the superiority of Nature to art—of its greater truthfulness (346). Much of the book, of course, hinges on the question of the authenticity of art, and on the question of its reliability as representation, as was the case also in *Moby-Dick*. The central ambiguity that Melville's hero faces, the question of whether the mysterious Isabel is in fact Pierre's half-sister, is mirrored in the ambiguity of the various portraits—the two paintings of the elder Glendenning encountered in the early chapters of the novel and the portrait of the anonymous stranger they see in the gallery in New York at the end, who seems suddenly to look as much like Isabel as Pierre's own father had. The whole question of the authenticity of the art that appears to support Isabel's claims is played out against a historical back-drop of New York in the 1840s and 1850s, when the galleries were known to be full of European fakes; Melville makes something of this then-current history in the concluding pages of his novel, when Pierre, Isabel, and Lucy visit a New York gallery on their way to the Battery. But the question of the authenticity of the visual arts, particularly of painting, in America, is simply another version of what was for Melville an even more central question, namely, the authenticity of the literary arts in which he was himself engaged, and which he portrays in his novel in the various figures of the literary artists living in the "Apostles," most notably Pierre himself and the troubling figure of Plotinus Plinlimmon, whose reliability as a touchstone is repeatedly brought into question.[11]

The series of short works that Melville wrote for *Putnam's Monthly* and *Harper's* in the mid-1850s shows something of a shift to what might be called the "architectural phase" of his career, although as Curtis Dahl has shown, Melville's interest in the symbolic relation between character and architectural style can be seen even earlier.[12] To be sure, not all of the magazine pieces Melville published in this period hinge on architectural images, tropes, and settings. But a substantial number of them do, including "The Piazza," "Bartleby, a Story of Wall Street," "The Lightning-Rod Man," and "The Bell-Tower," which together represent more than half of *The Piazza Tales* (1853–56), and "Poor Man's Pudding and Rich Man's Crumbs." "The Two Temples," "The Paradise of Bachelors," "Jimmy Rose," "I and My Chimney," and "The Apple-Tree Table," which represent more than half of Melville's uncollected works of short fiction. Sanford Marovitz examines several of these stories (as well as the novels which precede them) in his essay on "Melville's Temples" for this volume, and finds both an increased emphasis on architectural matters and a new sophistication in the art of storytelling. For Marovitz, the two are closely related. Moreover, in most cases, it should be emphasized, the architecture in question is an architecture that Melville knew firsthand, though his treatment of the various architectural styles and landmarks, more often than not, seems informed by his reading as well—of Ruskin, in particular, and of the American architectural theorist and landscape painter Andrew Jackson Downing, whose *Architecture for Country Houses, Part I: Cheap Cottages and Farm Houses* (1850) Melville apparently knew quite well.[13] Examples of structures familiar to Melville range from the simple examples of the chimney at Arrowhead and the "piazza" he arranged to have added to his farmhouse in Pittsfield, to the Wall Street of New York where his brother worked as a lawyer and the "Temple First" of New York's Trinity Church, Richard Upjohn's Gothic Revival construction completed in 1846 and toured by Melville in January 1848, to the series of buildings in London which Melville visited in 1849, including the theatre of "Temple Second."[14] Additional examples are the elaborate living and working quarters of "The Paradise of Bachelors"; and the Guild Hall of "Rich Man's Crumbs."[15] Vicki Halper Litman and Timothy Dow Adams both argue that Melville was very much a man of his time, seeing—as both Ruskin and Downing had—the character of a building's inhabitant in its architectural form. But both scholars also show him, in other contexts, as criticizing this then popular notion on the grounds of its superficiality. Suffice it to say that discussion of what Downing called "tasteless temples" was very keen during the 1840s and 1850s, and Melville, in the stories of this period, can be assumed to be trying to capitalize on the timeliness of that interest.[16]

Extending these earlier findings, Bryan Short, in a comprehensive essay written for this collection, demonstrates that even Melville's early responses to architecture reveal a dichotomy in his aesthetic philosophy which by the mid-1850s had developed into an anti-architectural, anti-visual arts theory of literature. In Short's view, the gap between literature and the visual arts split wide open, for Melville, in "The Bell-Tower," only to be healed again in his 1856–57 trip to Europe and the Holy Land. That healing is evidenced in Melville's unexpected turn, once back in America, to lecturing on Roman statuary and in the equally unpredictable turn, soon thereafter, to the writing of poetry. But it is at best a complex healing, and the poems in *Timoleon,* for instance, Short says, should not be read as constituting a reaffirmation of the values of monumentality or the eternal ideals of Classicism so much as providing evidence of Melville's discovery of the vital immediacy and perspectivism of all art.

The short fiction of Melville's mid-career shows evidence of his interest in other arts besides architecture, as one might expect, but it does so, typically, in a masked way—so much so that it has taken a good deal of sleuthing to bring that interest into plain view. Two stories from this period—"Bartleby" and "The Tartarus of Maids"—carry evidence of Melville's knowledge of two famous paintings by well-known American artists: *Caius Marius Amidst the Ruins of Carthage* (1807) by the historical painter John Vanderlyn, and *The Notch of the White Mountains* (1839) by the celebrated landscape artist Thomas Cole. Melville is likely to have seen both of these works in person, if not in the original, then in a copy or an engraving. As Wyn Kelley and John Gretchko report in their respective essays here, Melville had ample opportunity to see the work of both painters in the late 1840s and early 1850s, most likely through the exhibitions of the American Art-Union in New York or its annual distribution of select engravings to its thousands of members, such as Melville's good friend, Evert Duyckinck.

Both Kelley and Grethcko, like Litman, Dow, Dahl, and Moore before them, portray a Melville who was well-versed in the artistic controversies of his time, whether they concerned the waning popularity (and changing conception) of historical painting or the growing favor of landscape art in America. Kelley argues that Melville found in Vanderlyn's *Marius,* and in the obituaries of the artist which appeared after his death in 1853, an image of the failed hero that entered into his conception of several of his characters from this period, especially Bartleby and Israel Potter; that image also played an important role in Melville's growing sense of the powerful influence of historical forces in bringing about the ruin of individual lives. Gretchko, in turn, argues that Melville transforms the language and imagery of Cole's *The Notch* into a cruel, winter landscape in "The Tartarus of Maids" with the objective, finally, of spoofing the whole notion of the sublime, which Cole's work, until his death in 1848, epitomized. Though Gretchko is working with very different sources, his view is consistent with the views of Moore and Klaus Poenicke, both of whom argue that in his introduction to *The Piazza Tales* Melville was critiquing the European notion that the sublime, as embodied in the mountains and wilderness of North America, was America's peculiar birthright.[17] More generally, in these various works of magazine fiction, Melville seems intent on undercutting, or ironizing, the "picturesque" or prettified view of life which then dominated American culture, and substituting his own ironic, or more balanced, one.[18]

Virtually all of the pieces of this period can be regarded as featuring the author's questioning of the prevailing picturesque values, in the arts and in life more generally. Nowhere is this more evident than in "I and My Chimney," which details the narrator's fight to protect his unfashionable old chimney from the attacks of a series of projectors—including, most emphatically, his wife; a local "modern" architect; and his neighbors generally, one of whom, signing his letters "Claude," objects to his chimney because it is a blight on the landscape. Repeatedly Melville argues in these pieces for a more substantive aesthetic, one that takes into account practical human needs and does not try to paper over the more unsightly aspects of a world marked by such evils as poverty. Yet as John Bryant shows in another essay in this volume, Melville in this period did not so much seek to abandon or destroy the popular conception of the picturesque as to "deconstruct" it—to view it in more complex terms which enrich rather than negate it, and bring it into active tension with the darker forces of the "real" that one is likely to see only in a close-up. This shift is, of course, in keeping with the larger cultural and artistic shift that occurred around mid-century, from the noble, poetic ideal of nature to a realistic view which had "quieter ambitions," in the words of art historian Barbara Novak, "and seemed to give nature itself more say in the dialogue between nature and art that determined the course of landscape painting."[19] Needless to say, a comparable shift toward "realism" was occurring about the same time in the literary arts as well, and not just in Melville's writings.

Melville's major-length works from this period—*Israel Potter* (1855) and *The Confidence-Man* (1857)—are attenuated, ironic pieces, and seem to reflect a diminished interest in the arts on Melville's part. But this is not entirely true. To be sure, there are incidental references in *Israel Potter* to sculpture and architecture in Paris, Pisa, and London (particularly Christopher Wren's St. Paul's Cathedral); and in *The Confidence-Man* to the Piazza, at Covent Garden, of Inigo Jones; to Schiller (the essays on aesthetics in particular); to the elaborate garden cemeteries of Auburn and Greenwood outside Boston and New York City; to the Memnon statue and "Murillo's wild beggar-boys" (244), both familiar icons to Melville; and to an unnamed statue in the Pitti Palace in Florence (which Melville had not yet visited). But two of the essays included in this volume, those by Hennig Cohen and Helen Trimpi, demonstrate that Melville's interest in the visual arts can sometimes be found in unexpected places, if the investigator is resourceful and conversant with the author's habits of composition. Cohen, who has published frequently on the visual arts in Melville's writings, argues that Melville's encounter in Europe with important paintings of the plague by Baron Antoine-Jean Gros and Nicolas Poussin as well as his knowledge, presumably indirect at this point, of the unusual wax sculptures of plague figures by Gaetano Guilio Zummo, inform Melville's treatment of the themes of the hero's sufferings and the plague, and of dying and the democracy of death, in *Israel Potter*. Trimpi, following up her recent eye-opening book, *Melville's Confidence Men and American Politics in the 1850s* (1988), which emphasizes the role played by graphic prints and political cartoons of the period in the construction of Melville's Mississippi River novel, points out fascinating parallels in her essay for this volume between various avatars of the confidence man and contemporaneous stage and graphic representations lampooning the degeneracy of the bourgeoisie—in particular, a series of famous lithographs, by Honoré Daumier and Charles Philipon, of the huckster figure, Robert Macaire. Like several other contributors to this collection, Trimpi demonstrates not simply that Melville was a man of his time, widely attuned to the issues of middle-class European-American culture, but that the sources and analogues of his work are more varied (and farflung) than even most Melville specialists have imagined.[20]

In late 1856, after Melville had done his part in arranging for the publication of *The Confidence-Man* in New York, he set sail on an extended, seven-month trip to Europe and the Near East. This closed one major chapter in his life. From this point on, for a little over thirty years, he would write no more fiction. At the same time, this trip opened a new chapter, one in which the visual arts were to play an even more significant role than they had before, in Melville's life and in his writing. So far as surviving evidence reveals, this second major trip to Europe—the last and by far the longest, most enriching such trip Melville would ever make—marks the high point in the history of his firsthand engagement with the arts. Perhaps not coincidentally, from this time on he would write only poetry, until his very last years, when he turned again to fiction, or to a mixture of poetry and fiction, in constructing *Billy Budd*. Much of the poetry Melville composed in the next three decades was informed by the impressions he stored up and the lore about the arts he acquired during this second major European tour and in the decades thereafter—poetry which added up to several substantial volumes: *Battle-Pieces and Aspects of the War* (1866), the most carefully considered series of poetic commentaries ever written on the events of the Civil War; *Clarel* (1876), Melville's religious/existential epic poem based on his trip to the Holy Land; *Timoleon* (1891), a series of meditations treating mostly artistic subjects; and *Weeds and Wildings, with a Rose or Two,* his late valentine to his wife Elizabeth. Much of the poetry from this period, with the exception of *John Marr and Other Sailors* (1888), takes the visual arts—painting, sculpture, architecture—for its subject. What is just as important, it seems to have been shaped by the notion made famous in Horace's statement, *ut pictura poesis est* (poems are like pictures). Not only was this trip longer and more leisurely than the earlier ones, it also took Melville through a very different terrain. He traveled to Turkey, Egypt, Palestine, and Greece, and on the way back, he journeyed for the first time throughout Italy, "Art's Holy Land," he later called it ("At the Hostelry," *Collected Poems* 315), making stops in Naples, Rome, Florence, Venice, Milan, and elsewhere. Melville himself was in a contemplative mood, or perhaps a contemplative stage in his life, not so eager, as he clearly was in 1849, to return to his wife and new baby; and the journal he kept on this trip was a substantial record, so substantial that it can hardly be summarized here, important as it is to this overview of the subject. The best general appraisal of this period is still to be found in Leon Howard's *Herman Melville: A Biography.*

Wherever Melville went in Greece and the Near East, what most attracted his attention were, first, the works of architecture and second, the panoramic views of buildings and monuments, as well as various incongruous or otherwise memorable street scenes. With certain exceptions, such as the fountain of Ahmed III in Constantinople, the sculpture interested him only rarely, the painting almost not at all. This is probably to be expected in a region best known for its stunning architecture and the extensive ruins and remains of its ancient cities, but it is worth noting nonetheless, because it confirms the architectural bent of much of Melville's writing from the previous few years. In Thessalonica, he "Went into the mosques," several of which, he noted afterward, were "formerly Greek churches" that had been altered by the conquering Turks, and he noted the Roman remains of a triumphal arch: "Fine sculpture at the base representing battle scenes" (70–71). He was rather vague about most details, however, and seemed to be most interested in storing up visual images—picturesque moments, panoramic views, strange sights or incongruities—from his wanderings. In Constantinople, where he spent almost a week, he recorded more than 25 pages of impressions, but gave most of his attention to the many mosques in the city, particularly the six-towered mosque of Sultan Achmet ("Nothing finer" [80]) and the famed Hagia Sophia, the great masterpiece of Byzantine architecture, as well as to the Hippodrome and the three courts of the Seraglio, the palace residence of the Ottoman sultans vacated in 1853 in favor of other quarters. The view from the Serasker Tower, a nineteenth-century watch tower, drew high praise: "From the top, my God, what a view! Surpasses everything. The Propontis, the Bosphorous, the Golden Horn, the domes, the minarets, the bridges, the men of war, the cypresses.— Indescribable" (82). He also particularly noted the fact that the houses, lacking windows on the first floor, were so conspicuously designed to keep out robbers. Throughout his travels, Melville never seemed so exhilarated as when he had a commanding view from some height, or so threatened by assassins and thieves as when he felt closed up or "buried" in some darkened enclosure or netherworld in the Near East, a set of responses B. L. Ra'ad carefully examines in his essay for this volume. Nowhere, however, did Melville feel so effaced as when contemplating the ancient pyramids of Egypt. They "still loom before me," he wrote afterward in his journal, "something vast, undefiled, incomprehensible, and awful" (119). Clearly, this was the sight that had the most profound, even disturbing, effect on him during his entire journey.

If, for Melville, Egypt and the pyramids were overwhelming, Palestine and the ruins of Jerusalem were an emotional letdown. "To some the disappointment is heart sickening," he wrote in his journal (154). He spent almost three weeks in the Holy Land, much of it in Jerusalem, and almost everywhere he went he felt much the same depressing effect of age and ruin in the buildings and landscapes around him. Wherever he cast his eye in this ancient world, he saw not evidence of a redeeming God or religion, but of the wasting hand of Time. Significantly, this is the wasteland setting of *Clarel*, Melville's long poem of the 1870s which takes as its subject the endless, winding spiritual quest of modern man.

In the ancient town of Ramlah, Melville visited the "ruined mosque" and tower and saw the "ruined church" of Lydda. Joppa, or Jaffa, was "antidiluvian"; it contained "no antiquities worth speaking of—It is too ancient" (131), with even the houses old and dark, "arched and vaulted" and made of stone. The remnants of what was alleged to be an ancient pier turned out, upon inspection, to "bear no appearance . . . of any ruins of any work of art" (133); they were just a pile of rubble, or so it seemed to him. In Bethany, in the hills outside Jerusalem, the tomb of Lazarus was "a mere cave or cell" (134). All throughout Judea—the "Wilderness" setting of part two of *Clarel*—the land appeared to Melville as barren, like the accumulations of "the mere refuse & rubbish of creation" (137). To his astonishment, the entire town of Bethlehem, when viewed from a distance, "looked exactly like arid rocks" and not at all like the holy city (139). And in Jerusalem, the Church of the Holy Sepulcher, for Melville the most important architectural structure in the Holy City, was a "confused & half-ruinous pile," a "sickening cheat." Time had so "nibbled" the sculpture on the original facade of the structure that it looked to him like "so much spoiled pastry" (150). In Jehosophat, "Jew graves stones lie as if indiscriminately flung abroad by a blast in a quarry . . . so old the Hebrew inscriptions can hardly be distinguished from the wrinkles formed by Time . . . capitals of pilasters rubbed off by Time" (143–44). Cemeteries so thickly surrounded Jerusalem that, for Melville, "The city [seemed] beseiged by [an] army of the dead" (144). The whole city, in fact, was a kind of tomb; "there are *strata* of cities buried under the present surface of Jerusalem," Melville at one point exclaimed (152). All is stone piled upon stone.

Two weeks after leaving Palestine, following stops in Beirut, Cyprus, and elsewhere, Melville arrived in Athens. He was suffering badly from several nights without sleep, thanks to an infestation of fleas on the ship carrying him to Pireus and a "tempestuous, cold passage" (170), but he was excited about the prospect of seeing the Acropolis, and the moonlight glimpse which he caught of it as he approached the city he later memorialized in "The Apparition," one of two poems on the subject of the Parthenon he published in *Timoleon*. His spirits revived quickly under the influence of the austere beauty of the ancient ruins of the capitol; in "Attic Landscape" he would write of its "Pure outline pale" (245). Even his sense of spiritual well-being improved dramatically, as is evident from both the journal and these later poems which treat the subject of the softening influence of the Parthenon in particular. Among other things, Melville was fascinated by the "Imperceptible seams" (171) in the construction of the great masterworks of Greek architecture, referred to in a poem titled "The Parthenon" as "Art's meridian" (247), and later he even wrote a little poem on the subject, called "Greek Masonry." As in other places on this journey he was also struck, even puzzled, by the incongruities he encountered, particularly by the "Strange contrast of rugged rock with polished temple" (170). What he saw here transcended anything that might qualify as the picturesque; the effect was much more stunning than that could ever be. Unlike the situation at Stirling Castle in Scotland, he reminded himself in his journal, art and nature at the Acropolis did not "correspond" (170); here the two were starkly at odds. Melville revisited the Acropolis at least two more times during his brief stay in Athens, and in the record of his last distant view of it, on the road back to the port of Pireus, it is obvious that he was very much taken by this exquisite example of ancient architectural achievement.

From Greece, Melville traveled to Sicily and then to Naples, noting along the way the rugged Calabrian coast, which reminded him of the chiaroscuro wilderness scenes of that very same coast painted by Salvator Rosa, the great master of the Neapolitan School. He seems to have been struck almost from the first by the extraordinary military presence ("soldiers—music—clang of arms") throughout the city, then still under the control of the repressive Bourbons. But like other visitors before and after him, he was impressed also by the "splendor" (178) and "magnificence" (179) of this huge and bustling metropolis—its "noble streets" and "lofty houses" (176); its "superb" palaces and villas and extensive gardens, as well as by the noise and vitality of its people. "Naples in the Time of Bomba" was one of two poems Melville wrote based on his stay in Naples; at one time it was intended for inclusion in a volume of poetry which he tentatively titled: "Parthenope/An Afternoon in Old Naples:/In the Time of Bomba/with/A Salutatory/Touching/New Italy and Old Romance/&c/Painters and the Picturesque/and so forth/More or less versified by Herman Melville from the/original suggestions of the noble/The Marquis de Grandvin" (*Collected Poems* 483–84). Melville was especially taken by Posilipo on the outskirts of the city, a "beautiful promontory of villas—along the sea" (180), and by the view of Naples and the bay from various other headlands in the surrounding hills. But he spent most of his time on this particular stop touring the Museo Borbonico (now the National Museum), the principal repository for objects taken from excavations at Pompeii and Herculaneum and containing also the famous *Farnese Hercules* as well as the colossal group, the Farnese Bull, which Melville called "glorious." While there he also saw an extraordinary collection of bronze statuary, including several caricatures (Plato, Seneca, Nero) that he later incorporated into his lecture on "Statues in Rome," as well as hundreds of paintings, most of which he "but glanced at," though he specifically mentioned seeing works by Raphael, Domenichino, and Correggio (183–84).

At the time of his 1849 trip to Europe, Rome was the city Melville wanted most to see, but having failed to secure the contract he wanted for *White-Jacket,* he could not afford to extend his travels that far. On this occasion, however, when he finally saw Rome for the first time, he found himself "chafed" and tired from travel and lack of sleep, and strangely unresponsive to the city: "Rome fell flat on me. Oppressively flat. . . . The whole landscape nothing independent of associations" (190). Like other travelers, he seems to have found the Eternal City overwhelming—so rich in history, the architecture so resplendent and diverse, that it was impossible to take it in all at once. In brief reflections which he entered sometime later in the final pages of his journal, Melville observed, "*More imagination* wanted *at* Rome than at home to appreciate the place . . . *Ruins look* as much *out of place in Rome* as *in British Museum*" (268). Initially, too, he was outraged by the absence of any connection between Life and Art in contemporary Rome—by the incongruity between the "ridiculous" fashion he saw on parade at the pleasure grounds of the Pincian hill and the "truth" of the Antinous statue only "a stone's throw" away at the Capitoline Museum (192). This same statue of Antinous would prove important years later in the construction of *Billy Budd.*

Once Melville got his bearings, however, he dutifully went his rounds of the city, and before long he began to take pleasure in what he saw. As was his habit, he went first to the most famous sights—in this case, to St. Peter's, which he found disappointing, at least its front view: "Interior comes up to expectations. But dome not so wonderful as St: Sophia's" (190). In the course of three and a half weeks, he made several return trips to the great basilica, the work of Michelangelo and others. And he made several trips to Bernini's beautiful St. Peter's Square, and to the several Vatican museums where he saw the Sistine Chapel frescoes of Michelangelo and the many Raphaels in the rooms devoted to his work. By the end of his first week in Rome, Melville was responding so freely and energetically to the many treasures of the Papal museums, including the large collection of marbles, that he found himself "Fagged out completely," and had to sit a long time "recovering from the stunning effect of a first visit to the Vatican" (200). This trip, together with several visits he made to the Vatican museums in the days following, formed the ruling idea for the lecture he put together in America several months later on "Statues in Rome." As Merton Sealts has argued, the project originated with the idea, recorded sometime later at the end of his 1857 journal, to "repeople" the Coliseum "with all statues in Vatican Dying

& Fighting Gladiators" (268), though in fact most of the works Melville was to mention in the lecture on statuary were to be found either in the Capitoline Museum in Rome or elsewhere in Italy, from Naples to Florence.

Outside the Vatican, Melville visited most of the important landmarks of Christian Rome, including the Basilica of St. Mary Major, the city's best remaining example of a Roman church; the Basilica of St. John Lateran, second in rank only to St. Peter's; St. Paul's Basilica, destroyed by fire early in the century but rebuilt in 1854; the Church of St. Pietro, containing frescoes by Piombo from drawings by Michelangelo; the Church of Santa Maria degli Angeli, designed by Michelangelo (and bearing a modest connection with *Clarel,* as noted in Horsford 210); Il Gesu, a Counter-Reformation church of the Jesuits, known as a little gem of Baroque styling; Santa Maria di Aracoeli (called "Gibbon's Church," in Melville's journal, because here the great historian was inspired to write of the decline and fall of the Roman Empire); and probably San Pietro in Vincoli, the site of Michelangelo's *Moses,* which Melville described in his lecture on Roman statuary.

Naturally, he visited several of the principal sights of ancient Rome, too, most notably the Coliseum, which he returned to on several occasions; the Baths of Caracalla, where Shelley "got his inspiration," as Melville said (192–93); Diocletian's Baths, the central hall of which Michelangelo had converted into the Church of Santa Maria degli Angeli, and the site of a great fountain with colossal statues popularly known as *The Horse Tamers*—"gigantic figures," as Melville said, "emblematic of gigantic Rome" (196); and Trajan's Forum, a colonnaded square that was the latest and largest of the many imperial fora constructed when the Roman Forum proved too small.[21]

Melville can hardly be said to have spent all or even most of his time exploring the ruins and ecclesiastical buildings of the Eternal City, important as they are to an understanding of the history of Western culture and art. He devoted several hours, over the course of several days, to visiting in the studios of living artists—painters and sculptors, including the well-known American portrait painter William Page and the British sculptor John Gibson, who gained a certain notoriety for tinting his statues. Others he saw were the American Edward Bartholomew, a painter turned sculptor, and Thomas Crawford, a sculptor known for his allegorical productions on American themes. So far as can be determined, Melville talked of Titian and Swedenborg with Page, who was obsessed by both. Melville discussed the possibility of perfection in art with Gibson and talked about biblical and classical sculpture with Bartholomew.[22] More importantly, Melville devoted much time—considerably more than to anything else—to touring Rome's many museums and galleries, with their rich mixture of classical and Christian artifacts. Obviously, he was becoming more and more interested in painting and sculpture, the latter especially, as evidenced by his lecturing on Roman statuary soon after his return to New York. Of the several museums in Rome known for their sculpture, the Capitoline Museum, with its Hall of Emperors (containing 83 statues of Roman rulers), was a particular favorite. Melville visited it twice, noting in his journal its *Dying Gladiator* (or "Dying Gaul"); an Antinous; and several of the figures later featured in "Statues in Rome," including busts of Demosthenes, Socrates, Seneca, Plato, Titus, and Tiberius. And on more than one occasion he explored the Villa Albani (now Villa Torlonia), where he encountered an Apollo, believed to be by Praxiteles; a Minerva; a representation of Aesop; and another Antinous, an important icon of male beauty for Melville and for the nineteenth century generally. The Villa Albani, which at one time housed an unusual collection of classical sculpture, is featured in Melville's "Statues in Rome" lecture and serves as the setting for a portion of "After the Pleasure Party," one of his most difficult poems, on the subjects of love and aging, art and female beauty.

Melville also made several trips to various palace museums notable both for their collections of paintings and for their architecture. These include the Farnese Palace, designed by Michelangelo and Vignola, among others, and noted for its seventeenth-century frescoes by Annibale Carracci and his school; Melville concluded that it represented "the finest architecture of all the palaces (private)" (194). He also visited the Palazzo Barberini, one of the finest Baroque palaces in Rome, containing then a small collection of pictures, including the famous *Beatrice Cenci,* which is attributed to Guido Reni and which Melville went out of his way to see there (200–01). He also toured the Corsini Palace, containing "very many first rate works" by Holbein (portraits of Luther and his wife), Carlo Dolci *(Magdalen),* Salvator Rosa (a battle scene and a Calabrian landscape), and others (202). Among Melville's other stops were the Sciarra Gallery, which contained works by Caravaggio *(Cheating Gamblers),* Claude, and Titian, and the Rospiglioso Gallery, with its famous gardens and the *Aurora* ceiling fresco by Guido. The Quirinale Palace of the Pope, site of even more extensive gardens than those at the Rospiglioso, and of Guido's *Annunciation,* was another destination, as was, perhaps most importantly, the Doria Pamfili Palace, containing portraits by Raphael and Titian, two large landscapes of Claude which, Melville reported rather surprisingly, "did not touch me," several examples of Breughel which "much pleased" him (208), and Veronese's *Lucrezia Borgia*: "no wicked look about her. good looking dame—rather fleshy" (208). Finally, he went to the famed Borghese Gallery. Much of the once exceptional collection of sculpture there had been looted by Napoleon and carried to Paris earlier in the century, but Melville still saw a good many paintings, including the famous *Danae* of Correggio and an unusual portrait of Caesar Borgia by Raphael; he admired the grounds and some of the garden statuary, and returned several times. He visited various other gardens as well in Rome and its environs, including the world-famous ones at Tivoli. At the same time he took in the nearby ruins of Hadrian's Villa, possibly the inspiration for the poem, "The Ravaged Villa," in *Timoleon*. As already mentioned, he also saw the gardens on the Pincio, the hill just inside the wall of the ancient city.

From Rome, Melville continued north to Florence, stopping along the way for a day in Pisa to see the famous structures in the Piazza del Duomo, including the cathedral, the interior of which he greatly admired, and the campanile, which inspired his playful poem, "Pisa's Leaning Tower," published in *Timoleon*. He spent a week in Florence, "the flower of Tuscany," and took great pleasure in its quiet beauty and the simple grandeur of its architecture and art collections. "Florence is a lovely city even on a cold rainy day," he wrote in his initial Florentine journal entry (217). After making a first visit to the galleries at the Pitti and then the Uffizi Palace (where he saw a bronze copy of Cellini's *Perseus*), he came upon the suddenly looming duomo and campanile "unexpectedly," and was "Amazed at their magnificence" (217). And on his last day in Florence he returned to the cathedral for a closer look, climbed up into Brunelleschi's huge dome, and found himself duly impressed by its "Magnitude," as he was by the monstrous frescoes of Vasari and Frederico Zuccari. In between times, he revisited the Pitti at least once, where he saw *The Three Fates* of Michelangelo and several works by Rosa, including a "Battle Peice" (sic) which proved important a few years later to the overall conception and title of his own large collection of poems on the Civil War. And he returned at least twice to the more public Uffizi, designed by Vasari originally to house the offices of the Medicis. Although he at first reported it was "Idle to enumerate" the many treasures he encountered in this Renaissance palace, he went on to write that he was "Not pleased" with the world-famous Venus de Medici, "but very much astonished" at a partially restored antique statue of a group of wrestlers he saw there; that he was "charmed" with one or another of the two Venuses by Titian; and that he found "interesting" the extensive gallery of signed self-portraits by Raphael, da Vinci, Titian, del Sarto, Dolci, Lippi, Dürer, Rubens, Van Dyck, Reynolds, and others (218–19). Melville also toured much of the Accademia delle Belle Arti, or the Academy, known especially for its collection of Giottos and Florentine primitives, "predicessors," as Melville said in a rare historical remark, "of the Peruginos & Raphaels" (219); he ventured into the Renaissance Church of the Santissima Annunziata, where he admired the frescoes of Andrea del Sarto, whose *St. Agnes* he had seen in Pisa; and he seems to have spent a long time in the Museum of Natural History examining the anatomical wax figures there, including some especially compelling ones by Zummo showing the grisly effects of the plague. "Moralist, this Sicilian," he said mordantly, at the end of an unusually detailed journal entry. Hennig Cohen, in his essay for this volume, provides a fascinating assessment of Melville's fragmented remarks, and places them in the context of other writings by Melville from the 1850s, particularly *Israel Potter*, which evidence a profound preoccupation with death and decay. Zummo's was not the only sculpture Melville saw while in Florence; near the end of his stay, he also visited the studios of Hiram Powers, an American who early in life had made wax models for a museum in Cincinnati and whose *Greek Slave* (1843), made just a few years after he came to Italy, quickly became the most popular work of sculpture in its time.

Melville next traveled to Venice, stopping en route at Bologna and Padua and, more briefly, at Ferrara and Revigo. In Bologna, he saw Raphael's famous *St. Cecilia,* among other paintings, though he did not comment on it. And in Padua he was particularly impressed by Fasolato's intricate statue of "Satan and his host" *(Fall of Lucifer)* at the Palazzo Papafava; the rich array of frescoes by Giotto at the early fourteenth-century Scrovegni Chapel; and the Romanesque-Gothic style Basilica del Santo, built in honor of the city's patron saint, Anthony. Presumably, it was this building which inspired Melville's "In a Church of Padua," his poem in *Timoleon* treating the Catholic confessional.

Venice apparently appealed to Melville as much for its public life as for its palatial architecture and galleries, for almost every evening he "sallied out," as he said several times, to the famous Piazza San Marco, where he sat and took in the surrounding scene, noting especially the musicians and singers and the ladies taking refreshments. To be sure, he did admire the architecture of the buildings on Saint Mark's Square, particularly the elaborate facade of the Basilica itself, though he was disappointed in the "Oily looking interior" of the aged church and in its equally "unctuous" marbles (227); and as is evident in his little poem, "Venice," he was much taken by the "marble garlandry" of the city's many "reefs of palaces" along the Grand Canal (*Collected Poems* 238–39). Venice, of course, is a city of churches as well as palaces, and although Melville saw the inside of only a few of the latter, he toured several of the former besides Saint Mark's, including the fourteenth-century Church of Saints John and Paul, where the Doges are buried; he also saw the eighteenth-century Church of the Jesuits, with its "Astonishing" marble drapery pulpit (230), the octagonal Church of Santa Maria della Salute, and Palladio's Church of San Giorgio Maggiore, with its elaborate wood carvings (233). On several occasions he took note of the stunning facades of the great palaces on the Grand Canal, especially the famed Casa d'Oro, the Hôtel de la Ville (greatly admired by Ruskin), and the Ducal Palace; and he took a boat to the island of Murano to visit the glass manufactories there. The one gallery he visited was the city's major one, the Galleria dell' Accademia, with its famous collection of Titians and Tintorettos, several of which he commented upon. Besides the scene at the Piazza San Marco, what struck Melville most was the discovery that the characteristic "rich, brown complexions" of Titian's women were "drawn from nature," that is, duplicated in the swarthy faces of the "Numbers of beautiful women" he saw in his wanderings through the city's footpaths (233).

In the remaining days of his extended tour of Italy, Melville stopped in several other cities of the north, chief among them Milan, Turin, and Genoa, before moving on through Switzerland to Germany and Holland, and then to England preparatory to his trip home. In Milan, Melville twice in a period of twenty-four hours sought out the magnificent white marble Duomo there, a massive yet delicate structure begun in the late fourteenth century as a Gothic cathedral but showing evidences of its eclectic history. After his second visit, he pronounced it "Glorious. More satisfactory to me that [than] St. Peters. A wonderful grandure" (238–39), and as both his journal and his poem, "Milan Cathedral," attest, he was smitten by its scores of pinnacles, gleaming "like to ice-peaks snowed" (*Collected Poems* 242), its numberless groups of carved angels and saints which he saw close-up on his roof-walk there, and its beautiful "burning" windows (239). In Milan, he also visited the famous Brera Gallery, with its extensive collection of north Italian paintings, including Gentile Bellini's well-known *St. Mark Preaching at Alexandria;* then he sought out the greatly faded glory of Leonardo da Vinci's famous fresco of the *Last Supper* at the refectory of the old monastery at the Church of Santa Maria delle Grazie, philosophizing briefly in his journal afterwards about the evanescence of the "glow of sociability" it allegorized in contrast to "selfishness so lasting" (238).

Melville spent just one day in Turin before moving on to Genoa, but he saw enough of the city to be struck by the extraordinary uniformity of its architecture, a consequence of its being rebuilt after a devastating war with the French in the early sixteenth century. He had a satisfying time examining the royal collection of paintings in the gallery of the converted Castello palace, now in the Academy of Science. He commented favorably on the work of several north Italian painters there, among them Crespi, Albani, Titian. But he seems to have been more taken by the work of several Dutch and Flemish painters, including Rubens (a copy), Van Dyck, the Breughels, whom he pronounced "always pleasing," though he identified them only in the singular, and, most importantly, Teniers, the "remarkable . . . effect" of whose work, Melville explained in a relatively rare comment on technique, "is produced by first dwarfing, then deforming humanity" (241). Though Melville had seen several Teniers works elsewhere, it is likely that this experience lay behind the writing of the poem "The Bench of Boors" in *Timoleon*. In Genoa, Melville saw little painting, but he was moved to comment on the strangeness of *"paintings of architecture* instead of realtiy [sic]." He also visited the great San Lorenzo Cathedral, and though he was disappointed in the palaces of "Genoa the Superb," finding them inferior to those elsewhere in Italy, he was struck by their open, inviting architecture, with courts and staircases and gardens in the front rather than inside a hidden courtyard, as in Rome. He was also interested to discover that the ancient port city was set in such bleak surroundings and had been so heavily built up over the centuries that it seemed to him "the capital and fortified camp of Satan: fortified against the Archangels" (245). As in other foreign cities, Melville visited the principal cathedral first, then the big galleries, and at some point took note of the distinctive overall impression which the local architecture and cityscape made on him.

After eight weeks of leisurely sightseeing in Italy, Melville headed north for his return trip home, quickly traveling through Switzerland, Austria, Germany, and Holland en route to London and finally Liverpool. Although here and there along the way he did pause to view a local attraction, such as the great nineteenth-century sculptor Thorwaldsen's monument to the Swiss guards in Lucerne and the Rhenish-style cathedral in Strasbourg, clearly the highlight of these last ten days on the Continent was the visit he made to the Trippenhuis Museum in Amsterdam to see the extraordinary collection of Dutch and Flemish realist paintings there. As Dennis Berthold demonstrates in his essay in this volume, Melville had been developing an interest in Dutch painting for several years; at its height it seems to have coincided with the swing toward realism and miniaturism in his own work, as seen in the shorter magazine pieces he turned out during the mid-fifties, even before his second European tour. But the visit to the Trippenhuis must have been a crystalizing event for him, for several of the painters whose work he saw there—Franz Hals, Rembrandt, Rubens, Jan Steen, Adrian Brouwer, Teniers, and several non-Dutch artists—make their appearance in his long, rollicking dialogue poem, "At the Hostelry," and together dominate the debate over the meaning of the picturesque in art.

In London, Melville visited the Vernon Gallery, with its notable collection of English landscape and portrait paintings, and the Turner Gallery, where he admired especially the "sunset scenes" and seascapes of Turner. However, the English painters did not make their way into "At the Hostelry" or any of Melville's other poems based on his travels of this period. Judging from his journal, the most fascinating sight he encountered in England was the mixture of pastoral and collegiate life at Oxford—the "*whole*some beauty" (266) he found there, the "Amity of art & nature." The "picturesque never goes beyond this," he wrote (259–60; 267). But apparently the shock of this discovery, noteworthy though it was to him, Melville was never able to work into his own writing. At best, the scene at Oxford was a paradigm of living beauty, "a mild & beautiful rebuke to chastize the sophomorean pride of Am[erica] as a new & prosperous country" (267). With that note, one of the very last in this 270-page journal, it is clear that Melville no longer possessed the innocent or "savage" eye he did when he started several months earlier; it had become, not exactly Europeanized, but more knowing and certainly more self-conscious as a result of his experience. And with that understated confession, he was ready to return home and get back to his work.

What Melville's work would consist of, it must have been hard even for him to say in the early days after his return. His trip had fitted him for little beyond what he had already been doing with his life. But it did give him something new to write, or talk, about—a subject, even a series of subjects, about which he could lecture, for a fee, in the cities and towns of America. Within weeks of his return, he was preparing for the first of three lecture tours he was to undertake in the coming months, on the unpromising, and for him unlikely, subject of "Statues in Rome." No manuscript of Melville's lecture survives. But as noted earlier, Merton Sealts has used extant reviews from local newspapers to fashion a reliable approximation of it, and of what turned out to be Melville's only other lectures as well, on "The South Seas" and "Traveling." Sealts's reconstruction tells us a great deal more about the subject than can be gleaned from a close study of Melville's journal entries from his time in Rome. It also reveals that he had, at least for this period of his life, become a rather staunch "classicist," and less a "modernist."

Melville appreciated many things about the statues of the Romans, not all of which are entirely consistent with one another. In the busts of various historical figures—Demosthenes and Socrates, Seneca and

Plato, Titus and Tiberius—he saw evidence of the worldliness or realism of the Roman outlook, the capacity, captured by the artists of these works, to see through outward appearances and "prattle to us" centuries later, as he said, "of much that does not appear in history and the written works of those they represent" (134). In some of these statues, such as the bust of Tiberius, the flaws or traitorous qualities of their subjects were harder to see; but Melville insisted that close scrutiny showed the Roman sculptors of the early period to be capable of extraordinary subtlety in revealing in their work the petty or mundane yet largely hidden qualities of these historical personalities at the same time they showed their more famous public side. This capacity is one that Melville, himself a powerful skeptic on the order of Montaigne, valued greatly. But what is notable about his lecture is that he so clearly valued, at the same time, the remarkable idealism of the Romans and of their art— their capacity to suggest the "heroic tone," as he said, of these public figures while hinting at their sometimes considerable failings. The one exception was the *Apollo Belvedere*—Roman in that it was a Roman copy of a Greek original—which Melville joined others in calling perfectly "divine" (138–39). The "crowning glory" of Roman art, as Melville reportedly called it, "gives a kind of visible response to that class of human aspirations of beauty and perfection that, according to Faith, cannot be truly gratified except in another world" (137).

This one example aside, it is, generally speaking, the complexity or variousness of art, and of Roman (and Greek) art in particular, that Melville valued most, the kind seen, for example, in the curious fact that the Romans, a notoriously ferocious people, could create some examples of animal sculpture marked by this same "ferocity" and others marked by a kindness and gentleness such as their successors, the Christians, were to claim as their own. Such complexity is seen virtually everywhere in the statuary that formed Melville's subject in this lecture. In the famous *Dying Gladiator* in the Capitoline Museum Melville saw evidence of "the mute Christian spirit" which he also felt to be incipient in the early Roman character; in the later sculpture he encountered in the sepulchral vaults of the Vatican, examples of "Hope," he said, "sit side by side with examples of 'Despair,'" and "Joy comes to the relief of Sorrow" (144). More than even Sealts suggests, I think this "doubleness" of vision, and not just the emphasis on the visionary or the ideal which is sounded at the end of his lecture, was the source of fascination for him in the subject of Roman statuary. In his effort, near the end of his lecture, to contrast the modern tendency to value science and technology with the ancient tendency to value the ideal, Melville left the impression that only the latter was of lasting value to him, when in fact most of his lecture is devoted to exploring the idea that the Romans were not one-sided but an intriguing mixture of sharp-eyed realists *and* visionary transcendentalists. Melville was, it seems, still in the process of formulating the ideas of the complex value and conflicting goals of art that he would try to capture in some of his later writings, most particularly in several of the brief poems in *Timoleon* (1891). His lecture, at least in the form it survives today, shows inconsistencies in tone and in definition of subject which suggest that he had not yet perfectly mastered his material or come to hold a consistent point of view toward it. But much of what Gail Coffler reports as finding in her luminous reading of *Billy Budd* at the end of this volume—the tensions between the ideals of Greek and Roman art, the combination of beauty and strength, the transcendent and the terrestrial—can be seen to exist in somewhat less finished, if also more explicit, form in this lecture of Melville's from more than three decades earlier.

A classical view of and attitude toward art is deeply embedded in several other works Melville composed in the decades following his second major European trip, most notably in *Battle-Pieces, Clarel,* and *Timoleon.* Moreover, such classical themes as power and restraint, or of power spent, and of conflict and reconciliation are to be found in these late works as well. But in *Battle-Pieces* (1866) especially, there is a new note, too, a sudden openness to American art and artists that goes beyond the treatment of American themes one might expect to find in a carefully structured collection of poems on the American Civil War. More than anything else, this new note appears to have been prompted by Melville's attendance at the fortieth annual exhibit of the National Academy of Design in New York City in the late days of the war, in April 1865, though it should be added that Melville had evidently, since the late 1840s, been attending the New York galleries that specialized in American realist art. At least two poems from *Battle-Pieces* take their subject from works that were included in this particular show: "The Coming Storm," which was based on the landscape painting of that title by Sandford Robinson Gifford, and "Formerly a Slave," which was inspired by Elihu Vedder's "Jane Jackson, formerly a Slave—Drawing in Oil-Color."[23] Moreover, according to Hennig Cohen, other works by American artists featured in the exhibit of the National Academy of Design also provided material for certain poems in Melville's collection. These included, or so it appears, either one of two (possibly both) paintings of Niagara Falls for Melville's "A Canticle," namely, DeWitt Clinton Boutelle's "Sunrise at Niagara," which, Cohen points out, was on display in the same room at the National Academy with Vedder's "Jane Jackson," or Frederic Edwin Church's "Niagara" (1857), an instantly famous "Great Picture," initially exhibited alone at Williams, Stevens, Williams and Company, a commercial gallery in New York. The picture made the American artist the most famous painter in the country.[24] Cohen also points out that the allegorical figure of "America," which appears in Melville's poem of that name, is likely to have been based on one or the other of two well-known sculptures (if not both) which he had seen in Italy, one by Thomas Crawford and the other by Hiram Powers. And Cohen demonstrates as well that Melville relied a good deal, at least in a generalized way, on some of the paintings of Civil War scenes on display at the National Academy and on certain of the illustrated news magazines of the day, particularly *Leslie's* and *Harper's,* to flesh out the events of the Civil War for himself (*Battle-Pieces* 287–89, 15–18).

Still another group of works that find their way into *Battle-Pieces* are not American but European, and are even more varied in style and genre. In Cohen's view, these include Titian's famous portraits, particularly his *Man with a Falcon,* in connection with the poem "Commemorative of a Naval Victory" (284–85); J. M. W. Turner's *Fighting Temeraire,* which Melville saw at the National Gallery in London in 1857, in connection with the poem "The Temeraire"; Guido Reni's ceiling fresco *Aurora,* which Melville saw in Rome in 1857, in connection with the poem "Aurora-Borealis"; the *Apollo Belvedere,* which Melville saw in the Vatican, in connection with "On the Slain Collegians"; and, finally, the "battle-pieces" of Salvator Rosa, which, as already suggested, probably provided the inspiration for the title, and even the organization, of Melville's collection.[25]

During the period from 1866 to 1876, Melville managed no significant travel; he worked as a customs officer in New York. But he read widely, particularly in the art histories and commentaries of the nineteenth century and earlier; and that reading, in combination with the memories of his 1857 trip to the Near East, provided an important part of the background he needed to write the long poem of this period, *Clarel.* *Battle-Pieces* shows Melville working more or less intuitively with materials from the visual arts and with certain analogies between poetry and painting, arranging his poems like pictures in a gallery and inviting his readers to consider them as a gallery-goer would a collection of oils or sketches on a common theme. *Clarel,* though it initially seems to concern itself far less with the visual arts than Melville's collection of Civil War poems, is, in an understated way, more deeply preoccupied with aesthetics, and reveals Melville's effort to formulate his own conception of the meaning and purpose of the arts in all their forms. Most particularly, in *Clarel* Melville makes powerful thematic use of several impressive landscapes and architectural structures he had seen during his 1857 trip to Palestine and the Near East, including the Pyramids of Egypt, the Church of Hagia Sophia in Constantinople, and the Church of the Holy Sepulcher and the Ecce Homo Arch in Jerusalem. The Church of the Nativity in Bethlehem is another important referent, as is the ancient rock city of Petra, unknown to the West until early in the nineteenth century, and, most notably, the desert or wilderness monastery of Mar Saba, generally considered "the most extraordinary building in Palestine" (Bezanson xxiv). Marovitz, in "Melville's Temples," looks closely at Melville's handling of the most central of these—the Church of the Holy Sepulcher, the Church of the Nativity, and the Mar Saba monastery—and shows how landscapes and architectural structures, in combination with heights and depths more generally, are used not just to set the stage but to define and dramatize the conflict of ideas that underlies the poem. Marovitz explains how Melville's use of architecture, by the time of *Clarel,* had become theatrical in artistically sophisticated ways. However, as in Melville's earlier works, there is also, in *Clarel,* a broad range of relatively straightforward allusions to the arts in various other forms, which the author uses to shape his characters and give definition to his themes, including several references to artists and works that were among his favorites. Melville mentions the Laocoön statue, specifically the serpent, for example. He cites prints by such varied artists as Piranesi (particularly the sixteen futuristic "Prisons," or *Carceri* [2.35]), Holbein, and Claude Lorrain. And he alludes to Guido Reni's *Beatrice Cenci,* the portraits of Titian, and the frescoes of Fra Angelico.

But the significance of the visual arts to *Clarel* is more than a matter of setting, character, and theme development, and more than a matter of allusion. While it is true that *Clarel* is, first and foremost, a poem about the spiritual quest of nineteenth-century mankind, it is also the case that, as a vehicle for that subject, the poem is deeply concerned about the nature of art, as Melville conceived it, and in particular about Melville's response to Matthew Arnold's influential conception of art from earlier in the century. In two essays from the early 1980s, Shirley Dettlaff and Douglas Robillard scrutinize Melville's system of aesthetics in *Clarel* and his thinking about the relation between literary art and the visual arts in that work.[26] Dettlaff argues that while Melville was powerfully attracted to Arnold's Hellenistic conception of art in the 1860s and early 1870s, he finally accepted it only up to a point, and that the result of his struggle can be seen here and there in many disparate segments of Melville's long narrative poem. Where Arnold pressed for a revival of the Greco-Roman emphasis on clarity and beauty in the arts, on the finite and knowable, Melville, in *Clarel,* showed himself to favor a more complex melding of the Hellenistic and the Hebraic (or

Judeo-Christian) conceptions, according to which clarity and purity of line, important as they are, are secondary to the need for art to "puzzle and raise questions," to "challenge the imagination" by pointing to the infinite, the mysterious, and the chaotic that lie beyond human understanding (Dettlaff 228). Though relying on terms which delineate a dialogic split between the Hellenism and Hebraism of Melville's aesthetic thinking rather than one within his understanding of the Greco-Roman tradition itself, this is much the same complex aesthetic noted earlier in connection with Melville's lecture on "Statues in Rome." Dettlaff argues that evidence for Melville's aesthetic theory, which might be said also to unify the Burkean dichotomy between the beautiful and the sublime, can be seen particularly in the narrator's description of the Church of the Holy Sepulcher (*Clarel* 1.28.25–34) and, more prominently still, in Rolfe's description of the sharply outlined buildings of Petra which had been carved out of the rough-hewn mountains of Judea:

> Mid such a scene
> Of Nature's terror, how serene
> That ordered form. Nor less 'tis cut
> Out of that terror—does abut
> Thereon: there's Art.
>   (2.30.41–45, also 17–18)

Robillard extends this view by arguing that Melville's reading of Charles Du Fresnoy's *De Arte Graphica* (1668) and John Dryden's "A Parallel of Poetry and Painting" (1695) enriched his understanding of the analogies between the sister arts, particularly in matters of pictorialism and allusion. These parallels contributed powerfully, Robillard argues, to the design of the poem, but they also offered "a surer grasp of complex and invisible truths" (118), the kinds of truths, or questions, that Melville's characters were struggling to articulate for themselves and their fellow pilgrims. The theory of art which Melville seized on in reaction to his encounters with the writings of Arnold, Du Fresnoy, and Dryden was, in effect, a theory of indeterminacy, one which was in keeping with the bold theme of spiritual wandering, or indeterminacy, at the center of his epic poem. Such a theory, it must be emphasized, is hardly unique to *Clarel,* however. It goes back to *Moby-Dick* and the period of Melville's appropriation of the "abstractionism" of Turner described by Robert Wallace in this volume and elsewhere. It is also pervasive, as B. L. Ra'ad argues in this collection, in much of the journal that Melville kept on his 1856–57 trip to the Near East, where austere, monochromatic landscapes and massive, crumbling structures combined, in Melville's imagination, to form scenes of desolation or "blankness," of a moral and spiritual "waste land," which anticipate the "abstractionism" of much painting and literature of the modern period.

Important as questions of art are to *Clarel,* they are nonetheless kept on the margins of the central story or played in a minor key. But in *Timoleon* (1891), the last work to be published in Melville's lifetime, many of those same questions are brought repeatedly to the fore and, for the first time in a single volume—by Melville or any other American poet of the nineteenth century—made the central subject. The title poem, in this respect, is misleading, for it focuses on a historical figure, the Greek general known as the scourge of tyrants, a figure having no direct connection to the arts. But the dedication to the American artist Elihu Vedder, whose work Melville had honored in *Battle-Pieces,* provides an important clue to the overriding theme of the volume, and more than hints at Melville's ruling intentions. As a whole, the collection is profoundly concerned with the character, meaning, and effect of art, and of the visual arts especially, so much so that *Timoleon* ought to be recognized as the high point of Melville's lifelong preoccupation with the subject. Out of a total of 42 poems in the volume, nearly two-thirds take the visual arts as a theme or major subject; this is in addition to three poems on the literary arts, one on music, and two on the subject of art in general. At least one and possibly two poems in the collection— notably, "The Marchioness of Brinvilliers" and, perhaps, "The Bench of Boors"—take particular paintings for their theme, specifically a crayon sketch of the Grand Mannerist Charles Le Brun, in the first instance, and of David Teniers the Younger, in the second.[27] Several other poems, as Douglas Robillard argues in his second essay for this volume, "Wrestling with the Angel: Melville's Use of the Visual Arts in *Timoleon,*" are concerned with the subject of literary pictorialism, specifically in ways that can be traced to Melville's reading in aesthetics—in Ruskin, Reynolds, Jarves, and others—during the years leading up to his completion of the collection. Others, such as "The Garden of Metrodorus," "Lone Founts," and "Disinterment of the Hermes" take ancient sculpture (or landscape gardening) for their subject. By far the greatest number, however, almost half the poems in the volume, focus on architecture. This group includes a large majority of the poems in the section titled "Fruit of Travel Long Ago," written in some form not long after Melville's return from the Near East in 1857 and revised over a period of several years thereafter. The architectural subjects touched upon include the pyramids of Egypt (in one poem); the Parthenon (in two poems) and the many columns, temples, and other structural remnants of ancient Greece (five poems); and the churches, private residences, and public buildings of medieval and early modern Italy (six poems). What these poems share is an inquisitive attitude about art; they take the view that the work in question is an occasion for contemplation, a challenge to the thoughtful observer, such as Melville himself, who would try to understand it or capture its moral (or social or historical) meaning from a modern observer's perspective.

Architecture, sculpture, works in stone—to judge from *Timoleon*, these interested Melville more, or stayed with him longer, than almost any other art form. Less ephemeral than paintings, less dependent on detail for their effect, they were at the same time more dramatic, easier to hold in the mind, and thus more congenial as subjects to write about after Melville had returned home. But it should be said, too, that, given the itinerary of his Near East trip in 1856–57, it was also the case that many, even most of the truly memorable works of art Melville saw were the architectural monuments of earlier cultures, works that had outlived their makers by generations, even centuries. Their longevity held a special power for him. Melville was much captivated by the simple beauty and strength, the sheer endurance, of these extraordinary, mostly anonymous constructions, and as Catherine Georgoudaki has argued, it is clear from these poems and from his lectures on Roman statuary that he viewed ancient Greek and Roman art in particular as symbolizing a set of values that were to be preferred to the values of materialism and utilitarianism (and even of Christianity) of his own time. As he had argued with energy at the end of his lecture on Roman statuary, the Coliseum and the *Apollo Belvedere* were superior to London's famed Crystal Palace and the American locomotive (*Melville as Lecturer* 151–54).

But what is most distinctive about the poems in *Timoleon*, I think, is their elucidation of two overriding ideas. First, for Melville, the surviving examples of ancient, medieval, and early modern European art suggest a kind of mystery—a set of noble values, to be sure, but also a way of seeing, feeling, and thinking that carries one beyond what can be perceived or known, even with the most educated eye. Second, it is the business of art to put the viewer in touch with that mystery. This is one meaning of the notion of an art of indeterminacy, of "abstraction," that characterizes much of Melville's aesthetic thinking from the time of *Moby-Dick* on. It is what made Melville a "romantic" in some contexts and, as time went on and his enthusiasms became muted, a "modern" in others. And, what is perhaps most telling, it is one of the things he seems to have valued in classical art as well, even though this is not what is typically thought to characterize classical art, despite its powerful strain of idealism. In spite of the conspicuousness of classical subject matter in these poems, then, *Timoleon* cannot be said to mark a univocal turn backward to classicism in Melville's aesthetics, as Morris Star has argued (116ff.). Like several of his earlier works, *Timoleon,* too, favors a distinctively romantic or "modern" art that puzzles or confounds, and takes us out of ourselves, even as it restores something to us, as Melville suggests in the well-known poem called "Art" from that collection:

> In placid hours well-pleased we dream
> Of many a brave unbodied scheme.
> But form to lend, pulsed life create,
> What unlike things must meet and mate:
> A flame to melt—a wind to freeze;
> Sad patience—joyous energies;
> Humility—yet pride and scorn;
> Instinct and study; love and hate;
> Audacity—reverence. These must mate,
> And fuse with Jacob's mystic heart,
> To wrestle with the angel—Art.

Not all the poems in this volume posit the same idea, of course, or even take the same point of view. But I take "Lone Founts," "Milan Cathedral," "The Parthenon," "Greek Architecture," and the last poem, "L'Envoi" (which announces an end to the search for the infinite, at least for this series of poems) to be representative of this persistent theme in *Timoleon,* one which is nonetheless related, of course, to the ancient theme of the yearning for immortality, for an understanding of the beauty, strength, and goodness that are eternal, no matter how ephemeral they may seem even in their most memorable incarnations. Not surprisingly, this is the theme also of Melville's final work, *Billy Budd.*

Before looking at *Billy Budd,* however, and its relation to the visual arts, some brief mention should be made of the subject in connection with the other major unpublished manuscripts that Melville left at the time of his death. Especially germane is "Daniel Orme," where the narrator speaks admiringly of the penetrating powers of two consummate portrait-painters, Titian and Gilbert "Stewart" (*Great Short Works* 424); but the visual arts are also a component of "Rip Van Winkle's Lilac," a landscape poem which constitutes part 3 of *Weeds and Wildings,* and of the two long poems in "Marquis de Gran Vin," titled "At the Hostelry" and "Naples in the Time of Bomba." John Bryant, in his nimble essay on Melville's aesthetics for this volume, discusses "Rip Van Winkle's Lilac," not in connection with any particular work of art Melville may have seen, but in the context of Melville's distinctive conception of the picturesque, a notion central to an understanding of the transformation that occurred in painting and printmaking in the century or so after about 1730. As Bryant shows, the chiaroscuro effect of the picturesque mode, with its play of light and darkness, of nature and culture, past and present, readily appealed to Melville's dialogic imagination. Like other essayists in this collection, then, Bryant places Melville's aesthetics in a "middle ground" between the beautiful and the sublime, between eighteenth-century geniality and modern *Angst,* the earthly and the transcendental, the seen and the unseen. But for him it is a "middle ground" of active tension rather than stasis, yet also one wherein the tension can be seen to have grown more subdued as the author himself came to value more and more the attitude of self-restraint.

Dennis Berthold, in his revisionist essay for this volume, provides a discussion of the other major unpublished art poem, "At the Hostelry," which takes much the same position. But rather than align it with the picturesque—the ostensible subject of this poem—Berthold places it in the context of the history of Melville's engagement with Dutch genre painting, whose domestic and fraternal values Melville celebrated with increasing zest. That vigor is most prominent, perhaps, in "A Squeeze of the Hand" from *Moby-Dick,* but it appeared elsewhere as Melville's career progressed through the 1850s and is particularly evident in the short fiction. "At the Hostelry" imagines a protracted debate on the subject of the picturesque among a varied group of well-known painters from the Dutch school—Jan Steen, Van Dyck, Adrian Brouwer, and Franz Hals among others—and various other European schools, particularly Italian and French. And while it does not take long for the participants to "deconstruct" the whole notion of the picturesque, Melville's admiration for the Dutch School is everywhere evident. Like Bryant, Berthold suggests there is a dialogic quality to Melville's aesthetic system, but Berthold's strategy is not to offer a comprehensive theory of Melville's aesthetics so much as a "counterweight" to the prevailing view that Melville favored the "grand style" in art and the tradition of philosophical idealism generally, to the exclusion of all else. From this point of view, the revolution that occurred around 1850 in the cultural and artistic valuation of art, from the ideal to the real or everyday world, had been brewing for many decades, and the artists who showed the way were the seventeenth-century Dutch painters whose work had been much denigrated in the eighteenth century by Sir Joshua Reynolds and others. Melville, we know, saw many Dutch paintings in Europe on each of his two major trips abroad, but he speaks of them in his journals as though he had long been familiar with them. His interest, therefore, would seem to go back at least to the 1840s, when he is likely to have seen paintings by the Dutch masters for the first time, either in private collections or in galleries such as the American Academy of Fine Arts, the Apollo, and the American Art-Union in New York, or the Athenaeum in Boston, all of which are known to have included Dutch paintings in their holdings.[28]

The two strands or traditions of art—the ideal and the real, the abstract and the representational—come together again in Melville's final work, *Billy Budd,* but this time in the form of Greek and Roman archetypes of male beauty and strength represented by the title character. This is the argument of Gail Coffler in the final essay for this volume, and as such it stands as a fitting conclusion. More than any other work, *Billy Budd* shows how deeply Melville's experience of the visual arts became imbued in his creative consciousness and how subtly that experience could be transmuted by his imagination into a story that seems to have such unrelated matters—history, politics, and family tragedy—at its core. In the course of his narrative, Melville in fact mentions explicitly very few works of art. He does refer to the well-known etching of his contemporary, Sir Francis Seymour Haden, *Breaking up of the "Agamemnon"* (69), in connection with his sketch of the old Dansker; he speaks of "a Greek medallion" and of certain anonymous prints of the conspiratorial Titus Oates (64) in his description of Claggart; and he alludes to the frescoes of Fra Angelico, which Melville had seen in Florence, and the *Farnese Hercules,* which he had viewed in Naples (140), both in connection with the young Billy.[29] But as Coffler shows, by far the most important works of art in the construction of Melville's "inside narrative" were two widely famous sculptural figures he had admired for several decades. One was a bust of the young Antinous, two versions of which he had seen in Rome and a copy of which he owned himself in his later years. The other was the *Apollo Belvedere,* for the nineteenth century one of the great icons of ancient Greek culture, but known only in the form of a Roman copy. Coffler's reading of *Billy Budd* suggests something of the dynamic interplay of intellectual and moral strength and sensual and eternal beauty that Melville, with the help of sculptural models such as these, came to recognize at least as early as *Moby-Dick* as constituting the basis of all art.[30] In Coffler's reading, *Billy Budd* is more than an exercise in moral philosophy; it is a treatise on aesthetics, one in which the author attempted to sum up a lifetime of engagement with the arts, at the same time he tried to create a lasting example of what he had come to believe about the subject.

One overriding question remains: was Melville, then, as Coffler's essay seems to suggest, essentially allied with the ancients in the last years of his life? Was he no longer a modern? Certainly the question of whether we are to regard him as an ancient or a modern in aesthetic sensibility or predisposition runs throughout most of the essays in this volume, as it does throughout much of the scholarship generally on Melville's relation to the arts. The answer, I think, simply has to be that he was both, and that he remained so until the end of his life. Like the

Victorian era he so strangely epitomized, Melville's aesthetic tastes were remarkably eclectic, his artistic interests unusually varied, his outlook complex. While some of the essays in this collection suggest that he was *only* one or the other, I think it is fair to say that none of the contributors would in the end want to argue that Melville was exclusively one and not the other. He was, it seems evident, both an ancient and a modern; he took all of Western culture as his heritage, including the America of his own day. Like his contemporary, Walt Whitman, he was infinitely curious and receptive; he, too, "contain[ed] multitudes." Necessarily, he was both idealist and realist; abstractionist and representationalist; indeterminist and determinist—as an artist himself and as a man with long-standing interests in virtually every kind of art. Characteristically, among the many prints Melville owned, one was a copy of Turner's *Apollo Killing the Python,* a work treating a classical subject by one of the first and possibly the greatest of the "moderns."

"The symmetry of form attainable in pure fiction," Melville wrote near the end of *Billy Budd,* "cannot so readily be achieved in a narration essentially having less to do with fable than with fact. Truth uncompromisingly told will always have its ragged edges; hence the conclusion of such a narration is apt to be less finished than an architectural finial" (128). Truth, not representational accuracy alone; verity, not verisimilitude; suggestiveness rather than precision—that, even at the end of his life, was Melville's touchstone, the recognition that art, as Willa Cather would later say, is what is implied or intimated, what is *not* on the page (or the drawing pad or the canvas) as well as what is on it. Like his contemporaries, Turner and Ruskin, Melville knew that in the greatest works of art there is something "indeterminate," something only the "savage" eye can see. "May it not possibly be," Melville asked rhetorically near the end of his introduction to the lecture on Roman statuary, "that as [the poet] Burns perhaps understood flowers as well as Linnaeus, and the Scotch peasant's poetical description of the daisy, 'wee, modest, crimson-tipped flower,' *is rightly set above* the technical definition of the Swedish professor, so in Art, just as in nature, it may not be the accredited wise man alone who, in all respects, is qualified to comprehend or describe" (129; emphasis mine).

Melville's Reading
in the Visual Arts

DOUGLAS ROBILLARD

elville's interest in the visual arts was a lifelong preoccupation, and, in pursuing it, he read widely in art history, aesthetic theory, and the lives and works of individual artists. The range of his concerns went beyond painting and sculpture to such peripheral areas as the craft of engraving, book illustrations, flower arrangements, pottery and ceramics, and gems. A careful reader, he often marked his books and sometimes used them for marginal commentary; and, though this system of marking is not an entirely reliable guide to either the amount or the quality of the knowledge that he derived from his studies, it does offer clues to the subjects that most caught his attention. Walker Cowen has made a strong case for the marginalia as an index to Melville's thought, observing that "the books establish a coherent and accurate impression of his intellectual life, his prejudices, and his enthusiasms" ("Melville's 'Discoveries'" 334).

Brought up in a genteel and knowledgeable household which considered pictures, illustrated books and art objects a natural part of its ordinary life, Melville would have learned early to think in pictorial terms. After the death of his father and the family's move to Albany, there were opportunities to see paintings, to discover books in the libraries, and, as William H. Gilman has pointed out, to share the company of painters and professional men who were interested in the arts (*Melville's Early Life* 72–76). Like others who have gone on to become literary artists, Melville had a grasping, vivid imagination that responded to the stimulus of the sister arts, and he could make much of a fleeting allusion, a picture or a print, a description, or a moral observation. With a capacious and exact memory, he stored up impressions which could be evoked later, in his own literary compositions. The process he followed in accomplishing this is personal and obscure, but, now and then, for the reader following after, there can be flashes of recognition. In *Redburn* (1849), the learned allusions to art objects that Redburn makes as he describes what he sees in the infamous House of Aladdin are a clever bit of fakery; but they must have been assembled from a body of reading which could inform the author about such recondite matters as the paintings on the walls at Pompeii, the private art collection of Tiberius, and the secret gallery of the temple of Aphrodite (*Melville's Early Life* 224).

To follow the story of how Melville became a sophisticated art-lover in the raw America of the nineteenth century is to give what amounts to an epitome of the new country's involvement in the arts, reflecting both its debts to the old world and its stubborn, patriotic dream of fashioning its own characteristic arts. There were moralistic arguments for and against the very existence of the arts, and a cultural nationalism demanded a distinctively American form for the arts, free from European influences. Many of the best American artists made the pilgrimage to Europe to study the old masters or to study with the best contemporary artists of the old world. Cultivated and not so cultivated American tourists went, guidebooks in hand, to the art centers in each country. During the whole nineteenth century, opportunities improved constantly for Americans to see, in their own country, the works of art displayed in galleries and exhibitions, in spectacles like the popular panoramas, and in the public arts, commissioned by the government and executed as often by European craftsmen as by native-born Americans. There was a ready market for prints, illustrated books and magazines, and casts of popular sculptures. These were the marks of a country not yet sure of its patrimony, obstinate about standing upon its own cultural feet, and quick to take offense from visitors who derided it as a wilderness.

We have only the scantiest records of Melville's earliest reading, but an important book that he might well have known was William Dunlap's *History of the Rise and Progress of the Arts of Design in the United States* (1834). Dunlap encouraged his readers to study the works of earlier writers on the arts, including

> Vasari, De Piles, Leonardo da Vinci, Albert Durer, Du Fresnoy (with notes by Reynolds), Winkleman, Mengs, Reynolds, Opie, Fuseli, Pilkington's Dictionary (with additions by Fuseli, who has, in all his works, immense learning on the subjects of which he treats, though sometimes displayed rather than used), and we must not forget Shee and Burnet. (1: 5)

This is an ambitious list of readings, even for a confirmed lover of the visual arts, but it is likely that some of Dunlap's readers tried it. Whether or not he discovered the list in Dunlap, Melville read, over a period of many years, the works of Vasari, De Piles, Du Fresnoy, Winckelmann, and Reynolds; and he may well have given some time to the study of Mengs, Opie, Fuseli, and Pilkington.

In order to assess what he actually did read and guess at how that reading may have affected his thought and writing, we must generalize. Establishing a useful terminology is difficult for those who encounter the arts, either as critics or as amateurs. The artists themselves can contribute significantly to discussions of their specialties, but these others often suffer from a lack of mechanical skills and, perhaps, no exact knowledge of the transaction between the artist and his creation. Disarmed in this way, Melville and others who wished to speak of the visual arts usually chose to express their perceptions in literary terms, since these lay ready at hand and were easily comprehensible to a public that read books but had little opportunity to see original works of art. Thus, when Oliver Wendell Holmes wrote of an exhibition in Boston and set out to describe Washington Allston's *Uriel in the Sun,* he quoted Milton's description of Uriel from *Paradise Lost.* Similarly, the tourist's guidebooks, like those of John Murray so familiar to Melville, were carefully constructed outlines of tours for the art lover, pointing out what one should see and admire, and supporting the recommendations with descriptions taken from literary works. These guidebooks established a kind of standard listing of what one must go to see: sculptures like the bust of Antinous, the *Apollo Belvedere,* the *Farnese Hercules,* the *Torso Belvedere;* the paintings of Raphael, Claude Lorrain, Salvator Rosa, Guido Reni, and the works of Teniers, Murillo, Rubens, Ruysdael, Hobbema, Titian, and Veronese.

Untraveled readers seemed to learn more from the writings of well-traveled amateurs or from literary works than from the best of art treatises. Melville's early "Fragments from a Writing Desk" cites Byron, Burke, Chesterfield, Campbell, and Shakespeare, and refers to paintings and sculptures that he can hardly have seen. The records of his reading between 1844 and 1849 are scattered, but his connection with Wiley and Putnam gave him the opportunity to read Ruskin, whose *Modern Painters* was published first in America by that firm. Wiley and Putnam also published *The American Whig Review,* and, though Melville may have disliked the magazine's politics, it seems likely that he could have scanned it for its articles on Hazlitt, Winckelmann, William Sidney Mount, and other topics having to do with the arts. Another journal, *The United States Magazine and Democratic Review,* often published articles and notes on such artistic matters as American painting and sculpture, the exhibitions of the National Academy of Design, and the art of the Vatican, as well as poems about Correggio and Raphael, and news of the Art-Union.[1]

In *Melville's Reading,* Merton Sealts has listed books drawn from the library of the Boston Athenaeum by Judge Lemuel Shaw during periods when Melville was visiting with the Shaws. The reasonable assumption is that, even if the books were not taken out specifically for Melville, they were, at least, available for him to read at the Shaw home. Some would bear upon his interest in the visual arts. There was Roger De Piles's *The Art of Painting,* an excellent seventeenth-century treatise on design, landscapes, perspective, and coloring; a worthwhile addition was a biographical dictionary of ancient and modern painters. Another text was Charles Eastlake's *Contributions to the Literature of the Fine Arts* (1848). Eastlake (1793–1865) was a painter of distinction, a president of the Royal Academy, and a learned writer; among the pieces in *Contributions* were an article on "basso-rilievo," a review of a biography of Raphael, extracts from his translation of Goethe's *Theory of Colours* and from his notes to Kügler's *Handbook of Italian Painters,* as well as his preface to his translation of Kügler's *Handbook of the History of Painting.* Eastlake's *Materials for a History of Oil Painting* (1847) was charged out in 1848 and John Burnet's *A Treatise on Painting* in 1849, both at times when Melville was visiting the Shaws.

A clearer picture begins to emerge of the kinds of reading Melville was doing in the visual arts by the end of the 1840s. His connection with the Duyckincks and their journal, *The Literary World,* put him in touch with New York artists and connoisseurs. Typical issues of the magazine carried newsy and chatty remarks about the art world and some serious, critically sophisticated commentary. Issues from the year 1847, for example, contained a lengthy critique of pictures at the Art-Union, with remarks about works by Cole, Durand, and numerous less gifted painters. During 1848 and 1849, issues featured stories about exhibitions at the Goupil Gallery, Washington Allston's picture of *Belshazzar's Feast,* and Benjamin West's *King Lear;* a notice of G. Henry Lodge's translation of Winckelmann; a letter from Margaret Fuller on American artists in Italy; and comments on Thomas Cole's *Dream of Arcadia.*[2] Items like these were appearing during the months before Melville sailed to England (1849–50) and converted his journey into an art tour. The business of his publication arrangements taken care of, he visited the British Museum, the National Gallery, Hampton Court, and the gallery at Dulwich to see works of art. Some of the people he visited were associated with the world of art. Samuel Rogers had a fine collection of paintings; Charles Robert Leslie, an American, had become thoroughly Anglicized and was a well-known painter.[3] Among the books that Melville acquired during the visit were several that improved his knowledge of art. From Murray, the publisher, he received guidebooks for France and Germany.

But the most interesting books that he brought back with him were Madame de Staël's *Corinne* and Goethe's *Autobiography*. An important feature of *Corinne* is the grand tour of Rome taken by the heroine and her lover, Lord Nevil, during which she lectures on the art and culture of the country. Careful descriptions of art works are given, along with observations upon history, religion, philosophy, and aesthetics. There are discursive passages on Italian literature, music, drama, popular art, festivals, and the national character. The book thus offers an impressive array of civilized and often brilliant comments, all focused by the attention given to art. This important feature of the novel was one of the reasons for its popularity. As Ellen Moers has pointed out, the book "did at least as much as *Wilhelm Meister* to arouse the passion for Italy among the English Romantics" (228). The book, and the author, aroused similar feelings among Americans as well. Thomas Jefferson, Gouverneur Morris, and James Fenimore Cooper's father corresponded with Madame de Staël. Meeting her in Italy in 1805, even before publication of *Corinne,* Washington Irving saw her as "a woman of great strength of mind and understanding by all accounts" (*Journals* 1: 284). Sophia Hawthorne read *Corinne* and could have conversed knowledgeably about it when Melville, living near Tanglewood in the months after his European visit, often visited with the Hawthornes (*French and Italian Notebooks* 905). Melville's copy of the novel has not come to light; it could be of immense interest if its markings and marginalia were to reveal what Melville found useful.

The case of Goethe and Melville seems ambiguous, considering the latter's clearly expressed dislike of much of Goethe's writings and thought. But his markings show his interest in the autobiographical writings, and, in the second volume, the added "Letters from Italy," a translation of the *Italienische Reise,* was given a particular scrutiny. Goethe's entries that Melville marked included his comments on Tintoretto and Veronese; on Palladian architecture and pictures by Perugino, Guido Reni, Titian, Domenichino, and Raphael; on Winckelmann's art histories and letters, the *Apollo Belvedere,* and a statue of Minerva. Goethe had a well-developed painterly vocabulary and wrote perceptively about the art objects that he viewed.[4]

An important book in Melville's collection was Edmund Burke's *A Philosophical Inquiry into the Origin of Our Ideas of the Sublime and Beautiful.* Although Burke's *Inquiry* does not deal specifically with the visual arts, its topics readily transfer themselves to any such study, and much of its language could be described as painterly, dealing, as it does, with light, darkness, color, shapes, and forms, and the part they all play in exciting emotions of the sublime and the beautiful. What it says applies specifically to the sublime in art that Melville admired: the landscapes of Salvator Rosa; the gigantic in Nature, which dwarfed humans in Turner's paintings; the awesomeness of an oceanic tempest portrayed by Salvator and Turner; the endless galleries of Piranesi's *Carceri;* the spectacular landscapes of the Holy Land in Bartlett and Allom; and the Flaxman illustrations for Dante. Others among Melville's choices in the works of art that he admired illustrate the ideas Burke put forward in his descriptions of the qualifications for the beautiful: the Guido Reni portrait, *Beatrice Cenci;* the Charles Le Brun sketch of the Marchioness of Brinvilliers; the Domenichino *Saint Cecelia;* the *Apollo Belvedere;* the Elihu Vedder drawing of the woman which was to serve as inspiration for Melville's poem, "Formerly a Slave." The language of Burke's treatise penetrated into the works of the early Romantic writers, and his conceptions apply profoundly to Melville's writings.[5]

Melville's journey to Europe and the East in 1856 and 1857 began as a pilgrimage to Palestine but continued as another art tour, mainly in Italy. The pattern of his activities was much the same as it had been during the 1849–50 journey. He visited museums, galleries, and exhibitions, and he met, or attempted to meet, artists and others concerned with the world of art. In Naples, he saw paintings of Raphael and Domenichino. In Rome, he went to the Vatican, the Sciarra Gallery, and the palaces where he could see paintings and statues. He talked to English sculptor John Gibson and tried to see the American James Jackson Jarves, who wrote extensively on art topics.[6] The stored impressions of these and other experiences were to serve him directly in his later writings. The lecture, "Statues in Rome," was one of his subjects in his brief nonliterary attempts to earn some money.[7]

A significant note by Evert Duyckinck indicates that in November 1859 Melville borrowed "Vasari & Lanzi 7 vols" from Duyckinck's personal collection (Sealts, *Melville's Reading* 74, 102). Giorgio Vasari's *Lives of the Most Eminent Painters, Sculptors, and Architects* would have been useful for Melville as he prepared his lecture, but it is possible that he had dipped into the book even before 1859. Likewise, Luigi Antonio Lanzi's *History of Painting in Italy, from the Period of Revival of the Fine Arts to the End of the Eighteenth Century,* in an 1847 translation, offered a sensible grounding for Melville in a chronological sequence of Italian painting.

When Melville acquired Madame de Staël's *Germany* on March 4, 1862, he was again broadening his knowledge of the arts. The book was exceedingly popular in America immediately after its original publication in 1814. George Ticknor read it early, and, influenced by it, learned German, translated Goethe's *Werther,* and traveled with Edward Everett to study in Germany. From there, he wrote to Thomas Jefferson, in 1815, that Germany's "literature is a kind of *terra incognita* to us . . . it does not enter into the system of our education" (Ryder xvi). Subsequently, American interest in Germany became widespread. The *Democratic Review* seriously suggested that German literature was a more suitable model for Americans than English literature and supported its claim by offering translations of Goethe, Schiller, Lessing, Moses Mendelssohn, and Clemens Brentano.[8]

Melville demonstrated his interest in Madame de Staël's book by giving it a close reading; over the course of the 850 pages of the text in its two volumes, he marked about 300 passages, indicating a strong interest in Schiller, Goethe, Winckelmann, Lessing, Schlegel, Kant, and Fichte. He exhibited a special interest in the passages on poetry, devoting many markings to discussions of Klopstock and of poetic style and versification.[9] In a way, this book does for Germany what *Corinne* had done for Italy: it serves as a useful, well-considered introduction to the art and culture of a nation. It contains very little that deals specifically with the visual arts. Rather, there is a generalizing commentary that could apply either to the visual or the verbal arts. A passage emphatically marked by Melville is of this kind:

> In the arts, we often speak of the merit of conquering a difficulty; it is said, nevertheless, with reason, that either the difficulty is not felt, and then there is no difficulty, or it is felt, and is then not surmounted. The fetters imposed on the mind certainly give a spring to its powers of action. (Cowen, "Melville's Marginalia" 11: 46)

Considering that, at the time he probably marked these works, around 1862, Melville was struggling with poetry, some of it dealing with his experiences with the visual arts, and was shortly to take on the "incubus" of *Clarel,* the passage surely reflects his thoughts about the merits of conquering artistic difficulties.

During the next few years, Melville was to invest substantial effort in the study of books about the visual arts. An important reason may have been his desire to incorporate this knowledge into his larger plans for literary composition. We tend to think of *Clarel,* and quite rightly, as a poem which draws deeply upon the Palestinian portion of Melville's travels. But the poem contains substantial passages which draw upon the author's experience of the visual arts. The Palestinian experience, vivid as it must have been, was no more meaningful for him than the Italian part of the tour, with its crowded days of viewing art objects, going to artists' studios, and refreshing his mind's eye with some of the masterpieces that he had seen previously only in the form of unsatisfactory prints.

What Melville seems to have learned while composing the lecture, "Statues in Rome," was that his topic was beyond the scope of his knowledge. The lecture, judging from what we have of it, is a good piece of work, for it would have been impossible for Melville to say something devoid of interest or originality as he explored his theme. But the lecture is the work of an intelligent amateur rather than a practiced writer on the arts. Melville needed only to compare his lecture with the writings of the professionals he had for years been reading—Reynolds, Ruskin, Haydon, Hazlitt, for instance—in order to see the difference. However, he did have a splendid gift denied the others. Weak in the theoretical and critical aspects of art commentary, he could embody pictorial, painterly, sculptural, and architectural elements in his poetic or novelistic design in an inspired way. He knew, to a fine point, the virtues of art allusion in verbal composition, including the laudable intricacies of concealed allusion. The web of referential prose in *Pierre,* for example, constantly reflects such artistic designs as Flaxman's illustrations for Dante, the Guido Reni portrait of Beatrice Cenci, and Sir Joshua Reynolds's art of portraiture. In the novel's account of Ralph Winwood, the portrait artist, there is conjoined a commentary upon American painting, the amateurish Art-Union, and the physiognomical school of portraiture that had its roots in the speculations of Lavater, Gall, and George Combs.

Melville's reading, and sometimes his rereadings, in the 1860s and 1870s show him moving between two worlds, or, perhaps, two conceptions of art. One of these is well represented by his purchase, in 1870, of *The Literary Works of Sir Joshua Reynolds,* a thick, two-volume compilation published by Bohn in London; this he read and marked quite extensively. The other conception could be represented by his acquisition, in 1865, of a five-volume set of John Ruskin's *Modern Painters.* In these works, Melville could study theoretical aesthetic views which clashed— the old, settled notions of art criticism as practiced by Reynolds and still accepted by many American readers, and the new, iconoclastic ideas of Ruskin.

Melville's marginalia in the Reynolds volumes can tell us something of where his interests lay in the 1870s. Doubtless, he read through all of Sir Joshua's "Discourses on Art," but he let the first five go by unmarked. In the sixth, however, he paused over a discussion of imitation and the study of artistic predecessors, during which Reynolds asserted that one learns from earlier works themselves, rather than from precepts formed by them. The fifteenth and last discourse, given by Reynolds at the Royal Academy in 1790, three years before his death, is a valedictory and retrospective view of his chosen art. Offering his remarks in a spirit of recollection and reminiscence, Reynolds emphasizes his view that the artist could make more valuable contributions to art criticism than could the critic who was not an artist. Melville marked passages in which the painter concedes the importance of original creative outbursts of inspiration, and he showed a special interest in a passage in which Reynolds points out that confidence in one's own mechanical skills might lead to boldness in the poetic or imaginative part of his work. In the passage, Reynolds employs a nautical metaphor, saying, "He that is sure of the goodness of his ship and tackle puts out fearlessly from the shore." Melville, as always the believer that "in landlessness alone resides the highest truth, shoreless, indefinite as God" or that "all deep, earnest thinking is but the intrepid effort of the soul to keep the open independence of her sea," marked Reynolds approvingly with triple sidelines.

Although the volumes that Melville owned and marked so assiduously carried only the name of Reynolds in the title, they actually constituted a compendium of discourses upon the arts. They contained the didactic poem, "De Arte Graphica" (1668) by Charles Du Fresnoy; John Dryden's preface to the translation he made in 1695 of Du Fresnoy's poem, the essay entitled, fittingly enough, "A Parallel of Poetry and Painting"; William Mason's 1783 translation of the Du Fresnoy poem with Sir Joshua's notes; and Alexander Pope's poem, "Epistle to Mr. Jervas with Fresnoy's Art of Painting." To judge by Melville's markings, it seems clear that he studied fairly carefully this considerable anthology of opinion and comment about the literary and pictorial arts.[10]

If he found useful hints in the seventeenth- and eighteenth-century ideas of *ut pictura poesis,* as represented by Du Fresnoy, Dryden, and Reynolds, Melville was also reviewing the more radical and disturbing ideas of the arts that had made their way into the world during his early development as a literary artist. In 1843, John Ruskin's *Modern Painters* was published in England. The American publishing firm of Wiley and Putnam, which had published *Typee* in 1846, brought out the American edition of Ruskin's study in 1847. Like other writers, Melville must have been keenly aware of the publicity surrounding it. Emerson read Ruskin's book while sailing to England in 1847; Whitman reviewed it for the *Brooklyn Daily Eagle* and Hawthorne also read it. During the 1850s, it had an enthusiastic following in America, more so, Ruskin thought, than it had in England. It was reviewed, debated, written about all over the country. So it may well be that by 1847–48, Melville had read *Modern Painters,* or, at least, knew its arguments, and that Ruskin inspired his early interest in the paintings of J. M. W. Turner.

However, by the time that Melville acquired his own set of *Modern Painters* in 1865, its four additional volumes bulkier and duller than the first, much of this early furor was in the past. We have only meager evidence about Melville's reading of this set of Ruskin, since there are few markings in his copy. He does seem to have made his way through the whole work, for there are a few marks in the first, second, and fifth volumes.[11] Again, as in his reading of Reynolds, Melville seems interested in passages in which Ruskin deals with originality and greatness in the composition of works of art. A marked passage in the first volume points out that the creative powers of the artist cannot be exerted on unworthy objects, and Ruskin makes a point of defining *excellent,* in his own way, as that which "required a great power for its production." Later, Melville takes note of a passage in which Ruskin attacks the theory of imitation and another in which the art critic asserts that imitation is not consistent with the truth. The paucity of markings in these many pages seems to suggest that Melville turned, naturally enough, to Ruskin for help with his own creative problems and did not find much aid; and, indeed, Ruskin's ideas, so bold and exciting in the 1840s, had begun to appear, to the readers of the 1860s, just a bit faded and subject to attack by later aestheticians.[12]

Perhaps the most interesting of the art books that Melville was studying at this period was *The Art-Idea,* by James Jackson Jarves. Published in 1864, the volume was given to Melville in 1871 by his brother-in-law, J. C. Hoadley. There are good reasons for Melville's interest in Jarves, a person with a checkered and fascinating career. In the 1840s, he had lived and worked in Hawaii and had published a *History of the Hawaiian or Sandwich Islands* and a volume of *Scenes and Scenery in the Sandwich Islands,* both in 1843. By 1851, Jarves had changed the direction of his life, moving to Europe, traveling about for a time, and finally settling in Florence. He wrote extensively on artistic and cultural matters. Articles appeared in *Harper's New Monthly Magazine* and were converted into popular books—*Parisian Sights and French Principles* (1852); *Art-Hints, Architecture, Sculpture and Painting* (1855); and *Italian Sights and Papal Principles, Seen Through American Spectacles* (1856). We cannot be certain that Melville read the articles or any of these books, but they were the sorts of things he might have scanned in preparation for his 1856–57 journey. He must have known something of Jarves, for he made an unsuccessful attempt to meet him in 1857 in Italy.[13]

Jarves was a serious collector of art and a thoughtful art critic, as some of his subsequent publications attest: *Art Studies: The "Old Masters" of Italy; Painting* (1861); *Art Thoughts* (1870); *A Glimpse of the Art of Japan* (1876); and articles like "American Museums of Art" (*Scribner's*, July 1879) and "Ancient and Modern Venetian Glass of Murano" (*Harper's New Monthly Magazine*, January 1882). Melville's markings in *The Art-Idea* indicate his attention. Jarves's sixth chapter theorizes about the freedom of Greek art and its "emancipation" from Egyptian art, citing an idea of evolutionary development to contrast the refined art works of polytheistic Greece with what Jarves calls the more primitive works growing out of monotheistic Christianity. Melville, turning over in his mind the journey to Palestine and the subsequent art tour of Italy, is given here a set of thoughts that he could have found of considerable value for his composition of *Clarel* and some of the art poems that would appear in *Timoleon*.

In chapter 14, Jarves discusses American artists, including some whom Melville knew. He is dismissive of Charles R. Leslie as having become too Anglicized. He praises the work of William Sidney Mount, especially his genre paintings; Melville had already taken note of the resemblance between these works of Mount and the Dutch school of genre paintings that he admired. Jarves's lengthiest commentary is reserved for Washington Allston, praising him for resisting the lure of Europe and returning to his own country to work, even in the face of neglect. A passage that Melville marked reads:

> the artistic fire was too deep within him to be put out even by the aesthetic chill of New England. What a man of the exquisite impressibility of Allston must have felt in this atmosphere can only be conjectured. He, however, nobly stood his post. (Jarves 172)

Melville's recognition here is moving, not only for its praise of the great American painter, but also for the quality of its self-examination. In 1871 he must surely have felt, with his own "exquisite impressibility," what had happened to him and his artistic labors. And, now, just at this time, he must have felt that he, too, was nobly standing his post, ready to compose the long poem that would cause him the most time, trouble, and work of his whole career, and that might stand as a summation of his thought.

Jarves's book seemed to offer Melville something that Ruskin and Reynolds did not. At the time of his writing, Jarves was criticized, not simply as a follower of Ruskin and a promulgator of Ruskinian theory, but worse, as a diluted Ruskin. Even so, he presented a motif that Melville might have found valuable, an interpretation of art from an American viewpoint. Jarves's contribution in this area is salient in its attempt to remake the history of art into evolutionary history, to get away from the notion of the arts as living within the ruins of empire, be they Egyptian, Greek, or Italian. He was trying to make his art history fit into a progressive social and political theory suitable for an emergent America. In *The Art-Idea,* he hastens through his discussion of classical and Christian art, only pauses over the glories of the Renaissance, and moves toward the latest, and possibly for him the best phase of evolution, represented by the American artist and the American art environment. That phase, Jarves thought rightly, had not yet developed. Of William Page, the American painter whom Melville had much wanted to meet in Italy, Jarves remarks that a great artist "is hidden somewhere, but he eludes actual discovery." Jarves did feel that there was promise in the work of a younger man, Elihu Vedder. Melville must have felt his own high assessment of Vedder justified here.

After the publication of *Clarel,* Melville's reading in the visual arts seems to have become less focused, less demanding than it had been before. He had, by then, studied many of the required materials for his own aims; and if it is true, as he had asserted in *Moby-Dick,* that "there is an aesthetics in all things," he had discovered the aesthetics of literary pictorialism.

His contributions to a studied theory of the arts were weaker. In the poem, "At the Hostelry," he rehearses the themes he had encountered in his studies of the visual arts by giving to the painters who take part in his poetic symposium their varied reactions to the idea of the picturesque. Swanevelt, for instance, enunciates the principles of Burke's sublime:

Like beauty strange with horror allied,—
As shown in great Leonardo's head
Of snaky Medusa,—so as well
Grace and the Picturesque may dwell
With Terror. Vain here to divide—
The Picturesque has many a side.
(*Collected Poems* 319)

Jan Steen, the great Dutch painter, is given a speech which serves as a summary statement of the themes of the poem:

to this I hold,
Be it cloth of frieze or cloth of gold,

All's picturesque beneath the sun;
I mean, all's picture; death and life
Pictures and pendants, nor at strife—
No, never to hearts that muse thereon. (329)

The poem, despite the great interest it holds for any student of Melville who is intent on drawing some sense of the master's brooding about the place of the arts in literary composition and in the world, is a disappointment, weak where it should be strong in its discussion of an important theoretical idea. Melville surely understood its weakness and thus probably chose not to publish the poem.[14]

By this time, in the late 1870s and the 1880s, Melville seems to have given up his habit of writing in the date of acquisition for the volumes he received into his collection. In addition, for the books that might interest the student of Melville's concern with the visual arts, there are no markings or marginalia in the pertinent volumes. As a result, one must be cautious about ascribing to Melville a keen or lasting effect from the books which now came to his attention.

From about 1879 to 1891, to judge from publication dates, Melville acquired a series of volumes written by John William Mollett, dealing with a wide range of subjects in art history and art criticism. Designed for the informed general reader, they seem intent upon giving understanding of the works of Rembrandt, Meissonier, Wilkie, and such painters of the Barbizon school as Corot, Daubigny, Millet, and Rousseau. The *Rembrandt* (1879) is a typical volume, a short monograph of just over a hundred pages that undertakes to give a life of the artist, a study of his predecessors, and a reasoned account of his paintings and etchings. There is a chronological listing of both, a bibliography, and 16 illustrations from Rembrandt's work. Mollett's companion study, *Sir David Wilkie* (1881), is of about the same length and follows a similar pattern, giving details of Wilkie's life and discussing briefly, with a number of illustrations, the range of his artistic work and an account of those of his pictures to be found at the time in the public galleries in England. The two volumes that treat *The Painters of Barbizon* (1890) offer sketchy accounts of the work of the several painters they discuss. It is difficult to know what, if anything, Melville might have learned from volumes such as these. They hardly rise above the level of guidebook commentary upon the artists and their works, and so it is scarcely a matter for wonder that Melville seems to have found nothing to engage his imagination and prompt him to reach for his pencil for a marking or marginal comment.

A volume by Georges Duplessis, *The Wonders of Engraving* (1871), was given by Melville to his wife in 1875. It certainly bears upon his interest in the engravings he was busy acquiring during much of his career. As Wallace has demonstrated, there are more than 300 separate items in the surviving collection that once belonged to Melville, and the variety of subjects and artists that he collected is very wide. There are excellent pieces of Dutch realistic art; Italian works ranging through pictures by Veronese, Titian, and Domenichino; a considerable number of works by Rubens and Turner; and a great number of miscellaneous pieces by many artists and engravers.[15]

The Duplessis volume, one of a series called the "Illustrated Library of Wonders," is ideal for the general reader who wants to learn something about the art of engraving. Its eight chapters deal with the origins of the art and give a survey of engravings in Italy, Spain, the Low Countries, Germany, England, and France. A final chapter, "Processes," discusses wood, copperplate, etching, dry point, mezzotint, and engravings in color. Its illustrations are chosen to exhibit the art and include pictures by Rembrandt, Paul Potter, Ruysdael, Hogarth, and Claude, all artists whom Melville seems to have admired.

In *Clarel,* Melville treats the subject of engraving with sympathetic knowledge and attentive detail. A view of Jerusalem is thus characterized:

> "Is yon the city Dis aloof?"
> Said Rolfe; "nay, liker 'tis some print,
> Old blurred, bewrinkled mezzotint."
> (1.37.29–31)

In section 35 of book 2, entitled "Prelusive," the author comments upon Piranesi's "rarer prints" and describes the infinite galleries so dear to the Italian artist, constructing mazes that match mankind's heart, "with labyrinths replete." At the conclusion of the passage, Melville writes:

> Dwell on those etchings in the night,
> Those touches bitten in the steel
> By aqua fortis, till ye feel
> The Pauline text in gray of light;
> Turn hither then and read aright. (33–37)

Here, the pictures have become hermeneutic texts for the bemused traveler. In a later passage of the poem, Melville refers to a less than satisfactory print, "lost, or else slurred," in its reproduction of the portrait of Beatrice Cenci. Here, he is recalling his own experience of seeing the original painting and comparing it to a print he had purchased; the reproduction inevitably loses some of the painting's best qualities.

In 1881, James Jackson Jarves presented a collection of Venetian glass to the Metropolitan Museum of Art. The museum, opened in 1871, offered New Yorkers a fine resource for their appreciation of the arts, and it would be hard to imagine that Melville did not take advantage of it. However, the record of what he is known to have read during the latter years of his life is thin. Bezanson suggests that Melville was "an avid skimmer of current journals and newspapers" ("Introduction," *Clarel* cvii). Many of the magazines of the later nineteenth century were lavishly illustrated, particularly in the articles they published on Titian, Turner, Elihu Vedder, Joshua Reynolds, and other artists. At some time during these late years, Melville acquired a copy of *Turner* (London, 1879), a biographical and critical study by William Cosmo Monkhouse. He also added to his collection Owen John Dullea's study, *Claude Gelée le Lorrain* (New York, 1887) and Frank Cundall's *The Landscape and Pastoral Painters of Holland* (New York, 1891). Cundall's informative volume deals briefly with the works of Hobbema, Potter, Cuyp, and other painters whose paintings had long interested Melville. He sometimes gave illustrated books as gifts: the Duplessis volume on engraving was presented to his wife, Elizabeth, as was *Childhood a Hundred Years Ago,* by Henriette Keddie (London, 1877) with illustrations from the paintings of Joshua Reynolds. Eleanor, his granddaughter, received Keddie's *Landseer's Dogs and Their Stories* (London, 1877) in 1891.

Robert Wallace has justly observed that Melville's "responsiveness to art was also a major strand in his intellectual development, one that scholars have yet to map out in a comprehensive way" ("Melville's Prints and Engravings" 62). During all of his mature life, he seems to have taken every opportunity to visit art exhibitions, galleries, and museums. His collection of prints, assembled over a period of years, is evidence of his desire to have round him, at all times, an assembly of art objects which could feed his imagination.

For more than fifty years, Melville read books about the arts. Their variety, as we see, is almost bewildering; he wanted to acquire an orderly view of art history, to study closely the lives and works of those artists who most moved him, to make his way through the profusion and variety of art topics that could have been open to him only in tantalizing and incomplete glimpses, and to assimilate the best critical efforts of professional artists. In this venture, as in others, he was persistent, marking passages which held his attention, and going back to them, no doubt, as he reread and studied his sources.

The effects of these efforts are best seen in Melville's own writings. Literary pictorialism is a vital element in most of his fiction and much of his poetry. *Moby-Dick* is enriched by the attention given to the portraiture of the whale. Poems in *Battle-Pieces* and *Timoleon* depend, for their effect, upon pictures by Turner, Vedder, Teniers, and Le Brun. Melville is an author who thought in painterly terms, and the result is a vivid embellishment of his literary art.

Bulkington, J. M. W. Turner, and "The Lee Shore"

ROBERT K. WALLACE

O f all the curiosities of *Moby-Dick,* Bulkington is one of the most mysterious. Ishmael first sees him in the Spouter-Inn in chapter 3. "This man interested me at once; and since the sea-gods had ordained that he should soon become my shipmate (though but a sleeping-partner one, so far as this narrative is concerned), I will here venture upon a little description of him" (16). Ishmael sees him again in chapter 23 ("The Lee Shore") as the *Pequod* heads into the open sea: "who should I see standing at her helm but Bulkington! I looked with sympathetic awe and fearfulness upon the man, who in midwinter just landed from a four years' dangerous voyage, could so unrestingly push off again for still another tempestuous term." This fearless mariner is a man of heroic stature. He embodies for Ishmael "that mortally intolerable truth; that all deep, earnest thinking is but the intrepid effort of the soul to keep the open independence of her sea." Yet he never appears again in the book; "this six-inch chapter is the stoneless grave of Bulkington" (106–07).

For decades, Melville scholars have attempted to find a real-life source for Ishmael's "sleeping-partner" shipmate. The editors of the 1952 Hendricks House edition offered four speculative guesses as to the "dedicatee" of chapter 23: one of Melville's actual whaling companions; his cousin Thomas Wilson Melvill; Jeremiah R. Reynolds; Edgar Allan Poe (606–07). In the 1960s S. A. Cowan argued that Bulkington embodies the Emersonian concept of self-reliance, Alan Heimert compared him to the Missouri politician Thomas Hart Benton, and William Powers saw him as the fictional embodiment of Henry Chatillon, the guide in Parkman's *Oregon Trail*. In the late 1970s Keith Huntress pointed to the writings of Henry Cheever as a possible inspiration for Bulkington and "The Lee Shore," whereas Curtis Dahl found a possible influence in a whaling ship that arrived in New Bedford in December 1840, as Herman Melville was about to embark on the *Acushnet*. Suggestive as they are, none of the above theories has laid the mystery of Bulkington to rest. He remains a powerful presence in *Moby-Dick*, but no critical consensus has yet been reached as to his source or to his precise range of reference, if any, beyond the pages of the novel. Melville scholars have so far left Ishmael with the last word on this mysterious figure: "Up from the spray of thy ocean-perishing—straight up, leaps thy apotheosis!" (107).

Ishmael's presentation of Bulkington is so anomalous that some critics have asked whether he is not a mistake, an excrescence from an earlier version of the novel which Melville somehow failed successfully to remove. This theory has been most elaborately forwarded by Harrison Hayford in his 1978 essay on the "Unnecessary Duplicates" in *Moby-Dick*. It has been most recently reiterated in the Northwestern-Newberry edition of the novel (1988; pp. 583, 656–58, 832, 849). Hayford surmises that Bulkington is a leftover from an earlier draft of the story, before either Queequeg or Ahab had been created. He imagines that Melville assigned the latter characters to the heroic role originally conceived for Bulkington and then dismissed the Bulkington figure from the text. Hayford is troubled by the "two vestiges of Bulkington" that remain in chapters 3 and 23, but can offer no explanation "beyond the humdrum one that Melville, like lesser writers, found it hard to throw away good words he had written" (148). I propose an alternative explanation. Rather than seeing Bulkington as a vestigial fugitive from an early version of the story, I wish to suggest the possibility that Melville added him as a deliberate augmentation of the mature story, a *necessary* duplicate who adds a dimension that would otherwise be missing. Specifically, I propose that Bulkington is one of the many tributes in *Moby-Dick*, none of them explicit, to the life and the art of the painter J. M. W. Turner (1775–1851).

Turner's name is nowhere present in *Moby-Dick*. But scholars have recently begun to suggest, and even to document, important affinities between Turner's art and Melville's masterpiece. Beaver in 1972 suggested that Turner's *The Whale Ship*, exhibited at the Royal Academy in 1845, six years before the publication of *Moby-Dick*, possesses the same kind of "indefinite, half-attained, unimaginable sublimity" that Ishmael sees in the painting he encounters in the Spouter-Inn at the beginning of chapter 3 (711). Independently of Beaver, Richard S. Moore in 1982 compared the style of the Spouter-Inn painting with that of two Turner oils: *The Whale Ship* (BJ 415) and *Snow Storm—Steam-Boat* (1842, BJ 398).[1] In addition, he argued that Melville's fictional painting may actually have been influenced by what the novelist knew of Turner's paintings. Moore is persuasive in demonstrating that the "nameless yeast" by which Ishmael characterizes the water in the Spouter-Inn painting is an adaptation of the "accumulated yeast" by which John Ruskin characterizes the water of *Snow Storm—Steam-Boat* in *Modern Painters I,* published in America in 1847 by Wiley and Putnam (the American publishers of Melville's *Typee*). Moore is less persuasive in arguing that Melville may actually have seen *The Whale Ship* and *Snow Storm—Steam-Boat* in London in 1849—and therefore was influenced by these works directly (127–29). One problem is that Moore locates *Snow Storm—Steam-Boat* in the National Gallery, which Melville did visit, when it was actually in Turner's private gallery, which he apparently did not.[2] Another problem is that Melville makes no mention of Turner or his works in the journal of his London visit in November and December of 1849.

My 1985 essay in *Turner Studies* established a number of Turner paintings to which Melville undeniably did have access in London. He saw *The Battle of Trafalgar* (1822, BJ 252) at Greenwich Hospital. He saw the four Turner oils in the Vernon Collection: *The Golden Bough* (1834, BJ 355), *Venice—the Dogana* (1842, BJ 396), *Venice—the Grand Canal* (1833, BJ 349), and *William, Prince of Orange, Landing at Torbay* (1832, BJ 343).[3] At the private collection of Samuel Rogers he saw an early *Seapiece* in oil, the *Stonehenge* watercolor, the *Study of the Quarter-Deck of the Victory,* and numerous rare and valuable engravings. Melville also had access to an extraordinary group of Turner connoisseurs during his last week in London, especially during the Paradise of Bachelor dinners (December 19 and 22) and the Samuel Rogers breakfasts (December 20 and 23). Rogers, in addition to being a collector of Turner, had published two volumes of poetry with celebrated Turner vignettes (*Italy* in 1830 and *Poems* in 1834). Peter Cunningham, present at both of the "Paradise" dinners, had evaluated a number of Turner paintings in his 1849 *Handbook of London;* in 1852 his "Memoir" of Turner was to be the first published biography of the painter. The painter C. R. Leslie, present at the December 22 dinner, was a strong proponent of Turner's late style, having made the arrangements for the 1845 purchase of *Staffa: Fingal's Cave* (1832, BJ 347) by James Lenox of New York. Richard Ford, also present on December 22, was a collector of Turner watercolors who had visited the painter's private gallery in August 1845, soon after *The Whale Ship* and *Whalers* (BJ 414) had been returned from the Royal Academy. John Murray, co-host of the dinner for Melville on December 22, had in 1846 hosted Turner at a May 19 dinner celebrating the exhibition at the Royal Academy featuring Turner's *Hurrah! for the Whaler Erebus!* (BJ 423) and *Whalers (boiling Blubber)* (BJ 426). A. W. Kinglake, present with Murray and Turner at the dinner in 1846, joined Melville and Rogers for the post-Paradise breakfast on December 23 (Wallace, "Sultry" 6–9, 13).

Whether by accident or design, the guests at the above breakfasts and dinners were ideally suited for providing Melville with information about Turner, his seascapes, his private gallery, and his whaling oils. Melville may not have seen *The Whale Ship, Snow Storm—Steam-Boat,* or the private gallery with his own eyes, but he is likely to have seen them through the eyes of some, if not all, of the above companions. The Turner paintings and connoisseurs that he *did* encounter in London help to account for the sophistication with which the young novelist alludes to the painter and his work throughout *Moby-Dick,* even without mentioning his name. Ishmael's rather bold comparison of the pitch-poling Moby Dick to Eddystone Lighthouse in a storm in chapter 133 ("The Chase—First Day") alludes to a rare 1824 engraving of Turner's *Eddystone Lighthouse* to which Melville had access in Samuel Rogers's portfolio of engravings. More important in the context of the novel as a whole is Ishmael's depiction of the painting in the Spouter-Inn. This prose painting incorporates allusions to two contemporary reviews of *The Whale Ship* about which Melville is likely to have heard in London. Ishmael's "boggy, soggy, squitchy picture truly" alludes to the celebrated "lobster salad" epithet that *Punch Magazine* had tossed at the painting in 1845. His depiction of "a long, limber, portentous, black mass of something hovering in the centre of the picture over three blue, dim, perpendicular lines" is adapted from the equally renowned review of *The Whale Ship* that Thackeray had written for *Fraser's Magazine* under the pen name of Michael Angelo Titmarsh. Not only does Ishmael adapt much of his diction from Titmarsh, he also recreates the dynamics of perception by which each man stands before a painting that appears to be a wild chaos of meaningless color—until suddenly the whale, the boats, and the perilous grandeur of the chase become miraculously clear (Wallace, "Sultry" 11–12).

The above allusions, added to Moore's insight about Ishmael's adaptation of Ruskin's "accumulated yeast," provide precise sources for the generally "Turneresque" style of the painting in the Spouter-Inn. By knowingly alluding to what *Punch,* Thackeray, and Ruskin had written about the 1845 *Whale Ship* and the 1842 *Snow Storm—Steam-Boat,* Ishmael's language indicates that Melville had Turner very much on his mind as he composed the fictional painting whose aesthetic Moore rightly calls "a perfect emblem" of the entire novel (125). Ishmael's encounter with this Turneresque painting of "chaos bewitched" (12) at the beginning of chapter 3 is followed almost immediately by his first encounter with Bulkington, still early in the same chapter. Newly landed from several years at sea, Bulkington and his *Grampus* crewmates enter the Spouter-Inn "enveloped in their shaggy watch coats, and with their heads muffled in woollen comforters." Bulkington sits apart as his shipmates divert themselves by "capering about most obstreperously." When they see that he has "slipped away unobserved," they dart "out of the house in pursuit of him." And Ishmael "saw no more of him till he became my comrade on the sea" (15–16).

Hayford correctly notes that the "four-paragraph *Grampus*-crew episode" is "detachable, unintegrated with anything that precedes or follows" (139). This to him heightens the likelihood that it derives from a very early draft of the novel. I wish to explore the alternative possibility that this detachable episode was inserted at a relatively late stage in the compositional process—perhaps even as a way of associating Bulkington with the Turneresque painting that is introduced into the story a few pages before he is. Of course I would not venture to identify Turner with Bulkington on the basis of chapter 3 alone. Queequeg also materializes in the "Spouter-Inn" chapter, soon after Bulkington's departure. I would not for that reason link *him* with Turner. The strongest evidence for linking Turner and Bulkington comes in chapter 23, "The Lee Shore."

Just as the "nameless yeast" that Ishmael sees in the Spouter-Inn painting alludes to Turner's distinctive achievement as a painter of seascapes, so does the kind of "Lee Shore" reality that Ishmael pictures in chapter 23. Ishmael's depiction of a ship approaching a lee shore in a gale pivots upon the irony that "the port, the land, is that ship's direst jeopardy; she must fly all hospitality; one touch of land, though it but graze the keel, would make her shudder through and through." Topographically, the "lee shore" in this chapter is entirely extrinsic to the plot. The *Pequod* has passed far beyond the sandy elbow of Nantucket when Ishmael inserts this chapter; the ship is in no danger of being wrecked literally upon the kind of lee shore that Ishmael describes. Rather it is an imagined lee shore that Ishmael presents, symbolically representing the hazards and perils of the truth-seeking quest. One who seeks the truth must head out into the "howling infinite" of the open sea even though this tack deprives him of "safety, comfort, hearthstone, supper, warm blankets, friends, all that's kind to our mortalities" (106). This chapter is symbolic of Ishmael's intellectual quest throughout *Moby-Dick*. It also symbolizes Turner's intellectual quest throughout his life and art, as Melville would have known when writing this chapter.

In *Modern Painters I* Ruskin had celebrated Turner's portrayal of the "Truth of Water" in a general sense, arguing that in painting rivers or seas, storm or calm, surface or depth, Turner had no equal among his contemporaries or even his predecessors in the history of art. From the beginning to the end of his long career Turner's exploration of the "Truth of Water" embraced the topography and truth of the lee shore. The first sustained record of this interest is found in the sketchbooks he kept during his walking tours of the coasts of England, Scotland, and Wales in his mid-twenties. As Finberg notes, two small pocket-books known as "On a Lee Shore" 1 and 2 (c. 1801) are "filled with drawings of the heavy billows of the North Sea thundering on a lee shore"; Turner used one of these sketchbooks "on the Yorkshire coast, the other on the wild coast between Berwick and Edinburgh" (48). Two adjacent pages in the second book contrast the two primary dangers of the lee shore: one depicts "Fishermen launching a boat in a heavy sea"; the other shows a "Boat coming aground in stormy weather."[4] The "going out" and the "coming in" are equally dangerous to men willing to hazard that treacherous moment that suspends them, defenseless, between the chaos of the water and the solidity of the shore.

Turner's oil painting of *Fishermen upon a Lee-Shore, in Squally Weather,* exhibited at the Royal Academy in 1802 (BJ 16), pictures just such a moment. The small boat is suspended between the bare pole pushing against the shore and the massive wave that strikes the bow with such force that the small boy sitting there recoils with mouth agape (Fig. 1). The drama of the wave breaking against the bow is intensified by the bright sunlight which, through the gaping rent in the clouds, illuminates the white concussive spray against the dark surroundings. The perils of the "going out" in this work are contrasted with those of the "coming in" in the companion oil now known as *A Coast Scene with Fishermen hauling a Boat ashore* (c. 1803–04, BJ 144). In that work the young painter depicted the living line of the lee shore after it had been negotiated by five fishermen who are hauling their boat ashore. But two other fishing boats head out into the storm just beyond the breakers, giving visible testimony to a truth that Ishmael observes upon leaving New Bedford: "one most perilous and long voyage ended, only begins a second; and a second ended, only begins a third, and so on, for ever and for aye" (60).

The Peace of Amiens of 1802 allowed young Turner to extend his study of the lee shore beyond the shores of Great Britain for the first time. His celebrated oil painting of *Calais Pier, with French Poissards preparing for Sea: an English Packet arriving* (1803, BJ 48) is enlivened by his understanding of the double-edged dangers of the lee shore. The

Fig. 1. J. M. W. Turner, *Fishermen upon a Lee-Shore, in Squally Weather*, exh. R. A. 1802, oil on canvas, 36 × 48 inches. Courtesy of the Southampton City Art Gallery, Southampton, U.K.

perils of the "going out" are felt by the French fishermen pulling out from the pier, the small banner on the bare mast showing that they are sailing into the very teeth of the storm (Fig. 2). The perils of the "coming in" await the passengers on the cross-Channel packet from England; their postures and faces express their fear of approaching the pier as soon as the French fishing boats clear the way. The dramatic peril of all the men upon the sea is heightened by the brilliant light that falls upon the chaotic waters and swelling sails from the high gaping hole in the clouds. The presence of the pier, of course, eases the transition between the sea and shore in this particular work.

Young Melville is likely to have learned a great deal about young Turner's engagement with the perils of the lee shore during the last week of his 1849 visit to London. Peter Cunningham, whom he first met on December 19, was particularly drawn to these early manifestations of Turner's talent as a marine artist; his 1852 "Memoir" of the painter gives special attention to *Fishermen upon a Lee-Shore, in Squally Weather* and other early oils of fishermen near the shore (19, 23). The next morning, at the first of two breakfasts with Samuel Rogers, Melville would have seen one such painting with his own eyes. Rogers's one original Turner oil painting, known today as *Seapiece, with Fishing Boats off a Wooden Pier, a Gale coming on* (BJ 540), has been untraced since the sale of Rogers's art collection in 1856. Butlin and Joll take their title from the Christie's sale catalogue, where the oil was also described as "an early work of this master" and "wonderfully true to nature." In style and subject matter, it had obvious affinities with *Fishermen upon a Lee-Shore, in Squally Weather* (described in an 1842 Christie's sale catalogue as "a fishing boat pulling off from the shore, among the breakers, near a wooden pier, which another boat is approaching, under a grand stormy sky in a fresh breeze"). In showing Melville the *Seapiece* in his own collection, Rogers is likely to have located it in the context of the painter's early career (Wallace, "Sultry" 6).

Turner's exploration of the lee shore during the middle period of his career (the 1810s and 1820s) was expressed primarily in watercolors that were published as engravings in such series as *The Ports of England* and *Picturesque Views of the Southern Coast of England*. In Turner's *Ramsgate* for the former series (c. 1825, Shanes No. 72), the looming presence of a massive pier seems only to heighten the peril of the storm-lashed ship being swept toward it (Fig. 3). In *Deal, Kent,* engraved for the "Southern Coast" series (c. 1825, Shanes No. 45), Turner presents his purest and most striking image of the danger of the lee shore as approached from a ship offshore (Fig. 4). The rigid storm flags of Deal indicate a powerful wind blowing directly upon the shore; this long,

Fig. 2. J. M. W. Turner, *Calais Pier, with French Poissards preparing for Sea: an English Packet arriving*, exh. R. A. 1803, oil on canvas, 67½ × 94½ inches. Courtesy of the National Gallery, London.

Fig. 3. J. M. W. Turner, *Ramsgate,* c. 1825, watercolor, engraved by T. Lupton for *Ports of England,* 1827. Courtesy of The Turner Collection, Tate Gallery, London.

Fig. 4. J. M. W. Turner, *Deal, Kent,* c. 1825, watercolor, engraved by W. Radclyffe for *Picturesque Views of the Southern Coast of England,* 1826. Courtesy of The Turner Collection, Tate Gallery, London.

looming stretch of sand is a "lee" shore in the strictest possible sense (even the smoke from a chimney barely escapes its confines before being driven off perpendicular to the shore). The high crest of sand upon which the city is perched would be as treacherous to the keel of a ship in this sea as the long weaving bolt of lightning in the sky would be to its mast. Already one ship off shore is shown to be foundering; the mast of another is about to wash ashore; and the hovellers of Deal, who make their living off the wrecks upon their sands, are about to drag their own small boats into the lee-shore breakers. Turner here graphically depicts Ishmael's paradoxical lee-shore truth that "in that gale, the port, the land, is that ship's direst jeopardy; she must fly all hospitality; one touch of land, though it but graze the keel, would make her shudder through and through" (106).

Both of these engravings from the "middle period" of Turner's engagement with the lee shore were potentially available to Melville even after his return to New York in February 1850. The Astor Library, incorporated and open to the public in 1849 (Leyda 1: 286), owned both the *Ports of England* and the *Picturesque Views of the Southern Coast of England* (*Alphabetical Index* for 1851, p. 391). Melville had seen a third lee-shore depiction from the "middle" period in Samuel Rogers's copy of Thomas Lupton's engraving of *Eddystone Lighthouse* (c. 1817, Shanes No. 113). Engraved for the "Marine Views" project that was never completed as a series, Turner's powerful image was extant only in rare individual copies such as the one belonging to Rogers. Whereas Turner's *Deal, Kent* presents the lee shore in its purest generic sense, his *Eddystone Lighthouse* presents it *in extremis*. Here the shore consists only of the treacherous rocks upon which the lighthouse is built (Fig. 5). The direction and force of the wind (indicated by the smoke blown from the lighthouse) make this a "lee" shore for the dark ship attempting to pass behind the Eddystone on the horizon line to the left. The potential for shipwreck is graphically indicated by the broken mast floating in the dark waters before the bright vertical shaft of the lighthouse.

The third and most powerful period of Turner's engagement with the lee shore resulted in a series of oil paintings in the 1830s and 1840s that carry his aesthetic far beyond either the oil paintings of the early 1800s or the engravings of the 1810s and 1820s. One of the most powerful works in this group, *Wreckers,—Coast of Northumberland, with a Steam-Boat assisting a Ship off Shore*, was first exhibited at London's Royal Academy in 1834 (BJ 357). Its frightening lee shore is populated by a ghostly gathering of wreckers salvaging the remains of an unseen ship whose keel has already shuddered against the shore (Fig. 6).

Fig. 5. J. M. W. Turner, *Eddystone Lighthouse,* c. 1817, engraved by T. Lupton for *Marine Views,* 1824. Courtesy of The Turner Collection, Tate Gallery, London.

Far out in the steep sea, another ship is trying to avoid the same cruel fate with the aid of a steamship that is tugging it into the teeth of the onshore wind. This ship, like Ishmael's Bulkington, "fights 'gainst the very winds that fain would blow her homeward; seeks all the lashed sea's landlessness again; for refuge's sake forlornly rushing into peril; her only friend her bitterest foe!" (106). Melville is not likely to have seen *Wreckers* with his own eyes; in 1849 it belonged to Elhanan Bicknell, who had bought it from Turner in 1844. But many of his London interlocutors would have seen it not only at the Royal Academy but also in Bicknell's home; they are likely, too, to have told the young American whaler/novelist a good deal about Bicknell himself, the whaling entrepreneur who appears to have originally commissioned both *The Whale Ship* and *Whalers* (Butlin and Joll, pp. 206, 262).

Turner's unexhibited *Waves Breaking on a Lee Shore* (c. 1835, BJ 458) translates his published and exhibited lee-shore works onto a new psychological plane. Here there is no ship; there are no people. The

Fig. 6. J. M. W. Turner, *Wreckers,—Coast of Northumberland, with a Steam-Boat assisting a Ship off Shore*, exh. R. A. 1834, oil on canvas, 36 × 48 inches. Courtesy of the Yale Center for British Art, New Haven; Paul Mellon Collection.

Fig. 7. J. M. W. Turner, *Waves Breaking on a Lee Shore*, c. 1835, oil on canvas, 23½ × 37½ inches. Courtesy of The Turner Collection. Tate Gallery. London.

waves, rather than ships, are breaking against the shore (Fig. 7). In place of the wretched human scavengers in *Wreckers,* this shore has a pair of dark shapes that are blessedly inanimate. All of *its* drama is natural, as the impetuous force of water meets the immovable base of the shore. Turner here accepts marine chaos on its own terms—as Ishmael will do when he asserts in chapter 23 that "in landlessness alone resides the highest truth, shoreless, indefinite as God—so, better is it to perish in that howling infinite, than be ingloriously dashed upon the lee, even if that were safety!" (107). Turner apparently created the bracing strength and tonic truth of this powerful meditation for his own private consumption. One feels that in doing so, he has at last "bewitched" some of the marine chaos, some of the lee-shore strife, that had engaged him ever since his early sketching tours. The wind is as strong as ever, the shore as treacherous, yet the observing eye and swelling soul have become strong enough to internalize its naked power.[5]

Melville is not likely to have actually seen Turner's purest and most powerful painting of the "howling infinite" of the lee shore. Because *Waves Breaking on a Lee Shore* was unexhibited and unengraved, the only way the novelist could have seen it was by visiting Turner's private studio and gallery in December 1849. Had he been able to accept a December 19 invitation to spend Christmas at the home of C. R. Leslie, this might have happened; Leslie was one of the few individuals to whom Turner gave unlimited access to the private gallery on Queen Anne Street. Short of visiting the gallery himself, Melville had in Leslie the best possible source of information about the power and the range of its contents. Unlike Cunningham, Leslie admired Turner's late seascapes as much as his early ones. Writing to James Lenox of New York in 1845, Leslie had called Turner "the greatest living genius, not only in England but in the world; and whose genius is such that it may not be equalled in a century" (Wallace, "Sultry" 8, 16). Leslie himself would have had no difficulty imagining Turner at the helm of a ship. He habitually referred to the artist's "sturdy sailor-like walk" and thought that his Royal Academy colleague "might be taken for the captain of a river steamboat" (Leslie 137). This phrasing is taken from Leslie's *Autobiographical Recollections,* edited by Tom Taylor, another of Melville's social companions in London. In his journal entry for November 21, Melville records an evening spent in the company of Taylor, who was also a fixture at *Punch* in its "lobster salad" days.

Whatever Melville's exact knowledge of the specifics of Turner's lee-shore evolution, he knew enough of its essence to recreate that essence in writing chapter 23. Ishmael's tribute to Bulkington as a Truth-Seeker is expressed through Melville's appreciation of the topographical locale and spiritual force of Turner's lifelong encounter with the phenomenon of the lee shore. This particular tribute appears to have been formulated without the aid of such writers as Thackeray, Ruskin, or the anonymous *Punch* man. No commentator before the publication of *Moby-Dick* had addressed Turner's lee-shore subject with the power or precision of Ishmael in chapter 23.

Associating Bulkington with Turner sheds new light on several anomalies within "The Lee Shore" itself. The one-sentence opening paragraph of chapter 23 deliberately refers the reader back to chapter 3: "Some chapters back, one Bulkington was spoken of, a tall, new-landed mariner, encountered in New Bedford at the inn" (106). "The Lee Shore" returns us in more ways than one to the Turneresque essence of its Spouter-Inn predecessor.

After the long second paragraph stations Bulkington at the helm of the *Pequod* and defines the paradox of the lee shore as Ishmael understands it, the short third paragraph begins with a direct question to the reader: "Know ye, now, Bulkington?" I believe that Ishmael expects any reader who is well-acquainted with Turner's life and art to be able to answer in the affirmative. A. G. H. Bachrach, writing in 1981, has pointed out that Turner was the "supreme recorder" of the reality of the lee shore throughout the Romantic era in Europe. He also observed that "a picture of ships on a lee-shore," during that era, "would have been contemplated with the same feelings as that of an almost up-turned stage-coach in an Alpine pass, or a châlet about to be crushed by an avalanche" (22).

In the rhetorical question which ends the short third paragraph, Ishmael generalizes from the lee shore to the quest for truth itself. "Glimpses do ye seem to see of that mortally intolerable truth; that all deep, earnest thinking is but the intrepid effort of the soul to keep the open independence of her sea; while the wildest winds of heaven and earth conspire to cast her on the treacherous, slavish shore?" Such language is entirely applicable to Turner's entire career. So is its emphatic answer in the opening sentence of the fourth paragraph: "But as in landlessness alone resides the highest truth, shoreless, indefinite as God—so, better is it to perish in that howling infinite, than be ingloriously dashed upon the lee, even if that were safety!" (107).

Before concluding the short fourth paragraph with its hero's "ocean-perishing," Ishmael addresses him directly: "Take heart, take heart, O Bulkington!" This language suggests that Bulkington is someone who is alive and outside the book, even as Ishmael is writing. Turner was alive, though not well, in London as Melville was finishing the novel in June 1851. (A brilliant tribute to "J. M. W. Turner" in the June 1851 edition of the *Bulletin of the American Art-Union* had praised the painter for his "greatness of heart" and predicted that England's greatest artist had not long to live.[6]) If Melville was addressing Turner in this heartfelt apostrophe, he could hardly have done better than to do so in a paragraph that begins with Ishmael's stirring declaration about "landlessness," the "howling infinite," and the "highest truth, shoreless, indefinite as God." This is the truth not only of the *Waves Breaking on a Lee Shore* but also of *Snow Storm—Steam-Boat,* praised by Ruskin in *Modern Painters I* and acquired by Herman Melville, later in life, in R. Brandard's 1859 engraving (Fig. 8). Melville's recently catalogued collection of engravings at the Berkshire Athenaeum includes twenty engravings after paintings by Turner, most of them acquired after the publication of *Moby-Dick* (Wallace, "Prints" 81–82, 86).

J. M. W. Turner died in London in December 1851, two months after Melville's masterpiece was published in that city as *The Whale.* The last living account of him in the *Bulletin of the American Art-Union,* in the December 1851 issue, refers to "that large, bulky man who is just now descending the steps" of London's National Gallery (152). Bulkington, indeed.

Assuming that Bulkington was based to an important degree upon Turner, what does this add to our knowledge of Moby-Dick *or of Melville's art?* First, the association of Turner with Bulkington suggests that Bulkington's presence in the final version of the novel is more conscious and artful than is generally thought. Rather than an unnecessary duplicate left over from a very early stage of composition, Bulkington is in this view a highly sophisticated addition to the book after much of it had been written. This "detachable" persona could have been added to the book as late as early June 1851, when a letter to Hawthorne indicates that Melville intends to "take" his whale of a book "by the jaw" and "finish him up in some fashion or another."[7] Such a late addition would have been entirely in the spirit of revision advocated by John Ruskin in *Modern Painters I.* Ruskin advises the young artist (he and Melville were both born in 1819) to compose his most ambitious works with clarity, simplicity, and topographical accuracy. But

> finally, when his picture is thus perfectly realized in all its parts, let him dash as much of it out as he likes; throw, if he will, mist around it— darkness—or dazzling and confused light—whatever, in fact, impetuous feeling or vigorous imagination may dictate or desire; the forms, once so laboriously realized, will come out whenever they *do* occur with a startling and impressive truth, which the uncertainty in which they are veiled will enhance rather than diminish. (1: 420)

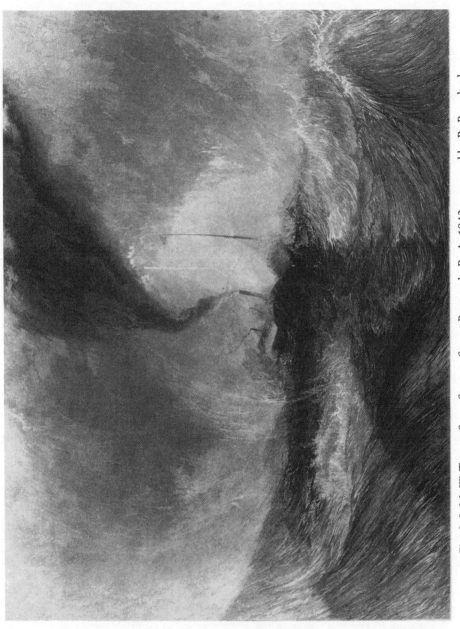

Fig. 8. J. M. W. Turner, *Snow Storm—Steam-Boat*, exh. R. A. 1842, engraved by R. Brandard for *Turner Gallery*, 1859. Courtesy of the Berkshire Athenaeum, Pittsfield, Mass.; the Herman

The indistinct aesthetic which Ruskin celebrates here is the aesthetic of Turner's late, great seascapes of the 1830s and 1840s. It is also the aesthetic of the Spouter-Inn painting and the Lee-Shore chapter.

The influence of Turner's aesthetic upon Ishmael's depiction of "The Lee Shore" allowed Melville to fully confront in *Moby-Dick* lee-shore realities that were present only peripherally in his earlier works. The closing pages of *Typee* feature a lee shore whose winds ("it blew strong upon the shore") intensify the drama, on the plot level, of the narrator's escape from pursuing natives (251). In *Omoo* the fishermen on the lee shore of Loohooloo work in the "long misty line of foam" produced by convergence of the "sullen ocean" and the shore (266). In *Mardi* the surfers on the lee shore of Ohonoo ride through a "scud and rack" resembling that of "the sea-beach, wreck-strewn, in a gale" (272–73). These passing images show the young Melville, in his late twenties, essaying to master the chaos of the lee shore in much the same way the young Turner had in his early sketches and oils. The plots of *Redburn* and *White-Jacket*, both written in 1849, gave him little opportunity to address the truth or topography of the lee shore. But neither did the plot of *Moby-Dick*, the book he began to write soon after returning from his London exposure to Turner's art and admirers in London. The lee shore in chapter 23, as we have seen, is an imagined essence, not an actual stretch of sand. The power of its "howling infinite" translates Melville's earlier understanding of the lee shore into a spiritual realm comparable to that of the late Turner. Inspired by Bulkington and artic- ulated by Ishmael, this vision of heroic perishing was made possible by Turner's own lee-shore evolution. Its powerful aesthetic entirely eclipses that of the conventional deliverance promised by the "angel's face" in the lee-shore painting in Father Mapple's pulpit in chapter 8.[8]

Related to the topographical chaos of the lee shore is the conceptual chaos that Turner's powerfully indistinct aesthetic enabled Melville to bring to the foreground of *Moby-Dick*. This, too, was present only marginally in earlier works. A striking image of psychic chaos occurs in *Omoo*, whose narrator momentarily dreams of "a grayish image of chaos in a sort of sliding fluidity"—until the buzz of a mosquito displaces the dream (216). During the calm in chapter 16 of *Mardi*, "the two gray firmaments of sky and water seemed collapsed into a vague ellipsis" whose "inert blending and brooding . . . seemed a gray chaos in concep- tion" (48–49). The chaotic potential of this image is powerfully unleashed by the gale in chapter 36, but it is immediately calmed when Annatoo is sucked into the sea. In *Redburn* and *White-Jacket*, Melville's depiction of watery chaos begins to feature the word and the concept of "yeast." Jackson's death-plunge in *Redburn* is marked by "one white, bubbling spot" that is "brewed into the common yeast of the waves" (296). During the gale off the Cape in *White-Jacket* "the whole ship is brewed into the yeast of the gale" (97). In these passages, written before the 1849 visit to London, Melville may already have been influenced by the "accumulated yeast" with which Ruskin had described the watery chaos of *Snow Storm—Steam-Boat* in *Modern Painters I*. But it is in the "nameless yeast" of the Spouter-Inn painting and in the "howling infinite" of the Lee-Shore chapter that Turner's indistinct aesthetic allows Melville to bring the raw annihilating power of Nature's inhuman chaos to the very foreground of his fiction. It remains there through the rest of the novel, from the "heartless voids and immensities" of chapter 42 ("The Whiteness of the Whale") to the gale-blown "Channel billows" that "recoil from the base of the Eddystone" in chapter 133, "triumphantly to overleap its summit with their scud" (550–51).

No painter before Turner had depicted reality as Ishmael sees it in the Spouter-Inn painting or the "Lee-Shore" chapter. Turner helped Melville to see this reality—first through Ruskin's prose, then through the paintings and connoisseurs encountered in London in December 1849. Melville, as a sailor, had himself seen the sea and the lee. Turner helped him to convert what he had seen, and felt, into art.

Given the importance I have posited for Turner's aesthetic in the creation of Moby-Dick, *why did Melville not make his tribute to Turner more explicit?* I believe that Melville expected (as implied by the question "Know ye, now, Bulkington?") that any reader familiar with the range and significance of Turner's achievement would recognize the Turneresque essence of Bulkington, the painting in the Spouter-Inn, and the "Lee-Shore" chapter. These covert allusions to Turner function in much the same way as do the ones to Shakespeare. Ahab's "bold and nervous lofty language," his tragic fate, and his relation with Pip at the end of the novel are universally thought to derive from Melville's knowledge of several Shakespearean tragedies to which Ishmael makes no explicit allusion. Direct allusions are unnecessary because any reader steeped in Shakespeare will immediately feel his shaping influence upon the text. Melville's use of Turner is comparable in intention and artistic control. The only reason it has gone unnoticed until recently is that relatively few Melville scholars know as much about Turner as they do about Shakespeare. A student of Turner who reads Melville's 1849 London journal recognizes that the breakfast and dinner companions whom Horsford terms "mediocre and undistinguished" from a literary point of view were eminently distinguished as connoisseurs of Turner ("London Literary World" 39). A student of the published criticism of Turner's seascapes in the 1840s will instinctively recognize Ishmael's response to the Spouter-Inn painting as an adaptation of Titmarsh's response to *The Whale Ship* and will read the "boggy, soggy, squitchy picture truly" as an allusion to *Punch*'s "lobster salad." Anyone who has seen Lupton's engraving of Turner's *Eddystone Lighthouse* (and is aware of its presence in Samuel Rogers's portfolio of prints when Melville visited him) will have no doubt as to the source for Ishmael's otherwise rather surprising comparison of Moby Dick with that lighthouse in chapter 133.

The student of Turner will recognize the above allusions as easily as the student of Shakespeare will read the relationship between Ahab and Pip as a variation upon that of Lear and his fool. Yet with Turner, as with Shakespeare, a certain amount of documentation is available to the critic who wishes to anchor the allusive essence to the novelist's life. Melville's "discovery" of Shakespeare in 1849 is documented by letters written to Evert Duyckinck from Boston and by markings and anno-tations in his copy of Shakespeare's works (Leyda 1: 288–91). His dis-covery of Turner appears to have begun with his reading of Ruskin's *Modern Painters* in 1847 or 1848 (Sealts, *Melville's Reading*, no. 430) and with his exposure to Turner paintings and connoisseurs in 1849. It is first made explicit in the annotation Melville wrote on the title page of Beale's *Natural History of the Sperm Whale,* inscribed on July 10, 1850: "Turner's pictures of whalers were suggested by this book."[9] The young novelist here lets us know that he knew *of* Turner's whaling works at the time he acquired the major cetological source he would use in writing *Moby-Dick.* In such chapters as "The Spouter-Inn," "The Lee Shore," and "The Chase—First Day" he shows us the use he could make of what he knew about these and other "pictures" by Turner.

Although Melville could easily have made the tributes to Turner in these and other chapters more overt, he may well have preferred to leave them shrouded in mystery. To have done so, to have left it to later students of this hieroglyphical novel to unravel this particular "cunning duplicate in mind" (312), is certainly in keeping with the spirit of the novel itself. The author, no less than his narrator, was obviously content with leaving Turner "but a sleeping partner [shipmate], so far as this narrative is concerned."

If Bulkington was a highly calculated allusion to J. M. W. Turner, why did Melville give him the name he did? One reason may be that Turner was, himself, widely known as a bulky man. Another may be that "Bulkington" was connected in Melville's mind to Bonington. The name Melville gave to the "dedicatee" of the "Lee-Shore" chapter effec-tively contasts Turner's bulk, both physical and artistic, with the stature of the young man, who, had he lived longer, might have challenged him as England's preeminent painter of the sea and the shore. R. P. Bonington

(1802–28), though a marine painter, tended to avoid the "howling infinite" of the lee shore or the "nameless yeast" of the open sea. His strong preference was "to depict Nature in her calm moments and in the splendor of a sunny morning rather than battered by storms and groaning under a squall of wind" (Dubuisson 118). Bonington was a particular favorite of many of those British connoisseurs, such as Peter Cunningham, who admired Turner's early paintings more than his late ones. Cunningham's evaluation of Turner's late Venetian oils in his 1852 "Memoir" conspicuously elevates Bonington at the expense of Turner and Ruskin. Turner's views of Venice, Cunningham writes, "noble *poems* as they are in many respects, are in parts grossly untrue. He twists buildings into places where in reality they are not,—and piles Mr. Ruskin's beloved 'Stones of Venice' in localities in which Mr. Ruskin I am sure is unable to maintain them." Cunningham suggests that to contrast Bonington's "noble 'View of Venice' in Mr. Munro's collection" with "the Turner in the Vernon Gallery" is to "see [the] outrages Turner in the eccentricity and abundance of his genius has thought fit to commit with materials requiring no such jugglery to make them more picturesque than they really are" (45–46).

Melville had an opportunity to compare originals by Turner and Bonington not only at the Vernon Gallery but at the private collection of Samuel Rogers.[10] He knew enough about Bonington to have created the name of Bulkington as a conscious variation upon his name. His penchant for painterly puns had been evident as early as *Mardi*, whose narrator claims that the whale-boat officers who drew pictures of whales into their log books at sea were "no Landseers" (95). The man who perpetrated this pun upon the canine specialist among Turner's colleagues at the Royal Academy was perfectly capable of grafting a bit of imaginative heft onto Bonington's name.

Melville's Temples

SANFORD E. MAROVITZ

> . . . for the temple is the crown of the world.
> *Pierre*

hat Herman Melville's temples are not limited to shrines is evident at once in his story "The Two Temples," where *temples* refers to a pair of very dissimilar sites, both of which for him had clear religious overtones. By the time one has finished reading the two parts of that story, the usual denotation of the word has been taken "out of joint," as it were, and ironically attributed not to the great church of the first half but to the theater of the second. Indeed, theater and drama for Melville seem to have held a holy charm, for as considerable evidence suggests, he read plays at times with an almost religious zeal, and he attended theatrical performances, especially when traveling in Europe, with extraordinary dedication. This may be confirmed easily enough with a glance through the journal he kept during his voyage to England and the Continent late in 1849, which provides an account of the numerous evenings he spent at the theater during those two months or so abroad as well as of the books he purchased overseas, including several volumes of plays from different countries and periods.

It is also true that if he spent many of his evenings at the theater, he passed a good part of the limited fall and winter daylight strolling through cities, examining the monuments of London and the Continent, with a particular interest in churches. These he explored with a sharp eye for detail, and on Sundays he generally remained for the services. For Melville, a man who could "neither believe, nor be comfortable in his unbelief," according to Hawthorne in 1856 (*English Notebooks* 433), God could possibly be found wherever the holy presence may be felt, whether in a conventional house of worship or a theater. Missing in one, divinity may be apprehended in the other.

77

Thus the "two temples," the first a church in which Christian brotherhood is nonexistent, and the second a theater in which flourishes the true spirit of Christianity that Melville sought for most of his life. Balancing thematically on lexical irony with the word *temples* as the fulcrum, they are at once individualized and matched. They resemble unidentical twins, one with a soul and the other without, not unlike "Monsieur du Miroir," the enigmatic sketch by Hawthorne that so engrossed Melville in *Mosses from an Old Manse.*[1] Structurally, too, the author has created parallels through his highly descriptive imagery, a complex of directional indications (height, depth, and penetration) with varying degrees of light and dark, brightness and shadow. In respect to these literary devices, Melville was employing kinds of imagery that he had often used before and would use again in much of his writing without loss of effect.

To be sure, from his earliest work through *Billy Budd* he often combined height, depth, and penetration imagery with variations in light and architectural reference to help dramatize his themes and situations. But in the fiction written before *Moby-Dick,* this dramatization is used primarily for highlighting, for generating increased emotional and imaginative effect; it has no necessary relation to theatricality and stagecraft. The sense of confinement, for example, of entrapment in the ships and huts of *Typee* and *Omoo,* is evident through a good part of both narratives, and in *Mardi* Hivohitee's bamboo pagoda and its environs offer an excellent illustration of the manner in which the early Melville could employ directional imagery—both natural and architectural—in a manner suggestive of allegory. In seeking the Pontiff, Taji and his companions first descend into a dark glen festooned with "noxious shrubs" along its dank sides and surrounded by deep woods; at the bottom a polluted brook runs, its source a vile-tasting spring smelling of sulphur. Extinct craters surround Hivohitee's slender structure, which rises story upon story through air "sultry and still, as if full of spent thunderbolts." The small room at the pinnacle is thick with a darkness through which neither Hivohitee nor anything else can be perceived; when Yoomy, the poet, the only one of the group who has climbed to the top, acknowledges that he cannot see, the Pontiff replies, "Then thou hast found me out, and seen all" (359–61). This unlighted space is not the Shakespearean blackness in Hawthorne's fiction that so fixed and fascinated Melville, the hellish blackness of night amid which the try-pots glow on the *Pequod,* but the negative dark that suggests only inscrutability and emptiness, the same sense of vacuity that the despondent Pierre believes to exist within the sarcophagus in the deepest confines of the Egyptian pyramid to which his probing imagination takes him: "appallingly vacant as vast is the soul of a man" (285).

In *Moby-Dick,* which Melville commenced approximately a year after he had rediscovered Shakespeare and apparently within weeks of returning from his first real sojourn in England and on the Continent, the heavy application of dramatic techniques and devices is far more evident than it had been in any of his earlier work. However, even there the nature of his dramatization differs considerably from that in his writing from *Pierre* on because in the latter work for the first time he employs an omniscient narrator, a divine practical joker who toys knowingly with the plight of his hero; from beginning to end, Pierre, the naif, becomes the butt of the narrator's—and presumably Melville's—ironic vision. Yet *Pierre* is less drama than melodrama on an operatic scale. Like *Moby-Dick,* much of it is developed as a sequence of dramatic scenes, but in *Pierre* the emotional extravagance of most of the central characters is heightened by the perspicacious taunts of the narrator. In *Moby-Dick* the experienced Ishmael constitutes half of a balanced portrait of the narrator, while the other half is represented by Ishmael the initiatee; together the two halves balance against all of the other characters, for all but Ishmael go down with the ship, and here Moby Dick serves as the fulcrum. For all of his dramatic devices as a storyteller, though, Ishmael's vision, however comprehensive, is limited. It may be true that he sees and overhears more than any conventional definition of literary realism would permit, but he describes the setting of each scene with its events and its dialogues from the perspective of one who has experienced rather than created it in his imagination. From the opening chapter Ishmael sees himself as having been duped by the Fates into believing that he has governed his actions through his own free will; like Pierre, he has become an acknowledged fatalist. But unlike this impulsive idealist, he learns to accommodate Fate and does not allow himself to become its fool. Although Ishmael is operated upon by Fate, he takes it in stride, whereas Pierre is victimized by it. The directing consciousness that tells Pierre's story moves him and all the other participants from one setting to another, presenting each scene as if it were actually being staged and commenting upon each episode as if that voice were indeed the voice of Fate.

In *Mardi* Taji's companions seek truth from Hivohitee's pagoda-like bamboo tower; in *Moby-Dick* Ishmael enjoys a transcendental vision at the masthead, a fall from which—as White-Jacket learns—brings one back to solid reality with a thunderous splash; and in *Pierre* the heroic young fool of virtue moves from his family estate at Saddle Meadows to the rear building of a church, the Church of the Apostles, another of Melville's temples. Across from Pierre's window is a seven-story church tower, an upper window of which frames the head of Plotinus

Plinlimmon, whose silent features magnetically attract yet bewilder the truth-seeking youth. Below him, Pierre can see nothing: "like a profound black gulf the open end of the quadrangle gapes beneath him" (271). "I look deep down and do believe," Starbuck says in *Moby-Dick* (406), shortly after Queequeg and the rest of the crew have descended deep into the hold of the *Pequod* to find the leaking oil barrels, so deep as to think of seeking the "coins of Captain Noah." They lift the barrels and other containers to the deck till "the hollow hull echoed underfoot, as if you were treading over empty catacombs" (395). Perhaps Starbuck's looking "deep down" instead of heavenward to confirm his belief suggests the root of his trials, his tragic flaw, for time and again in Melville's works the depths are associated with either thought-diving[2] or, by extension, the brooding blackness of mystery, tragedy, and death, as the "profound black gulf" of the courtyard below Pierre's window foreshadows. Even Ahab acknowledges of himself, "Gifted with the high perception, I lack the low, enjoying power" (147). To what kind of "enjoying" does Ahab refer? Presumably the kind that occurs at the Spouter-Inn, the narrow entrance to which is dominated by a painting that appears to have been created during the days of witchcraft; or the kind displayed below decks in the forecastle of the *Pequod* when the crew becomes riotous; or the kind that appears in the tiger-hearted depths of the sea where he is finally carried by Moby Dick, bundled silently into eternity. Is it going too far to suggest that he dies as a consequence of succumbing to the low enjoying power which he refuses to acknowledge yet which humanizes and thus flaws him, the sheer pleasure of a rebellious pride, like the arrogance that led to Satan's condemnation to the deepest pit of Hell?

The heights in Melville's writing are more ambiguous than the depths. They may connote divinity and heaven; or aspiration ("there is a Catskill eagle in some souls that can alike dive down into the blackest gorges, and soar out of them again and become invisible in the sunny spaces" [*Moby-Dick* 355]); or speculation (as in "The Mast-Head"); or alienation in pride or withdrawal ("Like most old-fashioned pulpits, [Father Mapple's] was a very lofty one"; he mounted the ladder to it "as if ascending the main-top of his vessel" and then stood "impregnable in his little Quebec" [*Moby-Dick* 42–43]). The Seaman's Bethel in New Bedford is, of course, another of Melville's temples; in the scene depicting Father Mapple the staging is superb with the preacher highlighted in the lofty pulpit and the walls surrounding the congregation decorated with marble tablets bearing the names of whalemen carried to their death at the bottom of the sea. Like other scenes in *Moby-Dick* that feature individual speakers with compelling force, it holds great dramatic power, but it is a set piece on the order of each one of the gams, self-contained within the longer narrative; it has a reflective, thematic bearing on the romance as a whole, but it is not crucial to the structure of the work, as it directly affects neither plot nor character development. With the writing of *Pierre,* however, Melville made each *dramatic* event and confrontation serve as a link to the next. Unlike Ishmael's circular progression toward the climax of the romance and what salvation he achieves, Pierre's Fate-driven descent to self-immolation is linear. Apart from those chapters in which he either gains background information from Isabel or wrestles with his unwilling imagination to create the great American novel, each episode brings him a long step nearer his fatal end in a subterranean prison cell. The narrator, voicing the consciousness that envisions from the beginning what disillusion Pierre is doomed to suffer, enables readers to perceive what Pierre himself perhaps never does—that intensity of mind and emotion cannot in itself fulfill the need of the ambitious young writer. Instead,

> Youth must wholly quit, then, the quarry for awhile, and not only go forth, and get tools to use in the quarry, but must go and thoroughly study architecture. Now the quarry-discoverer is long before the stone-cutter; and the stone-cutter is long before the architect; and the architect is long before the temple; for the temple is the crown of the world. (257)

If Pierre does not learn the lesson, Melville did, for all that he created after the publication of *Pierre* testifies to his calculated use of design, not the "careful disorderliness" (304) that Ishmael acknowledges as the structural basis of his narrative but a subtle dramatic order in which each object and character may be *envisioned* in relation to every other one, and these may be seen, as if staged and appropriately illuminated, in relation to objectively depicted components of the setting.

A glance at selected tales of the 1850s demonstrates the remarkable effect of Melville's move from digging ever deeper into the quarry of his experience to considering more deliberately the art with which he applied its resources. Simultaneously, it illustrates the increasing attention he gives to architectural heights, depths, and interiors as a means of enhancing his central themes and contrasts. Although he did not altogether forgo the use of an omniscient narrator during this period, for the most part he returned to the first-person teller he had employed in his first six novels. In the tales, however, his narrators are usually older men, those with a lifetime of experience behind them, recalling nostalgically at some times and with bewilderment at others either events from their own past or tribulations from the lives of people whom they knew. Because their chief role in their respective tales is that of representing, i.e., re-presenting, recollections they are drawing from memory and presumably crafting into the stories they tell, these narrators effectively control their material through their comprehensive empirical knowledge of it; consequently, they function as a director might on stage, evoking and placing characters amid the sets, knowing the "facts" of their narratives from the outset though not necessarily understanding all of the implications.

Most of the action in "Bartleby," for example, occurs in one restrictive office complex in which walls, inside and out, serve as controlling images. Appropriately, the edifice housing the second-floor office is situated on Wall Street and surrounded by tall buildings that tend to restrict the setting still further. Two office windows look out upon walls, one upon the white wall of an airshaft "penetrating the building from top to bottom," and the other upon a black wall about ten feet away with "lurking beauties" in its aged blackness and "everlasting shade" (14). To a large extent the effectiveness of "Bartleby" *depends* upon this walled-in setting, in which the characters move from dialogue to monologue among the barriers as if governed by a director on stage. When the scene shifts from the office to the Tombs, of course, walls continue to dominate; despite the narrator's pointing out the grass and sky visible from the prison yard, Bartleby acknowledges, "I know where I am" (43), and soon dies imprisoned, like Pierre, against the wall.

Melville's other short stories generally describe life in a similarly restrictive manner. Even "Benito Cereno," a tale of the sea, occurs chiefly within the narrow compass of a ship, and what dominates thematically is not the vast ocean but the shipboard confinement, with all of the objective imagery that supports it (i.e., ropes, chains, the inner walls of the captain's quarters).

In another of his diptychs, Melville associates a sense of enclosure with directional and architectural images to achieve the striking central contrast of "The Paradise of Bachelors and the Tartarus of Maids." Each half of the dual story is effective and meaningful in its own way, but together they generate a dramatic impact by means of the contrast, and that contrast is reinforced by the setting. In the first half the narrator attends a banquet for nine bachelors in an apartment located "well up toward heaven. I know not how many strange old stairs I climbed to get to it" (320); indeed, it proves to be "the very Paradise of Bachelors" (323), for it complements perfectly the lives of the comfortable drones dining within. In contrast, the working girls dreadfully exploited in "The Tartarus of Maids" labor in a paper mill situated in a deep gorge near the bottom of a hollow called "the Devil's Dungeon" (324); here, too, the epithet is apropos because the girls work in a dangerous, at times even fatal, mechanized environment as if Satan were driving them in the pits of Hell. Each of these two locales serves as a temple befitting one or another divinity, the first on the order of the Olympians and the other of Moloch or Satan. The stage director's role is less evident in either half than in the way the pair has been juxtaposed for a compelling dramatic effect.

The same purpose is fulfilled in "The Two Temples," though in this pair of stories heights are emphasized more for perspective than for the symbolic implications evident in "Bachelors" and "Maids." The basic contrast here is not between heaven and hell but between isolation and community. Climbing ever higher into the bell tower of one of New York's newest, wealthiest, and most fashionable churches during a Sunday service, the narrator peers through a screened but unglazed ventilation window down upon the service, which seemed to be "some sly enchanter's show" far below.[3] "Height, somehow, hath devotion in it" (306), he believes, but soon learns that such devotion has its price. When he finds himself helplessly locked in the tower and forced to ring the bell for aid, he notes a stained-glass window representing a Madonna and child, whom he perceives as "the true Hagar and her Ishmael" (308). Simultaneously he recognizes himself as outcast by the wealthy hypocrites professing to be Christian worshipers below. Having experienced this misfortune in one of New York's wealthiest churches, the destitute narrator reappears in "Temple Second" before a London theater; he longs to enter but lacks the price of a ticket. After a workman hands him one gratis, he climbs to "the topmost gallery of the temple" (313), from which amid the audience of working-class people he watches Macready perform below and realizes that he has found the charity in a London theater that he could not find in a church at home. Whereas he is driven from the first temple after descending from the bell tower, in the second he freely joins the enthusiastic crowd after the performance as the audience flows from the theater.

With his portrait of Bannadonna in "The Bell-Tower," his most Hawthornesque tale, Melville again employs a third-person omniscient narrator as he does in *Pierre*, but here the teller has a double focus upon both a single character and an architectural extension that represents him, the 300-foot tower itself. Typical of Hawthorne's driven antiheroes, Bannadonna is governed by the "unpardonable sin" to the extent that he attempts to compete with divinity by endowing a mechanism with lifelike qualities and erecting a structure commensurate with that aim. After placing a final stone upon it, he stands like Father Mapple, "erect, alone, with folded arms, gazing" proudly upon the Alpine summits in the distance (175). Soon he is slain by his own machine, and a year later the tower collapses, bringing its defective bell down with it.

In all of these stories, among others he wrote during the 1850s, Melville employed architectural imagery in conjunction with heights, depths, and enclosures as a means of developing scenes visually along theatrical lines. This imagery has the effect of stage sets amid which the central character moves almost as if shifted from place to place for dramatic enhancement under the guidance of a director. Perhaps this technique is most evident when the tale is narrated in the third person, as in "Benito Cereno" and "The Bell-Tower," but it is no less true of the first-person narratives as well, "Bartleby," for example, and the two diptychs briefly discussed above. In most cases, the heights are emphasized, though the depths are at least shown, usually but not always, for contrast. Most often, in these tales height connotes heavenliness: the bachelor's apartment in "The Paradise of Bachelors," as we have seen, is "well up toward heaven" (320), and in "Temple First," as the narrator says, "Height, somehow, hath devotion in it." The same association is evident in one of Melville's short poems, "Milan Cathedral," written after his journey of 1856–57 to the eastern Mediterranean: higher and higher the white spires climb, he writes, then asks, What could they symbolize in the builder's eye but "the host of heaven" (*Collected Poems* 242)? Often, however, height suggests isolation or alienation, and sometimes all of these implications may be evident in a single story, as, again, in "Temple First." The ambiguity of this height imagery may well reflect Melville's own enduring, unresolved ambivalence regarding such matters as "'Fixed Fate, Free will, foreknowledge absolute,' &c" (5), over which he meditated and brooded for much of his life.[4] Melville entered this Miltonic phrase in his journal not long after setting out on his first extended visit to Europe in 1849, but those concepts, deeply explored in *Moby-Dick,* were still central concerns several years later when he sailed again toward the Near East in the fall of 1856. This is manifest in his journal from that voyage and more tellingly in the major but often overlooked literary achievement to which it led, *Clarel,* published twenty years later.

Melville's numerous journal entries made during his second European tour reveal how often he was drawn to observe and comment upon sites dominated by striking heights or depths as if they served as sustenance for his brooding nature. After visiting a cave near Naples, for example, he wrote: "What in God's name were such places made for, & why? Surely man is a strange animal. Diving into the bowels of the earth rather than building up toward the sky. How clear an indication that he sought darkness rather than light" (186). Here the images of light, height, depth, penetration, and architecture ("building") are patently yoked with an explicit if rhetorical reference to God. Howard Horsford has noted that Melville had "an inveterate habit of climbing every tower or dome within reach . . . [and] terror or no, . . . never missed a chance to 'get *up* aloft'" ("Introduction," *Journal* 21). Like Hawthorne's narrator in the steeple ("Sights from a Steeple"), Melville appreciated the vantage he gained from peering out toward a far-distant horizon and down over a vast area below as if doing so gave him a sense of power, of control, like that of Bannadonna atop his 300-foot tower, or of greater knowledge through the broader field of perception. While touring Constantinople, he climbed "the Watch Tower within a kind of arsenal" near the bazaar, and he was exhilarated: "From the top, my God, what a view! Surpasses everything" (82). But looking out at the Alpine heights—"covered a long way down with snow"—as he sailed east in the Mediterranean about three weeks earlier, he was also well aware of the isolation such a perspective can bring: "The most solitary & dreariest imaginable" (66). The despair to which such alienation could carry him becomes evident in the 11-line poem he wrote on the Leaning Tower of Pisa, possibly projecting his own psychological insecurity at the time onto the precarious situation of the structure:

> The Tower in tiers of architraves,
> Fair circle over cirque,
> A trunk of rounded colonades,
> The maker's master-work,
> Impends with all its pillared tribes,
> And, poising them, debates:
> It thinks to plunge—but hesitates;
> Shrinks back—yet fain would slide;
> Withholds itself—itself would urge;
> Hovering, shivering on the verge,
>   A would-be suicide!
>   (*Collected Poems* 240–41)

This short poem is but one of many examples of the death theme that Edwin Shneidman and other Melville scholars have observed as recurrent in his work. Horsford points out in his introduction to the journal of 1856–57 that "ideas and circumstances connected with death, violent or by disease, recur constantly in his observations and in his imagery" (21); that suicide was in Melville's mind before as well as after he visited the Holy Land is clear from his description of the "rotten & wicked looking houses [of Constantinople]. So gloomy & grimy seems as if a suicide hung from every rafter within" (85). The "curious kind of timorousness [that] seems to have possessed Melville" during his tour of the Near East, according to Horsford, is perhaps even more apparent from his journal entries in Egypt than from those in Turkey, especially in his observations at the site of the pyramids in Cairo. These impressed him still more than the heights of towers and mountains during this voyage, for they nearly overwhelmed him with their sheer mass as well as their dimensions. Standing before them, he felt:

> oppressed by the massiveness & mystery. . . . A feeling of awe & terror came over me. Dread of the Arabs. Offering to lead me into a side-hole. . . . Long arched way,—then down as in a coal shaft. Then as in mines, under sea. . . . It was in these pyramids that was conceived the idea of Jehovah. Terrible mixture of the cunning and awful. . . . The idea of Jehovah born here.—When I was at top, thought it not so high—sat down on edge. Looked below—gradual nervousness & final giddiness & terror. Entrance of pyramids like shoot for coal or timber. Horrible place for assassination. . . . Pyramids still loom before me—something vast, undefiled, incomprehensible, and awful. Line of desert & verdure, plain[er] than that between good & evil. An instant collision of alien elements.[5]

As in other structures with profound religious significance, the pyramids are temples in which predominant directional images converge with imagery of darkness to connote the mystery and terror that accompany thoughts of death, thoughts often near the front of Melville's mind. And with these thoughts of darkness come images of light as well, which contrast with that somber theme by suggesting another side to death. Melville watches people climbing the pyramids and notes "Arab guides in flowing white mantles. Conducted as by angels up to heaven. Guides so tender" (118). The contrast is remarkable, and the ambivalence is clear; the pyramids serve here as an objective correlative to evoke the same kind of conflicting thoughts that Ishmael entertains in "The Whiteness of the Whale" in *Moby-Dick*. The Great Pyramid stands at once as the inspirer of dread and the origin of Jehova, an expression of the art of divinity and the art of man:

> Slant from your inmost lead the caves
> And labyrinths rumored. These who braves
> And penetrates (old palmers said)
> Comes out afar on deserts dead
>   And, dying, raves.
>
> Craftsmen, in dateless quarries dim,
> Stones formless into form did trim,
> Usurped on Nature's self with Art,
> And bade this dumb I AM to start,
>   Imposing him.
>   (*Collected Poems* 255)

It was the stupendous totality of the Great Pyramid that so affected Melville's imagination, not only the dimensions but the manner in which all parts of it collaborated to form one massive, nameless, metaphysical end.[6] To his eye, "The long slope of crags & precipices" rose more like rock strata than like man-made walls. "In other buildings," he wrote, "however vast, the eye is gradually innured [sic] to the sense of magnitude, by passing from part to part. But here there is no stay or stage. It is all or nothing. . . . Its simplicity confounds you." Through its "sheer immensity," the Great Pyramid affects the imagination as having been created neither by humankind nor nature but by

> that supernatural creature, the priest. They must needs have been terrible inventors, those Egyptians [sic] wise men. And one seems to see that as out of the crude forms of the natural earth they could evoke by art the transcendant [sic] (novelty) of the pyramid so out of the rude elements of the insignificant thoughts that are in all men, they could by an analogous art rear the transcendant [sic] conception of a God. But for no holy purpose was the pyramid founded. (123–24)

To him, the Pyramid was as unfathomable, inscrutable in its vast, fundamental enormity, as the whale is unknowable to Ishmael, for like the whale, it "refuses to be studied or adequately comprehended," however meticulously one measures and calculates, but "looms in my [Melville's] imagination, dim & indefinite" (123).

Doubtlessly, the profundity of his experience at the site of the pyramids did much to put Melville in an appropriate frame of mind for his travels in the Holy Land, to which he sailed within the week. Once there, he noted in his journal, "In pursuance of my object, the saturation of my mind with the atmosphere of Jerusalem, offering myself up a passive subject, and no unwilling one, to its weird impression, I always rose at dawn & walked without the walls" (145). During his stay of about three weeks in Palestine, Melville spent most of the first two in and around Jerusalem with several days (probably three) taken for a tour to Jericho, the Jordan, the Dead Sea, Mar Saba, and Bethlehem, before passing the final week in Jaffa awaiting the Austrian steamer that would carry him to Europe. The difference between the fragmentary descriptions of Christian sites that he entered in his journal and his representation of the same settings in certain passages of *Clarel* exposes the way he dramatized his experience in the Near East by drawing from the store of impressions with which he saturated his imagination, his total consciousness, as "a passive subject, and no unwilling one," during the short period of his stay amid the temples and shrines of the Holy Land.

As I have suggested with reference to his journal, it is difficult to recognize a definite pattern to Melville's varying responses to heights and depths because they seem to be determined both by his constantly shifting moods and his sustained tendency to ponder deeply and at length over metaphysical questions, epistemological and ontological problems, for which neither honest reason nor uncertain faith could provide satisfactory answers. In *Clarel,* however, where one finds greater consistency through his use of a central consciousness as narrator, the interplay between the directional and architectural images complements the emotional, philosophical, and psychological complex that underlies the work. With the aid of a coordinating central consciousness, this interplay dramatizes the poem by visually reflecting the manifold conflicts voiced by the participants (including the unspoken thoughts of the narrator), each of whom to a degree represents one voice or another of that little "company of selves" that Henry A. Murray recognized as inhabiting Melville's own psyche ("Introduction," *Pierre* xcv). These are the "selves" of the journal as well as of *Pierre,* about which Murray was writing when he made that observation. The controlling narrator positions the characters and projects their monologues in particular with the stark contrasts in emotive coloration that are achieved during the most forceful moments of a staged performance.

As in his earlier work, so in *Clarel,* Melville's architectural references, again coordinated with directional and light imagery, function as stage settings, at one time beshadowed in the gloom of inner darkness, as in the depths of the Christian shrines of Palestine, and at another colored by the sun at various stages of ascension or decline over the Judaean wilderness. As often in Hawthorne's writing, when the lights and shadows mix, as at dawn and dusk, they create an aura of doubt that ambiguously reflects the uncertainties of the moral situation in which the characters are enmeshed (*Clarel* 3.32.2–3). However, when the darkness is profound or the daylight clear, the situation is correspondingly despairing or at best vaguely hopeful, for generally in *Clarel* light over the stony wasteland suggests an existential indifference rather than the transcendent illumination that accompanies grace. Similarly, the depths and heights in *Clarel,* depicted with both architectural and natural reference, correlate with dark/light imagery both to enhance the dramatic effect and to project from other vantage points the sense of loss brought by dark mystery in place of divine truth on the one hand or by existential blankness in place of divine glory on the other. So neither the dim chapels nor the sunlit towers are supportive of faith, and the middle ground, the ambiguous level of shadowy skepticism at best and stark hypocrisy at worst, offers the honest seeker no support.

In the Holy Land, three Christian shrines are emphasized, though the directional and light imagery is as often employed with reference to natural settings as to architectural structures. Nevertheless, its application carries over in effect from one to the other so that the darkness of a natural cave is immediately called to mind by association when similar darkness is depicted in the grotto-like sancta beneath the Church of the Holy Sepulchre in Jerusalem and the Church of the Nativity in Bethlehem as well as in the deep stairwells of Mar Saba in the desert. These are the three main sites that Clarel visits on his pilgrimage, as they were central in Melville's own journey in Palestine. If, as Thomas Farel Heffernan has noted, the Church of the Holy Sepulchre was the chief attraction to Melville, it also caused him the greatest disillusion (52). As for the structure of his poem, the most important of the three sacred places is the monastery of Mar Saba, to which most of book 3 is devoted. Reading *Clarel* and the correspondent journal pages with particular attention to Melville's descriptions of these three holy sites discloses that many of Gordon V. Boudreau's observations on Melville's response to Gothic architecture may be extended to include also the major shrines he visited in Palestine and described in these writings.

Before Clarel undertakes his circular pilgrimage within the Holy Land—from Jerusalem and back through Jericho, the Dead Sea, Mar Saba, and Bethlehem—he spends several days wandering in and near the ancient temple city itself. The restrictive setting depicted as the poem opens suggests the eponymous hero's need to free himself from the rationalistic moral and spiritual dilemma in which he finds himself entrapped (Boudreau 68). Clarel is portrayed in a somber, confining cell-like room within the walls of the Old City as he is first becoming aware of those subtle "under-formings of the mind" (1.1.75) that will lead to his increasingly uncertain comprehension of surfaces as his journey progresses: "In chamber low and scored by time, / Masonry old, . . . / Much like a tomb . . . / A student sits, and broods alone." The student, Clarel, not yet identified by name, already assumes here the central role of a Hamlet, pensive, skeptical, alienated, brooding over the state of his world in the imagistic context of confinement and death. During the course of the poem he remains dramatically central, for it is in contrast to his queries and doubts that the viewpoints of all other spokesmen appear as possible alternatives—however extreme or reasonable and accommodating they may appear. Of course, Clarel is as effective a participant in the drama by overhearing the dialogues of others as he is by joining them with his own expressions of uncertainty and his questions. Moreover, as Shakespeare's audience is more aware than Hamlet can be of the conspiratorial thoughts and machinations uttered around him, so the readers of *Clarel* are aided by the narrator's exposition of views held by Clarel's fellow pilgrims and others, which are sometimes related in the form of silent monologues or dialogues spoken outside Clarel's hearing.

Whether expressed amid the stark natural settings of Palestine or at one of Melville's three major shrines, the very presence of these diversified viewpoints on sites suggestive of permanence intensifies the student's internal conflict and thus heightens the dramatic tension of the poem. According to John Wenke, "Melville's conflation of philosophical and psychological complexes highlights the mysteries and ambiguities of life. . . . For Melville, the philosophical idealism provides a generative force behind his symbolic method and his psychological examinations. . . . Philosophical complex and fictional counterpart fuse climactically as Melville's absolutistic questers [in this case, Clarel] pursue the idealistic lure" (585). Clarel's is another example of the age-old quest for permanence amid change, but time and again in *Clarel* the permanence is suggestive of death rather than ideality, and the changes that crackle across the surface of earthly existence only make Clarel's longing for an ultimate truth appear all the more futile. In his journal Melville noted, "There are *strata* of cities buried under the present surface of Jerusalem" (152), and outside the Old City walls at Siloam he observed the village "occupying the successive terraces of tombs excavated in the perpendicular faces of living rock. Living occupants of the tombs— household arrangements. One used for an oven. Others for granaries—" (143). Recognizing the apparent indifference among current villagers to the burial places of previous inhabitants, Melville was doubtlessly dismayed but not fully unexpectant when he saw coffee being sold beside the Ecce Homo arch beneath which Jesus passed (Fig. 1) and Christian pilgrims worshipping over the marble anointing stone in the Church of the Holy Sepulchre, an object to which W. H. Bartlett referred, in a book familiar to Melville, as one of several "palpable absurdities" that make one doubt the authenticity of the church as the site of the crucifixion (179). In *Clarel*, after the pilgrims have climbed to the roof of the Church of the Nativity in Bethlehem, the plainness and simplicity of the early church and its rituals are contrasted against the artifice and superficiality of the late nineteenth century, to which essential spiritual devotion of the past has succumbed: "The thing of simple use, you see, / Tricked out—embellished—has become / Theatric and a form. There's Rome!" (4.16.188–90).

In this respect, Clarel's central problem—and Melville's—is, according to W. H. Auden, a characteristic paradox among the Romantic poets. "On the one hand," Auden wrote, "the poets long to immerse in the sea of Nature, to enjoy its mystery and novelty, on the other, they long to

Fig. 1. Ecce Homo Arch. Reproduced from William M. Thomson, *The Land and the Book; or, Biblical Illustrations . . . of the Holy Land: Southern Palestine and Jerusalem* (New York, 1880).

come to port in some transcendent eternal and unchanging reality from which the unexpected is excluded" (82). There is a difference, however, in that the Nature Melville describes in *Clarel,* for all its mystery, is in itself more suggestive of a stark existential permanence than of vital imaginative transformations, and when integrated with the rock-and-dust-covered strata comprising the remains of dead civilizations it veritably desiccates the life force that once nourished each of those past cultures and all the once-mortal human creatures that created them. In *Pierre,* again in Auden's view, Plotinus Plinlimmon observes in his pamphlet that Christ was abhorrent to the Jews in Jerusalem because while there "he lived according to Heaven's time and they lived according to Jerusalem time" (67). Pierre, attempting to do the same, first in Saddle Meadows and then in New York City, is also estranged from his past and deprived of a future, not only the fool of Truth, Virtue, and Fate but the fool of Time as well, dying in his dark, cave-like cell beneath the level of the city streets.

During his visit to the Near East, both in Egypt and in the Holy Land, Melville depicted the folly of attempting to reveal the underlying spiritual core of Being, the true source of divinity on earth, by exposing the physical foundations through which the mythos and traditions of historic Christianity, in the eyes of countless believers over nearly two millennia, may be confirmed. In a text which Melville read and marked, Arthur P. Stanley discussed the Church of the Holy Sepulchre as "the most sacred of all the Holy Places; in comparison of which, if genuine, all the rest sink into insignificance; *the interest of which, even if not genuine, stands absolutely alone in the world"* (Cowen, "Melville's Marginalia," 526; checked and underlined by Melville in his edition of Stanley 453). Where Melville sought the sacred, he found the profane, and the Church *was* of interest to him, as his markings in Stanley testify. Moreover, again what he saw appealed chiefly to his sense of the theatrical. In his journal, he was characteristically sketchy and laconic in the entries he made following his visit to the Holy Sepulchre, duly noting: "Broken dome—anointing stone[—]lamps—dingy,—queer[—]small—irregular—caves—grots—Chapel of Finding of the Cross. Pilgrims—chatting—poor—resting" (141; Figs. 2 and 3). While inside the church he climbed a narrow set of stairs to a small chapel from where he could look over a balustrade down upon the Turkish guards mocking Christian pilgrims as they entered the building, the same vantage point held by the narrator overlooking a hypocritical church congregation in "Temple First." The chatting pilgrims themselves at the Holy Sepulchre, as portrayed in *Clarel* as well as in the journal, are too much in the contemporary world to seek or gain the kind of spiritual elevation Melville himself had hoped to find. Whether in the chapel above the main floor of the church or in one of the dim sacred grottos below—the Chapel of St. Helen and beneath that the crypt where she allegedly found the Cross—his response was more that of a skeptical observer than a true believer. Indeed, his attitude may well be defined through a journal entry he made after visiting the Dicksons, who had come to the Holy Land to convert the Jews into Christian farmers but had not a single example of success to show for their efforts: "The whole thing is half melancholy, half farcical—like all the rest of the world" (159).

The same was true of his experience at the Church of the Nativity. Following his stopover in Bethlehem, Melville entered briefly in his journal: "In chapel, monk (Latin) took us down into cave after cave,—tomb of saints—lights burning (with olive oil) till came to place of Nativity (many lamps) & manger with lights. View from roof of chapel &c" (139; Fig. 4). His descriptions of this church with its caves are enriched in *Clarel,* but his conclusion, as expressed during Clarel's view from the chapel roof early the next morning, again reveals a formal, theatrical perspective rather than the profoundly religious one that he might have been expected to gain following a pilgrimage to the presumed site of Christ's birth (4.16.188–90).

This sense of theatrical placement in coordination with variations in light and directional imagery is most patently evident in Melville's extended treatment of his stay at Mar Saba in the third book of *Clarel.* In his journal, the entire experience is rendered in a single long entry that emphasizes the striking contrasts of heights and depths that characterize the site:

> *St. Saba*—zig-zag along Kedron, sephulcril [sepulchral] ravine, smoked as by fire, *caves & & cells—immense depth—all rock—enigma of the depth—* . . . wall of stone on ravine edge—Monastery (Greek) rode on with letter—hauled up in basket into hole—small door of massive iron in high wall. . . . At dusk went down by many stone steps & through mysterious passages to cave & trap doors & hole in wall—ladder—ledge after ledge—winding—to bottom of Brook Kedron [about 600 feet below]—*sides of ravine all caves of recluses*—Monastery a congregation of *stone eyries,* enclosed with wall. . . . Went into chapel &c—*little hermitages in rock—balustrade of iron—lonely monks* . . . numerous *terraces, balconies—solitary Date Palm mid-way in precipice*—Good bye—over lofty hills to Bethalhem [sic]. (138–39; Figs. 5–7)

However terse and fragmentary his journal entry, both that passage and his extended description of the monastery amid its barren surroundings clearly illustrate the depth of impression Mar Saba made upon Melville during the short period of his stay there. The monastery dates

Fig. 2. Church of the Holy Sepulchre. Reproduced from William M. Thomson, *The Land and the Book; or, Biblical Illustrations . . . of the Holy Land: Southern Palestine and Jerusalem* (New York, 1880).

Fig. 3. The Holy Sepulchre (with Pilgrims). Reproduced from William M. Thomson, *The Land and the Book; or, Biblical Illustrations . . . of the Holy Land* (New York, 1858).

Fig. 4. Interior of the Church of the Nativity. Reproduced from William M. Thomson, *The Land and the Book; or, Biblical Illustrations . . . of the Holy Land* (New York, 1858).

Fig. 5. Mar Saba and Kedron Valley. Reproduced from William M. Thomson, *The Land and the Book; or, Biblical Illustrations . . . of the Holy Land* (New York, 1858).

Fig. 6. Mar Saba—Church and Courtyard. Photograph by the author.

to approximately 484 when it was founded by Saint Sabas, who is said to have been guided to construct it at its present location by a beam of supernatural light.[7] Originally it held but a few monks, but the number of its inhabitants increased to perhaps 14,000 during its early years, including those who dwelled in caves that punctuate the valley walls and in other buildings constructed in the surrounding area. Anyone who sees this holy site isolated beside the Kedron Valley will understand its impact upon the imagination of as sensitive and perceptive an artist as Melville, especially while undertaking a quest of faith. "Certainly, if there exist [sic] a spot where the wildest dreams of imagination appear realized,"

Fig. 7. Mar Saba—Stairwell at Entrance. Photograph by the author.

W. H. Bartlett proposed, "it is within this convent [i.e., monastery], overhung and surrounded by horrid precipices, full of arched vaults and caverns, adorned with lamps and pictures of saints and martyrs, . . . seen as they were by the gathering gloom of twilight" (226).

By the time Clarel and his fellow pilgrims arrive at Mar Saba late in the afternoon, this aspect of the monastery has been adumbrated by thoughts and visions of death that have accompanied them throughout the day. In the morning they find the corpse of Nehemiah, the aged prophet-like figure who had been traveling with them, at the edge of the Dead Sea, and before they can give him a decent burial, the body is covered by a sudden landslide, as though some divine power were claiming its own without the need of human intervention (2.34.146). While passing through the Judaean Mountains later that day, the pilgrims walk along a path beside a deep gorge, "Piercing profound the mountain bare" (3.1.93), reminiscent of the ravines that lead to Hivohitee's bamboo pagoda in *Mardi* and the paper mill in "The Tartarus of Maids." They peer into the gorge from "A ticklish rim" and see within "Two human skeletons inlaced / In grapple as alive they fell" (3.1.84–85), or so their position suggests. As the travelers approach Mar Saba, they watch monks descending into darkness holding banners and candles; later, after they have entered the monastery and relaxed in conversation, their merry talk is interrupted by the doleful hymn of monks below echoing through a darkened stairwell (3.9.57–59, 3.14.125ff). Ever attempting to fulfill his quest, Clarel climbs to the top of the monastery wall and seeks answers from "turret, crag and star," but all is "strange, withdrawn and far" (3.16.123–24). The most prominent implications of the imagery here— heights and depths alike—are somber, suggestive of isolation and alienation. Mar Saba appears ageless but more indicative of a barren earthly permanence than a heavenly afterlife beyond the edge of time.

With the monastery and its surroundings as his predominant source for the third book of *Clarel,* then, Melville has created his vastest, grandest stage, one upon which each of his major characters has a role, and the "solitary Date Palm" he identifies in his journal becomes a focal object for them all (Fig. 8).[8] Behind them is the narrator in full control of characters and setting, manipulating them—thoughts and placement— in relation to each other while using the palm tree as their inspirational center. As a spot of vital green in the midst of "dreary sterility" (259), it is a device recollective of the doubloon in *Moby-Dick;* but it is more than that, too, because whereas the golden doubloon is simply a thing of fixed material worth and consequently a reflector of each speaker's egocentric values, the living tree in a barren setting represents an integrative,

Fig. 8. Peter Toft, *The Holy Palm of Mar Saba,* 1882. Courtesy of the Berkshire Athenaeum, Pittsfield, Mass.; the Herman Melville Memorial Room.

assimilative source and power, an earthly object that suggests the transcendent, inspiring thoughts beyond those of mere self-interest.

In this scene four principal speakers address the palm in monologue from as many different vantage points. Clarel, standing beside the tree, can see the other three across the chasm, but those three are isolated and unaware of each other's relative proximity. A fifth speaker, Derwent, an Anglican priest and good-natured Protestant accommodationist, sips from the sacred font at the Kedron and converses with another guest at Mar Saba. He looks up at the palm, sees it as a benediction, and wishes it well for another millennium, but it does not move him to think deeply or address it more than briefly (3.25.67–70). The three more sober pilgrims observed by Clarel are situated at different heights on the opposite valley wall. Far below Clarel but above Derwent is Rolfe, to some degree a representation of Melville himself, a man of both faith and reason, one who thinks deeply and appears to be the most fully individuated of all the major characters. Rolfe's response to the palm is that of a sensitive, meditative person to an appealing aspect of nature: "It sighed to his mood in threnodies of Pan" (3.29.82). On a brink high above Rolfe, the Swedish Mortmain utters his quiet monologue of hopelessness and despair; he sees hate as dominating the world and believes that the palm is calling him toward forgetfulness (Lethe) and death (3.28.86–87). Not long after, he succumbs to the palm's influence and dies during the night. As Mortmain voices his despondent monologue, however, Clarel observes Vine lying alone immediately above him and doting on the past, in which lies "the true blessedness"; Vine invokes the palm as a thing of beauty and light that should abide like the Seraphim through whatever subversion and reversals the Fates may be planning (3.26.56–64). Meanwhile Clarel, centered beside the palm, converses with the misogynist Celibate ("Not fortune's darling, . . . / But heaven's elect"), after which he meditates on woman's role in life as spiritual, sexual, or both—with Ruth's image, of course, always clear in his mind. Clarel perceives the palm as a "martyr's scepter, type of peace" (3.30.72–73), an appropriate symbol to help resolve the conflicts in his own warring mind.

The beauty evolving from this positioning of characters in relation to the isolated date palm inheres in the way each in a few lines has effectively completed the portrait that the narrator has been gradually developing since the pilgrimage began; moreover, this has been accomplished with a remarkable sense of both dramatic effectiveness and formal integrity through Clarel's presence at the monastery proper, standing on a shelf of rock beside the tree: "While of each other unaware, / In one consent of frame might be" (3.30.140–41). Here heights, depths, and architecture are once again coordinated with Melville's subtle art of theatrical character placement as a means of both dramatizing the conflict of ideas and drawing unity from diversity in form.

Although Clarel's pilgrimage through the Holy Land does not provide him with the answers and assurance he seeks there, in the closing passages of the epilogue he is admonished by the omniscient narrator to keep his heart and not despair over the deep shadow that has necessarily accompanied the bright light of the modern age. The student may find at last that death is but the threshold to "victory" if faith in *"the spirit above the dust"* is maintained; indeed *Clarel* itself is a record of its hero's intellectual groping toward that realization, which may come "like a burning secret" escaping from the depths of the bosom where it has long been entrapped. The pilgrimage thus constitutes an internal search into mind and soul as well as an external quest in Palestine, and therefore one may infer from the narrator's suggestion of an immanent truth awaiting liberation that something may exist after all in that imaginary sarcophagus to which Pierre's impetuous but futile drive carries him. Pierre, of course, never allows himself to consider such a possibility, and Clarel may not be privy to the narrator's admonition. But because the reader is aware of it, Melville's dramatic poem ends ambiguously, perhaps to a slight degree even optimistically, rather than on the dark note that may be expected as a consequence of Ruth's death and Clarel's own sustained uncertainty.

Thus Melville's use of directional imagery in correlation with his sense of stagecraft is no less evident in *Clarel* than in much of the fiction after *Moby-Dick*. This combination increases the pictorial effectiveness of his architectural settings as accessories to the intellectual drama in which characters and ideas are dynamically engaged, though not necessarily through spoken dialogue. The effect is often further enhanced through the subtle use of light/dark imagery, which, under the pen of a less capable artist could be easily over-exaggerated into an undesirable Gothic or melodramatic chiaroscuro. But Melville's strengthening sense of form, particularly dramatic form, after the failure of *Pierre,* rarely allowed him to falter. It was his own frustrating moral, philosophical, and religious ambivalence that led to the increasing ambiguity of his work, but in the later writing the "company of selves" that constitutes his troupe of fictive players operates under his masterful direction as if it were on stage. By the time he completed *Clarel,* the world—"half melancholy, half-farcical" as he perceived it in the late 1850s—had truly become his theater.

"Like bed of asparagus":
Melville and Architecture

BRYAN C. SHORT

Jn a journal entry of April 21, 1857, Melville describes his first view of Strasbourg Cathedral: "To the Cathedral. Pointed—pinnacles—All sprouting together like bed of what you call it? asparagus" (125). His homely simile contradicts expectations; in *Mardi* he had written, "from its first founding five hundred years did circle, ere Strasbourg's great spire lifted its five hundred feet into the air" (229), and in *Redburn,* "I did not expect that every house in Liverpool must be a Leaning Tower of Pisa, or a Strasbourg Cathedral" (127). In spite of exalted prejudgments, gleaned perhaps from the John Murray travelers' handbooks he read (Star 56), Melville employs his depreciatory trope without irony or hesitation.

Melville's characterization of Strasbourg Cathedral resembles others of his touristic responses to architectural monuments in Europe and the Levant. In his earlier 1849 journal, he reports of "Richboro' Castle" in Sandwich, "an imposing ruin; the interior was planted with cabbages" (12). Cruising the Rhine, he reflects, "the old ruins & arch are glorious—but the river Rhine is not the Hudson" (38). In the later journal, the "Bank of the Bosphorus" in Constantinople is "like Brooklyn Heights" (62), and Milan Cathedral evokes "flies caught in cobweb" (121). As a tourist Melville often calls to mind the "frank Yankee" of Emerson's poem "America, my Country . . . ," staunch in

> his tenacious recollection,
> Amid the coloured treasures of Art

That enrich the Louvre or the Pitti house
Tuscany's unrivalled boast
Of the brave steamboats of New York.

(Ferguson 241)

Melville responds more strongly to scenes of contemporary or commercial life—ships, slums, marketplaces—and more elaborately to wine, food, and accommodations than he does to architecture. In describing the monuments he visits, he uses an often vague and perfunctory vocabulary marked by such adjectives as "great," "glorious," "fine" and "graceful." Melville's journals suggest a writer of limited interest in and sensitivity to the visual arts—a suggestion which flies in the face of massive evidence to the contrary, as this volume attests. Instead, Melville's responses to architecture reveal an imagination at war with itself, a visionary sensibility in conflict with the evidence of vision. Architecture shines a Drummond-light on this key dichotomy in his aesthetic as it develops and changes over the course of a long career.

The frankness of Melville's journal entries bespeaks a cautionary truth: Melville did not see himself as an architect. The parallels he draws between architecture and writing (or human creativity in general) are specific, carefully focused, and problematic. From the early descriptions in *Typee* to the intellectual discriminations of the *Timoleon* poems, architecture carries a set of connotations that undercut the equation of genres implicit in Willard Thorp's judgment that "there could not be another *Moby-Dick* or *Pierre,* but there was left the architectural skill which he had taught himself, beginning with *Typee*" (li–lii). Indeed, in mid-career Melville evolves an anti-architectural theory of literature, and his new sense of the dialectical interplay between the two arts helps him through the dark hours preceding his voyage of 1856.

The tone of Melville's response to architecture is set in *Typee* when Tommo describes the "remarkable monumental remains" he encounters in returning from the spring of Arva Wai. Tommo asserts, "I came upon a scene which reminded me of Stonehenge and the architectural labors of the Druid" (154). Kory-Kory explains that the "series of vast terraces of stone" is "coeval with the creation of the world; that the great gods themselves were the builders." Although Tommo attributes Kory-Kory's belief to ignorance, he concludes the ruins to be "the work of an extinct and forgotten race," and he admits that

> a stronger feeling of awe came over me than if I had stood musing at the mighty base of the Pyramid of Cheops. There are no inscriptions, no sculpture, no clue, by which to conjecture its history: nothing but the dumb stones.

How many generations of those majestic trees which overshadow them have grown and flourished and decayed since first they were erected. (155)

Tommo's rhapsody, in contrast to Melville's later touristic frankness, romanticizes the ruins on the basis of five qualities: muteness, surpassing antiquity, decay, putative divinity, and natural grandeur. Later architectural references play continually against these early figurative values; on their account, the archetypal architectural work is, and remains throughout Melville's life, the Egyptian pyramid. The *Typee* passage shows a striking similarity with imagery in "The Bell-Tower" and, later still, the poem "The Great Pyramid" in *Timoleon;* not a new set of visual elements but a reevaluation of underlying symbolism occasions the dichotomy which comes to characterize Melville's aesthetic during the 1850s.

Typee reveals conventional interpretive structures aptly described by Vicki Halper Litman in "The Cottage and the Temple: Melville's Symbolic Use of Architecture." Architectural constructions in Melville fall into stereotyped categories such as the homey cottage, the ideal Greek temple, or—to extend Litman's argument—the sublime pyramid. Yet underlying Melville's use of such stereotypes, which Litman admits can be ironic, lies an imagination, as Joyce Sparer Adler has shown, obsessed by "relation"—by abstract principles of order and opposition. Bainard Cowan's analysis of Melville's response to the possibility of allegory in *Moby-Dick* spells out a comparable view: "Ideas cannot be directly expressed but must be represented in concepts whose form in their interplay constellates the Idea" (120). I would expand Adler's and Cowan's line of thought to assert that Melville's use of architecture reveals the sort of imagination that Harold Bloom attributes to Wordsworth, characterized by "a cinematic dialectic in which natural sight and sound reach their horizon and blend into a seeing and hearing of processes that cannot, in mere nature, be seen and heard" (*Ringers* 38). Melville belongs among the visionary company who "do tend to make the visible at least a little hard to see" (37). However, the obscurity of Melville's visionary imagination, his tendency to supplant sight with "idea" or "relation," owes as much to specific, early figurative patterns as to the Romanticism outlined by Bloom. The negative synesthesia by which monumental visual art signifies muteness—"dumb stones"—in *Typee* sets the stage for the later anti-architectural definition of literature.

A good example of the relational nature of Melville's imagination, its visionary rather than visual orientation, is the way in which the Great Pyramid takes on the symbolic burden of divine origin when Melville, in his later journal, balances its aery "summit" with experience of its internal passages: "Then as in mines, under the sea. The stooping &

doubling. I shudder at the idea of ancient Egyptians. It was in these pyramids that was conceived the idea of Jehovah. Terrible mixture of the cunning and awful" (75). Melville's 1857 experience permits him to bring together the size and age of the *Typee* ruin with the height of "The Bell-Tower" and the subterranean depths implicit in the famous "Egyptian seed" image from his 1851 letter to Hawthorne (*Letters* 130)— as well as Bartleby's incarceration in "the heart of the eternal pyramids" (*Tales* 53), and the "mummy" imagery in *Pierre* (323). The actual experience of visiting the pyramid gains force in Melville's imagination through the manner in which it brings a series of physical qualities (size, age, height, depth) and their predetermined symbolic values into telling relationships which then produce a new visionary perspective or "idea": that the pyramid gave birth to the thought—at once cunning and awful— of Jehovah, that its sheer spatial scope engendered notions of an absolute temporal origin.

To summarize, Melville's responses to architecture exemplify the process by which his imagination begins in more or less conventional Romantic symbols, specifies and elaborates their figurative values, organizes relationships among them, and then tests them against actuality. In a remarkable journal entry of February 25, 1857, he admits that "Rome fell flat on me"; he summarizes bleakly, "the whole landscape nothing independent of associations" (106). Exhausted, he finds himself burdened by Coleridgean fancy, by a state of mind dependent on "associations" and unable to put into play the esemplastic power of imagination—the power to perceive an "idea" constellated out of the form of a complex conceptual/symbolic interplay. The journal entry demonstrates the remarkable degree to which Romantic aesthetic theory shapes Melville's mid-career understanding of his own personal experiences.

Melville's imaginative process becomes more complex and self-conscious during the period of time bounded by his 1849 and 1856 voyages. Theoretical speculation leads him to focus new attention on both the specific figurative structures that he has earlier engaged and the underlying principles on the basis of which such relationships attain literary meaning. The dichotomous interplay between the visual and the fictional emerges during this period. Architecture tells a limited but central part of the story; its magazine of specific symbolic relations and experiences gives it a unique role in Melville's aesthetic development.

Architecture breaks loose from its earlier stereotypes when Melville consciously poses to himself the question of its analogy with writing. At the end of his "cetological system" in *Moby-Dick*, after comparing his effort to the Cathedral of Cologne, he makes the famous judgment, "small erections may be finished by their first architects; grand ones, true ones, ever leave the copestone to posterity. . . . This whole book is but a draught—nay, but the draught of a draught" (145). In this passage he places the question of origins framed in *Typee* against the parallel question of ends. He explicitly contradicts an earlier passage which asserts that the "copestone" of the universe was put in place "a million years ago" (10); as "draughts" replace "erections," the indefinite past of architecture gives way to the indefinite future of writing. Muteness yields to articulation, "dumb stones" to endless revision. In the relationship between Hawthorne and Shakespeare in "Hawthorne and His Mosses," Melville proposes a similar model of cultural progress: the American present opens itself to the future through a literature which updates truths uncovered by past genius. Architecture, in contrast, takes on an increasingly funerary aspect in Melville's works. It blends the memorial with the immemorial; like the "cenotaph" that begins "The Haglets" in *John Marr and Other Sailors,* it increasingly commemorates the forgotten.

Melville's most clearly architectural tale, "The Bell-Tower," reflects both the changing symbolic value of architecture and the weight of Melville's theorizing. In his lecture, "Statues in Rome," as reconstructed by Merton M. Sealts, Melville reacts to St. Peter's: "The mind is carried away with the very vastness. But throughout the Vatican it is different. The mind, instead of being bewildered within itself, is drawn out by the symmetry and beauty of the forms it beholds" (*Tales* 405). Notwithstanding its problematic authenticity, this statement aptly summarizes the interplay of two Melvillean themes: the solipsistic bewilderment experienced by Pierre in his relationship with Isabel, and the sublimating effect of an artistic discipline by which Pierre attempts, unsuccessfully, to establish a future for himself. Both themes bear upon the parable of Bannadonna, and they resolve in a manner which widens the gap between literature and the visual arts. The dream of mind "drawn out by the symmetry and beauty of the forms it beholds" proves curiously alive in the memorial context of architecture even while *The Confidence-Man* casts fiction as a "bewildering" revision of apocalyptic texts.

Melville's separation of literature from the visual arts certainly owes much to what Bryan Wolf characterizes as "the peculiarly *linguistic* quality of sublime art in America" (156); if Melville were to accede to "the uncanny talent of words to usurp the place of things" (155), then it would be easy to see how a theory of literature as endless revision would end up showing the mind "bewildered within itself." However, this line of thought overlooks the specific nature of theoretical speculation in "The Bell-Tower" and fails to explain the reemergence of architectural *exempla* later in *Timoleon*. Melville had earlier addressed the rapacity of language in Wellingborough Redburn's musings on the proliferation of nautical terms:

> I wonder whether mankind could not get along without all these names, which keep increasing every day, and hour, and moment; till at last the very air will be full of them; and even in a great plain, men will be breathing each other's breath, owing to the vast multitude of words they use, that consume all the air, just as lamp-burners do gas. (66)

As Redburn matures, however, his fears melt away; Melville, in abandoning popular realism for Romance, sees himself as an artist of the "idea" that mediates between language and physical fact, of the "great art of telling the truth" which successive literary or cultural revision, step by step, discloses. Had he indeed lapsed into silence in 1857, the deconstructive view of language evident in *The Confidence-Man* might be blamed; but he wrote on, and his poetic works reach out to the visual world—Civil War events, the landscape of the Holy Land, all forms of art—with renewed forthrightness. "The Bell-Tower" marks the specific place of architecture in Melville's transitional consciousness.

The central question of interpretation in "The Bell-Tower" is whether or not Bannadonna can be taken, as Harold Bloom takes him, as the author's self-image (*Modern Critical Views* 5). Bannadonna, in Bloom's reading, tropes the failed hubris of Melville's career, perhaps evoking the "wicked" nature of *Moby-Dick*. The interpretive and biographical question can more clearly be framed, however, by first acknowledging that the failure in "The Bell-Tower" is an architectural failure that goes far beyond Bannadonna's sin; an earthquake, rather than any moral flaw of its builder, leaves the tower in ruin. Yet the larger failure in the story plays dialectically against Bannadonna's death in terms of the specific aesthetic issues that the tale raises.

The ultimate collapse of the tower, its destruction by natural forces, figures the chief failing of architecture as a discipline. Bannadonna is no mystic, alchemist, or theosophist but a "practical materialist" for whom "common sense was theurgy; machinery miracle; Prometheus, the heroic name for machinist; man, the true God" (*Tales* 184). He prefigures the power of the Great Pyramid, in which "was conceived the idea of Jehovah," as well as the distressing might of the ironclads in *Battle-Pieces* and the bitter Margoth in *Clarel*. Mechanic force usurps the past, tradition, and memory to produce a forgetfulness that returns human creativity to the mute archetypes of nature rather than revisionary cultural truths: "now with dank mould cankering its bloom . . . stands what, at distance, seems the black mossed stump of some immeasurable pine, fallen, in forgotten days" (174). Melville's conclusion, "and so pride went before the fall" (187), suggests the vanity of architectural willfulness, of the reduction of human perspectives, explicitly sought by Bannadonna (183), which results from the builder's wish to challenge nature, to originate the physical source of transcendent symbolic relations.

Bannadonna's death has an efficient cause in his belief in "a law in art, which bars the possibility of duplicates" (179). His theory has led him to cast a different facial expression on each of the great bell's "hours," and it is his supposed "striving to abate that strange look of Una" (185) which seals his fate. Artistic principle contradicts architectural ambition; as a "practical materialist" he seeks a replicable precision—associated with the "conquest" of nature—which his principle of non-duplication in art excludes. He dies at the hand of his own mechanical slave, distracted by contradictory theories.

Bannadonna's notion of non-duplication modifies the "ideas" which Melville associates with architecture. On a biographical level, it attributes Melville's failure to the unwillingness to duplicate his popular efforts. That failure is chastized by Romantic conventions which Bannadonna, in his architectural pride, imagines he controls; yet these conventions, in tracing the power of art to a nature challenged and thus imitated, signify their own inevitable relapse into decay, impotence, forgetfulness.

On the level of aesthetics, Bannadonna's principle of non-duplication prepares the way for what has been taken as the classicism of Melville's late verse. In the first of the "Parthenon" poems, natural imagery as a trope of architectural accomplishment gives way to history:

> You look a suncloud motionless
> In noon of day divine;
> Your beauty charmed enhancement takes
> In Art's long after-shine.
> (*Poems* 235)

The Parthenon gains its effect not as a mute or forgotten divine origin or exemplum of the natural sublime but from the "enhancing" power of its temporality. The second poem in the series, in comparing the Parthenon to "Lais, fairest of her kind," proposes the uniqueness of the temple:

> Spinoza gazes; and in mind
> Dreams that one architect designed
>   Lais—and you! (235)

Melville attributes the isomorphism of natural and architectural beauty not to universal aesthetic law but to the dreaming Spinoza, a counterpart to the transcendental youth who risks death in the masthead chapter of

Moby-Dick. "One architect" did not design both girl and temple; the human artist produces a unique form of beauty.

The non-duplicable beauty which Bannadonna advocates associates clearly with time, with the march of hours around the figures on his great bell. Melville suggests an analogy between historical time—a progression of unique moments into the future—and an art which parallels literature in escaping the memorial/immemorial nature of architecture, its Romantic concern for ultimate origins or mute images of forgotten divinity. The texture of human time gives artistic accomplishment a context, a fitting moment which cannot be duplicated. The notion is not classical but rhetorical; truth lies in decorum rather than Platonic forms. At the same time, the principle of non-duplication, specificity, or historical context leads Melville to rethink the "idea" of the architectural in more subtle terms than those given by the ending of "The Bell-Tower." If the entropic textuality of *The Confidence-Man* destroys the last vestiges of "architectural" Romanticism in Melville's works, then his 1856 trip reawakens an interest in the visual arts that explains his attempted career as lecturer. His sharp, if homely, responses prepare an escape from the association of architecture with mute, ahistorical monumentality and thus lay the groundwork for the later interplay of the visual and the linguistic in *Timoleon*.

Not surprisingly, what revivifies architecture in Melville's eyes is his sense of a new set of relational possibilities inhabiting his responses to the monuments he visits in 1856–57. The piquancy of his metaphors turns attention away from grandiose, preestablished symbolic values and toward the qualities of context and momentary truth. His homely figures return a human scale to the monuments he sees and give them a specific role in a parable of aesthetic education. Melville's journal shows him in the guise of "frank Yankee" coming to a personal belief in the changing (non-duplicated) symbolic potential of the monumental past—a narrative that he revises and elaborates in *Clarel* and, implicitly, in the "Fruit of Travel Long Ago" section of *Timoleon*.

Melville's 1856–57 voyage demands close attention for a number of reasons. It enables him to gain control over the question of origins by, in a sense, rewriting his 1849 journal in a way that gives new significance to the visual and architectural. It is as if Redburn had the opportunity to revise and update his father's guidebook. Melville's new standpoint does not entail a turn to realism; he retains his fascination with idea and relation, with seeing through the visible to a deeper truth; but the broader view opens up additional symbolic fields and a new sense of the unavoidable complexity of aesthetic values, both sources for the many-layered irony of his late works.

The journal of 1856–57 repeatedly situates architectural monuments within the double framework of, on the one hand, the human activity that teems around them and, on the other, the unique, growing sensibility of the narrator. In Constantinople Melville begins with the picturesqueness of the lifting fog: "Could see the base & wall of St. Sophia but not the dome. It was a coy disclosure, a kind of coquetting, leaving room for imagination & heigthing [sic] the scene" (58). The imaginative stimulation provided by architectural monuments partakes of immediate and mundane rather than sublime figures—coyness and coquetry rather than natural grandeur. As the voyage progresses Melville becomes increasingly sensitive to the tales, anecdotes, and situations of the people with whom he travels and whom he encounters along the way. The rich perspectivism of *Battle-Pieces* and *Clarel* follows naturally from his journal.

To the abstract relational categories that architecture evokes in his earlier works—high and low, vast and intimate, light and dark, mute and articulate, antique and new, original and revisionary, and many others—Melville adds the structures of subjective judgment—coy or bold, clear or obscure, sharp or tempered, individual or general, calm or agitated, cunning or awful, civil or barbarous, and so on. Nowhere in Melville's writings is the artistic so thoroughly and elaborately framed by the social. The later stages of the journal are filled with such asides as: "Same old humanity. All the same whether one be dead or alive" (101); "Shows that humanity existed amid the barberousness of the Roman time as it now among Christian barberousness" (106). Freed from a set of "ideas" attuned to archetypal, natural paradigms, Melville explores and tropes the diversity of aesthetic experience.

The extent of Melville's changed values in the 1856–57 journal emerges in a comment he makes in Genoa, well into the trip: "One peculiarity is the *paintings of architecture* instead of the reality. All kinds of elaborate architecture represented in fresco.—Machiavelli's saying that the appearances of a virtue may be advantageous, when the reality would be otherwise" (123). Ironic as it is, the statement acknowledges the logic and morality of effect, or appearances, as part of the "idea" of architecture. Monuments provide a setting or backdrop for human activity as well as examples of an inherent symbolic order. No longer do they have meaning purely in the manner of the Typee valley ruin—independent of transactions with the surrounding social world. Melville's description of the Leaning Tower of Pisa, for example, sets a Romantic tone reinforced by literary and natural allusion but finds resolution in a practical human perspective that casts an ironic shadow on its particular allure: "Campanile like pine poised just ere snapping. You wait to hear crash.

Like Wordsworth's moore cloud, it will move all together if it move at all, for Pillars all lean with it. About 150 of 'em. There are houses in wake of fall" (114). Exactly such effects of human scale as evidenced in the last sentence of the entry inspire the *Timoleon* poems that culminate Melville's responses to the visual arts.

References to art in Melville's 1856–57 journal demonstrate his incipient turn to Victorian aesthetic values—to what Robert Langbaum calls a "poetry of experience"; *Battle-Pieces* explicitly follows such a program (Short, "Form as Vision" 554). Architecture enables a clear picture of Melville's change in sensibility because of the way in which the architecture poems in *Timoleon* directly evoke journal material. "Pisa's Leaning Tower" offers a brilliant case in point:

> The Tower in tiers of architraves,
> Fair circle over cirque,
> A trunk of rounded colonades,
> The maker's master-work,
> Impends with all its pillared tribes,
> And, poising them, debates:
> It thinks to plunge—but hesitates;
> Shrinks back—yet fain would slide;
> Withholds itself—itself would urge;
> Hovering, shivering on the verge,
>   A would-be suicide!
>   (*Poems* 230)

"Pisa's Leaning Tower" exemplifies the effect of Melville's ongoing tendency to see through the visible to the visionary combined with his new perspectivism and the irony that attends his interest in the complex relation between artistic fact, idea, and human context. It overlays the experience cited in the journal with the overt phallicism—not so evident before—associated with "grand erections" in "I and My Chimney" and to a lesser extent "The Bell-Tower." Melville freezes the tower "on the verge" of its orgasmic "plunge" and "slide" eternally debating with itself whether to experience the death—in the Elizabethan sense—of sexual release. What the poem gains from Melville's conceit is a hyperbolically heightened sense of both the miraculous balance and architectural unity of the tower. The shared act of *coitus interruptus* calls attention to the harmony of columns and structure, all as if subject to a single desire.

"Pisa's Leaning Tower" looks through obvious architectural facts to a conceit which brings vividly to life, on the one hand, the structure of the monument and, on the other, an elaborate world of sexual symbolism. The tower remains "hovering, shivering on the verge." The combination of participles suggests the excitement in the situation described; the poem asks whether sexual pleasure lies in release or suspension, and it finds in this question an aesthetic "idea" whose power is proven by the unique fascination of the tower. To what extent, it queries, does the tower gain aesthetically from its ridiculous lean, clearly *not* "the maker's master-work"? To a similar extent Melville's poem employs its indecorous trope to tap an otherwise unavailable rhetorical power.

"Pisa's Leaning Tower" brings architecture to life in a dramatic, amusing, and yet telling manner; its phallicism risks making the reality of the tower "at least a little hard to see," and it cautions us against reading the art poems in *Timoleon* as an affirmation of classicism. Melville's Greek poems describe the classic effect and intent that color Greek architecture, but "Off Cape Colonna" rejects that architecture's complacency. Furthermore, if we recognize the care with which Melville ordered the poems of his final volumes (Short, "Memory's Mint"), then we must consider as meaningful the reversal of his 1856–57 itinerary that gives "The Great Pyramid" a last word before his persona returns, in "L'Envoi," to his own "towers." Melville accepts the typically Victorian challenge of bringing the specific character of classical Greek architecture to life, but his aesthetic no more rests with it than does Browning's with his various Renaissance personae. The *Timoleon* poems explore a variety of aesthetic perspectives without imposing a monistic vision on them; departure from natural archetypes inevitably leaves a complex context which blends subjective and objective, immemorial and remembered, tradition and revision, indissolubly together.

"The Great Pyramid" builds directly on Melville's journal entry of 1857 to describe a work of architecture which challenges nature by combining forgotten past with "future infinite." The monument appears at first blush to achieve exactly the sort of success dreamed by Banna-donna and to reimpose natural archetypes after the distinctly human values associated with the Parthenon in "The Apparition," the final poem in the Greek series:

> Diogenes, that honest heart,
>   Lived ere your date began;
> Thee had he seen, he might have swerved
> In mood nor barked so much at Man.
>   (*Poems* 240)

Melville's journal finds the Great Pyramid "cunning and awful"— qualities which would contradict the humanizing effect of the Parthenon; but the symbolic value of the monument shifts in the poem away from the dramatic tone of the journal and returns to the archetypal "dumb stones" of *Typee*. The poem describes its subject "turning the other cheek" to time and tide in a manner characterized by such terms as "blind," "aridly," and "unmoved." It echoes the "old implacable Sea" of the "Pebbles," which ends *John Marr and Other Sailors* (*Poems* 204). Its ending, however, twists Melville's symbolism in a way that signals what William Bysshe Stein calls a "shocking reversal of his earlier attitudes" (*Poetry* 135). Rather than tracing the "seemingly eternal presence" of the pyramid to nature, Melville asserts "a mortal hold on immortality." Thus, "what lives on in time are the fears which legend perpetuates or which human beings conceive in the darkness of their own thoughts." Stein concludes, "The Melville of 'The Great Pyramid' is in firm control of the values which give his life meaning and purpose. They are not in the Greek or Egyptian past; they are in the present—in his knowledge of the exigencies of fate" (136).

Stein's reading, although correct in large measure, depends on the same equation of architecture with human creativity which Melville has been so careful to avoid. The final stanza of "The Great Pryamid" comments on its preceding (in this case natural) symbolism, as last stanzas and lines in *Timoleon* often do, in a way that reflects the accrued symbolic complexity which architecture displays in his works:

Craftsmen, in dateless quarries dim,
Stones formless into form did trim,
Usurped on Nature's self with Art,
And bade this dumb I AM to start,
    Imposing him.
            (*Poems* 241)

By changing "Jehovah" of the journal to "this dumb I AM," Melville not only evokes the mute, forgotten stones of the *Typee* ruin but also brings ostensible originary power under the aegis of literature—of both Biblical text and "I AM" of the primary imagination in Coleridge's *Biographia Literaria,* purchased by Melville in 1848 (*Log* 1: 271). The pyramid gives birth not to the general human principle of creativity—Jehovah— but to a Romantic theory of logos which traces meaning to "dumb" sources. Coleridge relates imagination not back to nature but to the eternal or infinite, a commonplace in the post-Kantian theories of the sublime which inform Isabel's "bewilderingness" in *Pierre.* Nature is itself ever figurative; thus the evocation by an architectural monument of natural paradigms represents not a reflection of originary forces but self-troping, subject to the revisionary processes of literature or culture. Art "usurps" on nature by instituting symbolic relations which determine our understanding of time and creativity; architecture gains precedence by virtue of its magnitude and age; it threatens to silence other genres, to "impose" a dumbness validated by the Romantic literary tradition from which Melville has emerged.

"The Great Pyramid" recognizes both the power and danger of architecture as an exemplar of human creativity—its special, seductive, yet dissembling influence on the artistic imagination. In Melville's own career it has played just such a role: present at the beginning, it generates a set of visionary ideas which dominate his early symbolic explorations; these then interact with an emergent revisionary aesthetic associated with literature; finally architecture stands revealed as exemplary of exactly that contextualized, figuratively unstable creative process which its age and solidity seemed earlier to contradict. In the final *Timoleon* poem, Melville's last published words, the seeker after "knowledge" returns to his own sources of inspiration, to the "lasting love" found in a perspective that replaces wide visual experience with the comfortable "fold" of literature:

> But thou, my stay, thy lasting love
> One lonely good, let this but be!
> Weary to view the wide world's swarm,
>   But blest to fold but thee. (242)

Melville and John Vanderlyn:
Ruin and Historical Fate
from "Bartleby" to *Israel Potter*

WYN KELLEY

lthough John Vanderlyn painted his *Caius Marius Amidst the Ruins of Carthage* (1807; Fig. 1) at the height of his career as a painter of historical subjects, it foretells his later trajectory into increasingly bitter brooding over his personal ruin and the failure of historical art in the American marketplace.[1] Vanderlyn intended the painting as a dramatic portrait of a hero contemplating ruin and planning vengeance: as he explained in a letter, "I endeavoured to express in the countenance of Marius the bitterness of disappointed ambitions mixed with the meditation of revenge" (Lindsay 71). Vanderlyn succeeded in capturing not only Marius's mixed and powerful emotions but also a popular acclaim for himself far beyond what he achieved for any of his other works. Yet by the time of his death in 1852 he had for many years suffered poverty and neglect. Obituaries in *The Literary World, Harper's,* and *Putnam's* noted this neglect in language reminiscent of Vanderlyn's remarks on the brooding Marius: "I recognized in the man the lingering sparks of a lofty but crushed ambition, whose great disappointments were silently and uncomplainingly borne. . . . " References to an "ungrateful country," "long years of voluntary exile," and "the utter loneliness of his declining years" (McEntee 593, 594) show the way Vanderlyn's public persona had metamorphosed from the promising nationalist painter of his youth into a mythic figure of heroic decay. In his failure and death Vanderlyn received more sympathetic publicity than he had in years, and

Fig. 1. John Vanderlyn, *Caius Marius Amidst the Ruins of Carthage,* 1807.
Courtesy of The Fine Arts Museums of San Francisco; gift of M. H. De Young.

his *Marius* survived as "Vanderlyn's great work, and certainly one of the most celebrated historical pictures in the country" (Kip 231).

In many ways, the issues in Vanderlyn's life and art reveal central issues in New York culture from the 1820s to the 1850s—issues with which Melville became centrally concerned as well. The decline of historical art, the popularity of a romantic military figure in spite of that decline, and the attention paid to Vanderlyn himself as a figure of ruin came to a head in the 1840s and early 1850s at the same time Melville began to consider the themes of ruin and historical fate in his own work. Melville's use of these motifs and his references to Marius in his work suggest that the literary theme of failure came not only out of his own experience of commercial neglect in the 1850s but also in response to cultural and ideological trends. Vanderlyn, as an example of someone suffering from these trends, may well have played a role in Melville's conception of the failed hero from Bartleby to Israel Potter.

One question at the outset, of course, is the extent to which Melville knew of Vanderlyn's life and art. Melville and Vanderlyn inhabited the same world, even knew many of the same people, for several decades. Melville would most certainly have read the lengthy obituary in *Putnam's* that appeared at the same time as sections of *Israel Potter*. Beyond that lies room for abundant conjecture. Vanderlyn grew up in Kingston, New York, about halfway between Melville's two early homes, New York City and Albany.[2] He was the kinsman and protégé of De Witt Clinton, who also helped foster the political career of Melville's uncle Peter Gansevoort.[3] As a member of the American Art-Union in the 1840s, Vanderlyn would have encountered many people known, socially or through their writing, to Melville: the brothers Duyckinck, Charles F. Briggs, William Cullen Bryant, George William Curtis, Asher Durand, and William Gilmore Simms, all of whom in turn might have known of Vanderlyn's cranky temperament and professional hardships.[4] Furthermore, as a friend of the Duyckincks, Melville would have had access to books and information about American artists and historical art.[5] Vanderlyn's friendship with Washington Allston brought him in contact, through his biographer, with Melville's friend Richard Henry Dana, who collected Allston's papers after his death (Averill 183). And Vanderlyn's reputation enjoyed a considerable revival in print in the 1850s, after he died. It is hard to imagine that Melville could have avoided knowledge of his life or his most famous work, the *Marius*.

Melville's references to the historical Marius in *Moby-Dick* and "Bartleby, the Scrivener" may at first seem simple reflexes of an educated person. Plutarch's original would have been familiar to anyone who had attended school or who, like Redburn, owned an "old family Plutarch"

(*Redburn* 67). Just such an allusion appears in *Moby-Dick:* "In plain prose, here are four whales as well known to the students of Cetacean History as Marius or Sylla to the classic scholar" (205). Marius's historical character (157–86 B.C.), as the insanely violent Roman general who fled to Carthage and there proudly rebuked the governor who would deny him sanctuary, has less significance here than his usefulness as a familiar historical reference.[6] In "Bartleby," however, Melville invokes the figure of Marius much more subtly as a way of building Bartleby's character and situation. Speaking of Bartleby's lonely weekends in an office building, the lawyer-narrator exclaims: "And here Bartleby makes his home; sole spectator of a solitude which he has seen all populous— a sort of innocent and transformed Marius brooding among the ruins of Carthage!"[7] Marius as "innocent and transformed" suggests that Melville did not allude to Plutarch's Marius, a remarkably crude character, but to more contemporary portrayals which, following Vanderlyn's, transformed Marius into a Romantic figure of ruin. The emergence of the Marius figure as a Romantic rather than classical hero is one of the more striking examples of literary, aesthetic, and political developments in the 1840s.

John Vanderlyn (1775–1852) painted the *Marius* in Rome at a time when historical art and the neoclassical Grand Manner held center stage in European art. American artists of Vanderlyn's period—from Copley, West, Trumbull, and Vanderlyn's mentor, Gilbert Stuart, to Allston, Morse, and Dunlap—gravitated to Europe to study classical models and to paint in the styles of David, Correggio, and Reynolds (Craven 4–43). The Marius subject had already proved popular in France at the turn of the century, and America's preeminent painters tried it, too. Benjamin West, one of the most influential American practitioners of the Grand Manner, drew *The Slave and Caius Marius,* Samuel F. B. Morse attempted *Marius in Prison,* and Washington Allston, Vanderlyn's closest companion in Rome, painted Marius at Minturna and urged Vanderlyn to take on the subject himself.[8] Vanderlyn had every reason to believe, then, that his choice of subject and style placed him in the mainstream of contemporary art. In fact, Vanderlyn's *Marius* received such flattering attention in Rome that he took it to the annual exhibition at the Louvre in 1808, where Napoleon saw it and awarded it a gold medal.[9] Vanderlyn returned to America convinced that historical paintings would make him rich.

Unfortunately, Vanderlyn misjudged aesthetic fashions in America, and, as a result too of poor financial management, he became a spectacular failure. After some initial success, his career declined steadily as the American public lost interest in historical subjects and turned toward

Romantic landscapes and genre works. Allston himself abandoned historical painting, and landscape and genre painting by artists like William Sidney Mount dominated American art for the rest of the century. As Morse found, "the traditional themes of history painting, with their aristocratic implications, made little appeal to the rising middle-class patron and public." John Neal, in an 1824 issue of *Blackwood's,* called Vanderlyn's work "Frenchified" (Larkin 83, 84).

Nevertheless, Vanderlyn's associations with Stuart and Allston placed him solidly in the New York art world, and he participated in the founding of the Apollo Art Association and in the American Art-Union. His schemes to establish a Rotunda to exhibit his panoramic paintings— another art form that became passé the minute he tried it—were for a time patronized by Washington Irving, John Jacob Astor, and De Witt Clinton (Averill 113), to name just the few most familiar to Melville. Although Vanderlyn quarreled with the American Art-Union and lost his lease for the Rotunda, his *Marius* survived as an important work of historical and republican art. Especially in literary circles, it received considerable attention, where it was read as a Romantic portrayal of heroic ruin. Lydia Maria Child's poem, "Marius Amid the Ruins of Carthage," based on Vanderlyn's painting, presents the hero as a "lofty soul" and a "genius."[10] Other literary works drawn from Marius's life, including a verse play by William Gilmore Simms, view Marius not as the ambitious maniac of Plutarch's *Lives* but more like the pensive Byron of *Childe Harold's Pilgrimage,* a "ruin among ruins."[11] Vanderlyn's painting, while striving after the neoclassical models of late eighteenth-century art, fortunately included enough Romantic elements to make it enduringly popular.

For some writers of the 1840s, the painting also embodied political themes of the Jacksonian era. In 1840 the *Democratic Review* published a long anonymous piece entitled "Marius" that romanticizes Vanderlyn by allying him with Napoleon and romanticizes Napoleon by allying him with Marius.[12] All three are seen as democratic heroes whose military sympathies partake of an aesthetic/political sublime. In a vision that would later prove ironic, the writer imagines Napoleon seeing in "Marius" his own future exile and meditated revenge; Vanderlyn was to receive this kind of revisionist treatment too. In seizing on Vanderlyn's Marius as a kind of American Napoleon or classicized Jackson, the *Democratic Review* writer made the same sentimental and popular use of the motif that Child had and Simms later would in the year after Vanderlyn died. But the article also shows how easily democratic ideology appropriated history—making Marius into a plebeian fighting the aristocrats—and art for its purposes. It suggests how many strands—

historical, aesthetic, political, literary—Vanderlyn's painting managed to join.

But if the painting embodied and inspired popular themes, it was also canonized as an American work of the highest refinement and taste. In 1842, the American Art-Union in New York chose the *Marius* as the prize painting in its annual lottery and had an engraving of it distributed to all its members. In choosing Vanderlyn's work for the engraving, the Art-Union emphasized that the *Marius* had "become identified with the history of Art in this country." Among the members of the American Art-Union in 1842 were several men who later became friends of Melville's, including Evert Duyckinck, who in 1847 took Melville to an exhibit at the Art-Union. It is likely, then, that Melville saw at least the engraving, if not the original painting, sometime in the 1840s. Curiously enough, the engraving for 1843 was William Sidney Mount's *Farmers Nooning,* an example of just the democratic art that superseded Vanderlyn's.[13]

In any case, Melville's reference to Marius in "Bartleby" owes more to Romantic and contemporary notions of the figure than to the original classical sources. Like Vanderlyn and the contemporary writers, Melville selected the brooding Marius rather than the active ambitious Marius as the analogue to Bartleby's character. And of all the images of Marius available to Melville, Vanderlyn's seems the most apt for several reasons. First, knowing how strong was the impact of the visual arts on Melville's imagination, we can speculate on the effect this painting—or more likely the American Art-Union engraving of it in Duyckinck's collection—could have had on Melville's characterization of Bartleby. Vanderlyn's Marius, though nothing like the pale and ghostly Bartleby in appearance, has Bartleby's defiance and strength of character. Melville's repeated references to Bartleby's stony motionlessness, his monumentality, as if he were "the last column of some ruined temple" (33), bring to mind the ruined columns and temple of Vanderlyn's painting. Secondly, the example of Vanderlyn himself, who died in miserable poverty in 1852 just before Melville began "Bartleby," would have given the painting a new layer of irony. Any viewer after 1852 could read Vanderlyn's fate in the painting along with that of Marius and thus identify the painting as an image of personal and artistic as well as political ruin. Melville, in his circumstances, would certainly have been sensitive to such an irony.

In early 1853, Melville's career, like Vanderlyn's from the 1820s on, seemed in collapse. Like Vanderlyn he aimed for a market that didn't exist. In the first in a series of attempts to win back his earlier fame, he published "Bartleby" (1853), a portrayal of a man brooding silently over the ruins of his life and his culture. It would not seem a popular formula, but Melville's story was well received, and other similar tales followed: "The Happy Failure" (1854), "The Fiddler" (1854), "The Bell-Tower" (1855), and "Jimmy Rose" (1855).

Between these stories and *Israel Potter* (1854; 1855), however, a significant change in the formula occurred. Whereas the short stories concentrate on isolated instances of ruin, *Israel Potter* indicts a whole nation in the failure of his central character, an American patriot and a hero of Bunker Hill. After an early success as a courier for the American republic, Potter is captured by the British, escapes, but is detained in London for close to fifty years because of various historical and personal crises. His long exile ends, not in a triumphant return to a welcoming country but in final obscurity and poverty. More than Melville's other stories of failure, it ties the hero's downfall to historical forces and the ironies of historical fate. Melville's narrator speaks as a Marius who not only meditates on Potter's undoing but also condemns the country that permitted it.

Although the Marius echoes in *Israel Potter* are interesting in themselves, there are also echoes of Vanderlyn's biography, which received considerable attention in *Harper's,* the *Literary World,* and *Putnam's* in the year following his death. The obituaries for John Vanderlyn ring with sentimental regret for the passing of an anachronistic national hero. A similar tone, charged rather more with irony, reverberates in *Israel Potter.*

Several of the obituaries emphasized, as the American Art-Union did in 1842, how much Vanderlyn was identified with the early history of the American nation. The *Literary World* observed that with his birth in 1775 Vanderlyn's life was "coeval with the American Republic" (219), and other accounts referred to Vanderlyn's early and familiar intercourse with America's great national figures: he met Washington; he painted portraits of most of America's presidents in his period; he went to France as the protégé of Aaron Burr; and later in life, even after his prestige declined, he was chosen to paint *The Landing of Columbus* for the Capitol Building in Washington. Vanderlyn's devotion to historical subjects, even if he did not find a market for them, made him a vestige of a generation that monumentalized America's history and its heroes. Like Melville's grandfather, Thomas Melvill, he seemed, as in Oliver Wendell Holmes's poem on the subject, a "last leaf."

Israel Potter, too, is caught up in his country's history and then, like Vanderlyn, washed up on its shores a forlorn wreck. In battle he views Washington from afar and consorts intimately with Benjamin Franklin, John Paul Jones, Ethan Allen, and even England's George III. He returns to America on the anniversary of the battle of Bunker Hill and witnesses the dedication of the monument which is the only memorial of his heroic service to his country. But like Vanderlyn he has been forgotten. In the end, old and penniless, he contemplates the remains of his father's farm, now a rubble: "a little heap of ruinous masonry" (*Potter* 169).[14]

Potter also resembles Vanderlyn in that he had an important but shadowy relationship with a biographer-narrator. The original Israel Potter, whose narrative Melville bought in London in 1849, worked through Henry Trumbull to make his complaints public in 1824. Vanderlyn too, trying to advertise his desperate circumstances, acquired a biographer in 1848. Robert Gosman, a journalist from Kingston, wrote a eulogistic account of Vanderlyn's early years in Paris, ending with the triumph of the *Marius*. Interestingly enough, after Vanderlyn's death the manuscript circulated among several of Melville's friends. In his search for a publisher, Gosman approached Nathaniel Parker Willis, Richard Henry Dana (at just the time when Melville was also approaching Dana about an appointment in an overseas consulate), and finally the editors at *Harper's*. In December 1853, however, in the middle of all this, a great fire stalled *Harper's* operations for some time, and Gosman had to give up (Averill 182–83, Howard 211–12, Leyda 482–90).

Melville was also negotiating with *Harper's* that winter to publish "The Encantadas." Because of the fire, he went to *Putnam's* with "The Encantadas" and also *Israel Potter*, which he began writing in the spring of 1854. *Putnam's* accepted both, ran "The Encantadas" in March, April, and May 1854, and began running *Israel Potter* in July.

In June, between "The Encantadas" and *Israel Potter*, *Putnam's* published a tribute to Vanderlyn written by a fellow artist and friend, Jervis McEntee. Appearing as it does in a magazine with which Melville was immediately concerned, it seems likely to have come to his notice. The piece, called "John Vanderlyn," is quite similar to Gosman's manuscript in making Vanderlyn a fallen national hero. McEntee presents Vanderlyn in old age as a "genius" suffering "the melancholy effects of penury and want, silently endured" (593). The author is seized, as Gosman was in his narrative, with the historical ironies of Vanderlyn's life:

> Here was the companion of kings and emperors, the friend of Madison and protégé of Burr, with the frost of almost eighty winters upon his head, a heartbroken suppliant in the very village where he was born, and upon which he had reflected so much honor, discouraged and disheartened by the coldness and indifference he had everywhere met, come back to die in the place of his birth, to lay down his reverend head, a beggar among his ungrateful countrymen. (595)

Melville in 1849 had already called Israel Potter's story "the Revolutionary narrative of the beggar" (*Journals* 43). And he was well into writing *Israel Potter* when he would have encountered the *Putnam's* tribute to Vanderlyn. It does not seem likely, then, that he had Vanderlyn in mind until the later chapters and the preface were written. Yet the concluding chapters and the preface are precisely those sections that take up the Vanderlyn theme of ruin. The mocking address to the Bunker Hill monument, contrasting sharply with the lyrical, sometimes humorous, opening chapters, dwells heavily on "the hard fortunes of my hero" for which he "durst not substitute for the allowance of Providence any artistic recompense of poetical justice" (viii). Melville ironically awards Potter a monument, not only the Bunker Hill marker but also the "posthumous pension" of "ever-new mosses and sward" (vii). In a similar vein, though less ironically, the author of the *Putnam's* piece speaks of Vanderlyn's *Columbus* as "an unsatisfactory monument from the grudged and tardy bequest of an ungrateful country" (594). Potter's years in London, which Melville describes as marked by a squalor that "we too cross over and skim events to the end" (161), bring him to the same depths of poverty and oblivion that Vanderlyn suffered in "the utter loneliness of his declining years" (594). Vanderlyn, says McEntee, might dream of the "star of Napoleon, who had encouraged and flattered him . . . and Burr, his early patron and friend. . . . [L]ooking back on the days when he enjoyed their companionship and encouragement . . . he might well have sighed for the closing scene" (594). Israel Potter, too, reminisces about "the far Canaan beyond the sea . . . painting scenes of nestling happiness and plenty" (166). Both Melville's Potter and Vanderlyn are afflicted with the sense of a glorious past which both they and their country have lost. Both brood over the suffering they have endured in the service of a beloved but ungrateful nation.

The theme of ruin in *Israel Potter* is less personal, more broadly historical, than in Melville's earlier stories of ruin. Whereas Trumbull's Potter is a victim of social and political injustice, Melville's Potter suffers as well the impersonal force of fate; and *fate* appears much more frequently as a word and concept in Melville's Potter than in Trumbull's. In fact, the influence of fate seems inexorable, and Melville rather heavyhandedly peppers the novel with references to impending doom: "Little did he ween that these wretched rags he now wore, were but suitable to that long career of destitution before him. . . . The dress befitted the fate" (19); "fate snatched him on the threshold of events" (84); "he was destined to experience a fate, uncommon even to luckless humanity" (160). McEntee also speaks of the "incomprehensible Providence" governing Vanderlyn's life. Like Marius, Melville's narrator and the aged Vanderlyn dwell deeply, even obsessively, on fate's darkly perceived interventions.

Melville may have exploited the inflated rhetoric and aggrieved tone of the *Putnam's* piece on Vanderlyn for the purpose of parody. But *Israel Potter* also shows Melville working seriously with issues that plagued Vanderlyn's life and art. In choosing a historical subject Melville may have found something that Vanderlyn also sought through historical art: namely, an opportunity to imagine events not in terms of personal character or destiny (as an artist might do in a portrait and as Melville had done in his novels through *Pierre*) but in a more classical sense, as ordained by history.[15] Melville's later writings, particularly *Battle-Pieces*, sections of *Clarel*, and ultimately *Billy Budd*, show increasingly the intervention of historical events into individual lives. Vanderlyn's Marius brooding among the ruins of Carthage emerged in Melville's cultural milieu at a time when Melville himself began to see history as a force seriously to be reckoned with. It stands as a powerful image of Melville's brooding. But more than that it allows Melville's readers to conceive of his brooding—so often viewed as personal to the point of neurosis—as something sanctioned and heightened by contemporary art. In the brooding Marius, Melville might have seen a grimly heroic engagement with fate that corresponded to his own aspirations.

The White Mountains, Thomas Cole, and "Tartarus": The Sublime, the Subliminal, and the Sublimated

JOHN M. J. GRETCHKO

Jn the second and most unusual part of Herman Melville's two-part story, "The Paradise of Bachelors and the Tartarus of Maids" (1855), the word *white* in some form occurs sixteen times, *blank* seventeen times, *snow* six times, and *pallid* four times. Truly the predominant color and motif is whiteness, just as it is in *Moby-Dick*. What more fitting, then, that the locale of the "Tartarus" should be the White Mountains of New Hampshire and not, as commonly believed, Mount Greylock of the Massachusetts Berkshires? It seems clear that Crawford Notch is the predominant source of the mountain scenery for "Tartarus" and that Theodore Dwight is a probable source linking the story to *Moby-Dick*. Further, a sublime painting by Thomas Cole may well have influenced "Tartarus," as an examination of Melville's serious burlesque of the sublime will reveal.

Up to the time of Melville's writing *Moby-Dick* in 1850 and 1851, the White Mountains had maintained their image as a rugged and forbidding wilderness, still remote from eastern seaboard cities. Thomas Cole was preeminent among those who painted these mountains previous to 1850, and the first to capture public enthusiasm with two paintings in the late 1820s. When railroads in the late 1840s and early 1850s made this the most accessible wilderness in America, painters saturated the area, especially the New Hampshire towns of North Conway and West Campton. When photography crippled the art of portraiture, and tubed paint expedited direct painting from nature, nature became the new portraiture. It is in this era of immediate artistic and commercial development that Melville opens the sixth paragraph of chapter 1 of *Moby-Dick:*

> But *here* is an artist. He desires to paint you the dreamiest, shadiest, quietest, most enchanting bit of romantic landscape in all the *valley of the Saco.* What is the chief element he employs? *There* stand his trees, each with a hollow trunk, as if a hermit and a crucifix were within; and *here* sleeps his meadow, and *there* sleep his cattle; and up from *yonder* cottage goes a sleepy smoke. (796; emphasis mine)

The idea of using the positioning words *here, there,* and *yonder* could well derive from a chapter titled "The White Mountains" in *Sketches of Scenery and Manners in the United States* (1829), where the anonymous author, in reality Theodore Dwight, bewails the eroded mountain terrain of the Saco River valley: "*Here* is a rock rounded like a cannon shot. . . . *There* lies a mass of granite. . . . *Yonder* lies the rock from which it dropped off."[1] Melville adopts the positioning words in this instance to introduce an idyllic painting rather than the ragged ruination of the upper Saco valley, caused by avalanche and cataclysm, which he will describe in small degree in "Tartarus." The insertion of a hermit into a scene that is sublimely Claudian seems perverse, however, since a hermit, like a brigand and a beggar, was distinctly Salvatorean.[2] A landscape artist of that day, striving to achieve the effect of the sublime, generally would not have allowed such extremes to clash. Melville's hermit, whose presence is more suggested than real, shatters the pastoral scene just as George Inness did with his exceptional railroad in *The Lackawanna Valley* (1855). One of the goals of Melville, if not Inness, too, may have been to satirize the landscape artist's quest for the sublime.

Melville's scene, sans hermit, was a common painterly view of the White Mountains from the Intervale near North Conway on the Saco River. The painter Benjamin Champney is regarded as the catalyst in 1850 of the so-called "White Mountain School of Art." His friend, John Frederick Kensett, created what became the celebrated and signature Claudian image of the region, *The White Mountains—Mt. Washington,* which was acquired in 1851 by the American Art-Union and circulated as an engraving to its then more than 13,000 subscribers (Metropolitan Museum 150).

In his memoirs, Champney, who probably painted more White Mountain scenes than anyone else, noted that "North Conway and the neighborhood of Artists' Brook at one time became almost as famous as Barbison [sic] and the Forest of Fontainbleau. . . . Dozens of umbrellas were dotted about under which sat artists from all sections of the country" (160). By 1853 some 40 artists were quartering temporarily at North Conway. This was the beginning of the heyday of the American landscape movement. The railroads had brought the wilderness closer to Boston and New York; the landscape painters helped to subdue it. By century's close, some 450 artists in nearly 6,000 paintings had reproduced almost every conceivable feature of the White Mountains (Campbell xiii).

In his description of the Saco, Theodore Dwight compares its ruddy waters to another colorful but nameless river: "The first explorers of one of the rivers of South America . . . were shocked at the sight of its waters, which flowed to the coast dyed by certain plants upon its margin, with the redness of blood."³ Although the Saco's waters are not dyed but muddied by runoff from the White Mountains, they are tinged nonetheless, and their swift flowing along often narrow banks also suggests lifeblood flowing through its own channels. In "Tartarus" Melville's river is brick-colored and called Blood River, an intentional parallel with the Blood River in canto 12 of Dante's *Inferno*. Dwight's reddened waters were probably a catalyst for Melville's image of the red river.

For Melville, the word *bloody* itself has a conscious link to the White Mountains in *Moby-Dick*. In chapter 42, "The Whiteness of the Whale," in the midst of his litanies on the power of whiteness, Melville remarks how the White Tower of London uncannily pulls "on the imagination of an untravelled American," so much more "than those other storied structures, its neighbors—the Byward Tower, or even the Bloody" (998). This *bloody* is a familiar neighbor. Melville continues, calling up "those sublimer towers, the White Mountains of New Hampshire, whence, in peculiar moods, comes that gigantic ghostliness over the soul at the bare mention of that name, while the thought of Virginia's Blue Ridge is full of a soft, dewy, distant dreaminess." In leaping from the tangible to the sublime, Melville echoes Dwight, who follows his own observation on the waters with a paragraph on the sublime:

> When we meet, in a mountainous country, with those contrasts of beauty and wildness, gentleness and sublimity, which such regions generally present: the majesty and awfulness of the wide forest, the naked summit, the prone rock, and the overhanging precipice, make us the more admire and enjoy the rich valleys at their feet, and the calmness and coolness of the streams which water them. The feelings of sublimity become painful, after they have been long excited by the view of vast magnitudes, and useless extensions of height, depth, or level surface; but they are often relieved by our recurring to milder, calmer, and more encouraging objects, with which we generally find them intermingling. The comforts of a cottage, the pleasant aspect of a river's margin, the green nibbled turf under the shade of a grove,

alternately administer to us a calm which alleviates the painful exertion we make in contemplating things too great for our powers. (63)

Where Dwight feels the pain of sublimity in his experience of the White Mountains, Melville feels a gigantic ghostliness in the soul at the mere mention of the sublime mountains' name. Dwight reveals the limitations of the subject of the sublime when he excuses himself from further reflection on it on the grounds that it is something beyond human powers. Melville goes the purveyors of the sublime one better, by suggesting that he does not need the actual experience of the sublime to convey an understanding of this metaphysical state, and thus he very modestly derides the idea of the sublimity of these mountains. He then replaces Dwight's Arcadia with thoughts of the Blue Ridge, a return to the tangible once again.

The mountains' most important attraction for travelers in the early nineteenth century was Crawford Notch, a three-mile close-walled stretch of the upper Saco River valley. Although other geological formations called notches, or passes, were known to exist in New Hampshire and to a lesser extent in other New England states, when someone said "the Notch" almost everyone knew which was meant. Nathaniel Hawthorne writes in "The Great Carbuncle" (1836) that the Notch "is the gateway of the mountain region" (154). No other notch at that time produced quite the same powerful emotions as Crawford Notch did.

After their wedding day, August 4, 1847, Herman and Elizabeth Melville began their honeymoon, arriving the next day at Centre Harbor, New Hampshire, on Lake Winnipesaukee, at the southern border of the White Mountains. Melville, on the occasion of his only recorded trip to these mountains, writes: "Tomorrow [August 7], I think we shall leave for Conway & thence to Mt Washington & so to Canada" (*Letters* 65). In a letter to her mother, Lizzie confirms the itinerary by stage to Conway. Writing from Canada, Lizzie asks her mother if she has received letters sent from Conway and Haverhill (Metcalf, *Herman Melville* 44, 46). Two years later Melville, in his London journal, peered down on the city of London from on high and compared it to "Clouds of smoke, as though you looked down from Mt. Washington in a mist" (32). Chances are he would have made this private notation only if he had ascended Mount Washington during the honeymoon journey; certainly the mountain had ready accessibility from the Notch. Since one of the Melvilles' destinations apparently was Mount Washington, their route from Conway had to have been through Crawford Notch. That Melville saw the Notch previous to his journey to the Levant in October 1856 is evident from a statement in his journal from that trip: "Pyramids not in line. Between, like Notch of White Mountains" (118).

There were three stage routes from Conway, one west to Centre Harbor, another to Maine, and the other north to the White Mountains through the Notch. Hosea Ballou II writes in an essay on the White Mountains for April 1846: "At Conway, all the regular stages for the White Mountains pass the night, so as to reach the Notch-House, thirty-two miles distant, the next day, a little after noon" (118). The Melvilles, then, on or about the evening of August 8 and perhaps on several evenings thereafter stayed at one of four inns: (1) Thomas Crawford's Notch House, where Henry David Thoreau and his brother John apparently stayed in September 1839 (and Francis Parkman in 1841), described by Ballou as a decent two-story inn with outbuildings; (2) the Mount Washington House or Fabyan's, a spacious, elegant hotel with outhouses;[4] (3) the White Mountain House, a two-story inn, not very well kept (all three of these at the base of their own private trails to the top of Mount Washington); or (4) a brand new lodging called Willey House, three miles south of Thomas Crawford's. These were the only accommodations in this wilderness. An exhausting eight- to nine-hour horseback trip to Mount Washington's peak and back would have demanded lodging close by. Of all inns, the Notch House possessed the most romantic setting and was at the base of the preferred bridle path to the summit of Mount Washington. The Notch House also provided horses and a guide, a service evidently matched only by the Mount Washington House. Thus it appears that only two inns would have met the newlyweds' needs. All these inns served commercial travelers year round on this well-traveled artery between Vermont and Portland, Maine.

Both approaches to the Notch, one from Conway in the south, the other from the north, had special merit. The abolitionist-journalist Nathaniel Peabody Rogers describes in a newspaper article of 1841 the strikingly different emotional response one was likely to have to each approach:

> The White Mountain Notch, it is said, is best seen passed . . . from Conway up. You then ascend it instead of descending, and get the sublime impressions of an *enhancing* approach to those awful piles in the great architecture of God. The other way you get the terrible and the appalling, as you *precipitate* from the level where flows the infant Saco, down through the jaws of the sundered mountain, and seem to be plunging almost to the bottomless abyss—with those frightful masses of fallen rock on every hand, bidding you gaze up to behold other hideous masses toppling to their descent (174).

The Reverend Thomas Starr King, for whom a White Mountain has been named, exhorts the tourist in a very florid account, *The White Hills* (1859), as the mountains were formerly called, to ride down through the Notch from the Notch House for the most impressive view, even if the traveler had already come up through it from the south (202). Evidently King, who had stayed at the Notch House in 1849, was less interested in ascending to the sublime than he was in descending into the horrific, equally awesome, Tartarean abyss. In short, the Notch was an important tourist attraction, especially for a sublime experience.

One of Thomas Cole's visits to the mountains resulted in his magnificent *The Notch of the White Mountains (Crawford Notch)* (1839), which depicts the beginning of the Saco valley (Fig. 1).[5] Melville's prose painting in chapter 1 of *Moby-Dick* seems to depict the opposite end of the valley. Melville's initial interest in the paintings of Thomas Cole stems at least from May 4, 1847, when he became a subscription member of the New York Gallery of the Fine Arts. This institution featured 11 Cole paintings, the most important part of the Gallery's works (Gretchko, "Melville and the New-York Gallery" 7). Although the *Notch* was not among the Gallery's Coles, Melville had the opportunity to view Cole's work from the week of April 1 through mid-May of 1848 at the important Thomas Cole Exhibition in New York City.[6] The American Art-Union borrowed 83 Cole paintings to honor this famous American artist, who had died two months earlier. Melville had this picture either in mind or in some kind of reproduction before him (perhaps as a drawing or lithograph but not as an engraving), when he began "Tartarus." His narrator rides a six-year-old horse named Black, parallel to the black horse in Cole's *Notch:*

> Turning to the east, right out from among bright farms and sunny meadows, nodding in early June with odorous grasses, you enter ascendingly among bleak hills. These gradually close in upon a dusky pass, which, from the violent Gulf Stream of air unceasingly driving between its cloven walls of haggard rock, as well as from the tradition of a crazy spinster's hut having long ago stood somewhere hereabouts, is called the mad Maid's Bellows'-pipe. (323)

Melville's connections in this passage with Crawford's Notch are far from coincidental. As in Cole's painting, the road turns to the east, or right side of the frame, passing what could be a farmhouse or small barn in a meadow sun-splashed despite the obvious autumn setting, as indicated by the deciduous trees changing color. The dusky pass is the northerly entrance into the Notch. Melville's Gulf Stream echoes Dwight, who quotes from the notes of a traveler about a rapid gust followed by large drops of rain reminiscent of a storm in the actual Gulf Stream (67). And in local lore the Notch itself had even been called a Gulf (King 205). *Cloven* is a suggestive word in this context because of the subliminal

Fig. 1. Thomas Cole, *The Notch of the White Mountains (Crawford Notch)*, 1839. Courtesy of the National Gallery of Art, Washington, D.C.; Andrew Mellon Fund.

presence of the devil in Cole's work just to the left of the pass. An overhanging rock at this point in actuality was called the Devil's Pulpit (Eastman 81). Nearby was a great stone face called the Old Maid of the Mountain (Eastman 81), not to be confused with the Old Man of the Mountain, which is west of these Notch mountains. The creation of Melville's crazy spinster may have been influenced also by Dwight, who writes: "At no great distance from the [Notch] house, a rising ground brings to mind the melancholy fate of a young woman, who here terminated an enterprise to which she was incited by an ardent lover" (64). The legendary girl is one Nancy, who has since given her name to a brook and a mountain, a bit further removed from Dwight's questionable location. Nancy froze to death pursuing her recreant beloved. Later another candidate for the honor of inspiring the legends around this story will emerge. Although the word *Bellows'-pipe* in Melville's story may indeed have been influenced by a feature of Mount Greylock in the Berkshires, as scholars have attested, the more likely impetus came from Hawthorne who, in "The Ambitious Guest" from *Twice-told Tales* (1842), writes: "the Notch is just like the pipe of a great pair of bellows" (326).

Melville's story next begins to wend its way into the Notch, from north to south:

> Winding along at the bottom of the gorge is a dangerously narrow wheel-road, occupying the bed of a former torrent. Following this road to its highest point, you stand as within a Dantean gateway. From the steepness of the walls here, their strangely ebon hue, and the sudden contraction of the gorge, this particular point is called the Black Notch. The ravine now expandingly descends into a great, purple, hopper-shaped hollow, far sunk among many Plutonian, shaggy-wooded mountains. By the country people this hollow is called the Devil's Dungeon. (324)

The horseman in Cole's painting has ridden from the north. The actual road was usually a torrent after a heavy rain. The pond in the foreground of Cole's work is the headwaters of the Saco River, here a mere creek (now culverted), which flows through the Notch. This is the watershed between the Saco and Ammonoosuc river systems. Melville's Dantean gateway, possibly influenced by Cole's subliminal devil, is in reality the Gateway of the Notch, at the highest point of the road, then a mere twenty-two feet wide through which both road and Saco passed. The gateway was greatly expanded for a railroad in 1875.

The Notch itself was generally described as grim. The Reverend Benjamin Willey describes it thus in 1856: "The entrance on each side is guarded by high overhanging cliffs, and the walls adjoining the road

Fig. 2. Detail of Mount Willard from Cole's *The Notch of the White Mountains (Crawford Notch)*, 1839. Courtesy of the National Gallery of Art, Washington, D.C.; Andrew Mellon Fund.

rise up perpendicularly fifty feet" (18). The Notch is a narrow rent extending about three miles, a hollow sunk among wooded Mount Willard, Mount Willey, and Mount Webster, the large forbidding mountain choking the pass in Cole's painting. High up the south side of Mount Willard is a cavern known as the Devil's Den, which can be seen from the Notch. In the painting another subliminal devil can be detected halfway up the right side of Cole's mountain (Fig. 2). For literary effect Melville may have taken the Devil's Den and bestowed it upon the bottom of the Notch itself, perhaps contributing to a statement made later by the boss of the Devil's Dungeon papermill when he observes a reversal in the natural order of things: "it is colder here than at the top of Woedolor Mountain" (335). Although certain features of Mount Greylock in the Berkshires do seem to correspond to features of the mountain scenery in "Tartarus," Greylock's notches are not exemplary and rarely are identified on maps. Certainly no road connects a notch with its Bellows Pipe and Hopper.

To date no identification has been made of the cataracts described in "Tartarus":

> Sounds of torrents fall on all sides upon the ear. These rapid waters unite at last in one turbid brick-colored stream, boiling through a *flume* among enormous boulders. They call this strange-colored torrent Blood River.[7] Gaining a dark precipice it wheels suddenly to the west, and makes one maniac spring of sixty feet into the arms of a stunted wood of gray-haired pines, between which it thence eddies on its further way down to the invisible low-lands. (324; emphasis mine)

This rather prominent Dantesque topography is not typical of Greylock. The torrents which the narrator hears are almost certainly the Flume and the Silver Cascade, called the Second Flume,[8] which tumble down the western side of Mount Webster into and essentially forming the Saco, which, as we have seen, Dwight compared to the redness of blood. It is possible that at this time the Saco itself may have leapt a considerable distance. The Reverend Samuel Eastman in *The White Mountain Guide Book* (first published in 1858) describes both cascades falling several hundred feet in broken descent. Of the Silver Cascade he writes:

> Like most of mountain falls, it rather glides over the surface of the ledge than leaps in a clear, unbroken sheet from the summit to the base. At first the water is diffused over a broad surface, and in times of drought is divided into several small streams. Before it reaches the base, however, all the water is compressed into a very narrow channel. (89)

Nor are these the only falls contributing to the Saco and its invisible lowlands. In the next "Tartarus" paragraph, Melville moves the reader through the Notch and offers a further suggestion concerning its identity:

> Conspicuously crowning a rocky bluff high to one side, at the cataract's verge, is the ruin of an old saw-mill, built in those primitive times when vast pines and hemlocks superabounded throughout the neighboring region. The black-mossed bulk of those immense, rough-hewn, and spike-knotted logs, here and there tumbled all together, in long abandonment and decay, or left in solitary, perilous projection over the cataract's gloomy brink impart to this rude wooden ruin not only much of the aspect of one of rough-quarried stone, but also a sort of feudal, Rhineland, and Thurmberg look, derived from the pinnacled wildness of the neighboring scenery.[9]

A major event in the history of the Notch occurred on the night of August 28, 1826, when violent storms burst over the mountains causing massive slides of rocks, water, and loosened trees, leaving many valleys in hideous ruin. At the southern approach to the Notch, Samuel Willey and his family had built their mountain home, which also served as a haven for travelers. The Willeys became unnerved by the sounds of sliding rock and left their house to seek safety further away from the mountain base. Their unfortunate decision led the family and two others, a total of nine people, to be killed in the avalanche and ensuing flood. Ironically, despite enormous destruction to the area, their home remained untouched. This tragedy stayed in public consciousness long into the nineteenth century, partly because of the extraordinary irony of the event and partly because the ruination long remained as a reminder. To the south of the Willeys' house, and considerably further than Melville's cataract, the swollen Saco tore through a sawmill built by Abel Crawford. The remains of the mill plus its black-mossed logs tumbled together were undoubtedly still to be seen even 20 years later, during the Melvilles' honeymoon. Hawthorne in "The Ambitious Guest," from *Twice-told Tales,* writes of the Willey misfortune: "Who has not learned their name? The story has been told far and wide and will forever be a legend of these mountains. Poets have sung their fate" (333). Hawthorne was right; the story is still being recounted today. Melville himself, as poet, had written of the legend; in *Clarel* (1876), Nathan, an American turned Zionist, traumatically recalls the death of his uncle in this very slide (1.17.83–98).

After the narrator in "Tartarus" pushes down in a southerly direction through the Notch, Melville seems to turn again to Cole's painting, which depicts the gateway at the northern extremity: "Not far from the bottom of the Dungeon stands a large white-washed building, relieved, like some great *whited sepulchre,* against the sullen background of mountain-side firs, and other hardy evergreens, inaccessibly *rising* in grim terraces for *some two thousand feet*" (324; emphasis mine). Melville's large, whitewashed building may be based on Cole's rendering of the white Notch House, which appears from a distance forlorn, even sepulchral. James Fenimore Cooper made the familiar Biblical phrase, *whited sepulchre,* famous in some circles in chapter 8 of *Home As Found* (1838), where John Effingham, a supposed bachelor, exclaims from a boat on the Hudson River, "Whited sepulchres! . . . All outside. Wait until you get a view of the deformity within." This Puritanical phrase from Matthew, occasioned by the view of the strikingly beautiful exteriors of Hudson River homes, became a stock phrase for Cooper's unsettling assessment of disingenuous American society. Was the Notch House the honeymooning Melvilles' new home as found? The second set of italicized words in the passage quoted above lightly parallels words from *The Course of Empire, Voyage of Life and Other Pictures of Thomas Cole, N. A.* (1853) by the Reverend Louis Legrande Noble, who loosely quoted extracts from Cole's journal for October 6, 1828, the date when Cole first ventured through the Notch: "We now entered the Notch, and felt awe-struck as we passed between the bare and rifted mountains, *rising* on either hand *some two thousand feet* above us" (97; emphasis mine). If Melville had read about Cooper's effusive evaluation of the *Course of Empire* series of paintings as related in Noble's biography, he may have had reason to recall Cooper's phrase from *Home As Found*.

Up to this point Melville has been establishing the setting of the story. The narrator's adventure then begins in earnest on a cold Friday noon in January. Dante similarly began his *Inferno* on a Friday, Good Friday, and both he and Melville's narrator found themselves in a forest. By noon the following day the narrator espies Woedolor Mountain, which probably represents Mount Washington; while many mountains in the vicinity deserve the appellation, Mount Washington is a prime candidate because it is rarely free of storms. An average wind of 35 miles per hour prevails even in summer, with hurricane-force winds one day in three. Melville writes: "This far summit fairly smoked with frost; white vapors *curled* up from its white-wooded top, as from a chimney" (325; emphasis mine). This is fairly descriptive of the *Notch* painting. The next sentence from Noble's biography reads: "With the exception of a few *curling* round the airy pinnacles, the clouds had now dispersed, and the sun shown down brilliantly upon the scene of wild grandeur" (97; emphasis mine). Cole may have referred to his own similar words in his journal when he painted the scene 11 years later. While the parallels with Noble's biography are enticing, more evidence is needed to link Melville firmly with it.

In "Tartarus" the narrator speaks of his good horse Black having "started at a sudden turn, where, right across the track—not ten minutes fallen—an old distorted hemlock lay, darkly undulatory as an anaconda" (325). Melville embellishes the time element here to emphasize the immediacy of the event, but the blasted anaconda-like tree can be said to undulate in the lower left corner of the painting. A case, too, could be made for undulations of a snaky severed root to the immediate right of the horseman. Dwight, too, speaks of a time when his "horse started, as if struck by a musket ball," and of the disappearance of the "venerable old hemlock" (76).

The narrator gains the Notch when "the violent blast, dead from behind, all but shoved my high-backed pung up-hill. The gust shrieked through the shivered pass, as if laden with lost spirits bound to the unhappy world" (325). Close observation of the area within the Notch gateway itself in the painting shows the mist taking the appearance of a ghoulish face with white hair, perhaps one of those "lost spirits." Abraham A. Davidson believes that Cole, because of his dovetailing of images in *The Titan's Goblet* (1833), was the first American painter to employ the double image, bridging the centuries from the time of such early practitioners as Hieronymus Bosch and Giuseppe Arcimboldo (21). In the same year that Melville's "Tartarus" was published, one John Spaulding more disconsolately portrayed the Notch:

> For two thirds of the year a more desolate place can hardly be imagined than this Notch. Dismal winds moan through the leafless trees, and through the fissures of the rocks; and methinks the poor storm-bound traveller here in fancy has heard the genii of the mountain, sending through this gorge a deafening chorus of most frightful music. (50–51)

There yet remain several seemingly unrelated matters to clarify in "Tartarus." In numbing weather, for example, the narrator discovers that his cheeks are freezing. "Two gaunt blood-hounds, one on each side, seemed mumbling them. I seemed Actaeon" (329). The allusion, of course, is to the hunter Actaeon, who rashly watched the virginal Diana bathe. For his wanton profaneness Diana promptly changed him into a stag (a symbol of lust) who was then killed by his own dogs. Melville's allusion seems at least partly to originate with another topographical feature called Diana's Bath, much further down the Saco near North Conway.[10] Melville finds the myth appropriate since he portrays the young women workers at the hamlet's papermill as virgins. If the narrator feels guilt at violating their presence, then it follows that he believes his punishment is the pain from his reviving cheeks.

The narrator expresses shock at the passivity of the papermill women tending the violent machinery, "mere cogs to the wheels" and "mares haltered to the rack" (328, 329). A pert boy named Cupid, acting as factotum, glides among the busy women. Melville may be indebted for this Cupid to Frederika Bremer's *Homes of the New World* (1853), another suggestive title, like Cooper's. Bremer's brief description of a child nicknamed Cupid who was stirring up a circle of ladies who were themselves talking and sewing by lamplight suggests a parallel to the Cupid of "Tartarus."[11] Because Melville had met Bremer at Hawthorne's, in August 1851, he would have been drawn to Bremer's title (Leyda 2:927). It may even have prompted him to recall his own new honeymoon home, where Cupid had reigned.

It is appropriate that Melville's narrator possesses some kinship to the factory workers. Because he can be easily identified as a member of the Shakers, a sect known for its celibacy, he shares with them the state of virginity. The Shaker connection is based on several pieces of infor-mation. For one thing, Melville informs us that this man had crossed the mountains for some 60 miles in order to gain a better price on the paper he needs for the small envelopes used in mailing out orders for garden seeds.[12] His business must be considerable since he used several hundred thousand envelopes in a year. One of perhaps two groups who had a seed business that large at that time were the Shakers. Starting the trade as early as the 1790s, the Shakers were one of the first to earnestly begin the business in the United States (Andrews 66, 81). They are said to have been the first to put up seeds in small envelopes, which were often printed in colors. The envelopes of Melville's seedsman were "mostly made of yellowish paper" (324). By the 1850s others may have gotten into the seed business in New England, but they were less significant by comparison. Those reading Melville's story at that time would have immediately recognized the seedsman as a Shaker, for the Shakers were the premier seedsmen of their day. They were known to grow quality seeds, and their products were distributed all over the country. That the narrator is a virginal Shaker is reinforced when he says of the girls at one point, "Then these are all maids," and then adds that "some pained homage to their pale virginity made me involuntarily bow" (334). Melville may have regarded the Shaker act of dispersing seeds about the country as a grand example of sublimation, that is, of sublimated sex, to be sure, but not necessarily of that alone.

———— The overriding symbol in "Tartarus," as in *Moby-Dick,* is whiteness. Richard S. Moore makes much of the fact that whiteness contributes to the horrific sublime in *Moby-Dick* (159–60). Whether this is so or not, one essential sentence in chapter 42, "The Whiteness of the Whale," states in no uncertain terms that whiteness is *beyond* the domain of the sublime: "yet for all these accumulated associations, with whatever is sweet, and honorable, and *sublime,* there yet lurks an elusive something in the innermost idea of this hue, which strikes more of panic to the soul than that redness which affrights in blood" (994; emphasis mine). True, whiteness may add horror to the already terrible, such as the ferocity of a bear or shark. But the sublime takes one only to the threshold of whiteness and leaves the viewer in awe. An understanding of the significance of whiteness requires more than a sublime experience, more than a feeling of the eternal.

In his important description of the Spouter-Inn painting in chapter 3 of *Moby-Dick,* Melville says, using equivocal and arresting phrasing, that there was an "indefinite, half-attained, unimaginable sublimity about it that fairly froze you to it" (805). Melville's word *unimaginable* probably has no ulterior intent. However, it is a strange choice since the sublime requires imagination, a pictured object.[13] Moreover, given Melville's varied use of the term *sublime* in *Moby-Dick,* where he applies it to Queequeg (847), uses it to describe Daggoo's sense of smell (954), has Ahab make sport of the notion (1336), and even twits the idea of the sublime in the passage borrowed from Dwight concerning the White Mountains, the significance of the whole idea of the sublime in this novel should be reexamined. This is even more emphatically the case when it is recognized that the famous tongue-in-cheek humor of *Moby-Dick* and much of Melville's other work appears to be inconsistent with the sublime. As Melville's friend George Adler wrote in a translation of the work of Jean Paul (Richter) for *The Literary World* of April 19, 1851, "the comic is the mortal enemy of the *sublime*" (309).

This seeming ambiguity in Melville's attitude toward the sublime afflicts "Tartarus" as well as *Moby-Dick*. A mural in the Great Room of the Society of Arts in the Adelphi in London, titled *Elysium and Tartarus,* one of a series of famed late eighteenth-century monumental paintings by James Barry, a close friend of Edmund Burke, may have prompted Melville to name his two-part story, "The Paradise of Bachelors and the Tartarus of Maids." Barry's work exemplified the Burkean sublime. Melville could have read about the mural and seen part of it depicted in Charles Knight's *London* (5: 365–68), a multivolume set which he purchased in London in 1849 (Sealts no. 191), and which he used as a source in "Paradise" (Gretchko, *Melvillean Ambiguities* 16–17). Regarding the "Tartarus," Carol Hovanec very insightfully remarks that it "has the design of a sublime painting" (48). She stresses point by point how Melville's description of the Notch most obviously conforms to the sublime of Edmund Burke (45–46). When the narrator of the story stands before the behemoth machinery inside the papermill, Hovanec observes that his "diction is again reminiscent of the sublime ('awe,' 'gazed,' 'strange dread,' 'terrible,' 'unbudging fatality,' 'spell-bound,' 'mournfully,' etc.)" (47). The narrator's ludicrous experience of the sublime before the machinery in the Devil's Dungeon or hell will yet be examined. If it proves that the White Mountains themselves and Crawford Notch in particular were regarded as quintessentially sublime experiences in Melville's America, then this story will eventually come to be regarded as an even more specific parody of that sublimity.

Scholars have pondered how it could have been possible that "Tartarus" ever made it past censoring eyes and into print in mid-nineteenth-century America. The same eyes that did not discern the sexuality of *Moby-Dick's* "Cassock," the grandissimus to the grandissima of the "Tartarus," could not admit to seeing any in "Tartarus." For these eyes the sexuality became sublimated or repressed. Consider what they missed. Here, as scholars have attested, the Bellows'-pipe can be an anus, *notch* was slang for vagina, the Dungeon is easily the womb, and the Blood River is blood from defloration or menstrual flow. *Mill* was slang for woman or her genitals. Even "White Mountains" occurs as breasts in

Mary Ann Temple . . . History of an Amorous and Lively Girl, a pulp novel published circa 1849 (David Reynolds 218). As the penetrating narrator wends his way into the papermill hamlet and tours the papermill, it becomes apparent that the mill's machinery imitates the reproductive process. However, if America at that time had admitted the story's sexuality, it would also have had to admit the concomitant violence as well, as in the act of rape, and try to reconcile the two. "Before each [female worker] was vertically thrust up a long, glittering scythe, immovably fixed at bottom to the manger-edge. The curve of the scythe, and its having no snath to it, made it look like a sword" (329). Melville first hints at violence when he introduces the Blood River, in part derived from Dante's twelfth canto of the *Inferno,* where the sins of violence are punished.

At a little lower layer the symbolic Amazonian woman of the Tartarus, which the narrator, Jonah-like, enters, may be Elizabeth, Melville's own wife. This is hardly farfetched since most of Melville's writing is highly autobiographical. If the Melvilles climbed Mount Washington, as it seems they did, then these newlyweds would have required nearby accommodations after their exhausting endeavor. The Notch House has an excellent chance of being that very inn, the white building in Cole's picture which Melville may have turned into a whited sepulchre of a papermill, a euphemistic womb. Melville could be the Shaker who comes to his intended as a virgin, thus making for an even closer identity between the narrator and the author himself. His wife may be the mad maid, the crazy spinster, here deflorated.

But at an even lower layer, beyond the sexual motif, whiteness remains a symbol in its own right. In *Sartor Resartus* Thomas Carlyle writes that "all Forms whereby Spirit manifests itself to sense, whether outwardly or in imagination, are Clothes" (215). The snowy White Mountains form a blanket for the Tartarus, just as whiteness colors the outside of Moby Dick. "The Blanket," as a middle chapter of *Moby-Dick,* suggests that for Melville whiteness is indeed at the center of things. Whiteness as a symbol or form is a void or blank. Melville imbues it with life by creating a vehicle, Moby Dick, which permits him to analyze that whiteness.

In "Tartarus" the "virgin" machinery in the papermill may be regarded as a metaphor for the analyzer himself, who procreates thought. The virgin in world mythology may very well prove universally to be an archetype for the generator of thought. Thus the narrator experiences the sublime not so much before the mill's machinery as before the machinery of his own mind or brain. In effect, he is awed by the power of the mind, its disquieting and unquenchable searching, its interminable reasoning, its insatiableness, its birthing or creation of thought. The sublime here stems essentially from a deification of the mind. It is a kind of narcissism whereby the narrator is awed by his own sense of awe. In the end, then, this insane self-involvement is Melville's parody of the sublime.

Every sublime process has an object, which manifests itself in the mind as a thought. The two, of course, are one; outer really is inner. We should now be alerted when, late in the story, Melville introduces John Locke, who was fundamental to the eighteenth-century construction of the sublime. The narrator (who technically can be said to remain "virginal" until the whole experience is over and he withdraws from the vaginal Tartarus) sees paper dropping from the mill's machinery and thinks, "All sorts of writings would be writ on those now vacant things." He is then reminded "of that celebrated comparison of John Locke, who, in demonstration of his theory that men had no innate ideas, compared the human mind at birth to a sheet of blank paper; something destined to be scribbled on, but what sort of characters no soul might tell" (333). However, what indeed is scribbled on the mind is not a Lockean mirror of "reality." Such a philosophy of mechanism, as Locke's was thought to be, and empiricist aesthethics, like Burke's, both foster objectivity. But objectivity is in truth nothing more than a mental impression or conception. The "virgin" generates objects. All thought is simply a mental object. Thinking creates an object in the mind. As the paper passes through the machinery the narrator seems to see "glued to the pallid incipience of the pulp, the yet more pallid faces of all the pallid girls." He is reminded of "the tormented face on the handkerchief of St. Veronica" (334). Thus for the imagination of the narrator the "virgin" machinery seems to generate an image that is particularly reminiscent of Christ. And by that allusion Melville indicates that what the "virgin" generates is "Christ" and that that image, or mental object, is subjective. Without objectivity there is certainly no Burkean sublime.

Moby-Dick and "Tartarus" are very closely related in their primary symbol, namely whiteness, whether it is applied as in the first instance to a whale ("like a snow hill in the air," chapter 1; "a hump like a snow-hill," chapter 133; with a "great Monadnock hump," chapter 135—Monadnock being in New Hampshire but not of the White Mountains) or as in the second instance to white mountains or hills. The white whale and the white mountain are, in effect, interchangeable. That Melville frames *Moby-Dick* with this metaphor indicates its extraordinary importance to him. Both Moby Dick and the Tartarus are, symbolically, the same jaws or vaginae dentatae. This theme may also be suggested in Cole's painting in an ancillary fashion where the fallen limb and blasted tree in the lower left corner seem to form a jaw. That jaw may reflect the Notch itself, which Nathaniel Peabody Rogers called "jaws" (174). Cole's painting of a quester-horseman about to enter his challenge may have been a trigger to the writing of one of the most important quest books ever—*Moby-Dick*. The "Tartarus" may then be a subtle record of the process which led to the making of Melville's masterpiece. It might also be regarded as a strange comment on the creativity which ensued from the author's honeymoon.

We as questers enter the metaphorical vaginal notch of Cole and Melville. We must be consumed by the thought process if we are to understand what we are and where we are. We must lose ourselves in extension, or object, which is a sublimation, in order to achieve by reflection a freedom. In short, we must be consumed by the process in order to understand it. Ultimately, it is only with the help of the heart—whose actions are conspicuous by their virtual absence from both "Paradise" and "Tartarus"—that we meld with the Void, or Ultimate Transcendent, that ungraspable phantom of life, and thereby counterbalance this process.

Toning Down the Green: Melville's Picturesque

JOHN BRYANT

The least-developed approach to Melville has been the study of his aesthetics, and perhaps with good reason.[1] To begin with, any formulation of a "Melville aesthetic" would have to account for the remarkable range of conflicting impulses evident in Melville's attempts to assimilate comic and tragic visions, the beautiful and sublime, the Hellenic and Hebraic. The problem is exacerbated by the author's reticence to expound upon artistic principles. Like a "scared white doe in the woodlands," his aesthetics must be grasped through certain "cunning glimpses": a few reviews, lectures, poems, and discrete passages from the fiction. With fragments for primary documents, we can only strike *toward* a Melville aesthetic. An important step in that journey is the picturesque.

In both his early, professional years and his quiescence, Melville visited galleries in Europe and America, lectured on art, amassed a large collection of prints, and wrote poetic disquisitions (never published in his lifetime) on painters and the picturesque. His excitement for the visual arts is undeniable, and yet the general view is that the author disdained the picturesque as a reflection of America's shallow optimism. Landscapes that mask the problems of mind and culture with impossible blendings of otherwise obdurate oppositional forces were to Melville inherently false. For Ishmael, a good painting is a "soggy, boggy, squitchy" affair, not an overly patterned iconography of light and dark. Moreover, paintings that "prettify" squalor—the "povertiresque" as Melville put it in *Pierre*—are at best worthy of satire. But given its controlled management

145

of the rough and unexpected, the curious and irregular, the seemingly unpolished picturesque was consonant with Melville's "half melancholy, half farcical" approach (Leyda 549). Thus, if Melville attacks the picturesque at times, it is only to clarify its deeper ethical and aesthetic potentials. For him, the picturesque provided a critical vocabulary of being and creation. It was a dynamic chiaroscuro that empowered him to "fuse" both bright and dark sides of his vision into what Hawthorne in "The Old Apple Dealer" had called "the moral picturesque." In this problematic sketch of a "generally negative" Bartleby-like figure, Melville's friend advises that "Every touch must be *kept down,* or else you destroy the *subdued tone* which is absolutely essential to the whole effect" (459, emphasis mine). In discussing his own version of this "moral picturesque," Melville would also argue, and in similar language, for "toning down the green" in both life and art. What emerges, somewhat unexpectedly, then, is an artist of self-containment and restraint for whom an aesthetics of repose was essential. Of course, with Taji or Ahab burning before us, it is difficult to conceive of their creator as a reposeful classicist. And, strictly speaking, he was not. But with Babbalanja and Ishmael at our ear, we begin to recognize in Melville's picturesque sensibility a well-modulated fusion—tense yet calm—of anxiety and mirth.

Melville touches upon his aesthetics of repose in such early works as *Mardi,* his *Mosses* review, *Moby-Dick,* and "The Piazza." Later, in several late or posthumous poems (notably "Art," "The Enviable Isles," and "At the Hostelry"), his approach to the picturesque became an explicit topic of debate. Because the picturesque could mute or contain the sublime, Melville's chiaroscuro ran counter to the traditional picturesque sensibility that heightened the sublime. This is particularly clear in two works: the early, much-admired tale "The Piazza," and one of Melville's last, most complex but least-known achievements, "Rip Van Winkle's Lilac." But before turning to them, it is important to examine how Melville's moral chiaroscuro employs the principles of fusion and repose, and why it was, therefore, in his hands a retrogressive mode.

Writing in 1885 to James Billson, Herman Melville declared himself "neither pessimist nor optomist [sic]" (Davis and Gilman 277), and while the aged author was probably giving a more positive construction to his personality than the events and publications of his earlier decades might merit, his insistence upon transcending both dark and bright visions is consistent with his earliest impulses to mix, combine, or unite the conflicting instincts of doubt and faith that perpetually drove his art. In short, Melville strove for a "mingled brew" in art, and as Edward

Rosenberry points out, a crucial problem for critics is finding the right language to express this fundamental, tragicomic blend. It is difficult to comprehend Melville's complex interaction of "Hellenic cheer, Hebraic grief" (*Clarel* 1.28.34) without resorting to metaphor. Berthoff, for instance, offers a chemical trope for the author's "power to hold apparently contradictory discoveries in mind at once, in *free solution*" (38; emphasis mine). And more recently Shirley M. Dettlaff has proposed a "balance" (rather than full Arnoldian synthesis) of the two in which Melville's ornamental Hellenism is "subsidiary" to his Hebraism (228). But neither the chemist's "free solution" nor the assayer's "balance" adequately characterizes the dialogical situation at hand, wherein Melville's voice of urgent self-exposure begets a voice of restraint that in turn begets renewed "flashings-forth" and "calms." Melville, too, searched for the right metaphor to express this chiaroscuro, and, as we shall see, his choices—the "marge" or shoreline, sea-calms, and the dawn—stress liminal and perpetually interpenetrating states of mind (not static "balances" or amorphous "free solutions") that are inherently picturesque.

Melville drew upon and modified a picturesque tradition that was already in his day essentially passé; and, in view of the generally accepted placement of the movement in modern art, his version was decidedly retrogressive. Paintings typically identified as picturesque first appeared in the seventeenth century, but they are as diverse in style as Salvator Rosa's moody depictions of banditti amidst Italianate ruins and Claude's bright landscapes. No serious attempts to clarify the concept appeared until the late eighteenth century, when William Gilpin penned his analectic musings. And though Edmund Burke's study of the sublime does not deal with the picturesque, subsequent essayists (in particular Uvedale Price and Richard Payne Knight) attempted to define the term by either modifying or rejecting Burke's alignment of the beautiful and sublime with the corresponding human instincts of love and fright.[2]

In expanding Burke's view to encompass the picturesque, Uvedale Price explored a middle ground. If, as Burke argued in the physiological extension of his aesthetic argument, beauty relaxes the nerve fibers that control emotion and the sublime tightens them, then, Price extrapolated, the picturesque leaves them naturally suspended. The emotion aroused is neither pleasure nor pain but "curiosity," and the artistic elements that naturally arouse this sensation are "roughness and sudden variation joined to irregularity" (Hussey 13).[3] Associationists (including Gilpin but most energetically Archibald Allison and Richard Payne Knight) argued against the Burkean approach, stating that the picturesque is that which we associate in the mind with framed pictures. It is, therefore, a visual habit, a painterly way of seeing the world and transforming nature into a coherent landscape.⁴ As stimulating as it was, the controversy between Price and Knight languished as the European vogue for the picturesque passed. Although Price's criterion of roughness and irregularity held in suspense is congruent with Melville's moral chiaroscuro, the concept of the picturesque became in general parlance a quaint derogation of the associationist view meaning little more than "pretty as a picture."

Christopher Hussey's renewed discussion of the "The Picturesque" in 1927 identified the concept as a transitional mode that allowed artists and viewers (from about 1730 to 1830) to adjust their habits of viewing from an appreciation of the "soft and pleasing repose . . . characteristic of the beautiful" (67) to that of the craggy, awe-engendering sublime. Broadly stated, it was a development away from the rational to the imaginative (or intuitive), from seeing with the mind to seeing with the feelings.⁵ Along with Uvedale Price and Hussey, Martin Price has more recently acknowledged the mixed nature of the picturesque, but in delineating what he calls "The Picturesque Moment," he explores a frame of mind that encompasses a variety of cultural phenomena: nostalgia, literature, humor, as well as the "preserving [of] the significant ruin" (261). The picturesque familiarizes the sublime (265), but, like wit and humor, it involves a playful dissociation of object and meaning (279), leaving us suspended between "the full tragedy of the sublime . . . [and] the serene comedy of the beautiful" (277). Nevertheless, the picturesque promotes an energy of mind, "an intensity of awareness" in its middle ground that is "primarily moral." The tension in Martin Price's picturesque moment, then, is a sense of order, or "the limited idea of unity" (279), giving way to accident, change, and chaos.

Price's picturesque resembles Melville's own intense, transitional sensibility, but the author's "moment" is counterdirectional: it points back toward the restraint of beauty rather than forward to the self-exposure of the sublime. Melville's appreciation of classical restraint clearly emerges in his discussion of Laocoön. Melville first viewed the Greek sculpture at the Vatican Museum on his return from the Holy Land in 1857 (Howard 249) and incorporated his reflections on it in his lecture "Statues in Rome" (Sealts). Like Lessing, Melville recognized that the sculpture's ancient artist had made his god-sent, marble snakes conform to sensuous lines; he had captured Laocoön's expression not in mid-scream—eyes bulging, mouth agape, face disfigured—but just before his scream. Not merely the triumph of form over emotion, this muting engages us more deeply in the central figure's predicament, for the subduing of a graphic reality within reposeful forms heightens the effect of terror by igniting our imagination, leaving us perpetually, even easefully suspended in anticipation of horror. Melville, too, was impressed by the statue's outward representation of "eternal mildness," by its "tranquil, subdued air such as men have when under the influence of no passion" (Sealts no. 150). Laocoön's anguished face, for him a "symbol of human misfortune," partakes of this repose (Bryant 154).

Melville saw this much, and more, for the ancient sculpture epitomized his modern condition of deteriorating faith. Poor Laocoön: he saw through the facade of the Trojan Horse; his spear proved its threatening hollowness; he saw the truth, spoke it, but was killed. Melville, who had spoken the truth in numerous fictions and was probably contemplating at the time of his visit to Rome an abandonment of fiction writing, saw himself writhing amidst the marble snakes. Laocoön's artist had lived during the fall of Roman imperialism and the rise of Christian hegemony. Similarly, Melville's millennial age of a now-ineffectual Christianity seemed to be giving way to newer, still-evolving philosophies. Both ancient and modern artists were caught in periods of anxious transition. Thus, Melville wrote that the ancient marble seemed to embody "the doubt and dark groping of speculation in that age when the old mythology was passing away and men's minds had not reposed in the new faith" (Sealts no. 139). The author saw through the anguish of the sculpture to that of the sculptor and found a restrained projection of his own sense of loss and anticipation.

Melville recognized in Laocoön the powerful effect of subduing the "doubt and dark groping" of Gothicism and selfhood. The Hellene's wrestling with those theological and ontological snakes reappears in the more Hebraic (and picturesque) imagery of Melville's remarkable, truncated sonnet, "Art":

> In placid hours well-pleased we dream
> Of many a brave unbodied scheme.
> But form to lend, pulsed life create,
> What unlike things must meet and mate:
> A flame to melt—a wind to freeze;
> Sad patience—joyous energies;
> Humility—yet pride and scorn;
> Instinct and study; love and hate;
> Audacity—reverence. These must mate,
> And fuse with Jacob's mystic heart,
> To wrestle with the angel—Art.
> (*Collected Poems* 231)

It would be inappropriate to argue that Melville's apparent substitution of a Blakean "angel" for snakes in his depiction of the artist's struggle with art bespeaks a yearning for transcendent serenity, for on the surface of it, there is no repose in "wrestling" with a demonic angel. Rather, we find Melville's sense of repose lodged within the "mystic heart," a crucible that can contain the fiery fusion of "unlike things," the artist's contrary instincts of "Humility—yet pride," his bright side and dark. Similarly, the heart (a homophone of *art*) fuses beauty and terror. The final effect is one of tense, not somnolent, repose. This crucial element in Melville's aesthetic—the subsuming of head within mystic heart, the fusion of light and dark, the ascendency of art over self—is a retrogressive version of Martin Price's picturesque moment stressing restraint rather than sublimity. His aesthetics of repose "softens" the sublime; it places limits on chaos, confines self-indulgence, and restrains dark groping speculation. In short, it is a return to Laocoön.[6]

Melville pursues the complexities of this dynamic of fusion and repose (a mating "in placid hours") in his recurrent picturesque imagery. His poem, "The Enviable Isles," for instance, draws out a key ethical dilemma implicit in the picturesque. Here, the artful fusion of the sublime and the beautiful corresponds to a fusion in life of awareness and joy, but at the same time Melville offsets any anticipation of a static balance of bright and dark sensibilities by alerting us to the perils of too much repose:

> Through storms you reach them and from storms are free.
>   Afar described, the foremost drear in hue,
> But, nearer, green; and, on the marge, the sea
>   Makes thunder low and mist of rainbowed dew.
>
> But, inland, where the sleep that folds the hills
> A dreamier sleep, the trance of God, instills—   (204)

The danger of this Tennysonian lotus-land is that the reposeful "trance of God" will "lull all sorrow and all glee;" it is a siren song luring us to deadly sleep. Full repose anaesthetizes the intellect, transforming us into "dimpling" dreamers, or worse, "unconscious slumberers mere." But implied in the opening stanza is a workable norm in which the poet, or any thoughtful soul not "dimpling in dream," may situate himself at that picturesque spot "on the marge" where, turning from the sea, he may be shocked by "thunder low" and yet enlivened by "rainbowed dew." The essence of Melville's picturesque lies in this coastal or "marginal" point of view, which encompasses and sustains the perpetual interpenetration of dubious "billows" and hopeful "beaches." The tension inherent in Melville's marge has its most memorable ethical application in his better-known image of the two-sided tortoise. As the jokey narrator of "The Encantadas" puts it, one must keep the bright side up, "but be honest, and don't deny the black" (56).[7] In life as in art, repose and awareness must be actively conjoined.

Melville explores the problem of consciousness and repose in his more complicated metaphor of the sea-calm. Like the Doubloon in *Moby-Dick*, a calm at sea mirrors the characters who perceive it. In *Mardi*, for instance, the archly Byronic Taji is vexed by calms; they freeze us in "the outer confines of creation, the region of everlasting lull, introductory to a positive vacuity;" they bring on "thoughts of eternity" and soul anxiety (10); they make us "madly skeptical" and "almost . . . an infidel" (9). A sea-calm is an "inert blending and brooding of all things"; it is a "gray chaos" (48) that activates the "instinct" for loneliness, misanthropy, and mere self-preservation. If Taji extracts sublime terror from an "everlasting lull," Babbalanja provides a more complex blending: "This calm is like unto Oro's everlasting serenity, and like unto man's last despair" (267). Where Taji experiences only doubt, Babbalanja finds a Burkean suspension of hope and doubt. His calms are picturesque.

Ishmael concurs with Babbalanja. Despite Melville's careful research into whiteness (*Moby-Dick* ch. 92), his analysis of the sublime is delivered through the reposeful voice of Ishmael, who calmly claims he can be "social with [a horror]" (16). Rhetorically, then, the awe-full whiteness of the whale is "kept down" by the "picturesque" voice of a "genial desperado" (196), and the final effect is a distinctive narrative tone carefully suspended just short of Burke's frightful sublime. Ishmael's voice, then, is invested with a reposeful accommodation of anxiety and mirth. It is itself a "calm." In "The Fountain" (ch. 85), he imagines whales "sailing through a calm tropical sea." They are "misty monster[s]" brooding over "incommunicable contemplations," and yet the "vapor" they spout is "glorified by a rainbow." Ishmael's perception of this intermingling of vaporous "doubts" and glorious "intuitions" creates "neither believer nor infidel, but makes a man who regards them both with equal eye" (314). Such a man as Ishmael can find "mute calm" and "eternal mildness of joy" in a pod of whales and can subsume their reposeful dalliance within the "tornadoed Atlantic of [his] being" (326).

In "The Gilder" Ishmael extends his metaphysics into aesthetics. The "dreary quietude" of a sea-calm, he notes, "mixes with your most mystic mood; so that fact and fancy, half-way meeting interpenetrate, and form one seamless whole" (405, 406). Here, Ishmael's calm does more than mingle consciousness and nature, or doubt and belief; it is itself a mode of creativity—and one that his captain cannot achieve. Ahab, like Taji, cannot endure a calm. Although he, in fact, longs for "blessed calms," he is continually wearied by the inevitability of "a storm for every calm." And worse, "there is no steady unretracing progress" through the stages of man's developing consciousness (from infant bliss to mature awareness) but rather an endless round of recycling through each successive stage, again and again, with no "final harbor" in sight. Ahab cannot rest easy, as can Ishmael, in manhood's last phase of maturity, "the pondering repose of If" (406). What Ahab lacks is what Melville himself strived to achieve in the creative process, the "calm . . . silent grass-growing mood" that the artist needs to compose (Davis and Gilman 128). This vital aesthetic sea-calm, discovered in Ishmael but denied to Ahab, is the picturesque moment of Melville's repose.

But perhaps Melville's most effective metaphor for delineating the dynamics of his picturesque sensibility is found in his discussion of Hawthorne (that "great intellect in repose") whose unique commingling of mirth and deep thought is like a perpetual, universal dawn. Here, light and dark are not merely balanced; they interpenetrate and thereby clarify each other. Hawthorne's dark awareness, Melville writes, "gives more effect to the ever-moving dawn, that forever advances through it, and circumnavigates [the] world" (540). In speaking of Hawthorne, Melville *spoke* himself. Although art cannot negate "Puritan gloom," it can "advance through it." Like the sea-calm, it is an ongoing fusion of "unlike things": rainbow and thunder, calm and tempest, light and dark. Thus, Melville's chiaroscuro dawn is a process of mutual restraint.

Finally, Melville transforms his metaphoric delineations of marge, calm, and dawn into elements of characterization found in three brief but memorable portraits of artists in "At the Hostelry." In this ambitious examination of the picturesque, Melville delights in the infinite inter-pretations given to the term. At the request of a Marquis de Grandvin, a dozen or so artists (some great, several not) assemble to haggle over aesthetics. Despite their varying styles, familiar elements of Melville's moral chiaroscuro clearly emerge. For Tintoretto, the picturesque requires that "Some decay must lurk / In florid things" (323). Spagno-letto's definition echoes the Encantadan tortoise: "Let sunny frankness charm his air, . . . And, mind ye, don't forget the pall" (328). And under Steen's "vineyard, lo, a cavern!" (330). In each case bright and dark intermingle. Moreover, the Ishmaelean geniality of Grandvin and Jack Gentian (their very names project mirth) dominates the poem. The Mar-quis focuses immediately upon the moral dilemma that the picturesque attempts to resolve:

> In best of worlds if all's not bright,
> Allow, the shadow's chased by light,
> Though rest for neither yet may be. (313)

His image recalls the "ever-moving dawn" of Hawthorne's mirth, but leaves us, once again, with the rest-less debate between opposing realms, the kind of tension that iron-railed Ahab, caught up in the damning cyclicity of evolving states of being, cannot endure. Spagnoletto and Lippi both exhibit the conflict of opposing styles: for both the "furious and serene" are "at odds" (319). The Dutch painters Steen and Swanevelt, however, strike a balance of sublimity and beauty: the former champions "*Wine and brine* / The mingled brew" (329); the latter praises Leonardo's Medusa wherein "Grace and the Picturesque may dwell / With Terror" (319). (Swanevelt's Da Vinci, like Ishmael, can be sociable with a horror.) But punctuating the debate are the impenetrable silences of the Great Masters themselves, who listen but never speak: Rembrandt is "reserved in self-control"; Leonardo is entranced by "light / Rayed thro' red wine in glass—a gleam / Pink on the polished table bright" (332), and Michael Angelo is mutely withdrawn sipping water. As Babbalanja notes, "Truth is voiceless" (*Mardi* 286), and in the silence of the Masters, picturesque moments of repose evoke a sense of self-control, clarity, detachment, and the sensual yet tense stasis of pink on bright polish.

In the works examined thus far, we have glimpsed the moral and aesthetic dimensions of Melville's uniquely retrogressive picturesque. As an artistic principle, his picturesque promotes a mingling of light and shadow symbolizing a tension between comic Beauty and tragic Sublime. In Melville's schema, the bright impulse toward artistic coherence struggles to gain ascendency over dark chaos, but it does not deny or negate darkness. Rather, by holding each other in restraint, the two sensibilities are more dynamically realized. As an ethical system, this moral chiaroscuro also argues for self-control: a subsuming of bitterness within a genial state of being. Thus misanthropy and philanthropy, nihilism and creativity, pessimism and optimism are, again, held in tense repose. But the peril of giving ascendency to repose is that excessive muting of form and mind leads to aesthetic and moral anesthesia. Repose is only useful when it is wakeful, and art without deep awareness is mere slumbering. Melville best dramatizes the problem of fusing repose and awareness in two picturesque works, "The Piazza" and "Rip Van Winkle's Lilac." Both sketches focus on portraits of the artist attempting to reassert ethical and aesthetic self-control. Each promotes a self-conscious voice of restraint.

Melville wrote "The Piazza," the title piece for his collection of stories *The Piazza Tales* (1856), at the end of his exhausting magazine years. Like "I and My Chimney," it is a recuperative sketch, the narrative of a man learning to control his expansive yet subversive vision within the limits of art. The final effect, as Johannes Bergmann notes, is a "calm despair" approaching a balanced, Irvingesque repose (268). The speaker begins in a restive mood. Through carefully planted asides, we learn of his sea past, his former delight in thunderstorms, and his present malaise, a morbid supersensitivity to nature. To him, the reflected sunlight from a mountaintop seems a spot of "hectic" upon a consumptive's cheek. Worms, he discovers, inhabit his newly planted bulbs. Nature is diseased, and there is a canker in his inmost creative spirit. But the speaker is on the mend: he builds a porch. His piazza faces north and in summer affords a cool view of Greylock—the sublime, mountain "whale" Melville studied while writing *Moby-Dick*. The intervening landscape is like a calm equatorial sea: vast, silent, lonely, reposeful. Fantasizing that the reflection from the mountain is the work of fairies, the speaker sets out, half-fanciful, half-serious, on a voyage to fairyland to grasp this light and reclaim its imaginative power.

On the surface of it, the recuperative venture fails, but though it does not provide the precise cure the speaker thinks he needs, he returns more certain of himself as both a thinker and an artist. Searching for a Titania to "cure this weariness" (444), he instead finds Marianna, an equally weary girl who from her lonely hovel fantasizes of "some happy one" living in palatial splendor on the speaker's piazza—a marble mansion, she imagines.[8] The girl's sterile life awakens our speaker from the vanity of his own desires. He has climbed beyond where singing birds fly: his fairyland is a wasteland of dry thunder and dead trees. Marianna's "strange thoughts" about the unknown piazza-sitter who stands before her are desperate fancies, the false longing for opulence that reflects and mocks the speaker's own illusions of sublimity and mountain fairies.[9] This mirroring calls attention to the speaker's narrowed perspective, and in his recognition of Marianna's illusions he begins his true cure. Marianna's lonesome mountain leads only to self-destructive "thinking, thinking—a wheel I cannot stop" (452). And neither "prayer" nor "pillow," neither religion nor mere slumber, can ease the constant headstrong speculation. "Better feel lone by hearth, than rock," she advises, and the speaker soon departs. Wishing that he could be Marianna's "happy one of the happy house," the speaker abruptly interrupts his self-pity with a peremptory "—Enough" that returns us instantly in two concluding paragraphs to home, hearth, and piazza.

The speaker's "Enough" (a jolting "*basta!*") derails his gloomy self-involvement and transports him both psychologically and aesthetically back to the piazza. It is a conscious insistence upon narrative control which, in calling attention to itself, does not bruise the fiction's coherence but, in fact, heightens our understanding of the artist's sudden awakening to the need for self-restraint. Ironically, what he must awaken himself to is the tense repose essential for the careful fine tuning of head and heart. As in the poem "Pontoosuce," the return is a "letting go" of selfhood. The piazza, then, becomes the restorative vantage point, the broader perspective, from which the artist can distance himself from his own disillusionment with nature and the sublime in order to control the chiaroscuro world he must now inhabit.

From the beginning and throughout, the speaker characterizes his piazza in consciously ambivalent terms. At first, it appears to be the perfect arena for the commingling of contrary needs: "the coziness of in-doors with the freedom of out-doors" (437). It allows one to "ease about" and serves as a bench upon which one might view "the picture gallery of nature" (438). It is a spot for repose. But the piazza is perhaps too easy, too reposeful, and nature too handily contained. In older days, the speaker muses, men stood before God; now they pull up an "easy chair" and amidst "tranquillity and constancy" think they worship Beauty. The piazza is a squatter's heaven, a modern contrivance reflecting the "failing faith and feeble knees" of the age. The speaker's journey off his piazza, then, is an attempt to retrieve a deeper faith in the "piety" of beauty through a direct contact with nature. He climbs the mountain in search of sublimity, finds more loneliness, despair, and illusion than at home, and returns to his piazza, but with a better idea of how to use it.

It is now a different piazza: a "royal box," not a gallery bench from which we watch nature's pageant, an "illusion so complete" (453). But at night when the theatrical curtain of darkness ends the play, "truth comes in" and the play of the mind begins. Like Ahab, the speaker walks his "piazza deck," haunted by Marianna "and many as real a story": it is an apt prelude to the haunting "Bartleby" and the rest of *The Piazza Tales*. In the end, the piazza itself becomes a stage upon which the speaker may control the successive interpenetrations of nature and mind. It is an inland *Pequod* sailing against mountain truths but dry-docked in the lowlands. It is a more valuable proscenium than the speaker first perceived. No longer an easy chair for slumber, it is the embodiment of an active picturesque point of view wherein bright illusions of nature commingle with the dark awareness of lonely despair.

Found in manuscript and published posthumously in *Weeds and Wildings,* the printed version of "Rip Van Winkle's Lilac" is less polished than "The Piazza" but structurally more complex. It is an encomium for Washington Irving, an artful and affectionate rewriting of Rip's return, an apologia of (and therefore an apology to) his wife, a blast at American materialism and Puritanism, a bold insistence upon the picturesque sensibility, a deeply textured tapestry of narrative lines complete with flashbacks and returns, and a unique combination of prose and poetry that anticipates Joycean streams ("Riverward emerging toward sunset . . ."). Yet the small attention this work has received verges on gross neglect.[10] It is also valuable as one of the few Melville texts for which a manuscript exists. Robert Ryan's textual analysis of the 30-page manuscript reveals that, like *Billy Budd*, "Rip" began as a poem preceded by a brief headnote which in time grew into a narrative sketch that dwarfs the original poem. The prose-plus-poem piece, as manuscript and as edited text, affords a unique glimpse of Melville's reliance upon a picturesque sensibility both in his rhetorical strategies and in his creative process. Interestingly enough, in juxtaposing manuscript and final edition, we experience two readings of "Rip." Caught up in a picturesque moment, we find ourselves situated between conflicting modes of expression: poetry and prose.

The prose sketch consists of three scenes: Rip's return from the hills, a sensual flashback to his early marriage years, and a flashforward from those years to a period just before Rip's return when a wandering painter sketches the dilapidated Van Winkle house. The verse section is Rip's monologue on a lilac he has planted; the third-person narrator interrupts to reflect on Rip's legacy. Melville's numbering of the manuscript pages indicates that the author first expanded the prose by inserting the vagabond painter and Dame Van Winkle sections, and then altered the poetry by reducing Rip's monologue and adding the narrator's final lines. Thus a simple retelling of Irving's tale grew into commentaries on art, love, and the artist's place in America.

Without the Dame and Artist episodes, the sketch is a simple matter of Rip's return (in prose) and bewilderment (in verse) over the lilac blooming beside his house where once an intractable willow stood. Unlike Irving's Rip, who deduces his slumber by the length of his beard, Melville's Rip achieves self-awareness through his lilac which, planted the day before to appease his wife, has grown beyond reason: "'*That* [L]ilac was a little slip, / And yonder [L]ilac is a tree!'" (*Collected Poems* 291).[11] But Melville interrupts Rip mid-quandary, and returning to his original prose narrative voice but speaking now in verse, he allegorizes the lilac's growth. We learn that in later years after Rip's death neighbors transplant innumerable cuttings of the bush so that the fragrance of Rip's initial planting transforms the entire valley into one "Paradise embowered" or "Lilac Land." As the lilac spreads, it confirms the persistence of youth and love. In addition, Rip's gay and fragrant bush (triumphant over a somber, adjacent willow) suggests the lasting presence and control of art and the continual resurrection of nature. It is a realization through art of the fairyland of nature never found in "The Piazza."

There is little doubt that part of Melville's message in the poem is to his wife. Melville's Dame is not Irving's shrew, but rather a trim-waisted, winsome beauty. The prolific lilac planted in early years represents the flourishing of Rip's love for the Dame, as well as the December rejuvenation of Herman's love for Elizabeth, whose middle years with the writer had not been smooth. Perhaps, too, Melville had in mind the shape of his own all-too sleepy writing career when he recast Irving's famous character. At the probable time of the composition of "Rip," Melville had been living in virtual obscurity for 20 years, but in the late 1880s a few enthusiasts were reading him and seeking him out. Plans were in the works for a new edition of *Typee* and perhaps other texts. Despite his retreat from the public, Melville had never given up writing, and he must have felt gratified, if not vindicated, to see a small revival of interest in him. On his desk he had kept a motto: "Keep true to the dreams of thy youth" (Metcalf 284). In some small degree, the simple creed was beginning to ring true; Melville, like Rip, was cautiously awakening to new possibilities; and again like Rip, he was "One tenant old where all was new,— / Rip's Lilac to its youth still true" (292). Although Rip's "picturesque resurrection" prefigures a Melville revival that did not, in fact, occur until the 1920s, Melville nevertheless saw in Rip's "Lilac Land" the reflowering of his own "poor good-for-nothing" years as a writer. In Rip he projected his own second coming.

But as intriguing as these biographical speculations may be, "Rip Van Winkle's Lilac" is better regarded as a statement of aesthetic principles as well as a demonstration of those principles at work, both for writer and reader. The principal aesthetic focus is on "a certain meditative vagabondo, to wit, a young artist, in his summer wanderings after the Picturesque" (287). The "vagabondo" is another "good-for-nothing" Rip; and both painter and Rip are versions of Melville—a lover, farmer, traveler, artist, and failure. The artist stumbles on the dilapidated Van Winkle home sometime after the Dame's death and just before Rip's return. The picturesque abode that attracts him is the product of factors he cannot fully know: Rip's inertia, the Dame's youthfulness, and time's decay. Melville's omniscient speaker explains that due to Rip's indolence the house had never been properly shingled and because of the overhanging willow "thin mosses" had begun to age (and also humanize) the structure. Not out of any "hard utilitarian view," but because of a "spirit of Paradise" that disdains aging (285), Dame Van Winkle had tried to chop the gloomy willow down, but she like Rip had given in to the "obtuse soft toughness" of the "immemorial" tree. As recompense Rip had planted his lilac, but in time the willow fell and decayed into the picturesque "umber-[hued] mound of mellow punk, mossed in spots, with wild violets springing from it" that the vagabond paints (286).

The leaning cottage, the rotting chiaroscuro mound, the victorious lilac, in short the fusion of ruin and growth, are the natural materials for the artist's composition. However, his attempts to render the subject on canvas are interrupted by "a hatchet-faced" man on a "lank horse" who insists the painter turn his attention away from Rip's ruin to the white, respectable, and godly church located on a distant hill (287). Like William Gilpin, who disparaged white, the artist abhors the cadaverous church. He much prefers the marble of ancient Greece "mellowed by ages, taking on another more genial tone" (288) that reminds us simultaneously of the marble Laocoön and the willow's mellow punk, and which also evokes a lively sense of pantheism despite nature's decay. But the pale rider, a "hard utilitarian," would deny such "paganish dreams": his sterile protestant ethic and sterile church are his protection against heathen nature. The painter's assertion that "decay is often a gardener," that there is salvation in the picturesque rather than in "something godly," is to the intrusive Puritan mere "gibberish."

The vagabond responds with detached irony: "what should we poor devils of Bohemians do for the Picturesque if Nature was in all things a precisian, each building like that church, and every man made in your image" (289). But as he invokes the picturesque and his irony begins to corrode his serenity, the artist quickly interrupts himself to return to his art—"bless me, what am I doing. I must tone down the green here." Since the essence of Melville's picturesque is self-control, his "toning down" is as much a restraint upon his animosity toward Puritan pragmatism as it is a muting of his pallette. The interruption echoes an earlier narrative interjection dealing with the same conflict between utilitarianism and art when, in defense of Rip's indolence, Melville as narrator finds himself on the verge of launching into a diatribe against our pragmatic society. Rip's genial virtues, he notes, are of no "practical efficiency" in a husband or in "the work-a-day world" where one "must needs energetically elbow his way therein, . . . or else resort to the sinuous wisdom of the serpent" (284). Melville does not allow himself to expand the subtext of this "wisdom"—that success is a confidence game—into a full critique of America. "Enough," he exclaims, and returns to his loving couple.

For a moment, as Melville verges on this critical digression, we are made to see the author dropping his narrative mask and abandoning the control over his sketch that his third-person distancing naturally promotes. Briefly, for one word, he steps out of the well-controlled action, but the very word—"Enough"—turns us back to the original story. Of course, there is a "sinuous wisdom" in Melville's narrative ploy. An uncharitable social truth emerges just as it is beaten down; a rant is defused, but the message is nonetheless delivered. As with the "Enough" we found in "The Piazza," this is Melville's narrative strategy for "toning down the green"—for maintaining distance and control, for mellowing an ejaculative style into a more natural, genial yet still dark voice. Thus, for the narrator and artist in "Rip," the "green" secrets of one's self are subdued even as they are exposed. Melville's greenness, then, is neither exalted nor denied but rather cagily muted. These parallel instances of erupting ego and restraint in "Rip" are two of the picturesque moments in retrograde that give light to Melville's aesthetics of repose.

This striving for repose or toning down is evident not only in the finished text of "Rip" but also in the creative rewriting Melville performed on his manuscript. Melville's alterations in "Rip" reveal his prolonged search for the right words to describe the vagabond artist and, by extension, himself. On leaf 27, for instance, he plays with various epithets: "the resigned one" becomes a more resourceful "patient one." Both, however, are cancelled, and on leaf 29 the painter emerges as "the sedate one." In this instance and in others, Melville seems to replace loss and resignation with a sense of sedate repose. A significant change on leaf 23 also emphasizes Melville's toning down of language. In attempting to strike a contrast between the pale precisian's boasts for his church and the mute magnificence of nature, Melville first describes "the blue peaks of the Kattskills" as looking "serenely down" upon the vain Puritan. Later he plays with the adverb, substituting "sublimely" for serenely and then finally "placidly" for sublimely. Serene, sublime, placid: in modulating between mild repose and sublime awe, the writer ultimately tones down the sublime, preferring instead placidity, an echo of the "placid hours" in the poem "Art" that must precede the fusions of creativity that lend "form" to "dream." Drawing upon his appreciation for the picturesque, Melville was honing his narrative voice to conform to an aesthetics of repose. In his last days as in former years, the process was a hard but fruitful battle.

Finally, our reading experience of the published text called "Rip Van Winkle's Lilac" is complicated by our knowledge of how Melville assembled the work—knowledge that comes to us by chance (most Melville manuscripts have not survived) but which nevertheless exists. Viewed as a linear narrative, "Rip" is a progression of genres and narrative voices. Its movement from prose to poetry and subsidiary modulation from third- to first- and then back to third-person voice constitute a virtual recapitulation of the major creative phases of Melville's development as a writer, specifically his experimentations after *Moby-Dick* with third-person voice and his shift to poetry after *The Confidence-Man*. It is as though Melville were attempting to encompass the principal voices and literary forms of his career and allegorize their development. But the genesis of "Rip" shows a different progression. Instead of prose giving over to poetry, the opposite occurs in Melville's creative process. Rip's poetic monologue yields a prose headnote that grows into a three-scene sketch while the monologue itself shrinks. The manuscript suggests, then, that Melville started with poetry but was drawn to the writing of prose fiction. And indeed the similar genesis of "John Marr" and *Billy Budd, Sailor* corroborate this notion.[12] In short, the linear narrative and genetic history promote diametrically opposed, yet equally valid reading experiences. Reading the printed "Rip" as a narrative, we progress from prose sketch to poem, but reading the manuscript "Rip" as a record of Melville's creative process, we move from poem to prose.

Only by inspecting the manuscript itself can we gain this privileged reading experience. Assuming that such a vantage point is aesthetically valid,[13] we find ourselves caught in what is best described as a "picturesque moment," for we are encouraged to keep in tense but reposeful suspension opposing fictive realms: the fluidity of prose and the concreteness of poetry. What sustains the reader and allows for a transcendence of the dialogical conflict in this reading experience is our awareness that, whatever "Rip" we choose to read, Melville's genially restrained, third-person speaker threads both prose and poetry together. "Rip" is not a confusion of genres; it is, in a sense, Melville's ultimate artistic chiaroscuro of sketch and poem. It is, as well, a complex allegory about a sketcher turned poet standing on the aesthetic "marge" between prose and poem. But as readers, we must recognize that any unitary allegorical interpretation of the work as exclusively a movement toward prose or toward poetry fails to acknowledge the complex interpenetration of forms inherent in Melville's latter-day artistic sensibility.

"Rip Van Winkle's Lilac," then, is a picturesque work about the picturesque sensibility which, in the juxtaposition of manuscript and text, promotes a picturesque reader response. In this case, the picturesque is not only a way of seeing but also a way of reading.

When Hawthorne wrote that Melville could "neither believe, nor be comfortable in his unbelief" (Howard 240), he created one of our more cherished "portraits" of the artist as one fated to "wander to-and-fro over these deserts." This is the restless Melville, the unbeliever, that continues to capture our modern sensibility. But this is only a partial portrait. We tend to overlook the implied believer or at least the desire for faith implicit in Hawthorne's characterization, just as we disregard the aesthetic importance of repose in Melville's work. Finally, the artist was as calm as he was restive. In a sense, Hawthorne's articulation of

Melville's problem with belief is only a theological extension of Melville's deeper picturesque sensibility, one that will not settle exclusively on either the beautiful or the sublime, comedy or tragedy, belief or doubt. Melville preferred "mingled brews": the chiaroscuro of darkness suffused with light, the tragicomedy of romance, the Tahitis and Enviable Isles encircled with beaches "on the marge" between tempest and repose. To fully appreciate this aesthetic we must recognize that despite Melville's insistence that art should plunge deeply into the sarcophagi of metaphysical truths, he also worked to restrain his "ontological heroics."

Melville's narrative voice in its many tonalities is invariably a hard-fought accommodation of the conflicting impulses of genial repose and dark truth-telling. It reflects the artist's longing for, yet wariness of, both restraint and self-exposure. For him, art must occupy a middle ground between dream and form, and too much control or too much fancy can deaden the final effect. By casting, as some critics do, Melville's persistent geniality as an ironic indictment of optimism, we ignore his carefully poised tensions between anxiety and mirth. Melville saw himself as a "meditative vagabondo" wandering after the picturesque. There is the promise of joy, restraint, and sincerity in this self-portrait, and if we are to acknowledge the undeniable presence of the picturesque in Melville's aesthetic, we must also recognize the function of repose in the artist's complex need to fuse "unlike things."

"Why talk of Jaffa?": Melville's *Israel Potter,* Baron Gros, Zummo, and the Plague

HENNIG COHEN

*W*hy talk of Jaffa? Melville poses this cryptic question near the beginning of *Israel Potter.*[1] His most obvious purpose is to avoid a dreary recitation of Israel's misfortunes as a British captive. For similar reasons, near the end of the novel he resorts to "omitting the particulars" (161) of Israel's London miseries, recorded in painful detail and particularity in his basic source, *The Life and Remarkable Adventures of Israel R. Potter* (Providence, R.I., 1824). Melville explains that such experiences are "necessarily squalid. Best not enlarge upon them" (*Israel Potter* 161). Besides, Israel, despite his remarkable adventures—and misadventures— is a common sort of man, a private soldier, and the "gloomiest and truthfulest dramatist seldom chooses for his theme the calamities, however extraordinary, of inferior and private persons . . ." (161). Melville's secondary purpose is to exploit the possibilities of the Jonah story, including its mythic dimension, the journey into darkness and the emergence into the light of revelation. His fundamental purpose is to define the role of the common man as hero in a democratic society born of revolution.

Melville arrived at and departed from the seaport of Joppa or Jaffa (both spellings were current and Melville alternates between them) when he visited the Holy Land. He associates this city, to which Jonah fled instead of proceeding to Nineveh as instructed (Jonah 1.1–4), with fatality and isolation. Thus in his journal of January 20, 1857, he wrote: "I am the only traveller sojourning in Joppa. I am emphatically alone, & begin to feel like Jonah. The wind is rising, the swell of the sea increasing. . . . " Impatiently awaiting a break in the weather which would permit his departure, he continues on January 22: "The genuine Jonah feeling, in Joppa. . . . it is only by stern self-control and grim defiance that I contrive to keep cool and patient."[2]

Melville refers to Jonah in his prose fiction more often than to any other biblical figure, Jesus and Adam included, and most memorably in *Moby-Dick* when Father Mapple retells his story (ch. 9). Father Mapple emphasizes Jonah's initial impatience and ultimate acceptance. Israel Potter tends to accept his lot and adapt to it, cool and patient from the outset. This diminishes the dramatic impact of his misfortunes but facilitates his surviving them. Other important references to Jonah and to Joppa occur in "The Honor and Glory of Whaling" (ch. 82), in which Ishmael cites the biblical story to enhance the stature of whalemen, and "Jonah Historically Regarded" (ch. 83), a comic refutation of contemporary biblical scholars whose historical arguments cast doubt on the spiritual import of the Book of Jonah.[3] The disasters that befell Joppa are recorded in legend and history. Hence G. M. Mackie writes in *The Dictionary of the Bible:* "Joppa was a constant sufferer in the famous wars of the Jews with Syria, Egypt and Rome." And: "Since the time of the Romans similar vicissitudes have marked the history of this unfortunate seaport."[4]

Jaffa is not mentioneed in *Life and Adventures,* but Melville's rhetorical question has its origin in a passing reference to an outbreak of smallpox among the prisoners the narrative contains (20). According to the historical Israel Potter, when he and his fellow prisoners were landed at Portsmouth, England, they were "conveyed to the marine hospital on shore, where many of us took the small-pox . . . which proved fatal to nearly one half our number." In fact, neither Potter himself nor his fellow captives appear to have had an especially hard time. Americans were a novelty and incited sympathetic attention. A "letter" to the *London Chronicle* of January 27, 1776, from an Englishman who visited their ship describes them as "at free liberty, victualled the same as the ship's company . . . their old cloaths were changed for new, at the expence of the Government. . . . one is dead of the small-pox."[5] Potter did not contract the disease, and after a month's confinement "on board a Guard Ship" at Spithead, he was assigned to row a barge and soon thereafter made his escape. Melville has the fictional Israel Potter "placed in the marine hospital . . . where half of the prisoners took the small-pox." He then raises his question about Jaffa and adds a description of Israel's imprisonment "on board a hulk" at Spithead (15). No qualifying "nearly" and a guard ship transformed into one of the infamous prison hulks. Israel "in the black bowels" of the hulk is "like Jonah in the belly of the whale" (15). By mildly modifying his source and employing a tone almost casual, Melville heightens the horror of Israel's situation, introduces a question that at first seems curious if not farfetched, and suggests mythic resemblances.

Israel's sojourn in London, "In the City of Dis," the title of chapter 24, parallels Jonah's experience in the belly of the whale. But Israel is an ordinary man. In apposition with the great kings of tragic drama, he is a "plebeian Lear or Œdipus" (161), a contradiction in terms since he cannot be both plebe and hero in the Shakespearean or Sophoclean sense. He is not the tragic hero of a royal drama. He is a "plebeian" whose poverty-stricken life is unremarkable. Neither is he a Hebrew prophet, though when he entered the city his "heart was prophetically heavy" (160); nor is he a mythic hero. The whale that swallows him is the poverty of London. But even so, his is a descent into the infernal region, a "subterranean" world where the Thames is "Phlegethon" and the city itself is equated with "Hades," "Erebus," and "Hinnom" (159–60). The narrative voice asserts bluntly: "In poverty,—'Facilis descensus Averni.'" The prophet Jonah, as he is aware, likewise undergoes a journey to Hinnom, for in his words it is from "out of the fish's belly . . . out of the belly of hell" that he prays for deliverance (Jonah 2.1–2). Israel's descent is not at all points comparable with that of Jonah into the black bowels of the whale or the epic heroes into Hades or Lear and Œdipus into the darkness; nonetheless it does like them lead to his self-realization, for he comes to understand and accept the place in the order of nature fate assigns to "inferior and private persons" (161).

Aside from whatever personal responses to Jaffa Melville might have had and in addition to his interest in the Jonah story, he was reminded of Jaffa by a famous, and in some ways notorious, nineteenth-century painting, *Napoleon Visiting the Plague Hospital at Jaffa* (1804; Fig. 1) by Baron Antoine-Jean Gros (1771–1835). Purchased by the state and prominently exhibited,[6] Melville could have seen it when he visited the Louvre (1849–50 *Journal,* November 30, 1849), a familiarity perhaps reinforced by readily available prints after the painting. The canvas is immense (17 feet 5 inches by 23 feet 7 inches), comparable in scale to the battle pieces Napoleon would commission, some of them by Gros, to exalt his victories and himself.[7] Gros made every effort to achieve historical authenticity, and Napoleon himself, who had commissioned the painting, approved his preliminary sketch.[8] It was first shown at the Paris Salon of September 1804, where it was an immediate sensation, and it has since been acclaimed Gros's "masterpiece" and a "key work

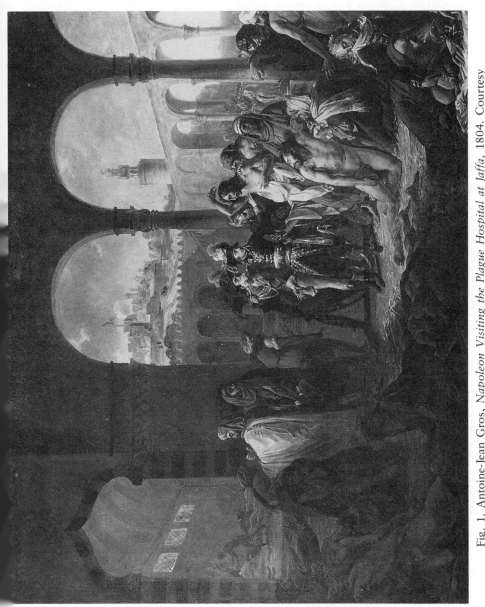

Fig. 1. Antoine-Jean Gros, *Napoleon Visiting the Plague Hospital at Jaffa*, 1804. Courtesy of the Louvre, Paris; Giraudon/Art Resource.

of the Romantic movement."[9] Its original shock effect was due to a topicality and an almost clinical realism which, in combination with its melodrama and the disturbing suggestiveness of its subject, placed it within the tradition of the sublime. It aroused, in Edmund Burke's vocabulary, a sense of terror and wonder. And it was remote, even exotic, and at the same time immediate. This immediacy was enhanced because it is also a history painting, then the most esteemed of the genres, and the story it told was contemporary and sensational in its own right.

In 1799, during the Egyptian Campaign, Napoleon's troops stormed Jaffa, massacred its inhabitants, and, acting on his direct order, put to death the Turkish garrison, which had surrendered. The matter has been much discussed. It has been argued that Napoleon deliberately sought to inspire terror and that he did not want to exhaust his dwindling supplies and encumber his retreat with prisoners. Whatever his reasons, Napoleon added to the accumulation of horrors associated with Jaffa since biblical times. Meanwhile, and more directly pertinent, an outbreak of the bubonic plague threatened to produce panic in his army. In a remarkable demonstration of leadership, Napoleon visited his plague-stricken soldiers in the pesthouse at Jaffa, inspiring them by this gesture of compassion and fearlessness. To prepare for the retreat, however, he ordered that the incurably sick be poisoned, though gently, with opium.[10] Napoleon's enemies made the most of the murderous events at Jaffa. His apologists, among them Baron Gros, countered with portrayals of Napoleon's heroism in the pesthouse. Gros shows him touching the bubonic sore of a soldier, a compelling figure who, like Napoleon, radiates an almost supernatural aura (Fig. 2).

By touching the sore Napoleon was ostensibly proving that there was little danger from the spread of infection, at least to himself. But much more was involved. Gros is validating the elevation of Napoleon to the imperial rank that would be celebrated by his coronation in December 1804 and with it his sacred powers of kingship. In touching the bubo of the soldier the painter places Napoleon in the tradition of the king as miraculous healer.[11] Louis XVI had performed the ancient rite of the "king's touch" at Versailles, and now the sacred power had passed to his successor. But legitimacy is not the full story. By implication Napoleon is identified with Louis IX, Saint Louis, who likewise fought the heathen in the Holy Land. Furthermore, the situation suggests an analogy between Napoleon and Christ raising Lazarus from the dead.[12] But Gros, exhibiting an almost Melvillean sensibility, is ambivalent in his adulation of Napoleon. The two figures confront each other, separated by a column and framed within respective moorish arches. In the distant background, above a bloody-red plume of Napoleon's headdress,

Fig. 2. Detail from Gros's *Napoleon Visiting the Plague Hospital at Jaffa*. Courtesy of the Louvre, Paris; Giraudon/Art Resource.

is what appears to be a Turkish fort flying the French tricolor. Above the bare head of the soldier is a tower, seemingly a minaret, surmounted by a cross. Gros's focus on the soldier detracts from his declared subject. Napoleon is immaculate in his glittering uniform and the soldier is dishevelled, stripped to the waist, and barefooted, but the soldier supersedes everyone else, even Napoleon, in magnitude and vibrancy. Though doomed to death, he is intensely alive. Gros celebrates Napoleon, yet he has sympathy for the plague victim whose frenzied attitude may well express at once his fear of the disease, the awe inspired by the temerity and calm majesty of Napoleon, and the desperate hope that he may, like Lazarus, escape the grave. Gros recognizes that the soldier is a sacrificial victim. His countenance is curiously Christlike; he, not Napoleon, has a crucifixion in his face, and as if to verify his martyrdom, there is the saracenic tower above him with its cross. Lazarus or Christ, in Melville's day the painting and the event elicited the idea of resurrection. For example, James Lloyd Stephens in his popular *Incidents of Travel in Egypt, Arabia Petrae, and the Holy Land* (New York, 1837), sounds this note in a description of the convent in Jaffa where Napoleon "touched the sick of the plague, restored the drooping courage of his soldiers, and almost raised the dying from their bed of death" (2:191). Melville might have read Stephens, for he and Stephens were both travel writers and Horace Greeley had compared *Typee* and *Omoo* "with the best of Stephens's Travels."[13]

On the whole, Melville says little about Napoleon, but before he wrote *Israel Potter* Melville had portrayed him in decidedly negative terms. The voyagers among the allegorical islands of his Mardian archipelago sight a "rocky islet" from which "Bello's standard waved." It had been the initial burial place of a "Mars and Moloch," a "god of war, who didst seem the devouring beast of the Apocalypse," and whose shadow "lingers in old Franko's vale" (*Mardi* 553). In the thinly veiled allegory, the islet is St. Helena, Bello is the British king, Franko is France, and the "rifled tomb" is that of Napoleon.[14] Napoleon's body was removed from St. Helena to Paris in 1841 for reburial in the Invalides. In *Redburn* Melville includes Napoleon, along with Milton's Satan, in a catalogue of "diabolical" figures and terms him "a martial murderer" (276); and in *Moby-Dick* he concludes his description of the killer whale with the observation that "we are all killers . . . Bonapartes and sharks included" (143).

From the standpoint of *Israel Potter,* the importance of Napoleon is not that he should be regarded as a killer but that Melville recognized him in the Gros painting as the archetype of the imperialist hero and therefore the exploiter of the common man. The painting is a much more dramatic statement, but the soldier Napoleon touches could be an Israel Potter. Napoleon is the culture hero of imperial France who cynically manipulates his soldiers. Benjamin Franklin and John Paul Jones, culture heroes of the American Revolution, are more benign in their treatment of Israel, but they bend him to their purposes and they, not he, engross public acclaim and achieve legendary status. Paul Jones's raid on Whitehaven, one more occasion of extravagantly heroic behavior on the part of Israel, common soldier and seaman, "made loud fame for Paul, especially at the court of France whose king sent Paul a sword and a medal. But poor Israel . . . what had he?" (*Israel Potter* 113). What indeed? Here, in a second question, is the suggestion of an answer to the earlier one, "Why talk of Jaffa?" The power structure, imperial and republican, used plebeian heroes, then all too often cast them aside. At Whitehaven, literally "Using Israel for a ladder. . . ," Paul Jones had scaled the fortress walls, the first rung in the ladder of his fame (101).

Other representations of the plague that Melville might have known are of related interest. Among them is *The Plague at Ashdod* (1630–31) by Nicolas Poussin, also in the Louvre and recognized as "one of his most influential paintings."[15] For instance, this painting was a source for one in a series of wax sculptures by the Sicilian artist, Gaetano Guilio Zummo (1656–1701; also spelled *Zumbo*), probably an ex voto offering commemorating the Naples plague of 1656, that would impress Melville profoundly (Fig. 3). *The Plague at Ashdod,* like the Gros painting, has religious and moralistic overtones. Its subject is the divine retribution visited on the Philistines for their seizure of the Ark of the Covenant (1 Samuel 5). While it would not be correct to describe plague paintings as an established genre, the subject was fairly familiar in European art,[16] and taken up by academic painters in the United States contemporary with Melville. An example is the New York portrait painter, Peter Paul Duggan (c. 1810–61), whose *Lazar House* was exhibited at the National Academy of Design in 1849. Melville was in touch with the art life of New York and attended exhibitions of the National Academy, on occasion making literary use of paintings he saw there.[17]

Melville retained his interest in the plague motif. Late in life, he bought a copy of Defoe's *History of the Plague in London* (1722),[18] and wax representations of the plague by Zummo that he saw in Florence in 1857 fascinated him. He would have been introduced to Zummo at least as early as 1849 when he read with enthusiasm Caroline Kirkland's *Holidays Abroad* while on the voyage to London. Mrs. Kirkland was sensitive to the peculiar appeal of these "small waxen figures showing every advance of decay in the human subject, which, for those who like such sights, are wonderful." It is almost as if she had Melville, whom

Fig. 3. Gaetano Giulio Zummo, detail from *The Triumph of Time*. Courtesy of the Museo Zoologico de "La Specola," Florence.

she knew, in mind.[19] They also caught the eye of Longfellow and Hawthorne, among Melville's American contemporaries, and before that the Marquis de Sade and Goethe. They attracted popular attention as well. The *Penny Cyclopaedia,* which Melville used in *Israel Potter* for descriptions of the British coast, titillated its readers with an article on Zummo's "group showing the effects of the plague . . . as extremely repulsive to look at as they are remarkable for their ingenuity of execution." Melville dined with its editor, identifying him in his journal as "Charles Knight . . . the Publisher of the Penny Cyclopedia, & concerned in most of the great popular publications of the day."[20] Zummo was acclaimed in his own time for the technical elegance of his wax sculptures, especially his anatomical models, but his portrayal of the ravages of the plague, and notably of decomposing cadavers, attracted unusual attention.[21] His contemporaries saw in his wax works an essential wholesomeness, a view, for somewhat different reasons, Melville shared. In the seventeenth century, science and the arts were in close proximity and reinforced each other. Zummo's realism was an imitation of nature, a replication both aesthetically and scientifically satisfying. Moreover, the contemplation of death and decay was intellectually edifying and spiritually uplifting.[22] Zummo's faithfulness to natural history and the moral implications that he projects are comparable to the evocative realism of the Gros history painting. Gros, for his part, shares Zummo's interest in the processes of nature. The figures in his drama move toward death in natural stages, descending in gradations from the vitality of Napoleon and his generals, to the stricken soldiers who look toward him, and on down to the dying at his feet. This gradation is repeated in the costuming and posture of the figures, which extends from the erect, splendidly attired generals to the nudity of the moribund, supine bodies.

The religiosity of Zummo's wax sculptures is all too obvious. They are reminders of human vanity and the corruptibility of the flesh.[23] Melville, for his part, saw in them, as he had seen in *Israel Potter,* human dissolution operating within the laws of nature, and he was attracted by the evident democracy of death: "—all ruins—detached bones— mothers children old men, intricacy of heaps" (Fig. 4). And: "In a cavernous ruin. Superb mausoleum . . . putrid corpse thrown over it" (Fig. 5). These notes are indicative of his journal entries at the time, and can be found along with the observation that a classical tomb of some forgotten grandee serves as the background for the rotting remains of commoners to the fore (entry for March 27, 1857). On behalf of Israel Potter and his kind, who delve "half buried" in the claypits, their metaphorical graveyard, Melville had asked another rhetorical question, "What signifies who we be—dukes or ditchers?"[24] He repeats the question and

Fig. 4. Gaetano Giulio Zummo, detail from *The Plague*. Courtesy of the Museo Zoologico de "La Specola," Florence.

Fig. 5. Gaetano Giulio Zummo, detail from *The Vanity of Human Greatness.*
Courtesy of the Museo Zoologico de "La Specola," Florence.

amplifies it at the end of the chapter: "What signifies who we be . . . ? Kings as clowns are codgers—who ain't a nobody? . . . All is vanity and clay" (157). The bodies of kings and commoners alike return to the earth. The skeptical phrase, "all is vanity," is recurrent in Ecclesiastes, but it is qualified by the observation that "the Earth abideth for ever" (1.2–3). In the earth and as common clay all are equal. But the Earth is also life everlasting, for life rises out of the Earth.

Death is a democrat, and the earth is at once a deathbed and a seedbed, a Potter's field for all mankind. Melville chose the traditional tombstone inscription, "Requiescat in Pace," as the title of the last chapter of *Israel Potter,* a benediction applicable to the soldiers of both the American Revolution and the Napoleonic wars, who in his estimation shared the common lot and share a common grave (163, 165). "Bartleby, the Scrivener," like *Israel Potter,* is a magazine story about the life and death of a forgotten man. The text of his obsequy ("He's asleep, ain't he?" . . . "With kings and counsellors . . . " [*Piazza Tales* 45]) is another reflection of the egalitarianism of death. Melville is recalling the words of Job 3.13–14, a favorite passage from a favorite book.[25] In *Mardi* a philosopher had addressed the bones of chieftains in the royal cemetery: "Grim chiefs in skeletons . . . ! Ye are but dust; belike the dust of beggars; for on this bed, paupers may lie down with kings . . . " (238); in *Moby-Dick* he had compared common sailors asleep in the forecastle with gravestone effigies "of canonized kings and counsellors" (426); and in *Pierre,* describing the funeral of an impoverished farmer, Melville related the passage from Job to the levelling force of death: "Oh, softest . . . of Holland linen is the motherly earth! There, beneath the sublime tester of the infinite sky, like emperors and kings, sleep, in grand state, the beggars and paupers of the earth! I joy that Death is this Democrat . . . " (278).

In equating dukes and ditchers, Melville has secularized the words of Job and given them a political application. His nineteenth-century readers would have been conscious of their egalitarian significance from their acquaintance with ideas popularized by Volney's *Ruins* (Paris, 1791).[26] The essence of the Romantic vogue that Volney exemplifies appears in his "Invocation" to the genius of "solitary ruins" who "confounding the dust of the king with that of the meanest slave, had announced the sacred dogma of Equality" and in a "vision" that reveals the fusion of all religions when the truths they hold in common are recognized.[27] Melville's cognizance of the ruins motif is apparent in a submerged reference in "Bartleby." The scrivener, in a setting "as deserted as Petra,"[28] is compared with "Marius brooding among the ruins of Carthage" (*Piazza Tales* 28; Figs. 6 and 7). Melville is citing the title of a celebrated portrait of the Roman Republican hero, in his old age a fugitive, painted in 1807 by John Vanderlyn (1775–1852; see Fig. 1 in Kelley, ch. 6). In *Israel Potter,* Melville describes "the incessant decay" of the rugged British coastline in language reminiscent of Volney, a natural ruin "showing in shattered confusion detached rocks, pyramids, and obelisks, rising half-revealed from the surf—the Tadmores of the wasteful desert of the sea."[29] The ruins of great civilizations and natural ruins, like the dissolution of dukes and ditchers, evince the equality that exists in the cyclic processes of nature, natural processes that include regeneration. Jonah, Melville writes in *Moby-Dick,* was "tombed in the whale's belly . . . " (364), and the Jonah story was the antetype of the Resurrection: "For as Jonas was three days and three nights in the whale's belly; so shall the Son of man be three days and three nights in the heart of the earth" (Matthew 12.40).

The context of Melville's typological reference to Jonah, as already noted, is facetious. Melville is playing with the question of the "historical story of Jonah" (364, 366), and while *Israel Potter* is rich in biblical reference to resurrections, the most explicit of them is likewise colored by its seriocomic context. When Israel returns from Paris and Benjamin Franklin to Squire Woodcock's country house, the squire conducts him to the entrance of a secret passage "like the marble gate of a tomb" that leads to a hiding place (67). "Am I to be buried alive here?" he asks in comic trepidation, to which the squire, with a smile, replies, "But your resurrection will soon be at hand," on the third day at the latest, he promises, bidding him, in a pun, "adieu" (68). The hiding place for Israel is a "blind tomb" in which he is "coffined" (70).

Like Jonah and Christ, Israel spends three days and nights in his tomb, from which he rises to find that the squire is dead. The rest is farce. He steals the squire's clothing, pretends to be his ghost, and escapes from the country house. This modulation from melodrama to comedy should be remarked. The comic underpinnings here and throughout *Israel Potter* are of a piece with much of the magazine fiction Melville was writing at this time. Its mix of the serious and the comedic is comparable, for example, to the sketches of "The Encantadas," another place of wandering and deception, replete with its "Tartarus," its "Potter's field," and an epitaph that is something of a joke (*Piazza Tales* 125, 127, 173). Low comedy is a characteristic of the commoner, not the king.

Once again on the road, Israel exchanges the elegant clothes of the squire for the rags of a scarecrow. This change of clothing, and the many others that precede and follow it, is a further indication of his ability to adapt to the environment in which he finds himself. On one other occasion, as he nears London and his subterranean life there, Israel dons the clothing of the dead, the rags probably of "some pauper suicide" (153). Again he is shaping himself to the demands of the circumstance, responding organically. That he wears the fine garments of a deceased country gentleman and then a pauper suicide's rags as the nature of the situation requires, conveys both the democracy of death and the continuity of life. Israel Potter may suggest comparison with the resurrections of Jonah and Christ but the comparison, like that with the mythic heroes who descend into and rise out of Hades, does not fit Israel so well as the clothing he picks up in his wanderings. The proper parallel of the plebeian hero is neither biblical nor epic nor tragic but the cycle of nature.[30] The structure of *Israel Potter* is circular, and it goes hand-in-hand with the characterization of Israel himself. The legendary heroes—

Fig. 6. *Opposite:* Frontispiece to the first edition of Volney's *Les ruines, ou Meditations sur les révolutions des empires* . . . (Paris, 1791). Courtesy of Haverford College, Haverford, PA.

Fig. 7. American version of the frontispiece of Volney's *Ruins; or, Meditation on the Revolutions of Empires* (Boston, 1840). Courtesy of the American Philosophical Society, Philadelphia.

Benjamin Franklin, John Paul Jones, and Ethan Allen—move forward toward their objective, and in this respect are like Ahab. Israel's aim is to make the most of happenstance, and he wanders in circles. He is like Ishmael, a sailor before the mast, and another wanderer and survivor. Ishmael, too, circles back from the end to the beginning. Israel's linear chronicle from birth to death is a return to the hearthstone of his infancy. The line of time is the circle of eternity. Israel expresses his understanding of his place in the natural order with his last words, "The ends meet," and his instructions to the plowman to plow the ruins of his homestead (169).

Therefore for Melville the Zummo wax figures are not merely a memento mori, nor are they religious in the usual way. Nor are they in essence morbid or necrophilic, though most American visitors to Florence found them so. Longfellow, for example, had turned away in disgust because he thought Zummo "revelled in the hideous mysteries of death, corruption and the charnel house"; Hawthorne, in the main conventional in his perceptions of Italian art, concurred but felt that the figures were "singular and horribly truthful."[31] The truth of their realism—anatomical knowledge heightened by artistic skill and deepened by political and moral content—was what intrigued Melville. "Moralist, this Sicilian," he wrote of Zummo in his journal (March 27, 1857). Gros, on the other hand, though engaged in dramatizing the legend of Napoleon, was a moralist in spite of himself. Zummo and Gros confirmed Melville's view that human decomposition, even under the horrific circumstances of the Neapolitan epidemic of 1656 or the Jaffa pesthouse, is a stage in a natural process. This sentiment Melville epitomizes at the end of *Israel Potter*, the final sentence of which equates the death of the old soldier and a familiar natural icon, the blasted tree—"He died the same day that the oldest oak on his native hills was blown down"—and it is this sentiment that justifies his raising the Jaffa question near the beginning.[32]

Daumier's Robert Macaire
and Melville's Confidence Man

HELEN P. TRIMPI

Jn an earlier treatment of Melville's satirical "portrait gallery" of politicians, journalists, and preachers of the 1850s in *The Confidence-Man* (1857), I observed his adaptation of certain methods of caricature from graphic prints of the period—specifically his use of a setting or situation to make a satirical point, his identification of a type or individual by some allusive element of physical appearance or speech, and his use of theatrical or mythical prototypes to comment on character and action (Trimpi, *Confidence Men* 30–38). These methods were intrinsic to his intentions in reflecting upon the contemporary political scene during the presidential election year of 1856, much as the intention of English and American political prints of the earlier part of the century had been to comment, usually in a partisan manner, on political personalities, parties, and events. I also argued earlier that Melville's Confidence Man—a shape-shifting trickster—has analogues in the theatrical traditions of Harlequin, who in both Continental commedia dell'arte and in English Pantomime had become a perennial stage type designed for mockery of various human foibles and vices—personal, social, and political ("Harlequin-Confidence Man" 164–70). Harlequin had also become a common allusion in graphic prints, to the idea of political changeability or tricksterism. Yet another significant analogue in the visual arts and the theater to be found in *The Confidence-Man*—one suggestive of larger questions about the meaning of Melville's commentary on his mid-century milieu—is the figure of Robert Macaire. Macaire, who had been created by the great French actor Frédérick Lemaître in the 1830s as a comic personality and vehicle for social and political satire, was acted on the French, English, and American stage for three decades and was still being performed at four theaters in New York City during the months we presume Melville was writing *The Confidence-Man*.[1] In graphic art he became the subject of a famous series of a hundred lithographs created by Honoré Daumier and Charles Philipon for Philipon's Parisian periodical *Le Charivari*, 1836–38.[2]

As the quintessential French *blaguer* (swindler, huckster, hoaxer, con man), Robert Macaire is uncle, if not father or brother, to Melville's masquerading Confidence Man. The many similarities of function and significance between the two figures bear looking into and suggest an indirect, if not a demonstrably direct, influence of Daumier's prints upon Melville's American character and also some possible reasons for the emergence of both as important symbolic figures in the popular graphic works of a major French artist and in the mature fiction of a major American writer—both within a 20-year period. There is presently no evidence that Melville owned or had immediate access to the French lithographs. The list of his collection of prints remaining in the Berkshire Athenaeum does not include any Daumier (Wallace, "Melville's Prints" 72–86). However, this list probably records only a portion of what he collected and there is no reason to exclude the possibility that he might have seen one or many of the famous prints in other collections or in printsellers' shops in New York, London, or Paris. On the other hand, he surely would have been aware of the personality of Robert Macaire as a theatrical type for social and political comedy, and he may well have been drawn by its existence there to look at or to buy some of the Daumier prints, which were widely distributed and collected from the time of their first appearances. Whether the filiation of Robert Macaire to the Confidence Man would have been through the stage figure or through Daumier's graphics is not easily determinable. Melville's fiction shows the certain influences of both stage techniques and graphic techniques in such an intermingled way that they cannot always be sorted out. However, certain techniques of his literary caricature can be directly linked to Daumier's prints in a way that theatrical influence does not fully account for.

What will concern us here, then, is the range of similarities and differences between two versions of a fictional character-type who engages in constant role-playing and deceit as a means of getting ahead in society. To see the nature of the relationship, readers of Melville familiar with the various roles that the Confidence Man assumes should glance first at six of the roles that Robert Macaire assumes, in the lithographs reproduced here: as banker and stock-promoter in "Bertrand, j'adore

Fig. 1. Honoré Daumier, "Bertrand, j'adore l'industrie." *Le Charivari*, 20 August 1836. Courtesy of The Fine Arts Museums of San Francisco, the Achenbach Foundation for Graphic Arts, California Palace of the Legion of Honor; Bruno and Sadie Adriani Collection.

l'industrie" (Delteil no. 354; Adhémar no. 2) in Figure 1; as private investigator in "Monsieur, on m'a volé un billet" (Delteil no. 364; Adhémar no. 37) in Figure 2; as speculator in industrial shares in "Robert Macaire au restaurant" (Delteil no. 372; Adhémar no. 4) in Figure 3; as teacher and model for other swindlers in "C'est tout de même flatteur" (Delteil no. 431; Adhémar no. 18) in Figure 4; as shareholder in "Robert Macaire actionnaire" (Delteil no. 435; Adhémar no. 29) in Figure 5; and as speculator in bitumen for street paving in "Dis donc, Macaire"

Fig. 2. Honoré Daumier, "Monsieur, on m'a volé un billet." *Le Charivari*, 6 November 1836. Courtesy of The Fine Arts Museums of San Francisco, the Achenbach Foundation for Graphic Arts, California Palace of the Legion of Honor; Bruno and Sadie Adriani Collection.

(Delteil no. 441; Adhémar no. 42) in Figure 6. What observations might Daumier (as well as Philipon, who wrote the legends for Daumier's drawings) and Melville have been making about a prominent aspect of public life in their time—observations that might possibly have a perennial application, too?[3]

In *Daumier and His World,* Howard Vincent compares the Parisian world of Daumier to the United States of the same era. It was, he says, a "fertile period of social dreaming, with the Utopian idealism of Saint-Simon, . . . Fourier, and Proudhon." It was also a time of financial speculation, business schemes, of swindling in stock issues, and of speculative enterprises of all kinds. During this time the publisher and artist Charles

Fig. 3. Honoré Daumier, "Robert Macaire au restaurant." *Le Charivari*, 28 December 1836. Courtesy of The Fine Arts Museums of San Francisco, the Achenbach Foundation for Graphic Arts, California Palace of the Legion of Honor; Bruno and Sadie Adriani Collection.

Philipon (1800–1862) started, first, the illustrated opposition paper *La Caricature*, a weekly that ran from 1830 until it was suppressed in 1834 for political reasons by King Louis Philippe, and, second, *Le Charivari*, a daily which began in 1832 and, by avoiding direct political caricature, survived much longer. In both, the most famous and successful caricatures were the regular series of 100 lithographs of Robert Macaire that appeared in *Charivari* from August 20, 1836, to November 25, 1838. As Vincent observes, Philipon and Daumier wanted to satirize a whole society, and they did so through "personification and symbol." For this they adapted the figure of Robert Macaire, who had been developed on the Parisian stage by Frédérick Lemaître out of a role in an unsuccessful

Fig. 4. Honoré Daumier, "C'est tout de même flatteur." *Le Charivari,* 11 March 1838. Courtesy of The Fine Arts Museums of San Francisco, the Achenbach Foundation for Graphic Arts, California Palace of the Legion of Honor; Bruno and Sadie Adriani Collection.

melodrama, *L'Auberge des Adrets.* Lemaître transformed a conventional bandit into a "buffoon, a blackguard with humor and dash, a witty scoundrel who could laugh at himself and his victims." Adapting his distinctive costume from an eccentric *clochard* whom he saw one night in the street, Lemaître brought to the stage a comedy in which two scoundrels, Macaire and his companion Bertrand, trick each other or connive together, and in the process various Parisian types are satirized (70–71).[4]

In the early lithographs in *Caricature,* Philipon and Daumier had ridiculed Louis Philippe, the "Citizen King," who led the government as

Fig. 5. Honoré Daumier, "Robert Macaire actionnaire." *Le Charivari,* 13 May 1838. Courtesy of The Fine Arts Museums of San Francisco, the Achenbach Foundation for Graphic Arts, California Palace of the Legion of Honor; Bruno and Sadie Adriani Collection.

a constitutional monarch from the expulsion of Charles X in the July Revolution of 1830 until the Revolution of 1848. Their attacks on the king and his ministers brought about fines and jail terms for both Philipon and Daumier and resulted in the suppression of *Caricature.* However, satire continued in the daily *Charivari,* especially through the immensely popular series of prints of Macaire and Bertrand, which circulated widely. (They were published separately at intervals as *Caricaturana.*) In these

Fig. 6. Honoré Daumier, "Dis donc, Macaire, que' que c'est que c'thé." *Le Charivari,* 13 May 1838. Courtesy of The Fine Arts Museums of San Francisco, the Achenbach Foundation for Graphic Arts, California Palace of the Legion of Honor; Bruno and Sadie Adriani Collection.

prints political caricature of specific government figures was avoided for more general and less dangerous topics: the worlds of journalism, finance, law, medicine, the arts, book-selling, small business, large business, and *puffisme* (advertising). As Philipon observed, writing in *Charivari* in 1836: "On the Exchange, in politics, in industry, in literature, and even in philosophy, one discovers everywhere Robert Macaire and Bertrand, meaning the swindler and his confederates." He dedicated the first litho-graph of Macaire to "those bankers, philanthropists, or contractors whose cash boxes, like prisons, are ever ready to receive but not to render up" (Vincent, *Daumier* 73). Vincent, who does not further explore the connections between Melville's Confidence Man and Robert Macaire, writes: "Macaire is the promoter *par excellence*. . . . He is the Confidence Man in an endless variety of confidence games. . . . Macaire has more appearances than Melville's chameleon Confidence Man; he has that character's wit and his pleasure in deception, but is free of his Timonism" (75). Vincent goes on to note Macaire's relationship to the clever servant of ancient comedy, and, in French dramatic tradition, to Molière's Scapin, the servant clown who enjoys "stratagem for stratagem's sake." He further observes justly that Macaire's speech "scintillates, overwhelms one with pun and word-play," adding that he is a "Mephistopheles of the gutter," who "delights in acquisition as pure operation and not as end." Finally, he emphasizes the centrality of Macaire as a "single symbolic summation" of the time, to which we in the twentieth century have, he feels, no parallel.[5]

In the extensive contemporary commentary on both the theatrical and the graphic versions of Robert Macaire, perhaps of most interest to us are the responses of William Makepeace Thackeray in English and of Charles Baudelaire in French.[6] Thackeray's essay, "Caricatures and Lithography in Paris," which appeared in *The Paris Sketch Book, by Mr. Titmarsh* (1840), is one of the best, because Thackeray was an artist and the illustrator of his own written work, and also because he was a careful (albeit prejudiced) observer of French society and art. He makes his principal topic in "Caricatures and Lithography" the Daumier-Philipon series. As a believer in royalty, Thackeray handles quite sympathetically the king's response to the provoking treatment he received in the prints in *Caricature,* relating the well-known story of Philipon's courtroom defense of himself by transforming, through four sequential sketches, the heavy-jowled features of the king into a pear—the famous caricature of *"La Poire"* (pear or dolt). He contends that of all the types of roguery in which the French excel the British, the one whose greatness exceeds all others is that of Robert Macaire. In Thackeray's words, it has come to be considered "the type of roguery in general; and now, just as all the political squibs were made to come of old from the lips of Pasquin, all the reflections on the prevailing cant, knavery, quackery, humbug, are put into the mouth of Monsieur Robert Macaire" (65).

Thackeray notes how the artists took over from Lemaître Macaire's "most picturesque green coat, with a variety of rents and patches, a pair of crimson pantaloons ornamented in the same way," his "enormous whiskers and ringlets," his "enormous stock and shirt-frill, as dirty and ragged as . . . can be," his "relic of a hat very gaily cocked over one eye, and a patch to take away somewhat from the brightness of the other."

Noting a relationship to English Pantomime, he observes of Bertrand
that he is the "simple recipient" of Macaire's jokes and makes vicarious
atonement for his crimes, acting, in fact, the part in the pantomime
taken by Pantaloon, who is entirely under the fatal influence of Clown.
Like Clown and Pantaloon in the pantomime, Macaire and Bertrand
"are made to go through the world; both swindlers, but the one more
accomplished than the other." He notes the immense popularity of both
the stage and the graphic versions of Macaire, and summarizes the
powerful effect of the prints especially in making both characters "believ-
able as historical personages"—almost as if they really existed (65–67).

Thackeray describes in detail Daumier's satiric lithographs of French
stockbrokers and speculators, explaining their backgrounds, and then
he cites Macaire's one venture into "religious" exploitation:

> "Mon ami," says the repentant sinner [Macaire], "le temps de la commandite
> va passer, *mais les badauds ne passeront pas* (O rare sentence! it should be
> written in letters of gold!) *occupons nous de ce qui est éternel.* Si nous
> fassions [sic] une religion?" On which M. Bertrand remarks, "A religion!
> what the devil—a religion is not an easy thing to make." But Macaire's
> receipt is easy, "Get a gown, take a shop," he says. (67)

Thackeray is referring to the print, "Robert Macaire Schismatique,"
whose legend begins with Macaire's parody of Christ's words, "En vérité,
en vérité! Je te le dis, Bertrand."[7] Although Thackeray dismisses French
satire on religious cant as weak in comparison with British wit on the
subject, readers of Melville can see in Macaire's broad definition of a
new "religion" similarities to the Confidence Man's solicitations as an
itinerant evangelist, in the form of the Deaf-Mute, who sells a sloganized
version of Pauline wisdom, and as an Herb-Doctor, promulgator of the
"religion" of "Nature." Moreover, we can hear a French version of the
American comic aphorism (attributed to Melville's contemporary, P. T.
Barnum), "There's a sucker born every minute," in Macaire's remark that
"Les badauds ne passeront pas; occupons nous de ce qui est éternel."

Thackeray draws his readers' attention to differences between French
follies and British, including a description of a lithograph that features
a "male beggar" who suggests Melville's American version of this type—
John Ringman, the Man with a Weed, who solicits his Masonic "brother"
Henry Roberts for money.[8] His characterization of the French series as
the "Macaire Picture Gallery" may be compared to Melville's satirical
portrait gallery of American confidence men—if we bear in mind that
the Confidence Man's actual "countenance and figure" change in his eight
different appearances, while his intent does not:

The countenance and figure of Macaire, and the dear stupid Bertrand, are preserved . . . with great fidelity throughout; but the admirable way in which each fresh character is conceived, the grotesque appropriateness of Robert's every successive attitude and gesticulation, and the variety of Bertrand's postures of invariable repose, the exquisite fitness of all the other characters, who act their little part and disappear from the scene, cannot be described on paper, or too highly lauded. (68)

The perennial charm (and truth) of the *blaguer/badaud* (swindler/ fool) relationship comes clear in Thackeray's remarks on the Macaire series. He notes the adaptability in British stage comedy of the Clown (or Harlequin) figure to any kind of topical political or cultural object of satire, and points to the comparable adaptability of Robert Macaire to all kinds of similar phenomena in French society. (The Confidence Man is similarly adaptable to the same kind of activities in the American milieu of Melville's time.) Thackeray concludes his essay: "Well hast thou said, O ragged Macaire,—'Le jour va passer, *mais les badauds ne passeront pas*'" (68)—a sentiment that is echoed in the remark of Melville's narrator in chapter 14 of *The Confidence-Man:* "The grand points of human nature are the same today they were a thousand years ago. The only variability in them is in expression, not in feature."

Although the Macaire sequence in *Charivari* ended in 1838, the *Caricaturana* sets circulated for a long period thereafter. Baudelaire, in his essay nearly 20 years later, "Of the Essence of Laughter, and Generally of the Comic in the Plastic Arts" (1855), and in his review, "Some French Caricaturists" (1857), speaks of Daumier as graphic artist in the highest terms. In the former piece he chastises "pedagogues" and "pedantic corpses" for having "let the comedy of Robert Macaire pass them by, without seeing in it significant moral and literary symptoms" (141). In the later "Some French Caricaturists," he reviews the graphic work of Carle Vernet, Nicolas-Toussaint Charlet, Henri Monnier (creator of M. Prudhomme), Grandville, Gavarni, Trimolet, Charles-Joseph Traviès (creator of Mayeux), and Jacque, but he gives the most space and highest praise to Daumier, singling out from the enormous body of work that he did (including 17 series of lithographs) the series on Macaire. Alluding to the royally enforced shift from political to social satire, Baudelaire writes:

The political pamphlet gave way to comedy. . . . [The] grand epic of *Robert Macaire,* related by Daumier in flamboyant vein, followed the revolutionary fury and contemporaneous allusions. And so caricature took on a new character, and was no longer particularly political. . . . It impinged on the domain of the novel. (222)

In Baudelaire's opinion, "Daumier extended greatly the limits of his art. He has made a serious art of it; he is a great caricaturist." In the future, if Daumier is to be understood for his true worth, he needs to be analyzed "both as an artist and as a moralist" (223).

Such commentary on Daumier's Robert Macaire series enables us to see how his use of the trickster type differs from Melville's as well as how it resembles it. *The Confidence-Man,* as conceived by Melville, is a more powerful synthesis, because it brings together into a single narrative structure both the broad appeal of satire on types, which the Macaire series had, and the more temporal, particularized satire of individuals—the kind that Daumier and Philipon had published earlier in *Caricature* and for which their periodical had been suppressed. The complexity of Melville's allusive structure in *The Confidence-Man* has, so far as present research can tell, no precise parallel in literary or graphic art, existing as it does simultaneously on three levels of satirical implication: general human types, regional or national types, and individual persons involved in political events of the 1850s (Trimpi, *Confidence Men* 244).

To illustrate the relationship of the Macaire series to *The Confidence-Man,* several general comparisons need to be made, and then several specific comparisons between typical examples from the series on Macaire and a single important episode in *The Confidence-Man.* Since many other parallels between the two works are obvious, as are many of the objects from the period which they hold up for ridicule, they will be only mentioned here.

One notable general similarity is that of the episodic and repetitive structure of *The Confidence-Man* to the sequence of individual prints, each featuring a single principal figure, typical of the periodical publication of Daumier's series. In "Dickens and the Traditions of Graphic Satire" John Dixon Hunt has noticed that there is a resemblance between the episodic structure of Dickens's *Sketches by Boz* and *Pickwick Papers* and the sequence of plates typical in graphic publications of the period (131). Daumier's sequence on Macaire evidently was produced without any definite conception of when it would end or even whether it would have a formal ending. It has been suggested that Melville conceived his work originally for periodical publication and that he intended a sequel or sequels to the work. In the absence of complete evidence we must deal with the text as it stands, and it may be argued that he conceived of it as a completed sequence of episodes, based on the idea that there were several ways in which one figure—archetypal, mythical, or allegorical in its implications—might assume various disguises in the course of a single day (April Fool's Day) to work his swindling tricks on various passengers on a Mississippi steamer. Since the narrative begins at dawn and ends just at or after midnight, some readers, including myself, discern not only a completed time sequence but also a framing effect in the appearance in the last episode of the Juvenile Peddler, who forms a symmetrical contrast (as another version of the Pierrot mask) to the youthful Deaf-Mute of the opening scene. Moreover, the portentous action of the Cosmopolitan in extinguishing the lamp in the Gentlemen's Cabin in the last scene seems to suggest a definitive conclusion to the action as a whole. If the latter view is what Melville intended to suggest, then the narrator's remark that "something further may follow of this Masquerade" may be taken not to hint at further episodes but more ominously at the potential for social and political disaster to the nation in the machinations of the contemporary individuals who have been satirized in the foregoing episodes. In contrast, although the Macaire series contains a print near the end in which Macaire and Bertrand, carrying money bags, are shown fleeing to Brussels (a notorious refuge for escaping scoundrels), the series itself ends inconclusively with a print in which Macaire, still presumably in France, presides over the funeral of a defunct *commandite* (limited partnership).[9] It is not, apparently, so neatly rounded out as a single artistic conception as *The Confidence-Man* is.

Another overall similarity between *The Confidence-Man* and the Macaire prints is the depiction of a swindler carrying on his operations in many different walks of life, for neither Daumier nor Melville confines his satire to the commercial world. The disguises that the Confidence Man puts on include several standard American types: an itinerant evangelist, a performing black beggar, a poor but genteel gentleman with marital problems, a charity solicitor, a stockbroker, a patent medicine salesman, an employment agent, and a gentleman "cosmopolitan" of no apparent profession. That each one seeks to establish a confidential relationship—one of trust involving the exchange of money—is what links them to Robert Macaire, who in each of his roles, whether as stockbroker, land or mining speculator, solicitor for a "philanthropic" cause, matrimonial or investigative agent, lawyer, book-seller, medical doctor, or other, always seeks to collect funds which he has no intention of returning to his victim. Both writer and artist seem to say not that all commercial men and only commercial men are knaves, but that nearly all men act like the worst kind of commercial men.

The third important similarity is that the swindling action both in the Macaire series and in *The Confidence-Man* depends for depth and brilliance of effect on the manipulation of language as well as on the visible appearance and action of the swindler. Witty dialogue, involving plays upon words and names, allusions to topical themes, and revelation of character through language, is a major source of meaning and humor in both. Although Baudelaire deprecated Philipon's contribution to the Macaire series, it is safe to say that for the popular audience at the time of *Charivari* and *Caricaturana* the wit of the legends formed an integral, perhaps essential, part of the meaning of the prints and hence of their appreciation of them. The legends consist sometimes of speeches only by Macaire, sometimes of dialogue between him and Bertrand, and sometimes between him and one or another interlocuter. For the modern researcher, the effort to discover the full meanings of the prints in the context of the period presents some of the same problems as the attempt to discover Melville's meanings in *The Confidence-Man,* and leads to the disclosure of many more detailed similarities in both subject and method.

On the other hand, there are significant differences, too, in conception and execution in the two works. Perhaps the most important is that Melville's work is a satire concentrated on a contemporary political situation of grave national importance—one more immediately serious than the Parisian social and economic scene in the 1830s. The main subject of *The Confidence-Man,* as I have argued in *Melville's Confidence Men and American Politics in the 1850s,* is the political and philosophical debate in the 1850s between the antislavery movement as it emerged in the newly formed Republican party (a sectional political party) and the proslavery response as it hardened and expanded into the platform of the Democratic party in 1856. That situation moved toward polarization in the election of 1860 and soon thereafter resulted in the secession of the Southern states and the Civil War. In contrast, the subject of Daumier and Philipon's series is not so sharply focused and potentially volatile, and of course did not issue in a tragic national cataclysm.

Moreover, although apparently narrower in its concentration on the American political situation in 1856 and on the many public figures involved in it, this focus constitutes only one level of Melville's comprehensive structure. For, the individuals he alludes to are depicted *through* regional and professional types and, ultimately, through generic types as well. Melville thus satirizes the special and the local in relation to the universal, the general, the enduring.[10] Daumier, by contrast, though he might on occasion allude to a specific person, has not related his trickster in any systematic way to specific persons linked together in contemporary life. Perhaps, as a result, his sequence was more immediately apprehensible than Melville's narrative, and more popular. To put the matter simply, it was less complicated. Paul Valéry touches upon the generalizing quality of Daumier's art when he compares him to

Michelangelo and Rembrandt, saying that like "most powerful writers," they are "creators of types." To say that Daumier's satire is more generalized is not to take anything away from him as an artist, but only to distinguish the more loosely conceived immediate quality of his work from the more tightly conceived, impeccably detailed, and minutely referential work of Melville. Such political commentary as Melville presents in *The Confidence-Man* has suffered more than Daumier's the limitations of all detailed topical satire. Its meaning was evidently not understood by many at the time of publication; and the book has been largely overlooked or underestimated subsequently. Like Goya's sequences of prints, *Los Caprichos* (1799) and *Los Disparates* (1821–24), which were aimed at satirizing specific individuals in Spanish public life, Melville's pasquinade has suffered from the demands of its form, and has had to rely instead upon its more general, perennially true meanings for whatever enduring life it has had.

There is a noteworthy symbolic dimension in Melville's treatment of the role-playing, shape-shifting figure that Daumier does not exploit, perhaps because French culture lacked the Puritan mythology of the Devil. Like much American political caricature of the period, Melville's portrayal of the Confidence Man employs the symbolism of historical demonology, with its connotations of spiritual and moral evil, while Daumier's Robert Macaire simply embodies the symbolism of a morally wicked human type. Only one print—namely, that of Macaire as "schismatique," the "founder of a new religion"— carries connotations suggestive of spiritual evil and even these are light-hearted in tone. Melville's conception of human character reveals more obviously the historic philosophical change from the traditional idea of mankind made in the divine image to the nineteenth-century Romantic notion of mankind made in the image of the Devil. It may be recalled that one of the standard attributes of the Devil in historical demonology is that he is a creature capable of assuming many different shapes. Such an attribute was useful to graphic artists, especially to American political caricaturists, but not to Daumier or Philipon.[11]

These differences aside, both artists seem to have found in contemporary journalists or publicists especially appealing targets for their satire. Of the eight different disguises which the Confidence Man employs, five allude to important editors in the world of American journalism in the 1850s or earlier: Benjamin Lundy of the *Genius of Universal Emancipation,* William Cullen Bryant of the *New York Evening Post,* Thurlow Weed of the *Albany Evening Journal,* Horace Greeley of the *New York Tribune,* and Henry Ward Beecher of the *Brooklyn Independent.* For one of these men, journalism was the central occupation and the source of his influence and fame: Horace Greeley, caricatured by Melville as the Philosophical Intelligence Office agent, was the founder and editor of the *Tribune* and a promoter of various public causes—political, social, and philanthropic. Satirizing the same profession, several of the Philipon-Daumier prints turn upon Robert Macaire's skillful use of promotion techniques. In particular, one of his most readily identifiable targets is the Parisian journalist, publisher, and commercial entrepreneur Émile de Girardin (1806–81). The prints that allude to Girardin form interesting parallels to Melville's caricature of Greeley in chapter 22 of *The Confidence-Man.*

Like Greeley, Girardin was an immensely successful journalist, who, according to Jean Adhémar, was "one of the first to realize that the press, especially the cheap, large circulation press, was a powerful business tool and means of launching new ideas." He founded a series of newspapers and published almanacs and atlases. Girardin's genius lay in convincing the public that all his enterprises were highly philanthropic, for "at that time the public was said to be 'ready to help enterprises with a moral purpose and directed by honourable men.'" These ostensible goals were precisely like those announced by Greeley, who was widely ridiculed by some who were skeptical of his motives. Girardin's most successful paper was *La Presse,* a cheap conservative journal, founded in 1836, just five years before Greeley's *Tribune,* and one which depended, like Greeley's *Tribune,* upon advertising to cover its publication costs. Girardin used his journalistic profits to launch various joint-stock companies. After the failure of several of his property and industrial securities concerns, in which he let the guilt fall on his colleagues, he was "regarded as the swindler *par excellence,*" although he managed to continue his publishing activities (Adhémar 8–12). Philipon and Daumier attacked Girardin and his *puffisme* in several of the prints early in the series, beginning with the first one in *Charivari,* "Bertrand, j'adore l'industrie" (see Fig. 1).[12] The satire of Girardin differs from Melville's satire of Greeley, however, in several important respects. Melville's is based on the American journalist's actual physical appearance as represented in literary descriptions and graphic prints of the period (and possibly also on personal observation), while evidently the features, posture, and clothing of Robert Macaire were not individualized to caricature Girardin but remain consistent with the established appearance of Macaire as he had been acted by Lemaître and adapted by Daumier and other artists earlier in *Caricature.* The caricatures in *Charivari* seem to be individualized more through the allusions in the legends, presumably composed by Philipon, than through Daumier's drawings.

In the first in the series, "Bertrand, j'adore l'industrie. Si tu veux, nous créons une banque," Macaire proposes to Bertrand that they start "une vraie banque! Capital cent millions de millions, cent milliards de milliards d'actions." And when Bertrand wonders about "les gendarmes," Robert answers, "How foolish you are, Bertrand. Is a millionaire ever arrested?" Of this print Adhémar notices that Philipon claimed that shares in the Banque Industrielle, which had just been issued by Girardin, were adversely affected by the impact of the print in *Charivari* (Adhémar 233). Apparently, because of the topical language in the legend, the readers of the periodical were able to recognize that it was specifically Girardin's actions which were being satirized. Likewise, in another print, entitled "Nous sommes actionnaires de l'institut agricole et archi-colles de Goëtho . . . et d'une foule d'autres opérations philantropique," Macaire's costume is the usual one, based on Lemaître's, and his features include the insouciant eye-patched expression and brassy posture of the ex-bandit.[13] But that Girardin is the target of the print is clear from the references in the legend to the Société Sanitaire and Société du Physiono Type, both connected with Girardin, and to the "institut agricole Goëtho," which is the actual name of a "philanthropic" organization founded by Girardin for the ostensible purpose of benefiting working boys in Paris (Adhémar 233, 239). "Messieurs et Dames!" is a third print early in the series and concerns the sale of stock in coal companies; the legend contains an allusion to the Saint-Bérain coal-mining company established by Girardin (Adhémar 233).[14] Adhémar's association of these and other prints with Girardin is made through the legends, which allude directly to the famous journalist's activities in the public world of affairs, while the physical appearance of Macaire as drawn by Daumier remains consistent with that established early in the series. Whether Girardin's appearance might have been caricatured in some aspect of Macaire's face, posture, gestures, body shape, or costume, in some prints it is difficult to say. Adhémar believes that Philipon did not ask Daumier for a "direct caricature" of Girardin, whose "round head and pince-nez"—known through portraits—are not caricatured in the prints. However, it may be noted that several of the prints that refer to Girardin's activities, unlike those just discussed, show Macaire with an especially rotund belly and stocky figure, details which might be taken to allude specifically to the corpulent physical appearance of Girardin. As a publisher and book-seller he is ridiculed in "Robert Macaire Libraire" (Delteil No. 367; Adhémar No. 24); as a teacher of business methods in "Robert Macaire Professeur d'Industrie" (Delteil No. 377; Adhémar No. 91); and as a journalist in "Robert Macaire Journaliste" (Delteil No. 356; Adhémar 36). Though his identity cannot be entirely confirmed in each of these,

Girardin would seem to have been a popular subject for ridicule in the prints of Daumier and Philipon.

Both French society in the 1830s and American society in the decade or two after produced prominent figures who exercised great influence over various areas of public life through the manipulation of the news and through advertising. Even in an era of censorship, at least one major French journalist (Girardin) was selected for criticism by Philipon and Daumier. By contrast, thanks to a freer press, several were selected by Melville, including the powerful publicists Weed, Bryant, and Beecher, in addition to Greeley. In each case, moreover, the satirist represented the historical figure in question as a trickster, a perennial human type, one that had a longstanding life in theatrical art as Harlequin (*Arlecchino, Arlequin*) in Italian and French commedia dell'arte and English Pantomime, as Robert Macaire in Parisian theater of the 1830s, and as "the Confidence Man" in the comic entertainment performed at Burton's Chambers Street Theater in New York in 1849 (Trimpi, *Confidence Men* 243). The advent of the popular press gave grand new scope to the activities of an old human type and to the satire on that type which quickly followed.

A more general question raised by Daumier's and Melville's use of the theme of tricksterism in public life is suggested by a remark of Paul Valéry concerning Daumier's lithographs: "Taken together, his caricatures give the impression of a Dance of Moral or Intellectual Death" (159). Why did a major French artist in the 1830s and a major American writer in the 1850s utilize the theme of an essentially empty, role-playing personality to embody major statements about the public life of their respective cultures? One answer may be that out of the early nineteenth-century analysis of the human condition in economic and deterministic terms, which had been made by such influential thinkers as Marx and Fourier, there emerged a new, very limited conception of humanity. The idea of mankind defined principally as an economic and materialistic entity whose social and personal relationships are conditioned by its economic and material needs and by its natural status as an animal with a relatively complex brain, was first suggested by Hobbes. His influential comment in *Leviathan* on the natural condition of mankind as a state in which there is "continual fear and danger of violent death; and the life of man solitary, poor, nasty, brutish, and short" (ch. 13), came to be expressed in the shorthand formula, "Every man a wolf to every other man." According to this logic, all others may be regarded as sheep for each individual to consume or make private use of in any way he can manage. Mankind as a natural exploiter is aptly characterized as a wolf, or better yet as a fox, because such animals suggest to the imagination wily, quick deceptiveness. Melville's narrator in chapter 1 of *The Confidence-Man* comments with quiet irony on those pessimistic skeptics who think that in "new countries" (such as Western America of the Mississippi Valley in the nineteenth century) "where the wolves are killed off, the foxes increase" (4). Whether the Confidence Man behaves as a wolf or a fox on the *Fidèle* seems to depend on his particular mood or on the susceptibilities of his particular victim as "sheep." In any case, throughout the narrative he lacks an internal personality. He is a "hollow" man (in T. S. Eliot's perceptive phrase), indeed, whose masks appear to be his only character.

An interesting anticipation in art of such a limited conception of humanity—namely, as nothing more than a role-playing personality—is the enigmatic group of drawings of the commedia dell'arte mask Punchinello made by Giovanni Domenico Tiepolo entitled *Divertimento per li regazzi*.[15] In these 104 drawings, produced late in Tiepolo's long life (1727–1824), the humpbacked, long-nosed figure of Punchinello, wearing his usual conical hat and loose floppy clothing, is the central figure in scenes depicting various aspects of Italian life, as well as a variety of professions and walks of life, at work and recreation, and at different periods of life from birth to death. That a close relationship exists between this series and the theater of the eighteenth century, especially between the drawings and the portrayals of Punchinello on the Venetian comic stage, is obvious, but the exact nature of the relationship has not been established (Vetrocq 12–13, 19–20). Clearly Tiepolo had something to say about the Punchinello type as role-player that was dictated by more than the practical utility (or amusement) of such a theatrical device on stage. I suggest that Punchinello may have been meant to represent a concept of mankind, or a definition of humanity, that the artist saw as underlying all the stages in peoples' lives and all the typical activities and professions in which they engage alone and in society. But why Punchinello, we find ourselves asking while lingering over these haunting drawings? Why is the cynical, deformed, hunchbacked, selfish, skeptical, (originally) Neapolitan character, so well-known on the traditional commedia dell'arte stage, represented as the common element in all human activity? Why, unless Tiepolo meant to evoke Punchinello's characteristic cynical melancholy and brutality as an all-pervasive characteristic of mankind, as observed in the social and intellectual milieu of his time?

Similarly, both Daumier and Melville apparently used theatrical types to characterize humanity generally in their time. Each artist drew—significantly—upon a shape-shifting figure, notable for his wily, amoral, exploitative nature. Daumier seized on Robert Macaire, who had been developed on the French stage but later was integrated into the role of Harlequin and into the structures of English and American Pantomime. Melville modeled his Confidence Man on the comic shape-shifter of commedia dell'arte and of the harlequinades of American stage, of which we may surmise John Brougham's "The Confidence Man" was an independent and less successful variant. That both chose such a type may indicate that each saw it as a dominant national—and perhaps universal—type of man. That we do not see either Macaire or the Confidence Man as infants and children or in all roles of human existence, as Tiepolo portrayed humanity in his Punchinello series, may mean that each allowed for the possibility of other types of humanity as well. But this type seems to have most effectively embodied what they observed in their fellow creatures. The dominant national type for Daumier, as well as for Melville, was a confidence-seeking swindler—a wolf or fox, who played upon the trust of his fellows.

The appearance of the theme of the role-playing swindler as a major subject in mid-century France and the United States coincides, of course, with the growth of the idea of democratic humanity and with the democratic faith that any person can become anything and rise to any position that he or she desires by means of native talent and effort. The Confidence Man and Robert Macaire are expressive of the dark side of the generally optimistic view of unlimited human potential in a free and democratic society. Ambition for fulfillment of one's highest and noblest capacities, when seen from a more knowing, even jaded perspective, can be viewed as opportunism, self-promotion, and hucksterism. The dark side of Emerson's "new Man" is also suggested here. Along with the fluidity of class and status that the rise of the middle-class and the advent of democratic government brought about, we see the emergence of the concept of a "classless" individual—one who may be born in one class but can easily leave it and become a member of another by his own efforts. Who, then, was he? If all persons are equal, how can we tell one from another—except by clothing, speech, external appearance? And if these are the major indices to one's social identity, how easily might they be manipulated, not just by the unscrupulous but by the average person as well?

It should be remembered, of course, that in *The Confidence-Man* there are other types of men and women. The Confidence Man is only one, though he is the central one and controls the action throughout. Harlequin, the shape-shifting trickster type, is only one of the perennial types of mankind, but in the context of the democratic system, he is the one who is most likely to thrive. He may even dominate when he succeeds in his efforts at self-promotion. Democratic society permits, even encourages, the versatile trickster—the manipulator of language, especially in journalism and in the worlds of politics and business—to prosper. Both Daumier and Melville, I think, saw this development in the public life of their time and depicted it, satirized it, in their art.

Finally, I should like to suggest that in both Daumier and Melville the artist's perspective on such a deformed conception of man is unquestionably that of the critic and satirist. Both see beyond the deformed conceptions of individuals who think of themselves and others in such terms. Each takes advantage of the satirist's traditional critical freedom to point out the knavery of such schemes and the folly of their dupes. Although the Classical-Christian idea of humans as beings who possess a consciousness of the divine that transcends the purely social role, and who are responsible for the condition of their souls, is not directly present in the world of the Confidence Man or of Robert Macaire, the worlds they depict are judged from that older, deeper, and truer perspective. Were they not, we as readers and viewers would hardly know how to judge them.

Melville's Art:
Overtures from
the Journal of 1856–1857

BASEM L. RA'AD

Jt is a curious phenomenon of Melville criticism that the journal of 1856–57 has not received much attention as a useful source of study in more than a literal way.[1] For this record of Herman Melville's visit to Europe and the Levant occupies a unique position not only chronologically in his career, standing as it does in those most difficult middle years, but also in terms of its content as a reasonably explicit treatment of two Old World regions of crucial relevance to his work. Nowhere else in the canon do we have such an extended nonfictional source of observations on a range of natural and man-made structures, on landscapes, on cities and religious sites, and on architecture, gardening, sculpture, and painting—observations that are instinct with significance for the development of artistic expression during a transitional phase in the last century. The journal, in fact, constitutes in its totality (hurried and misspelled as it is in vivid telegraphese) a treatise of substantial proportion. As a result, it would be difficult to form a comprehensive view of Melville's aesthetics without a full exploration of it.

But, at the same time, critical evaluation of the 1856–57 journal remains problematic. Not only has there been no serious recognition of its aesthetic content, but discussion of it has also remained incredibly thin and biographically biased. The few scholars who have paid any attention to the document either concern themselves with what it tells them about Melville's psychological condition or cite his literal uses of the journal in subsequent lectures and in the poetry.[2] More seriously, the biographical bias has been largely controlled by an impression of Melville that owes much of its credence to Hawthorne's statement in *The English Notebooks* that Melville's "writings, for a long while past, have indicated a morbid state of mind" (432). By seeing Melville as a defeated and distressed writer, such criticism precludes the possibility of finding any kind of progressive development or larger scheme in his career and results in narrow views about his aesthetic affiliation.

There is an assumption that Melville's thinking at the time is to be construed as some kind of aberration, whereas it is more likely that we misunderstand what Melville's contemporary literati may have meant by "morbid state." There is in fact a way of explaining Melville's mode of expression (and Hawthorne's description of it) in terms of an aesthetic phenomenon. For John Ruskin, such a "morbid state" is an essential element in the artistic generation of the "noble grotesque," and it is in this grotesque (rather than its common variants), "as it is partly the result of a morbid state of the imaginative power, that power itself will be always seen in a high degree" (*Works* 11: 189). Even Hawthorne himself associates "morbid sensibility" with a man of genius in "The Artist of the Beautiful" (*Mosses* 458). Once we accept the possibility of a different interpretation for Melville's "morbidity" we begin to see a forward-looking sensibility at work. Various manifestations of Melville's thinking, that is, take on an altered complexion when we examine them in the context that will be developed here—of Melville as a conscious aesthetician, an American innovator who gives unexpected turns to familiar concepts, a theorist of structure, and a post-Romantic precursor of the iconography of the modern wasteland and of trends in artistic practice we more readily recognize as the "abstract" in painting and the "modern" in literature.

Critical opinion has yielded little since Howard C. Horsford's introduction to his 1955 edition of *Journal of a Visit to Europe and the Levant*. Horsford assesses the journal as largely "mere record," with "conventional" guidebook views of only rare literary merit, and a total effect which "reflects Melville's depressed physical and mental state" (11–12, 15–16, 18). This assessment remains pretty much the same in the recent Northwestern-Newberry edition of Melville's *Journals* (184–85). A Melville biographer considers the journal of 1856–57 "much more terse and unadorned than the journal of 1849. Unlike Thoreau, Emerson, or Hawthorne, he was satisfied with catalogs of sights and events, incomplete sentences, unpolished paragraphs" (Miller 288). Still others have harped on Melville's "unselfconscious" obsessions, feelings of constriction and entombment, which one critic has boldly described as "almost pathological." Views of Melville's resigned silence or his quarrel with fiction depend on questionable biography to support them. They also neglect the evidence of Melville's continued public involvement as a writer and of the structural and thematic continuities between an early work such as *Mardi* (1849) and a late one such as *Clarel* (1876).[3]

Even on a biographical level, these claims of a great depression seem exaggerated when compared to an actual report by Evert Duyckinck, who found Melville "warming like an old sailor over the supper" and "right hearty" prior to his departure on October 11. It is true that family and friends were making every effort to "prevent the necessity of Herman's writing" and to set him up in a profitable occupation (Metcalf 160, 164). The financial and other pressures on the unpopular author were so extreme that the trip had to be arranged and funded. But while Melville may have had much to complain about, it is dangerous for us to continue to psychoanalyze (or to Ahabize) someone whose art was dedicated to exposing self-deception and whose insights even today unfold constantly before us. To do so is to assume that Herman Melville could not have written with purpose and meaning under conditions of stress. Rather than hypothesizing some kind of imaginative collapse at work in this period, we should try to see if we can find in it evidence of Melville's continued development of his aesthetic views.

It becomes clear how consciously Melville scribbled into his notebooks if we examine a passage often cited as proof of his pathological obsessions to see what other interpretations it can sustain:

> *Saturday Dec 13th*. Up early; went out; saw cemeteries, where they dumped garbage. Sawing wood over a tomb. Forests of cemeteries. Intricacy of the streets. Started alone for Constan<u>ple</u> and after a terrible long walk, found myself back where I started. Just like getting lost in a wood. No plan to streets. Pocket-compass. Perfect labryth [labyrinth]. Narrow. Close, shut in. If one could but get *up* aloft, it would be easy to see one's way out. If you could get up into tree. Soar out of the maze. But no. No names to the streets no more than to natural allies among the groves. No numbers. No anything.[4]

What is clear here, consistent with remarks elsewhere, is Melville's concern with the principles of city planning and landscape gardening. In the case of this city, Constantinople, he is commenting on its disorganized effect and its directionless overgrowth—what he later calls its "wilderness of traffic" and the "confusion" of its accumulated habitation (59, 63).

Melville also expresses negative feelings toward the opposite of this confusion, which he found in the symmetrical gardens of Rome. For him the gardens are joyless because their "forms of foliage" are "freaks" of nature "quarried" in shapes of architectural imitation; Rome makes a "lonely man . . . feel more lonely" in the sense that it is, like Jerusalem, a place where the "whole landscape" generates "nothing independent of associations" (110, 158–59, 106). The impact in Jerusalem of physical, historical, and religious stagnation Melville feels reflected in those "lofty walls obstructing ventilation," the "insalubriousness" of the "pent-up air," with whose "limitation" the townspeople themselves seemed as impatient as Melville (86–87). On viewing the island of Tinos, Melville notes how the "houses seemed clinging round its [the hill's] top, as if desperate for security, like shipwrecked men about a rock beaten by billows" (71). Rarely in his observations of landscape and architecture does Melville find what he calls the unity of "art & nature," the harmonious blend of unaffected human endeavor and pure form, although scenes in Venice and at Oxford for him approach the ideal combination (*Journals* 128, 156, 120; *Collected Poems* 238–39). Melville, then, was not merely reacting to enclosures and oppressive environments but rejecting them as symptoms of sordidness in the social landscape and their locations as unnatural constructs where reflection cannot be freed from association.

"No open space—no squares or parks," writes Melville of the same Constantinople streets (61). Clearly, rather than being the obsessions of a sick man, such remarks show Melville in an analytical frame of mind, theorizing on the psychology of habitation and on aspects of public landscape. In so doing, he was exercising his considerable reading in the visual arts and in architectural aesthetics.[5] He was also writing in an atmosphere of growing fellowship among literary men, artists, and architects whose objective was to promote American originality. Horatio Greenough (alias Horace Bender, 1805–52), a protégé of Emerson, best represents America's original effort in his attack on imitation and the introduction of inorganic, nonfunctional elements in architectural design (though his conclusion is not uninfluenced by Carlyle's *Sartor Resartus*): "If I be told that such a system as mine would produce *nakedness,* I accept the omen" (Greenough, *Stonecutter* 202). Greenough also challenged traditional assumptions by suggesting that "beautiful" and "deformed" are relative terms. In "American Architecture" (1843), an essay which echoes some of Emerson's "Thoughts on Art" (1841), he uses animal skeletons and skins as examples that the "great principles of construction" are based on "adaptation" (Small 94, 57–58). Andrew Jackson Downing (1815–52) was another influential architect whose treatises on landscape gardening and the suburban cottage have had a lasting impact. Downing, though less controversial in his views, offers the useful example of a chimney to illustrate the concept of relative beauty: "A chimney may be an ugly chimney, and yet give a truthful expression to a dwelling; or it may be a finely formed chimney, and thus become a beautiful truth" (*Country Houses* 32).[6]

Despite this mid-century milieu of enthusiasm, America remained oriented mainly toward Europe and England for aesthetic guidance and example. And this orientation was based on an assumption that America's landscape and its culture were inferior to Europe's. Such a view was expressed by England's most prominent aesthetician, John Ruskin, who in 1856 described what distinguishes European landscape: "the charm of romantic association can be felt only by the modern European child. It rises eminently out of the contrast of the beautiful past with the frightful present; and this depends for its force on the existence of ruins and traditions, on the remains of architecture, the traces of battlefields, and the precursorship of eventful history. The instinct to which it appeals can hardly be felt in America" (*Works* 5:369). On other occasions, Ruskin was even more derogatory in his remarks about America's lack of picturesque qualities as he identified them (Shepard 186; Landow 138).

In this position, Ruskin was not only expressing an English bias but also speaking for many Americans who made the grand tour of Europe or became expatriates there. They did not attack "America" with quite the same vehemence as Ruskin did, but they were at least defensive about what they saw as its aesthetic shortcomings. Hawthorne's preface to *The Marble Faun* (1859), in justifying his choice of Italy as the setting for his story, uses exactly Ruskin's language to show the impossibility of "writing a romance about a country where there is no shadow, no antiquity, no mystery, no picturesque and gloomy wrong, nor anything but a commonplace prosperity, in broad daylight, as is happily the case with my dear native land." (We recognize today that Melville wrote such a romance in 1852.) Even James Fenimore Cooper, who in fiction romanticized the American wilderness, had difficulty in reconciling European conventions with local scenery at a formal level and continued to repeat the formulas acquired from abroad (Nevius 104). We can see the popular appeal of such imported ideals in a contemporary collection entitled *The Home Book of the Picturesque* (1852), which reprinted an introductory essay by Cooper and another by Irving. In his essay "American and European Scenery Compared," Cooper apologizes that "time and association" as well as "labor," elements of the common picturesque, were as "yet wanting to supply the defects of nature" in America (55, 89). This is the comparison Hawthorne also makes between the "softer turf, . . . more picturesque arrangement of venerable trees" in Italy and "the rude and untrained landscapes of the Western World" (*The Marble Faun* ch. 8, p. 71).

Such positions and such ideas about America are totally deplorable to the narrator of Melville's "I and My Chimney," who snipes at travelers for their conditioned responses to scenery and ruins abroad. "All the world over," he says wryly, "the picturesque yields to the pocketesque." The same travelers who ridicule his blotchy "naked" chimney "would travel across the sea to watch Kenilworth peeling away." The narrator's whimsical "horror of industry," or what is called "sordid labor" in the 1856–57 journal, confirms Melville's systematic antipathy to the catch-words of the popular picturesque—not just as a patriotic gesture and not only because they violated his perception of the land but, more importantly, because they also ran against the great principles he affirms again and again of the durability and power available in natural phe-nomena unspoiled by human interference and "associations" (*Piazza Tales* 356–57, 361; *Journals* 156, 89, 106). Elsewhere, Melville undermines the elitism and commercialism of the picturesque (*Pierre* 20.1.276–77; *Collected Poems* 317, 335). Melville's rejection of the familiar distinction between "Past" and "Present" (*Pierre* 1.3.8–9), by way of a defense of America, led him to redefine antiquity (as he does in *Mardi* ch. 75, "Time and Temples") as something dependent not on human effort or created structures, since man can only work with what has already been aged by time, but rather on natural archetypal forms. Thus, despite almost total European authority in matters of taste, Melville reached a powerful aesthetic stance which transcended the available categories.

Melville's anti-associationist position relates in a remarkable way to the function of blankness in his iconography and to the distrust he shows of safe connections. This aspect of Melville's thinking sets him apart from many of his contemporaries in that it is emblematic of a turning point, then in its early stage, in the perception of the human condition and in artistic expression of it. Paul Shepard writes, confirming W. H. Auden's conclusion, about this artistic reversal of values: "Once the ship represented society, the garden, the normal human environment; and the trip on the sea and desert, a necessary evil. By the nineteenth century these meanings had been reversed: the voyage was the normal state of man."[7] Melville reflects these new values in his fiction and poetry. It is not surprising, for instance, that he sees in Rock Rodondo, in the third sketch of *The Encantadas,* a "dead desert rock" while "other voyagers are taking oaths it is a glad populous ship" (137; see Fig. 1). He thus prefigures an artistic sensibility we now recognize more readily as char-acteristic of the present century.

We see how far Melville strikes out into new ground by looking at a singular moment in the Hawthorne-Melville relationship that has

Fig. 1. Peter Toft, *Rodondo, the Encantadas,* c. 1880. Courtesy of the Berkshire Athenaeum, Pittsfield, Mass.; the Herman Melville Memorial Room.

become something of a critical commonplace. It concerns that walk the two men took on a deserted beach north of Liverpool in November 1856, Hawthorne's account of which is the only one cited to arrive at various conclusions about Melville's spiritual state (what some have called his "disturbed condition") and about the nature of his relationship with Hawthorne.[8] Hawthorne sees Melville's skepticism, his persistent arguing about "Providence and futurity," in terms of traditional iconography, as similar to the condition of "wandering to-and-fro over these deserts, as dismal and monotonous as the sand hills amid which we were sitting" (*English Notebooks* 432–33). But Hawthorne's idea of the desert condition is formulated by centuries of civilized and religiously oriented topography that harks back to Bradford and before. Regardless of any submerged ambiguity that might be found in his writing about the subject, Hawthorne sees the natural wilderness, as in Hester's "moral wilderness" and her roamings in the "desert places" of heart and intellect, as belonging to "an unredeemed, unchristianized, lawless region . . . that wild, heathen Nature of the forest, never subjugated by human law, nor illumined by higher truth."[9] Clearly, for him the "ideal landscape" is one where "enough human care" has been bestowed "to prevent wildness from growing into deformity" (*Marble Faun* ch. 8, p. 72).

Melville's response, in contrast, is revolutionary in the sense that it subsumes wildness and desolation. Melville describes the scene in simple but significant words: "*Wednesday Nov 12* At Southport. An agreeable day. Took a long walk by the sea. Sands & grass. Wild & desolate. A strong wind. Good talk" (*Journals* 51). It seems he views such a deserted setting with obvious attraction and no great trepidation. Even in this cryptic record, we detect a system of contrasts, of carefully defined physical, mental, and aesthetic qualities—of "sands" as opposed to "grass" as they express both an inner and a universal landscape. For Melville the human condition is expressible in exactly the kinds of features Hawthorne could not accept.[10] While it is true, as Hawthorne suggests, that Melville's dilemma has its source in religious and existential skepticism, the very desolation that reflects this skepticism becomes an extended mode of expression and a means to penetrate beyond ordinary distinctions. His was a triple burden mirrored in this modern sense of desert: the condition of necessary doubt dictated by both intuition and science, the cognizance of man's historical responses to the original desert condition in the form of myths and structures, and finally Melville's own artistic isolation as a result of such knowledge.

"Sands & grass" as coexistent symbols of mind and civilization, of sordid reality as opposed to verdant hope, and utter newness as opposed to torpid decay, take many forms in Melville's complex iconography. We can see them constantly all over the fiction and the poetry expressed in the dualities of reef/moss, sea/shore, rock/ivy, skeleton/vine, or other variations of these motifs. At a crucial point in *Mardi* when Taji attempts to dispel the shadow of the submerged Aleema (whose name translates as "knowledge" or "tradition") and to allay Yillah's fears and his own forebodings, he creates a fanciful past for her, but only half deceptively: "Think not of him, sweet Yillah. . . . Look on me . . . you have not been forgotten by me, sweetest Yillah. Ha! Ha! shook we not the palm-trees together, and chased we not the rolling nuts down the glen? . . . All the past a dim blank? Think of the time when we ran up and down our arbor, where the green vines grew over the great ribs of the stranded whale" (ch. 45, pp. 142–43). The same stranded whale recurs in one of the most intriguing episodes in *Moby-Dick,* "A Bower in the Arsacides," where the white skeleton is again intermixed and hemmed around by "trees . . . living flowers . . . shrubs, and ferns, and grasses . . . himself all woven over with the vines; every month assuming greener, fresher verdure; but himself a skeleton" (ch. 102, pp. 449–50). A condition of bliss exists, which human beings are loath to leave, once the backbone of reality has become overwhelmingly covered up in green myths.

In a letter to Mrs. Hawthorne, Melville uses a metaphor for life as "a long Dardanelles," with its shores of flowery hope, that leads to a "desolate & vacant" sea (*Letters* 147). When Melville landed on the actual shores of the Dardenelles, his aesthetic eye found similar representations of the universal condition in a more concrete and formalized set of entities attached to real scenes. His view from a steamer up the Bosphorus is filled with "contrasts": "The palaces . . . The white foam breaks on these white steps as on long lines of coral reefs. . . . The Cyprus [cypress] a green minaret, & blends with the stone ones. . . . the intermingling of life & death" (*Journals* 64–65).

While verdure and desert, their varieties and colors, remain dominant as contrasting landscapes in Melville's representational scheme, the 1856–57 journal and later *Clarel* confirm that there is a constant regression in verdant intensity in his writing, coupled with an emphasis on solid barrenness and decayed forms of greenness. This sense of barrenness stands in stark contrast to the verdure of Polynesian landscapes pervasive in his earlier experience. At Scotland's Dunbarton Castle Melville notes an "isolated rock . . . covered with sod & moss." In Egypt he is keenly aware of the "[c]ontiguity of desert & verdure," the "instant collision of the two [alien] elements" (50, 74, 76). Jaffa's "rocks & sands" have a "barren & dreary look," and Jerusalem looks "like a quarry—all stone" (72, 89). What ultimately impresses him most is the pervasive "all but verdure" impact of the "bleached" parts of Palestine, like Lima's "white veil," with its suggestion of a wasteland state ungraced by desert purity or verdant cover or green decay: "You see the anatomy—compares with ordinary regions as skeleton with living & rosy man. . . . No moss as in other ruins—no grace of decay—no ivy—the unleavened nakedness of desolation" (83; *Moby-Dick* 193).

Varieties of natural barrenness are appropriate reflections of the individual mind at present and, by retrogression, the condition of primeval humanity ("Man sprang from deserts," says Rolfe in *Clarel* 2.16.109). It is therefore the "doubt" generated by deserts (*Clarel* 2.11.16), as by a "calm" at sea (*Mardi* 9), which forces the human mind into the creation of green myths. Melville suggests that the typical posture of humanity is that represented by the Sphinx, a posture of avoidance— "back to desert & face to verdure" (*Journals* 76). By implication, then, all structure and all vegetation are additions to the basic nakedness which the conscious mind is now forced to face. In terms of Melville's skeleton/ vine image, the skeleton has again become exposed, a geological and a metaphysical uncovering, and must now appear in ungarnished starkness. The surface of civilization has been penetrated to the point where the mind comes to a full confrontation with the emptiness of origin. In this sense, the whale's whiteness can be interpreted as a form of barrenness to which our ordinary perceptual faculties respond. When Ishmael speaks of the "visible world" he no doubt means the green world—both the human and mythic world of created structures and the scientific world of normal perception, green being the accessible center of the color spectrum. Once one goes beyond the cover of color "laid on from without," strips the paint from "deified Nature," frees objects of their "associations," removes the "subtle deceits, not actually inherent in substances," then the "dumb blankness" becomes "full of meaning" and "the palsied universe lies before us a leper" (189, 195).

It is no wonder then that we find Melville succumbing with inevitable attraction to the sense of barrenness, not lamentingly but compulsively, in an inverse way similar to Ruskin's "strange pleasure" at the "noble unsightliness" of the Calais towers (*Works* 6:11–12). Melville's calculated "object," clearly stated, is to offer himself up as "a passive subject, and no unwilling one" to the "weird impressions" of desolate landscapes (*Journals* 86). The experience of doubt-inducing wastelands, suggestive of origin, also involves a necessary engagement in truth: "Patmos is pretty high, & peculiarly barren looking. No inhabitants.—Was here again afflicted with the curse of modern travel—skepticism. . . . When my eye rested on arid height, spirit partook of the barrenness.—Heartily wish Niebuhr & Strauss to the dogs.—The deuce take their penetration & acumen. They have robbed us of the bloom" (97). Melville is not really "deprecating" Niebuhr and Strauss, as argued in the historical note to the Northwestern-Newberry edition of the *Journals* (185). Rather, he is accepting their findings, somewhat grudgingly, because the knowledge they have provided disallows conventional support and forces acceptance of an "all but verdure" landscape as the true one (83).

Melville divides space into its content of structures created throughout human history ("art") and that larger preexistent space which consists of original structures ("nature"). Human structures are measures of expression or means of protection, while in already available structures exist all archetypes. In developing his unique architectural ideas along these lines, Melville adapts and extends contemporary aesthetic thinking in areas which relate to primal forms and patterns, space allocation, and relativity in applications of truth and beauty. In doing so, he confirms the existence of ideal forms only in natural precedents, and he insists on the allocation of available space in ways consistent with such precedents. All natural landscapes are architectural structures, and Melville therefore measures all types of human architecture by the extent to which they affect us "like Nature"—that is, how truly they represent "reality" (*Journals* 78, 91, 123).

All past human efforts are temporal and relatively insubstantial; they can only be considered permanent to the extent that they approximate nature. To describe humanity's negligible history, Melville uses the metaphor of the arid island and the tortoise in "The Encantadas" and in *Clarel*. "The Island" is the cultural world as suggested by the inexplicably worn condition of its rocks, which resemble "a shrine" (*Clarel* 4.3.33–35). Its singular creature, the tortoise, is an obvious reference to humanity (repeatedly called "he"), and the arch of its encrusted shell is symbolic of human history: "Of huge humped arch, the ancient shell / Is trenched with seams where lichens dwell, / Or some adhesive growth and sere. . . . / Searching, he creeps with laboring neck, / Each crevice tries, and long may seek" (4.3.63–77). Clarel concludes that humanity cannot hope to "solve the world" by persistent creation of alternative systems and structures (109–14).

When Pierre, isolating himself to write a book, begins to see through "the first superficiality of the world"—that is, when he comes to one further stage of his consciousness—he develops an appreciation of the "universality of thought" but has not quite reached that "ultimate element" which would gain him full release. At this pre-ultimate stage, he can only "by presentiment" perceive that "most grand productions of the best human intellects ever are built round a circle . . . digestively including the whole range of all that can be known or dreamed." In the extended simile Melville employs to illustrate the clarity of artistic inclusiveness (elided in the quotation above), the circular structure used is not a classic dome or a Burkean rotunda but, so typically Melvillean, the ringed atolls of the sea: "primitive coral islets which, raising themselves in the depths of the profoundest seas, rise funnel-like to the surface, and present there a hoop of white rock, which though on the outside everywhere lashed by the ocean, yet excludes all tempests from the quiet lagoon within" (21.1.283–85). Whether he uses original forms or forms of the circle, dome, and pyramid common in romantic iconography or the structural models of earlier aestheticians, Melville insists on identifying these figures with primal patterns such as the hoop of white rock or the rib cage of a whale or other natural antecedents.

In its imagery and observations, the 1856–57 journal confirms the arboreal and skeletal architecture so pervasive in the fiction, particularly in *Mardi*. The dome of St. Sophia in Constantinople is described as "[s]uspended from above like fully blossomed tulip from its stem" (158). Elsewhere, Melville speaks of the "[t]uft of sculpture . . . —Palm tree" in connection with Roman columns and a "bouquet of architecture" formed by the grasses growing in the midst of monuments (99, 114). The mosques on the "domed hills of the city" are modelled after the primitive tent, an Ishmaelite abode: "The Mosque is a sort of marble marquee of which the minarets (four or six) are the stakes. In fact when inside it struck me that the idea of this kind of edifice was borrowed from the tent" (63, 60). The Great Pyramid itself, whose angularity would have been anathema to Burkean aesthetics, is seen as the perfect analogy to the Great Whale and the Mount of Titans, just as these are described in pyramidal terms earlier in the fiction.

St. Sophia and the pyramids Melville admired as public landscape. He rejects as "absurd" a contemporary theory that the pyramids were constructed as a defense against the desert because this would destroy their meaning for him as pure forms that grew out of the original desert condition ("Might have been created with the creation"), and he considers St. Sophia's interior "a positive appropriation of space" in that it suggests natural expansiveness: "Owing to its peculiar form St: Sophia viewed near to, looks as partly underground; as if you saw but the superstructure of some immense temple, yet to be disinterred" (*Journals* 67). Melville's obvious concern with building specifications in the short fiction has been noted (Litman; Adams), but the controlling principles of his architectural imagination are still to be understood. If people are to build, says Melville, their buildings should not be removed from original form nor should they present unnatural constriction or unrealistic polish. Walls, fences, and public gardens embody human fears and an artificial sense of order

(*Journals* 77, 86, 110). "Walls are superfluous," says Borabolla (*Mardi* 287). The classical Acropolis is too smooth in contrast to its rugged background, whereas the pyramids ("No wall, no roof") gain advantage from their roughness. Human architecture has grown less likely to achieve essential structure, as Melville observes about London's Crystal Palace: "Overdone. . . . Vast toy. No substance. Such an appropriation of space as is made by a rail fence. Durable materials, but perishable structure" (*Journals* 99, 78, 128). Here again we find the key expressions that echo throughout the works: the preoccupation with "space" and the "appropriation of terra firma" in "I and My Chimney," with the concept of "duration" in *Mardi,* and with structure in the poem "Greek Architecture." Durability is based on nature and tested by time, and strength of creation comes not by innovative "lavishness" or sheer magnitude but by adherence to basic form and natural archetypal force (*Mardi* 228–29; *Collected Poems* 248; *Piazza Tales* 357).

Melville's views point to a departure from traditional aesthetic values and an altered sense of beauty. To put the matter differently, I would posit two questions: what makes an ugly chimney so important to protect, and why should those aspects of the "anomalous" whale which violate all precepts of classical art and of "landscape gardening" act instead to create "an added grandeur" (*Moby-Dick* 291)? While the revisionist process may have begun elsewhere in Europe and America, it took a peculiar and necessary turn in Melville's thinking.[11] For an American aesthetician like Melville trying to defend *his* nature against slighting attacks and to reconcile it with his artistic perceptions, the logical solution was to divorce beauty from its classical ideals and to separate the picturesque from the requirement of past association.[12] In addition to creating an imaginative rendering of such an altered sense of beauty, Melville modifies the common concept of the picturesque to suit his purpose. Explicitly in the 1856–57 journal, he expresses a distaste for past "associations" and the "sordid" aspects of human enterprise, and so undermines the popular picturesque to the extent that it can no longer function as a product of history and tradition (89, 106, 156). Here, he contradicts Ruskin, who (somewhat inconsistently) recanted from anti-associationism after realizing the importance of association to his theories (Landow 101–10).

The new American defense was simple and it was most definitively Melville's: the "anomalousness of America" (like that of the "anomalous" whale!) is additional proof that its newness "possess[es] the divine virtue of a natural law" (*Pierre* 1.3.9). While Melville ultimately grows disillusioned with America's promise (that "squandered last inheritance," *Clarel* 4.21.166) and with any pretense at human certainty, he extends his original defense into a universal position. Thus, by way of this revision, Melville insists on locating the truth in structures that retain natural precedence without erasing traces of origin, structures which extract from aridity the essence of self-sufficiency, simplicity and mystery. What shows the pyramids as ageless is the absence of green in them. What makes ruins "picturesque" is that they are aged by time rather than colored by association, the materials once extracted from ancient geological layers now returned to a less structured state intermingled with natural verdure: "Singular melting together of art in ruins and Nature in vigor. Vines overrunning ruins. Ruins here take the place of rocks" (*Journals* 104). A blotched, grotesquely shaped chimney becomes a compulsive construction (perhaps ironically so) in that it represents the individual's challenge, a local place of created mystery which the narrator refuses to yield to public scrutiny or certainty. For the real purpose of all perception, in whatever object or landscape, is to achieve an understanding beyond categories: "In nature point, in life, in art / Where the essential thing appears" (*Collected Poems* 318).

These observations lead to the question of whether we can find a frame of reference to explain Melville's artistic preoccupations and the total effect of his art. Difficulties in identifying an operative aesthetic scheme have not eased since Fitz-James O'Brien's frustrated complaint in 1857 that Melville persists in "hiding his light" in "a grotesque troop of notions" (Branch 364, 367). Perhaps we have here an impression similar to that elicited by critics of J. M. W. Turner's abstract art who dismissed his later paintings as "not like Nature," a criticism to which Ruskin responded back in 1844 that "Turner *is* like nature, and paints more of nature than any man who ever lived" (*Works* 3: 51–52; Herrmann 10; see Fig. 8 in Wallace, ch. 3, p. 120). It seems that, with modern art in particular, the interpretive process, like the creative process for both painter and writer, straddles a problematic gap between the imagination and the representation, and the interpreters of art often fail to accept the forms the artists find most appropriate in their own right.

It has accurately been observed that the isolated studies of Melville and the arts leave "much . . . to be done before a full synthesis can be achieved of the literary use to which Melville put his experience with art" (Wallace, "Melville's Prints" 63). Dettlaff's coverage of the scattered criticism recognizes this lack of a "definitive . . . comprehensive study" of Melville's aesthetic theories, though it concludes that previous "studies have identified most of those tenets" ("Melville's Aesthetics" 625, 658). The criticism is, in fact, generally limited in scope to single works and confused in its use of support from Melville's extensive readings, often relying on sheer critical assertion that fails to distinguish between what Melville thought art was as opposed to how he intended to practice it. There have been attempts to assign Melville to a single aesthetic category. It has been customary to think, on partial evidence, in terms of Melville's "classicism" (Horsford, "Introduction," *Journal* 12) and how Melville follows Burke (Glenn), though an attempt has been made also to "assess his classicism" and show how he asserts that, to quote the platitudes, "true art unifies the sublime and the beautiful . . . beauty and truth" (Dettlaff 212, 217, 228). In architecture, Melville's "utopian ideal of art" in the example of the Greek temple is contrasted to his non-utopian "ideal farmhouse" (Litman 636–38), and proof of his interest in the "biological analogy" is attempted (Adams 265). In another case, it is the "art analogy" (Robillard, "Visual Arts in Melville's *Redburn*" 43). Various forms of the sublime have been proposed, including the Puritan-adjusted Coleridgean "ultimate sublime" (Richard S. Moore 155, 203) and the Kantian-derived American "egotistical sublime" (Wolf 144, 155, 164). Attempts have also been made to identify Melville with Goethe's "demonic" (Milder) or with the common applications of the "grotesque" as variously defined by Wolfgang Kayser (Cook, Bainard Cowan 126).[13]

The key to Melville's aesthetic outlook, however, does not lie in any one set of influences or sources but rather in a permanent attitude toward artistic creation in painting, architecture, and fiction. A link that could clarify this outlook can be found in a historical development in art representation that needs to be explored. Just as the picturesque and sublime aspects, external ruggedness and natural immensity, became contrasting sources of relative beauty, the prevalence of the picturesque concept was a necessary step in the evolution of the "grotesque" or, what we may call now, "abstract" idea of art.[14] Part of this formula is suggested by Christopher Hussey: "The movement away from the conception of art as knowledge began in the eighteenth century with the discovery of visual properties. The Picturesque is a stage in this movement towards abstraction" (51). In reference to this artistic deviation from simple imitation, Kenneth Clark suggests something further: "The painting of landscape cannot be considered independently of the trend away from imitation as the *raison d'être* of art" (231). Such a movement occurred, one could stipulate, as artistic perception of the world necessarily altered the forms of art. In a way, the roughness and irregularity typical of the external picturesque was transformed into an inward feature of art. It was, that is, no longer possible to represent reality by direct imitation. Or, as Melville realized, it was impossible to maintain "Art's pure Acropolis in hold" (*Collected Poems* 332).

By using the term "grotesque," I do not mean to associate it with its common meanings and their various applications by critics.[15] Terrifying phenomena are incidental, not essential, to what I understand Ruskin to mean when he includes the grotesque as the last of the three true ideals in art, citing Spenser, Shakespeare, Scott, and some great painters as practitioners of the form. Ruskin, in fact, defended the grotesque against earlier assumptions that it consisted merely of "fanciful and terrible ideas . . . horrid phantoms . . . [in]capable of producing a serious passion" (Burke 63–64, 174–75). For Ruskin, the truest grotesque, an appropriately "imperfect" mode, gains modern importance from its positive kind of imaginative "confusion" in the presence of truths difficult to grasp, resulting in the juxtaposition of symbols and "gaps" in "bold and fearless connection . . . left for the beholder to work out." Clearly, what Ruskin describes in *Modern Painters* (a work dedicated to the defense of Turner) is an "abstract" quality—a term that was less accessible then, to be sure, though Ruskin uses it incidentally (*Works* 5: 130–32, 138, 139).

It is in this abstraction that Melville's art should be located and the connection to Ruskin and Turner invoked for the purpose of clarifying its meaning. Wallace has confirmed evidence that the Spouter-Inn painting in *Moby-Dick* was inspired by Turner (10–14). Turner in painting and Melville in fiction both signalled the growing disinterest in normal representational modes. In painting verbal landscapes, Melville by the nature of his perspective manipulated methods characteristic of the late Turner, methods precursory to impressionism and other modern trends (Clark 195; Shepard 126; *New . . . Encyclopedia* 4375; Lynton 14). Both expressed deep affinities with the sea and nature as force, both manipulated the vortex as symbolic form and whiteness as a significant color, and both captured the qualities of ambiguity and secret truth in their works (Clark 182, 189, 195). Several journal entries testify to Melville's intent to paint a scene, rather than merely "frame" it (Wolf 143), as in this abbreviated moonlit view of Mount Olympus from ship: "When it was far astern, its snow line showed in the moonlight like a strip of white cloud. Looked *unreal*—but still was there" (57; emphasis mine). In another instance, he observes how the scenery appears "all outline. No filling up" (97).

Perhaps even more significantly, the shared admiration for the art of Piranesi identifies Turner and Melville as subscribing to a similar view of the world and of art. Turner was partly responsible for the resurrection of Piranesi in England (Hofer viii). Melville's admiration for Piranesi takes a central literary form in *Clarel,* where the cumulative maze-like effect of obsessive imaginative hints indicates that true representation of reality is best achieved by implication and a necessary distortion: "The inventor miraged all the maze, / Obscured it with prudential haze; / Nor less, if subject unto question, / The egg left, egg of the suggestion" (2.35.29–33). Melville suggests here and elsewhere that the ability to brave this reality is the ultimate test of the individual.[16]

——— The connection between Melville and Ruskin's grotesque is intriguing as well. For Ruskin, "contemplation of evil" and of death, the aspects of "skeleton" and "whiteness," and a cognizance of nature's powers are all prerequisite for that condition of mind which produces the grotesque (*Works* 5: 131; 11: 185–86). Ruskin's chief examples of the grotesque, namely Dürer, Holbein, and Teniers (*Works* 5: 131), are all mentioned in the 1856–57 journal, and Melville notes in particular the "remarkable Teniers effect . . . produced by first dwarfing, then deforming humanity" (122). A similar effect is produced in the bas relief by Bastianino: "The legs thrown out in various attitudes. Capital. Grotesque figures" (117). Apart from the appearance in the 1856–57 journal of several other grotesque features (73, 89, 91, 128), perhaps the example of "Jacob's" dream as a grotesque is most striking in that Ruskin uses it as the perfect instance of truth imaginatively "narrowed and broken by the inconsistencies of the human capacity," while Melville in "Art" sees the creative process as that impossible effort to "fuse with Jacob's mystic heart" into pulsing life "unlike things" (*Works* 11: 181; *Collected Poems* 231).

By placing Melville in this aesthetic context, we can hope to begin to reconcile many elusive elements in his thinking and his fiction. For one thing, it enables us to better appreciate why Melville lost his popularity and frustrated his critics, and why he regained recognition in the twentieth century. It also helps to place his works as much in terms of earlier influences as in terms of features we readily recognize in such writers as Conrad, T. S. Eliot, Kafka, Camus, Faulkner, or Stevens, or in painters like Rousseau and Gauguin.[17] It becomes possible to bring to light more lucidly his recurrent symbols and to explain his digressive structures, or what has been called his typically "disrupted narrative" (Spanos 137; Dryden 216), as in fact calculated, suggestive, and predicative constructs designed to render what intrinsically "must remain unpainted to the last" (*Moby-Dick* 265), thus creating a conjunction of disparate elements in an endless journey of abstract dimension.

Hawthorne was puzzled by Turner's paintings, "blotches of color, and dabs of the brush, meaning nothing," whereas Melville strongly identified with them (and with Hawthorne). "There were many," wrote Hawthorne,

> . . . which I positively could not comprehend in the remotest degree; not even so far as to guess whether they purported to represent earth, sea, or

sky. In fact, I should not have known them to be pictures at all. . . . I mean to buy Ruskin's pamphlet at my next visit, and look at them through his eyes. But I do not think I can be driven out of the idea that a picture ought to have something in common with what the spectator sees in Nature. (*English Notebooks* 614)

One wonders at the implications this difference might have to the two authors, who both proclaimed to be writing "romance."[18] Obviously, a large part of the difference lies in Melville's intention, as in *Pierre,* to create his type of romance from the "Present" and its landscape. The hyperbolic preface to *Mardi* (1849) and the letter to John Murray indicate a decision to depart from normal factual representation in his handling of the romance form. The strategy for his "*real* romance" was a "new" one ("original if nothing more . . . with a meaning too"), a strategy by which both fact and symbol are blended into a fiction at once (*Letters* 70–71). His fictional world is a nature "transformed" but one to which we still "feel the tie" (*Confidence-Man* 183). Its truth, as confirmed in Melville's last novel, cannot be conveyed by the "symmetry of form" and will therefore "always have its ragged edges . . . [and] is apt to be less finished than an architectural finial" (*Billy Budd* 128). It is a world necessarily "twisted and contorted," whose real "strangeness" is as what is seen through a misted icy pane "held against a world of hoary grass."[19] Unlike traditional romance, Melville's art is an abstraction designed to render reality by ambiguous and suggestive means, not on the basis of the suspension of disbelief but rather on a system of suspended suggestions.

Melville and Dutch Genre Painting

DENNIS BERTHOLD

Jn the late sketch "Daniel Orme" (1883), the narrator begins by praising the insights into character that great painters provide: "A profound portrait-painter like Titian or our famous country-man Stewart, what such an observer sees in any face he may earnestly study, that essentially is the man. To disentangle his true history from contemporary report is superfluous" (*Great Short Works* 424). In other words, a master such as Gilbert Stuart or Titian—the latter a painter Melville admired throughout his life—can see through the veneer of reputation into the essential soul of a person and portray it on canvas. However, the narrator goes on to explain that he cannot hope to attain such ideality: "Not so with us who are scarce Titians and Stewarts. Occasionally we are struck by some exceptional aspect instantly awakening our interest. But it is an interest that in its ignorance is full of commonplace curiosity" (*GSW* 424). This distinction follows the conventional division that academic art critics made between high art and low art, what Sir Joshua Reynolds in his influential *Discourses on Art* (1797) called the "grand style" and the "comparatively sensual."[1] For critics in this tradition, the grand style was epitomized by the painters of the Italian Renaissance, especially Michelangelo and Raphael, while the sensual was usually represented by seventeenth-century Dutch painting, particularly genre scenes. So, while Melville names two painters in the tradition of high art, he omits those with the opposite tendency, the tendency the narrator himself pursues in sketching the lowly Daniel Orme, a retired sailor who has begun "to mellow down into a sort of animal decay" (424). The unstated inspiration for "Daniel Orme," as well as many similar sketches, descriptions, and brief but vivid scenes in Melville's writing is, I will show here, seventeenth-century Dutch genre painting.

There is a long tradition in Melville criticism of emphasizing Melville's philosophical idealism, his wrestling with "everything that lies beyond human ken," as Hawthorne put it (Leyda 529).[2] And while this is an important and undeniable tendency in Melville's writings, the anti-idealism epitomized by Dutch painting offers a significant counterweight that swings toward the direct treatment of ordinary life, a genre painting in prose that informs much of Melville's work during the 1850s and finds scattered instances in all periods of his career. This tendency is not just aesthetic: it is moral, political, and eventually deeply personal. It accords with Ishmael's mature belief, expressed retrospectively in "A Squeeze of the Hand," that "in all cases man must eventually lower, or at least shift, his conceit of attainable felicity; not placing it anywhere in the intellect or the fancy; but in the wife, the heart, the bed, the table, the saddle, the fire-side, the country" (349). Ishmael's list reads like a catalogue of Dutch artistic motifs, and mirrors, like Dutch painting, the values of an emerging Protestant republic: domesticity, appetite, personal comfort and security, individual liberty, family sentiments, and pastoralism. Recognizing Melville's personal and literary appreciation for Dutch art suggests a line of thought in his career that cherishes these commonplace virtues and that expresses them with descriptions and motifs employing a distinctively Dutch iconography.[3]

Such preferences held their own risks, for they were frowned upon by the art establishment as betraying vulgar and uneducated tastes. Among authors read by Melville, this case was most strongly made by James Jackson Jarves, a respected Christian art critic whose books Melville owned, annotated, and evidently admired. Adding religious strictures to conventional Reynoldsian principles, and probably echoing John Ruskin,[4] the leading art critic of the day, Jarves criticized Dutch painting for lacking "a spiritual faith or life" (*Art-Idea* 130). By treating almost every subject with equal fidelity, from "foul kitchens and dirty maids" and "houses of picturesque ugliness" to scenes of "convivial or stately domesticity, a love of the pastures, canals, and seas so closely associated with their riches," the Dutch failed to guide viewers to higher ideals. Yet Jarves (unlike Ruskin) recognized and praised the democratic implications of such art. Rooted in "democratic liberty of choice as opposed to aristocratic exclusiveness and ecclesiastical rigor of selection," Dutch art grew naturally from the political and religious character of Dutch society. Its very defects—gross sensuality, excessive materialism, vulgarity—made it appealing to "common sentiments and feelings, and failings, too, for it was essentially human, and loved the earthly natural, and spoke out, in earnest sincerity, what the people believed and liked, good or bad, just as their hearts dictated. There was but little high art in this," Jarves continued, "but it was a right beginning, leaving the popular mind to choose its own loves, and, through its own experience, to advance gradually from lower thoughts and feelings to higher" (*Art-Idea* 129). Thus, while Jarves condemned the absence of idealism in Dutch painting, he recognized its appeal to untutored audiences. In his last book (1864), he reluctantly acknowledged the power of popular taste: "Dutch art is too well-liked and known for me to dwell longer on it. Those whose aesthetics are in sympathy with its mental mediocrity will not desert it for anything I may say. Nor would I have them until they are prepared to appreciate a higher standard."[5]

Jarves's comments have led the contemporary American art critic Barbara Novak to observe that although "Dutch art did not have the intellectual credentials that would have rendered it acceptable to official criticism, . . . it was appreciated by the artists themselves and by private individuals who were not, it appears, very vocal" (*Nature and Culture* 232). While there is abundant evidence in the catalogues of art museums, private collections, and art galleries to show that Americans had ample exposure to Dutch painting, few people wrote about it or discussed its peculiar appeal. In his posthumously published *Lectures on Art* (1850), Washington Allston favorably compared Adrian Ostade to Raphael, yet had to assure his audience that by calling Ostade an artist he intended no disparagement of Raphael (90). And even so independent a mind as Nathaniel Hawthorne confessed in his Italian notebooks in 1858 that "It is the sign, I presume, of a taste still very defective, that I take singular pleasure in the elaborate imitations of Van Mieris, Gerard Douw, and other old Dutch wizards" (14: 317). Melville was one of these quiet admirers of the Dutch, and like his fellow artists Allston and Hawthorne expressed his admiration more openly later in life.

"At the Hostelry," probably composed in the early 1870s, just when Dutch genre painting (and genre painting in general) was solidifying its reputation in America, reveals Melville's complex attitude toward Dutch painting and its equivocal cultural status.[6] One of Melville's longest poems, "At the Hostelry" dramatically portrays nine earthy Dutch painters in boisterous and tipsy debate with their loftier Italian, French, and German counterparts. Their argument concerns the meaning and definition of the term "picturesque," a term that, by 1870, was less a rigorous aesthetic category than a catchword for popular, even vulgar art, as Jarves's usage above suggests. Predictably, the Dutch argue that the picturesque involves the realistic depiction of ordinary life, virtually a textbook definition of genre painting. Although a few other painters agree, the Italian masters Michelangelo, Leonardo, and Raphael, practitioners of the grand style, decline to argue. The debate ends inconclusively with a satiric analysis of *"The picturesque in Men of Mark,"* a reductio ad absurdum that implies how foolish aesthetic labeling can be.

Significantly, the Dutch are the most persuasive spokesmen for Melville's objection to aesthetic categories. When Jan Steen says, "For the Picturesque—suffice, suffice / The picture that fetches a picturesque price!" (Kramer lines 125–26), he echoes Melville's terms "povertiresque" in *Pierre* and "pocketesque" in "I and My Chimney." Steen, like Melville, knows that aesthetics serve commerce—the "pocketesque"—and thus he merrily dismisses abstract terminology by concluding, "All's picturesque beneath the sun" (line 433). Like Dutch art, the first popular and commercially produced paintings, the picturesque is simply a response to a changing marketplace, and is as flexible and fluid as taste itself. As Swanevelt, another Dutch artist, says, "Vain here to divide— / The *Picturesque* has many a side" (174–75). Aesthetic labels cannot contain the variety that results from the clear observation and reproduction of actual life, for nineteenth-century critics the leading characteristics of Dutch painting.

The important thing about "At the Hostelry," then, is that it explores the nature and appeal of Dutch painting and suggests that it deserves as much respect as ideal art. Claude Lorrain, for example, is too lost in "theory's wildering maze" (189) to participate in the debate, implying the social irrelevance of his style. And Tintoretto finds that picturesque paintings can come closer to nature than does his own work:

This Picturesque is scarce my care.
But note it now in Nature's work—
A thatched hut settling, rotting trees
Mossed over. Some decay must lurk:
In florid things but small its share.
You'll find it in Rome's squalid Ghetto,
In Algiers at the lazaretto,
In many a grimy slimy lair.   (260–67)

These are, of course, the very motifs that Victorian art critics disparaged. Here, they gain power as Tintoretto confers on them the authority of nature itself. By suggesting that the picturesque inheres in "Nature's work," he effectively sanctions Dutch painting and expands the meaning of the traditional ideal—one accepted by both Reynolds and Ruskin— of "truth to nature." Furthermore, his definition extends the permissible jlimits of art to include the social sphere—teeming urban ghettoes and public hospitals. Thus, Dutch genre painting can stimulate ethical concern by providing occasions, if not always motives, for human sympathy and understanding. No wonder that Adrian Brouwer, regarded as one of the most sensuous and vulgar of Dutch stylists, enthusiastically endorses Tintoretto's observation: "'Well put' cried Brouwer with ruddled face, / . . . 'Grime mark and slime!'" (268, 271). For Brouwer, any subject may be painted, for "In Art," he argues, "the sty / Is quite inodorous" (276–77). Brouwer then offers numerous examples of Dutch realism and variety, from Van Huysum's flowers and Teniers's "boors at inns" to Rembrandt's sooty, smoky portraits.

Such aesthetic eclecticism undermines the categorical aesthetics of Reynolds, who declared that

> to mingle the Dutch with the Italian school, is to join contrarieties which cannot subsist together, and which destroy the efficacy of each other. The Italian attends only to the invariable, the great, and general ideas which are fixed and inherent in universal nature; the Dutch, on the contrary, to literal truth, and a minute exactness in the detail, as I may say of nature modified by accident. (Quoted in Burnet 4:24)

But in a Protestant democratic society, the particular or individual *is* "the great," and when sympathetically presented, mirrors social and political norms better than the culturally remote saints and madonnas of Roman Catholic Italian art. The very qualities Reynolds disliked in Dutch art thus suited it to American tastes and values, what Emerson in "The American Scholar" called "the near, the low, the common," and gave it, as Jarves had grudgingly admitted, a cultural relevance Italian art could never attain.

Melville's first reference to a Dutch painting is in *Typee* (1846) where he alludes to David Teniers the Younger's *The Temptations of St. Anthony.* Tommo observes "a big black spectral cat, which sat erect in the doorway, looking at me with its frightful goggling green orbs, like one of those monstrous imps that torment some of Teniers' saints!" (211). As a painting that, according to Jane P. Davidson, combines religious themes with "genre" (36–38), the *St. Anthony* (Fig. 1) uses commonplace characters such as the old couple in the left foreground to connect its hagiographic theme with ordinary life. The couple's presence reinforces the reality of the grotesque demons that encircle the saint, suggesting that such nightmarish images symbolize literal truths observable in both humanity and nature, as Melville realized when he described Daniel Orme's moody mutterings as "grotesque additions like the wens and knobs and distortions of the trunk of an old chance apple-tree" (*Great Short Works* 428). Since Teniers painted between 100 and 200 versions of the *Temptations of St. Anthony,* it's uncertain just which one Melville had in mind. Figure 1

Fig. 1. David Teniers the Younger, *The Temptations of St. Anthony,* c. 1640. Courtesy of the Mayer van den Bergh Museum, Antwerp.

shows a representative, frequently reproduced version. By so graphically portraying spirit tempted by flesh, Teniers suggests the wickedness and corruption of fleshly delights, a dark truth that Tommo gradually comes to accept. Although Tommo is certainly no Saint Anthony, he does face repeated temptations, some of them—cannibalism—as grotesque and repulsive as the monstrous mental projections in Teniers's painting.

As his exposure to painting increased, Melville began to admire the energy and vitality in Dutch painting that suited it to depicting the violent world he so often celebrated. In *Mardi* (1849) he alluded to a painter famous for his depictions of hunting and battles when he compared killer whales attacking a right whale to a bull being attacked by dogs: "Had old Wouvermans, who once painted a bull bait, been along with us, a rare chance, that, for his pencil" (42). Melville's tastes are still in transition, for his narrator also wishes that the French marine painters Jean Gudin (1802–80) and Eugene Isabey (1803–86) could contribute a "blue rolling sea," and that Claude Lorrain could add a sunset "that would have glorified the whole." His knowledge of Dutch art is spotty, for while he is accurate in recalling that Philips Wouvermans painted hunting scenes, he alludes to a work that doesn't exist. Melville might be remembering the copy of Paul Potter's *The Bull* that was exhibited in New York and conflating it with a work by Wouvermans, a painter frequently exhibited there in prior years.

Such undiscriminating eclecticism continues in *Redburn,* a novel replete with allusions to specific painters: Murillo, Salvator Rosa, Guido, and Hogarth (247, 275, 228, 143). Although no Dutch painters are mentioned, the last allusion indicates that genre painting remains a key resource for Melville's writing. Moreover, Wellingborough Redburn's introduction to a world of toil, poverty, and misery undermines the efficacy of the grand style and draws him toward the more realistic descriptive techniques of genre. In the lengthy discussion of painting in chapter one, Redburn lists works influential in his youth. Among them are "rural scenes, full of fine skies, pensive cows standing up to the knees in water, and shepherd-boys and cottages in the distance, half concealed in vineyards and vines" (6). Such landscapes, reprinted in a large green French portfolio, recall the idyllic pastorals of Claude Lorrain, for example *The Herdsman* (Fig. 2), a work that duplicates precisely the iconography Redburn describes. According to H. Diane Russell, this etching—now called *The Cowherd*—was "greatly admired by print connoisseurs" of the nineteenth century and was widely reprinted (353). Redburn soon learns that actual scenes bear little resemblance to Claudian Arcadias, however; when he visits "a charming little dale" in England, he discovers "MAN-TRAPS AND SPRING-GUNS!" under the foliage (210). And the coast at Liverpool, instead of displaying beautiful mountain peaks shrouded in mists, shows "lofty ranges of dingy warehouses, which seemed very deficient in the elements of the marvelous" (127).

In sharp contrast to the ideal tradition, several of Redburn's own verbal pictures derive from the unflinching social realism of Hogarth and other genre painters. He compares an old toper to "a great mug of ale" with toasted brown cheeks and "the froth of beer bubbling at his mouth, and sparkling on his nut-brown beard" (167). The first English tavern he visits disappoints him with its dark narrow interior and view of a dingy courtyard (133), and the "general effect" of a brilliantly arrayed Lascar officer is "quite spoiled by his bare feet" (170). Particularly effective

Fig. 2. Claude Gellée de Lorrain, *The Herdsman*. Reproduced from *The Works of Eminent Masters* (London, 1854), 1:340.

are his moving descriptions of the poverty-stricken slums of Liverpool, with their rubbish-laden streets, soot-begrimed houses, dark alleyways, impoverished beggars, and, most telling of all, a dead infant clasped in its mother's arms, its face "dazzlingly white, even in its squalor; but the closed eyes looked like balls of indigo" (183). "*Grime* mark and *slime!*," indeed. Redburn's direct, honest pictorial style defies the dicta of Reynolds and challenges squeamish tastes by focusing on the distinctive particularities of a scene, even when it involves human suffering and death. Melville, like Redburn, is reeducating his eye to genre painting in order to find pictorial resources adequate to his increasingly realistic vision.

These early allusions suggest that Melville was aware of both the growing popularity of the Dutch and of genre painting in general. In 1843 the American Art-Union of New York City broke sharply with its traditional preference for historical painting and chose W. S. Mount's *Farmers Nooning* as its annual membership print, which meant that this simple genre piece was reproduced and distributed free to the Art-Union's thousands of members. As James Thomas Flexner has noted, Mount's painting "made the startling assertion that the life of ordinary Americans was picturesque and worth painting" (Cowdrey viii). Mount, who learned about Dutch painting from Washington Allston (Eliot Clark 54), was only the first in a long line of American genre painters who revealed the influence of the Dutch.[7] Richard Caton Woodville and Eastman Johnson perfected their genre technique by studying Dutch originals in private collections at home and in galleries abroad (Richardson 231–32), and Francis W. Edmonds expressed his admiration for the techniques of Dutch painting and commented favorably in his diary of 1840–41 on Sir David Wilkie's well-known genre piece, *The Blind Fiddler* (H. Nichols B. Clark, "A Fresh Look" 74). During the 1840s the Art-Union exhibited more and more genre pieces to New York audiences. In 1847, the year Melville attended the annual Art-Union show and met Mount (Leyda 262), the membership print selected was George Caleb Bingham's *The Jolly Flatboatmen,* a striking portrait of rafting on the Mississippi sometimes compared to Mark Twain's descriptions in *Huckleberry Finn.* Ten thousand copies were made and given to Art-Union members, among them Evert Duyckinck.[8] Because of the widespread availability of this painting, it is very likely that Melville saw it and sensed firsthand that new tastes were forming.

By the time of *White-Jacket* (1849), Melville's immersion in the boiling-pot of New York literature, art, and politics had educated him to the distinctive traits of genre painting: ordinary people enjoying ordinary activities. The smoking scene aboard the *Neversink* reveals greater familiarity with genre pieces and demonstrates how readily Melville exploited them in his art. Displaying knowledge of nationality as well as genre, the narrator fleshes out his picture of smoking sailors by alluding to both Dutch and English genre painters:

> It was a pleasant sight to behold them. Grouped in recesses between the guns, they chatted and laughed like rows of convivialists in the boxes of some vast dining-saloon. Take a Flemish kitchen full of good fellows from Teniers; add a fire-side group from Wilkie; throw in a naval sketch from Cruikshank; and then stick a short pipe into every mother's son's mouth, and you have the smoking scene at the galley of the Neversink. (387)

Melville has begun to appreciate the peculiar charm of domesticity in genre painting, and to distinguish it from the darker social realism of Hogarth. His allusion to Hogarth's *Idle Apprentice* series enforces the theme of shipboard brutality (377), whereas the light-hearted sketch of the smoking sailors shows that life on a man o'war has a pleasant side, too. The good nature evident in George Cruikshank's illustrations to Charles Dibdin's *Songs Naval and National* (1841; Buchanan-Brown, pl. 153) or in a popular painting such as Wilkie's *The Blind Fiddler* (Fig. 3) combines with the male camaraderie characteristic of Teniers, Steen, Brouwer, and many other Dutch painters to portray realistically and sympathetically essential shipboard values: geniality, comfort, and friendship.

With the sanction of the Art-Union given to genre painting, the stock of Dutch painting of all types—genre, landscape, seascape, still life— began to rise, and with it Melville's knowledge of Dutch art increased as well. On his visit to London at the end of 1849 Melville visited several collections of paintings. At Hampton Court he saw "Rembrandt's Jew" (probably *A Jew Merchant,* now considered the work of a pupil of Rembrandt) and mentioned the "Van Dycks" (16). He visited the Dulwich Gallery, a museum William Hazlitt praised for its fine collection of Dutch paintings, and among the "gems" by Titian, Claude, and Murillo he gave special mention to "The mottled horse of Wouvermans" (20). If he knew Hazlitt's views at this time, Melville may even have been led to the Dulwich to confirm Hazlitt's iconoclastically favorable opinion of the Dutch paintings there.[9] More important for Melville's writing than these fleeting visits to distant galleries were the increasingly abundant native visual resources. During the 1850s American art galleries exhibited more and more Dutch art (H. Nichols B. Clark, "Taste" 28). Even the famed Düsseldorf Gallery of the National Academy of Design, while nominally devoted to the historical realism of contemporary German painters and their students, exhibited Dutch paintings during its heyday, 1848–62, and the Crystal Palace Exhibition in New York in November 1853 hung pictures by Teniers, Ruisdael, Ostade, and Rubens alongside those of the Italian masters (Cummings 238).

The single most significant event for Melville's appreciation of Dutch art was the publication in New York of *The Illustrated Magazine of Art* (1853–1854). This periodical, at least one volume of which Melville annotated, ran a profusely illustrated series of articles on Dutch painters during its two-year history. The long and informative essays combined biography and criticism and commented favorably on Jan Steen, William Van de Velde, Jan Van Huysum, Adrian Brouwer, and Gerard Douw, to name only those Dutch painters Melville later characterized in "At the Hostelry." When the magazine ceased publication in 1854, a selection of articles was reprinted as *The Works of Eminent Masters,* a book that contained 185 engravings, 104 of them Dutch. Although Melville did not acquire a personal copy until December 1871 (Leyda 722), he may have seen one earlier or owned other volumes of the *Illustrated Magazine.*

Sir David Wilkie, *The Blind Fiddler*. Courtesy of the Tate Gallery, London.

The periodical seems to have influenced Melville's sketches of the 1850s, notably "I and My Chimney," "The Piazza," and "The Fiddler," and *Eminent Masters* was probably the chief resource for "At the Hostelry" as well as, in subtler ways, the Burgundy Club portraits and parts of *Weeds and Wildings*. Combined with the increasing cultural recognition of Dutch art, such resources led Melville to appreciate the Dutch as fellow artists striving to portray truth realistically in a thriving commercial and democratic society. He developed a more personal identification with these genial painters that eventually led him to empathize with their private struggles and their gradual aesthetic rehabilitation after years of neglect by the art establishment.

As his knowledge of Dutch painting increased, Melville located its peculiar appeal in its depiction of daily experience. It satisfied that "commonplace curiosity" the narrator feels in "Daniel Orme," and provided inspiration for sketching ordinary scenery and characters. The nautical setting of *Moby-Dick* forestalled Melville's genre painting in prose during the early 1850s: as Ishmael realizes in his analysis of the "Monstrous Pictures of Whales," neither the ideal painter Guido nor the genre painter Hogarth was capable of painting whales realistically (225). But the pastoral setting of *Pierre,* Melville's "rural bowl of milk," invited genre techniques, as in this long description of Isabel's farmhouse:

> But more near, on the mild lake's hither shore, where it formed a long semi-circular and scooped acclivity of corn-fields, there the small and low red farm-house lay; its ancient roof a bed of brightest mosses; its north front (from the north the moss-wind blows), also moss-incrusted, like the north side of any vast-trunked maple in the groves. At one gabled end, a tangled arbor claimed support, and paid for it by generous gratuities of broad-flung verdure, one viny shaft of which pointed itself upright against the chimney-bricks, as if a waving lightning-rod. Against the other gable, you saw the lowly dairy-shed; its sides close netted with traced Madeira vines; and had you been close enough, peeping through that imprisoning tracery, and through the light slats barring the little embrasure of a window, you might have seen the gentle and contented captives—the pans of milk, and the snow-white Dutch cheeses in a row, and the molds of golden butter, and the jars of lily cream. (110)

Dark forebodings of human suffering ripple under the surface of this particularized landscape: the "imprisoning tracery" that recalls old Glendinning's "stable slaves," one of them pointedly named Douw (30); the "contented captives" analogy; the warning of the lightning-rod. All of these Melville would associate with the "povertiresque," a false idealization of rural scenery that ignores human suffering, much as the poet Blandmour ignores the physical needs of the Coulter family in "Poor

Man's Pudding." But the specifically Dutch iconography of nourishing cheeses, butter, and cream offsets these images. When Melville finally speaks overtly of the povertiresque in Book 20 of *Pierre,* he omits all mention of the Dutch and instead associates this overly aesthetic style, a type of genre and landscape painting purchased at the expense of human sympathy, with the fashionable school of Thomas Gainsborough (276), whose romantic landscapes followed Claude in usually presenting "an arcadian view of country life" (Hayes 46). Many Dutch artists, in contrast, were aesthetically and economically more democratic. Some of them—Steen and Brouwer especially—lived the same lives as their subjects, a point made repeatedly in contemporary biographies and developed in "At the Hostelry." Their art therefore avoided hypocrisy and sentimentality and mirrored the particular truths of the painters' immediate milieu, as English genre painting, such as *The Blind Fiddler,* did not.

This social distinction forms the thematic basis for "The Piazza," where the narrator learns that distant panoramas offer the beauty of sublimity but obscure the ugly particularities of reality. When the narrator finally visits Marianna's gray, mossy, decaying house, it is like entering a painting and participating in the lives it depicts. He can no longer idealize the scene as would a Gainsborough or Claude Lorrain, but must confront its physical reality as well as its disturbing moral values. Like those Dutch painters who participated in the tavern brawls and rural poverty they depicted, the narrator learns to portray the impoverished life around him with sympathy and detail, as the obvious moral lesson of the sketch demonstrates. He learns, as did Rembrandt, that "truth comes in with darkness" (12), that bathing a scene in a misty Claudian glow veils reality in false aesthetic illusions. The close view, even though grotesque and disappointing, leads the spectator to a renewed capacity for human sympathy. The narrator has journeyed, as it were, from the purely aesthetic admiration for an idealized pastoral landscape by Claude to the personal moral involvement with a concrete, hard-edged close-up of a landscape by Jacob Ruisdael or Meindert Hobbema. Marianna's mossy, rotting gray cabin mimics the rural homes in many Dutch landscapes, and situates itself naturally into the world of Hobbema's *Wooded Landscape with Water-mill* (Fig. 4). Melville probably saw this painting at the Dulwich Gallery in 1849, and very likely read about it later in his marked copy of Hazlitt's *Criticisms on Art:* "Could we paint as well as Hobbema," Hazlitt wrote of *The Watermill,* "we should not envy Rembrandt" (392).

The landscape symbolism of "I and My Chimney" similarly distinguishes Claudian from Dutch treatments of nature and, despite the ironies

Fig. 4. Meindert Hobbema, *Wooded Landscape with Water-mill*. Courtesy of the Governors of the Dulwich Picture Gallery, London.

that surround the narrator, firmly link him with Dutch tastes and values.[10] The letter that appears in the village paper objecting to the beloved chimney as "a sad blemish to an otherwise lovely landscape" (376), is signed "Claude," a clear implication that the romanticized landscape style of the Italianate painter is inadequate to comprehend the homely realities of the ordinary American scene. In order to preserve his crumbling chimney, a symbol of domestic independence, art fused with nature, and the threatened artistic self, the narrator invokes imagery found in many Dutch genre and landscape paintings. He identifies with the chimney as an "old smoker," looking back to the lively smoking scene aboard the *Neversink* and forward to the drowsy, more sardonic enjoyment of tobacco in "The Bench of Boors" and "Herba Santa," a motif figured in Teniers's *The Smoker* (Fig. 5). And he admires the "truth to nature" represented by the chimney much as Tintoretto in "At the Hostelry" connected "Nature's work" with thatched huts, rotting trees, and decay, further tokens of the picturesque evident in *The Watermill*. Anticipating Tintoretto's analysis, the chimney-defending narrator declares that "of all artists of the picturesque, decay wears the palm" (356).

Perhaps the closest Melville came to composing his own Dutch genre painting in prose occurs in "The Fiddler," published in September 1854. This sketch celebrates the retired fiddler, Hautboy, and his easy acceptance of reality. According to Helmstone, the narrator, "Hautboy saw the world pretty much as it was, yet he did not theoretically espouse its bright side nor its dark side. Rejecting all solutions, he but acknowledged facts" (264). This is the same kind of moral detachment that many observers found in Dutch painting and that, by the end of Melville's sketch, makes Hautboy an artistic master worth following: Helmstone, a frustrated poet, tears up his manuscripts, buys a fiddle, and goes "to take regular lessons of Hautboy" (267). Melville makes Hautboy's matter-of-fact morality visually explicit in a description remarkably similar to Adrian Brouwer's painting *The Fiddler:* "Pressed by Standard," says Helmstone, "Hautboy forthwith got out his dented old fiddle, and sitting down on a tall rickety stool, played away right merrily at Yankee Doodle and other off-handed, dashing, and disdainfully care-free airs. But common as were the tunes, I was transfixed by something miraculously superior in the style. Sitting there on the old stool, his rusty hat sideways cocked on his head, one foot dangling adrift, he plied the bow of an enchanter" (266). There is no evidence Melville saw this painting by the earthy Brouwer; but a few months before he published "The Fiddler," an engraving of the painting (Fig. 6) appeared in *The Illustrated Magazine of Art* (vol. 3, Summer 1854). Merton M. Sealts, Jr., concludes that "The Fiddler" was probably composed in 1853, making it unlikely

Fig. 5. David Teniers the Younger, *The Smoker,* c. 1635. Courtesy of the Los Angeles County Museum of Art; William Randolph Hearst Collection.

Fig. 6. Adrian Brouwer, *The Fiddler*. Reproduced from *The Works of Eminent Masters* (London, 1854), 1:148.

that the engraving supplied a source for the sketch. Nonetheless, the similarities are striking. Hautboy's talent, like the riveting eye and implied music of Brouwer's figure, is rooted in a commonplace setting apparently hostile to art and yet still productive of an energy and spontaneity not always found in more congenial situations. And unlike Wilkie's *The Blind Fiddler,* Brouwer's picture shows the artist alone with his music, satisfying himself rather than an audience, a condition Melville increasingly accepted for his own writing. If Melville is satirizing mediocrity, as Donald Yannella has recently contended of "The Fiddler," it is remarkably good-natured, even jocund satire. Hautboy's unpretentious manner has its own charms, and Melville, like the Dutch painters who recorded such musicians, treats him with geniality and good humor.

On his second trip to Europe in 1856–57, Melville followed an itinerary that revealed his increased interest in painting of all types. He continued to exhibit eclectic tastes, as his journal mentions works by Claude, Rosa, Dürer, Holbein, Caravaggio, Titian, and many others. Melville's rare general comments upon artistic technique, however, indicate that he had begun to understand better the peculiar power of Dutch art. An entry written after his visit to the Turin gallery locates the excellence of Dutch painters in their penchant for the low, grotesque, and even ugly: "Rubens' Magdalen—excellently true to nature, but very ugly. Groups of children by Van Dyke—six in a row, heads,—charming. Teniers tavern scenes. The remarkable Teniers effect is produced by first dwarfing, then deforming humanity. Breughel—always pleasing" (222). While Melville's evaluation of these paintings is ambiguous, the entry shows that "truth to nature" does not always mean portraying the beautiful, the ideal, or the general. Nature contains beauty and ugliness, and the honest painter will portray both.

In Amsterdam Melville visited the Trippenhuis, whose collection later became the basis for the Rijksmuseum, the largest collection of Dutch paintings in the world. This experience reinforced Melville's association of the Dutch with geniality, a theme critics have long recognized in his writings. He noted Franz Hals's portrait of a painter and his wife (Fig. 7) and remarked on "The abandonment of good humored content.— Dutch convivial scenes. Teniers & Breughel" (127). The Hals portrait, long thought to be Hals and his wife, is actually the *Marriage Portrait of Isaac Abraham Massa (1586–1639) and Beatrix van der Laen (1592–1639).* But for Melville, an artist suffering through an unhappy period in his marriage, the erroneous title must have given the painting an especially poignant appeal. Hals's sensually rendered couple exudes a warmth, ease, and mutual satisfaction that eluded Herman and Elizabeth. Also on display were four Teniers paintings, including a *St. Anthony*

Fig. 7. Franz Hals, *Marriage Portrait of Isaac Abraham Massa (1586–1639) and Beatrix van der Laen (1592–1639)*. Courtesy of the Rijksmuseum-Stichting, Amsterdam.

and two tavern scenes, *The Old Beer Drinker* and *Bricklayer Smoking a Pipe*. In his journal, Melville singled out for mention two huge, conspicuously exhibited paintings, Rembrandt's *Night-Watch* and Paul Potter's *The Bear Hunt,* as well as Rembrandt's *Syndics* and Lieve Verschuier's *The Keel Hauling* (127). Other Dutch artists at the Trippenhuis whom Melville mentions somewhere in his works were Philips Wouvermans (nine paintings), Jan Steen (eight paintings), Gerard Douw (seven paintings), William Van de Velde II (five seascapes), Jan Brueghel (six paintings), and Brouwer (two paintings).[11] Although he saw Dutch paintings elsewhere on his 1857 journey, visiting the Trippenhuis and finding himself surrounded by hundreds of examples of the style must have stamped its leading features ineffaceably on Melville's ready mind.

Dutch painting took on more personal meanings for Melville after his European trip. His taste for the Dutch linked him with the democratic spirit in art, the personal lives of the painters, and, fortuitously, the aesthetics of his most admired compatriot, Nathaniel Hawthorne. In one of those minor shocks of recognition, Melville read chapter 37 of *The Marble Faun* in 1860 and found himself agreeing with Hawthorne's views on "The Emptiness of Picture-Galleries." Hilda, Hawthorne's innocent New England copyist, has spent a summer alone in Rome learning to live with her new knowledge of evil, an evil associated with human passion, sensuality, and love. Now unable to empathize with the old masters who once inspired her, she wanders aimlessly in the picture galleries, unmoved by the great religious paintings of the Italian masters and suspicious of their creators' spiritual integrity. In such a mood, the narrator says, a Mephistophelian "Demon" creeps over the viewer and heretically insists that Dutch sensuousness is superior to Italian intellectuality:

> If he spare anything, it will be some such matter as an earthen pipkin or a bunch of herrings by Teniers; a brass kettle, in which you can see your face, by Gerard Douw; a furred robe, or the silken texture of a mantle, or a straw hat, by Van Mieris; or a long-stalked wine-glass, transparent and full of shifting reflections, or a bit of bread and cheese, or an over-ripe peach with a fly upon it, truer than reality itself, by the school of Dutch conjurors. These men, and a few Flemings, whispers the wicked Demon, were the only painters. (336)

In his copy of the novel Melville commented marginally, "Most original & admirable, and, doubtless, too true" (Leyda 621). As with many of Melville's marginalia, some ambiguity lingers about the precise inspiration for the comment. But its presence demonstrates that he knew the philistinism still associated with a preference for Dutch art.

The late works that show the strongest affinities with the mood, values, and techniques of these earthy "Dutch conjurors" are the Burgundy Club Sketches, Melville's portraits of "good fellows" who live in a kind of "umberish haze" of wine and nostalgia. The sketches were composed in the mid-1870s and thus draw upon Melville's mature knowledge of Dutch genre painting.[12] Intended to frame "At the Hostelry," they draw on the techniques and themes of Dutch genre painting even while paying lip service to the significance of the Italians. The Marquis de Grandvin, for example, exhibits the qualities of "the Grand Style"

(*Great Short Works* 397) that make him appealing to men; but his uniqueness lies in his equal display of those "less exalted qualities" that make him appealing to women. His bisexual attractiveness combines the ideal and the natural, the Italian and the Dutch, and makes de Grandvin the most compelling and original member of the club. No wonder that "the landscape painter, B. Hobbema Brown," finds the genial Marquis a fascinating and admirable "godsend" (399). True to his allusive yet commonplace name, and like the narrators of "I and My Chimney," "Daniel Orme," and the Burgundy Club Sketches themselves, Brown recognizes that the combination of spiritual masculine grandeur and fleshly feminine commonplaceness makes for the most genuinely extraordinary personality.

Similarly, Major Jack Gentian, the Dean of the Burgundians, combines the noble qualities of a Civil War hero with the "less exalted" traits of comradeship and good cheer. As the narrator says, "Ah, Major, . . . I love thee; yes, and it is as much for thy queer little human foibles as thy not-so-common virtues" (411). Thus, while Major Jack declines to wear any official badges of his military service, even on May 30, the date commemorating the Union victory, he does appear that day on his balcony with a more realistic memorial of the campaign, a missing arm, "disposed more picturesquely, nay, somehow more conspicuously" (411). Here is the "Teniers effect" in prose, a portrait of a war hero that acknowledges and even prizes a deformity—as Dickinson might say, "Because I know it's true"—rather than the glittering badges of officially sanctioned honor. The major's empty sleeve is just the kind of detail that a Titian or a Stuart would omit and that a Teniers or a Brouwer would emphasize. And as with the major himself, the absence or presence of this detail has moral implications. The mild vanity Jack Gentian reveals by conspicuously displaying his sleeve on May 30 is a more honest and justifiable icon of his heroism than any medals could ever be.

Melville's allusion to Hobbema suggests how acutely he had come to see parallels between his own reputation and that of the Dutch. According to a biographical guide Melville purchased, Frank Cundall's *The Landscape and Pastoral Painters of Holland* (1891), Hobbema was obscure, a good friend of the more successful Ruisdael (read "Hawthorne"?), appointed gauger at Amsterdam, and buried in a pauper's grave (45). As Cundall's biographical sketch adds, Hobbema "had no pupils," and "his works were little thought of during his lifetime or even during the succeeding generation" (62, 47). These facts must have already been known to Melville when he characterized B. Hobbema Brown as "an inoffensive sort of theoretical misanthrope, with a treacherous flow of loving-kindness in him" whose landscapes are unappreciated "by the art-dealers, art-critics, and academic hanging-committees, to say nothing of the art public" (*Great Short Works* 399). From his reading in *The Works of Eminent Masters,* Melville knew that some Dutch painters had not achieved success in their lifetimes. He even sidelined the passage that described Brouwer's miserable death in a public hospital (147; Cowen, "Melville's Marginalia" 11: 455). Combined with contemporary academic criticism of Dutch painting, such biographical facts must have made Melville view the Dutch as companions in ignominy. Their ostracism was a sign of their dedication, originality, and insight. Brown's warm appreciation of de Grandvin's complex nature shows that life outside the bright circle of official renown allows one to transcend conventional aesthetic categories and see deeper truths than those purveyed by the academy. And just as Brown's paintings go unappreciated by the critics, so Melville's Burgundian sketches found no audience. Nevertheless, artists should continue to toil at their lonely craft as did Rembrandt, who, Melville noted in a copy of Balzac's letters, remained in his house for two years while learning to paint light and shade (Leyda 815).

Despite his midlife immersion in Dutch art, Melville never held an unqualified admiration for its hedonistic moral implications. His best-known poem on Dutch painting, published in *Timoleon* (1891), emphasizes precisely those aspects of Dutch art that offended genteel Victorian critics. As Jarves wrote in *Art Thoughts,* the Dutch tend "to materialize the understanding and sensualize the taste, without yielding any sustenance to the imagination" (182). And in *The Art-Idea* Jarves included a poem by George Walter Thornbury that begins "Never thoughtful, wise, or sainted,— / This is how the Dutchman painted" (290). In "The Bench of Boors," Melville writes a similarly inspired poem that portrays the intellectually numbing effects of life in the tavern with graphic detail and striking imagery:

> In bed I muse on Tenier's boors,
> Embrowned and beery losels all:
> > A wakeful brain
> > Elaborates pain:
> Within low doors the slugs of boors
> Laze and yawn and doze again.
>
> In dreams they doze, the drowsy boors,
> Their hazy hovel warm and small:
> > Thought's ampler bound
> > But chill is found:
> Within low doors the basking boors
> Snugly hug the ember-mound.

> Sleepless, I see the slumberous boors
> Their blurred eyes blink, their eyelids fall:
>> Thought's eager sight
>> Aches—overbright!
> Within low doors the boozy boors
> Cat-naps take in pipe-bowl light.
>> *(Selected Poems* 142)

The poem seems to substantiate Jarves's charge of "mental mediocrity." The vulgar language ("beery," "boozy") and the animalistic analogies ("slugs of boors," "basking boors," "Cat-naps") portray creatures too low and self-indulgent for even the most ardent proponents of artistic realism to accept.

Yet the poem might also be read as an ironic challenge to aesthetic idealism, for it was published at a time when Dutch painting had finally assumed more favorable status and one could confidently express a preference for the style without feeling he had "defective" tastes. From 1877 to 1881, *Harper's Magazine* ran an illustrated series praising the Flemish and Dutch masters and reprinting engravings of some of Melville's favorite works, including Rembrandt's *Night-Watch* and Teniers's *Temptations of St. Anthony.* The art books Melville assiduously purchased during the last decade of his life gave the Dutch more official recognition than ever before.[13] Even Thornbury's poem combines praise with criticism simply by listing so many pleasing images from Dutch works: "Cuyp's rich mellow gold I see,— / Teniers' silver purity" (Jarves, *Art-Idea* 291). And in 1887, Elizabeth Melville gave her husband an engraving of Albert Cuyp's "A Sunny Day," one of the nine Dutch landscapes or genre pieces in his personal collection of engravings (Wallace, "Melville's Prints" 80, and Fig. 3). This reorientation of tastes may have emboldened Melville to depict frankly the vulgarity of tavern life yet still find it preferable (although not necessarily superior) to the lonely and often torturous life of the mind. The clear light of intellectuality brings sight, but the coldness of thought brings pain, and the two combine to make the poet weary and anxious with sleeplessness. This parallels the reaction to the grand style Hawthorne had described in *The Marble Faun* and Melville imaged in his portrait of Leonardo da Vinci in "At the Hostelry":

> For Leonardo, lost in dream,
> His eye absorbed the effect of light
> Rayed thro' red wine in glass—a gleam
> Pink on the polished table bright;
> The subtle brain, convolved in snare,
> Inferring and over-refining there.
>> (lines 515–20)

Too much thought draws the observer away from the simple pleasures of life—here, the "red wine in glass"—and ensnares him in uncertainties of endless inference. In contrast, the mellow, hospitable "pipe-bowl light" of the smoky tavern soothes and comforts weary humanity, offering a middle state between dream and wakefulness that allows continued participation in human society. Technique assumes moral value as the chiaroscuro of a Teniers interior relieves the anguish of the overly cerebral life, just as Adrian Brouwer proclaimed in "At the Hostelry":

> Hey, Teniers? Give us boors at inns,
> Mud floor—dark settles—jugs—old bins,
> Under rafters foul with fume that blinks
> From logs too soggy much to blaze,
> Which yet diffuse an umberish haze
> That beautifies the grime, methinks. (282–87)

Many Teniers paintings could serve equally well to illustrate the typically Dutch iconography of Melville's brief verse, one of only four poems clearly inspired by a particular painter (the others are "Formerly a Slave," "The Temeraire," and "The Coming Storm"). Unlike the other three works, however, here the precise painting is unnamed, suggesting that the source is generalized.[14] "The Bench of Boors" combines elements of many Dutch tavern scenes, some of which are depicted in Teniers's *The Smoker* (Fig. 5) and others in an engraving of Brouwer's *The Drinkers* (Fig. 8) from *The Works of Eminent Masters*. Such life may be "low," but it is warmly human and sociable, as the two plates and Melville's snug, ember-hugging image suggests. The Dutch offer more than "an excess of sensual indulgence" opposed to an "excess of intellectual ardor," as William Bysshe Stein has said (*Poetry of Melville's Late Years* 96); rather, given the torture of thought, they pose a vital alternative to the cold and lonely life of the mind. If the poem mirrors sloth and self-satisfaction, it also represents comfort and geniality encouraged by liquor and tobacco, a commonplace theme in Melville's writing and particularly evident in his poetry. From the songs in *Mardi* through "Epistle to Daniel Shepherd" to "Falstaff's Lament" and "Ditty of Aristippus," Melville celebrated the appeal of bibulous camaraderie with motifs similar to those in "The Bench of Boors" and the paintings of Teniers, Brouwer, and other Dutch masters.

The iconography of Dutch genre painting also informs Melville's posthumously published collection of poems, *Weeds and Wildings* (1924), and suggests how powerfully appealing he found the theme of domesticity in his final years. Most of the poems praise ordinary nature—roadside flowers, woodland birds, butterflies, even a chipmunk. In subject

Fig. 8. Adrian Brouwer, *The Drinkers*. Reproduced from *The Works of Eminent Masters* (London, 1854), 1:149.

matter and descriptive accuracy, these vignettes parallel the still lifes of Jan Van Huysum, a typical "Fruit and Flower Painter" Melville celebrated in his uncollected poem of that title (*Collected Poems* 387). Other poems in *Weeds and Wildings*, like genre paintings, celebrate homely customs such as maple-sugaring and hanging Christmas stockings. In "A Dutch Christmas up the Hudson in the Time of Patroons," Melville creates a genre scene reminiscent of the Van Tassel homestead in "The Legend of Sleepy Hollow": as guests arrive for the holiday dancing and feasting, the narrator sits before the "ruddy hearth" and toasts apples. And the charming poem "A Dairyman's Child" is almost a perfect portrait-piece, all imagery and no narrative, like many descriptions in *The Sketch Book*. Melville personally acknowledged the parallels between such simple poems and Dutch painting in an 1877 letter when he compared Alfred B. Street's "The Old Garden" to "a flower-and-fruit piece by some mellow old Fleming."[15] This casual postscript evidences not only the continuing power of *ut pictura poesis*, but also the growing acceptability of Dutch verisimilitude.

Even more consciously Irvingesque is the prose-poem "Rip Van Winkle's Lilac," a landscape piece that focuses on the decay and picturesque beauty that overtakes Rip's "humble abode" while he sleeps. Echoing "I and My Chimney," the narrative describes the conflict between Rip and his wife over maintaining the house. Over time, the homestead becomes even grayer, mossier, and more rotten than Marianna's cabin in "The Piazza." The Van Winkle house eventually turns into a "tenantless ruin, hog-backed at last by the settling of the ridge-pole in the middle, abandoned to leisurely decay" (286). Yet, as in "The Piazza," artistic sensibility discovers "something of redeeming attractiveness in those deserted premises" (286). The willow tree by the house has fallen and been replaced by a lilac planted by Rip himself. So disposed, the scene catches the eye of an artist "in his summer wanderings after the Picturesque" (287). He sits down to paint it only to be accosted by a puritanical stranger who insists that he paint the new white church instead—a traditional New England icon with more acceptable moral associations. But the "Bohemian" artist maintains his integrity by recognizing, like the narrator of "I and My Chimney," that "decay is often a gardener" (288) and that Nature is seldom a "precisian" (289). Honest artists, following the practice of a Hobbema or Brouwer, avoid the sterile constructions of conventional society—the church is "a rectangular edifice stark on a bare hill-side" and reminds the artist of a "cadaver" (287)— and paint scenes of ordinary life, even if decay is a part of it. Eventually, we learn, Rip's house is replaced by a villa, implicitly leaving only the lilacs, the painting, and the story itself to memorialize Rip's home. The art of genre description, whether in prose or painting, democratically confers significance on the commonplace and testifies to its value by preserving its peculiar beauty and moral power for later generations.

Melville dedicated *Weeds and Wildings* to his wife, Elizabeth, calling her by the fictitious name "Winnefred." Nostalgically recollecting their life at Arrowhead, he seems to have found at last that domestic tranquility he admired in Hals's portrait of a married couple:

> How often at our adopted homestead or on the hill-side—now ours no more—the farm-house, long ago shorn by the urbane barbarian succeeding us in the proprietorship—shorn of its gambrel roof and dormer windows, and when I last saw it indolently settling in serene contentment of natural decay; how often, Winnie, did I come in from my ramble, early in the bright summer mornings of old, with a handful of these cheap little cheery roses of the meek, newly purloined from the fields to consecrate them on that bit of a maple-wood mantel—your altar, somebody called it—in the familiar room facing your beloved South! (482)

Simple joys take their place beside "the wisdom that is woe" as, late in life, Melville warmly celebrated the ordinary pleasures of marriage and domesticity. To be sure, there is some wishful thinking in such emotional indulgences; but by figuring his consolation in the motifs of Dutch painting, Melville reveals his continuing preference for the style. The example of *Weeds and Wildings* suggests that, at some deep level of feeling, perhaps one connected with his Dutch ancestry, his unspoken desire for family harmony, and his nostalgia for the rural peace of Arrowhead, Melville eventually took greater personal pleasure in Dutch art than in any other style.

The near view, the character sketch, the graphic domestic scene, all grow in significance in Melville's writing during the 1850s and influence his late poems and sketches. Both their verisimilitude and matter-of-fact moral tone reflect the techniques and values of Dutch genre painting and reveal Melville's growing affinities with this school of art. He knew how superficial and hypocritical such values could be, as suggested by "The Paradise of Bachelors" and "Poor Man's Pudding, Rich Man's Crumbs"; but he also knew that life could not be lived and enjoyed entirely on a cold spiritual plane, on the barren Acropolis of an overly idealized art. Too many landscapes were like those in the poems "Pausilippo" and "The Attic Landscape," beautiful scenes that yield no solace to the restless traveler. Too much thinking, as dramatized in *Billy Budd,* created only moral ambiguity and personal anguish. And in this final story, a dark brooding upon the conflicts between the natural and the ideal, Melville used the popular Dutch genre motif of contented card players to contrast the alternative possibilities of comfortable ignorance and anxious knowledge. Quoting "a writer whom few know" (presumably himself), he wrote, "Little ween the snug card players in the cabin of the responsibilities of the sleepless man on the bridge" (114). The ambiguities in *Billy Budd* make one wonder which approach to life Melville truly preferred. For all their vulgarity and seeming moral unconsciousness, the sensuous, earthy Dutch painters offered Melville a needed respite from the burdens of abstract and sometimes aimless thought, a snug harbor he returned to again and again throughout his career.

Wrestling with the Angel: Melville's Use of the Visual Arts in *Timoleon*

DOUGLAS ROBILLARD

n much of his writing, Melville displays a keen sense of the possibilities and limitations of literary pictorialism and, at the same time, his virtually unlimited interest in using its techniques. The earliest examples of this interest, found in the juvenile "Fragments from a Writing Desk," are imitative and mostly ineffective, a matter of literary allusion to works of art which the youthful writer had probably never seen. By the time Melville came to write *Redburn* (1849), however, he had greatly enhanced his repertory of representational techniques as well as his sophisticated knowledge of art objects, and the novel makes interesting use of a ship model, book bindings, the pictures of Salvator Rosa, Guido Reni, and William Hogarth, as well as whatever he knew of the decorations recently excavated at Pompeii, the alleged paintings owned by the emperor Tiberius, and the statue of Laocoön (Robillard, "Visual Arts" 43–57). By 1851, in *Moby-Dick,* he was offering a full range of pictorial semblances. The 1849–50 journey to Europe, with its lengthy art tour, and the intensive reading he had been doing before beginning on his most important novel, were coalescing with his evident genius for manipulating the devices of the literary arts. Vivid embellishments come to light in the novel: the painting of the whale at the Spouter-Inn; Guido Reni's treatment of the legend of Perseus and Andromeda; Captain Ahab as Cellini's Perseus; the many pictures of the pictorially elusive whale, sometimes monstrous, sometimes "less erroneous," preserved in a vast array of the visual arts, through paint, wood, sheet-iron, teeth, and stone (Pütz 161–66). The seascapes of Salvator Rosa and J. M. W. Turner are prominent sources for such literary pictorialism. Likewise, scenes and incidents in *Pierre* (1852) owe much to the art of portrait painting, and the descriptive portions of *The Confidence-Man* (1857) reflect the great contemporary interest in the enormous panoramic canvases of John Banvard and other producers of that evanescent American art form.

In 1857, after concluding the Palestinian portion of his solitary journey and pilgrimage that were so intimately joined to his sense of literary failure, Melville traveled back across the Mediterranean Sea, stopping briefly in Athens and then proceeding to Italy for what became an extensive art tour. The cryptic notations in his journal of that period reveal him as an eager tourist, bent upon seeing all there was to see of the art world as displayed at the Vatican, the Villa Albani, and the many palaces and exhibitions. He recorded visits to artists' studios, including those of John Gibson, Edward Bartholomew, William Page, and Hiram Powers; and he tried, unsuccessfully, to see James Jackson Jarves, the American connoisseur and art critic. The assemblage of these intimate and intensely felt impressions provided Melville with a suitable context for much of the writing he would later undertake. Almost at once, he began to use his art impressions by composing and delivering a lecture on "Statues in Rome." These earnest musings were those of a sensitive dilettante, acutely conscious of the many ways in which the visual arts were superior to the literary arts. Melville was thoroughly conversant with Lessing's dictum that the spatially conceived arts are holistically perceived, while literature must be comprehended sequentially, unfolding in time and, thus, often diluting some of its best effects.

It appears that Melville began composing some poems on art subjects around 1859. The section of *Timoleon* that he was to entitle "Fruits of Travel Long Ago" may consist, at least partially, of revisions of such poems. What seems quite clear is that Melville was finding the whole topic of the visual arts difficult, elusive, perhaps even intractable. It took a decade for him to exploit the Palestinian materials in the vast canvas of *Clarel,* but it would take about 35 years for the discordant elements of the *Timoleon* volume to fuse into a satisfactory artistic unity.

In the long period when these materials lay fallow, waiting upon his esemplastic imagination to give them final form, he made an extensive and ennobling effort to come to grips with the essential problems of literary pictorialism. He set out upon what amounted to a self-directed course of study in aesthetics by reviewing some of the major texts then available. In 1865 he acquired a five-volume set of John Ruskin's *Modern*

Painters and seems to have worked his way through the set, marking and annotating as he read. It is true that there are few markings in the volumes, but it is likely that Melville had known at least some parts of Ruskin for many years. The first volume had been published in 1843 to much discussion; and, when it was published in America in 1847, it was put out by Melville's own publisher at the time, Wiley and Putnam. If Melville did not then read the book, it seems fairly certain that he knew its arguments and was inspired by its championing of Turner to stir his own keen interest in the works of that great painter. Ruskin was widely criticized, quoted, and discussed in the periodicals of the 1840s, and Melville is likely to have read some of these pieces.

In 1870, Melville acquired a two-volume set of *The Literary Works of Sir Joshua Reynolds,* a large miscellany constituting a prospectus of seventeenth- and eighteenth-century aesthetic theory. The book contains Sir Joshua's own carefully conceived discourses on art, which Melville read, or perhaps reread, and marked with some care; Charles Du Fresnoy's *De Arte Graphica* (1668), an influential poetic treatise on painting; John Dryden's "A Parallel of Poetry and Painting" (1695), which served as a preface to his prose translation of Du Fresnoy; Sir Joshua's notes to William Mason's translation (1782) of Du Fresnoy; and Alexander Pope's "Epistle to Mr. Jervas with Fresnoy's Art of Painting."

In 1871, Melville's brother-in-law, John Hoadley, presented him with a copy of James Jackson Jarves's *The Art-Idea* (1864), an important book for Melville to be reading. Jarves was an American who had settled in Italy and wrote articles and books about European art; he expressed serious and worthwhile ideas about art and about the destiny of America and its developing arts. A perceptive collector of Italian paintings, he left a considerable legacy of pre-Raphaelite art to Yale University.

As Melville pondered, wrote, revised, and arranged and rearranged the poems that were to fit eventually into *Timoleon,* he continued to purchase art books and prints. After his retirement from his work at the New York Custom House in 1885, he was able to give more time to his poetry and other writings. Writing and assembling *John Marr and Other Sailors* (1888) and composing *Billy Budd* must have occupied much of his time, but he was able to bring the volume he called *Timoleon, Etc.* to publication in the summer of 1891. It was the last book he was to see through the press, and it must have cost him much effort, time, and spiritual travail.

A central theme of the volume is the life of art. Melville makes that sufficiently clear by his dedication of the book to Elihu Vedder (1836–1923), by then a prominent American painter. Long impressed by Vedder's art, Melville based "Formerly a Slave," from *Battle-Pieces,* upon one of Vedder's pictures. He later acquired a copy of *The Rubaiyat of Omar Khayyam,* illustrated by Vedder; and, in his dedication to *Timoleon,* he claimed his younger contemporary as "my countryman." Vedder must have seemed, to Melville, an idealized exemplar of the American as artist.

For the systematic study of the ways in which literature can draw upon the resources of the visual arts, a recent critic, Marianna Torgovnick, has constructed a scheme proposing that a continuum of usage of the visual arts in literary works proceeds through the decorative, the biographical, the ideological, and the interpretive, in an ascending order of importance.[1] Thus, she considers the decorative use of the arts of some interest but not nearly as crucial as ideological or interpretive uses (11–26). She tends, too, to find each of these elements separable; and her observation is probably accurate for the study of lengthy and complex prose fictions. She does not deal with brief, compact, and intense lyric and narrative poems. But we should note that, in any one poem, any and all of these elements might conjoin and merge, so that a single lyric might contain, within a tightly layered poetic construct, some elements, say, of the decorative and the interpretive, so commingled that they are hardly separable; or that all four elements, the decorative, the biographical, the ideological, and the interpretive, might be so joined in fusion that the parts are too involved to be easily separable.

Something of this intricacy is to be found in the 11-line poem, "Art," strategically placed within the *Timoleon* volume to allow its multiplicity of effects to glance each way in company with several other art-inspired poems:

> In placid hours well-pleased we dream
> Of many a brave unbodied scheme.
> But form to lend, pulsed life create,
> What unlike things must meet and mate:
> A flame to melt—a wind to freeze;
> Sad patience—joyous energies;
> Humility—yet pride and scorn;
> Instinct and study; love and hate;
> Audacity—reverence. These must mate,
> And fuse with Jacob's mystic heart,
> To wrestle with the angel—Art.

In spite of the lofty, generalizing tone of a piece that seems to be attempting to comment upon the lifework and travail of the artist, one discerns a powerfully autobiographical assertion of Melville's own labors and noble rewards, derived from a lifetime of exacting creativity.

The decorative element in the poem is manifest in its involved literary pictorialism in the concluding lines. The Biblical allusion to Jacob's victorious struggle with the angel is a familiar theme for Melville. In chapter 123 of *Moby-Dick* Starbuck levels a musket at the sleeping Ahab, then appears to have been "wrestling with the angel" and decides that he cannot kill the captain. Functional allusion, as Michael Wheeler observes, is a shorthand notation to suggest thematic cruxes, to "elucidate the meaning of each text and to indicate the literary modes and conventions in which its author works" (22–25). By his referential treatment of Jacob, Melville invokes a world of Biblical iconography, for the subject of Jacob's struggle with the angel was popular with painters who could render the spiritual contest in active, athletic terms. Melville would have been familiar with artistic representations of the scene; and, given his abiding affection for the art of Salvator Rosa, it seems at least possible that he knew Salvator's delineation of the tale of Jacob. When Lady Morgan published her biography of Salvator in 1824, the painting was in England, in the private collection of the Duke of Devonshire. Melville probably could not have seen the painting during his 1849–50 journey to England; but an engraving of the painting, executed by Richard Earlom, was available, and he might have studied this (Morgan 2: 366–68). To be able to visualize the struggle of man and angel as a picture rather than simply as a Biblical allusion is to understand more clearly Jacob's, and Melville's, difficult struggle and costly successes. Thus, in the brief poem, the decorative is more than simply decorative; it is certainly biographical and, by being thematic, it is also ideological and interpretive. The terms under which the artist must create force him to reconcile the discordances within the materials of his art, within the boundaries of his technical performance, and within the darkest areas of his psyche. He risks much by mating humility with pride and scorn, love with hate, and audacity with reverence. The mating of instinct with study is the province of the poet-scholar, an essential condition of his high calling. The fusion with "Jacob's mystic heart" is a reminder of a mysterious quality that we sometimes name "inspiration" or "afflatus," "daemon" or "epiphany." Hence, artistic creation is a struggle with divinity.

In his poems influenced by art subjects, Melville goes beyond generalization and exhortation to work closely with various forms of literary pictorialism. A short lyric, "The Marchioness of Brinvilliers," makes room for both painter and painting:

> He toned the sprightly beam of morning
> With twilight meek of tender eve,

Brightness interfused with softness,
Light and shade did weave:
And gave to candor equal place
With mystery starred in open skies;
And, floating all in sweetness, made
    Her fathomless, mild eyes.

Here the pictorialism is almost hermetic and nearly indecipherable except by the importation of external elements. The stance of the poem's narrator is that of viewer and commentator upon a painting or perhaps a print. Melville is working in an ancient, much used, and impressive tradition of poetry that includes Homer's description of the shield of Achilles and Keats's depiction of the Grecian urn. The term for such a poem is "iconic," and Jean Hagstrum's definition is exemplary: "In such poetry, the poet contemplates a real or imaginary work of art that he describes or responds to in some other way" (18).

In this case, the poet is describing a real work of art. Hennig Cohen and William H. Shurr have provided much helpful information about painter and painting. The artist is most likely Charles Le Brun (1619–90), an important painter and decorator in the court of Louis XIV. The Marquise de Brinvilliers was executed in 1676 after trying out her poisons on charity hospital patients and then killing several family members. Madame de Sévigné described the scene vividly in a letter of July 17, 1676:

> La Brinvilliers is in the air; after her execution her poor little body was thrown into a large fire, and her ashes dispersed by the wind, so that whenever we breathe, we shall inhale some particles of her, and by the communication of the minute spirits, we may be all infected with the desire of poisoning, to our no small surprise. (Aldington 1: 230)

Cohen remarks that there was a volume of Sévigné's letters in the Melville library; and it may well be that his poem is based, at least in part, upon the description. But the poem does focus upon a work of art, and it is likely that Melville saw such a work of art. Le Brun did a sketch of the infamous Marquise, and it might have been seen by Melville at the Louvre in 1849. Cohen suggests that an engraving might have been available (Melville, *Selected Poems* 238–39).[2]

The tale of an artist capturing the likeness of a murderess on the point of execution has a ring of apocryphal familiarity about it. One of the most famous and admired paintings of the sixteenth century is the portrait ascribed to Guido Reni and identified as Beatrice Cenci. It was a favorite among nineteenth-century American authors. Hawthorne thought it "the most profoundly wrought picture in the world." Melville, on seeing the painting in 1857, noted its "appealing look of innocence" and purchased a print drawn from it (*Writings: Journals* 108). It is, of course, the portrait's literary, historical, and psychological associations that attracted its eminent admirers. The Cenci story was reasonably familiar from its treatment in Shelley's verse drama. It cast some light upon a great and cruel age; and its portrayal of innocent beauty, paradoxically murderous, and, moreover, sacrificed to the legal system, must have been the cause of endless speculation about "the mystery of iniquity."

This mystery, from the Biblical phrase (2 Thessalonians 2.7), was much favored by Melville and was used as thematic matter in *Clarel*. In *Billy Budd,* contemporary with the *Timoleon* poems, he used the term again, in Captain Vere's remarks to the drumhead court. It figures, as well, in the highly ambiguous eleventh chapter of the novel, which attempts to account for Claggart's depravity and evil bearing, both hidden beneath a fairly comely and respectable exterior. Melville was surely fascinated by this discordant juncture of appearance and reality, of surface mildness and the little lower layer of murderous violence.

Melville often wrote about this mystery of discordance. In *Redburn,* Harry Bolton, sweetly innocent to all surface appearances, is thoroughly depraved, as his taking Redburn to the somewhat ambiguously evil house of Aladdin in London demonstrates. In *Moby-Dick,* the great white whale divinely swims like a benevolent lord of the sea, the wrenched hideousness of his jaw hidden from view. In *Pierre,* the "tolerable copy" of Guido Reni's picture of Beatrice Cenci initiates the reflection upon the "anomaly of so sweetly and seraphically *blonde* a being, being double-hooded, as it were, by the black crape of the two most horrible crimes . . . possible to humanity—incest and parricide" (ch. 26). Another version of the paradox appears in the poem, "Pebbles," at the conclusion of *John Marr and Other Sailors;* in the sixth section of the poem, the ocean is depicted as combining the "mad ramping of ravening waters" with "Christ on the Mount, and the dove in her nest." Thus, the pictorialism of "The Marchioness of Brinvilliers" offers the author another opportunity to assess the dark mystery that so haunts him. The language describing the portrait insists upon the immediate dichotomy of shadow and substance in painterly terms. The artist has "toned" morning colors with twilight shadows, in a subtle chiaroscuro of paint and character. The disposition of the elements of portraiture in facial expression allows the poet to observe the enigmatic fusion of candor and mystery in the subject; and he notes that, although the painter has been "floating all in sweetness," the eyes, though mild, are fathomless. The Le Brun drawing shows the subject in a pose of resignation, eyes uplifted heavenward.

The crucifix that she holds in her left hand intimates that she has made her peace with God.[3]

William H. Shurr remarks that "The beautiful surfaces are not to be trusted. The picture itself is a pasteboard mask and so is the poem" (244). This analysis is a reminder of Captain Ahab's denunciation of appearance, but it has more to offer, a comment on what appears to be Melville's very conception of the nature of poetry, or, possibly, of one important kind of poetry. The poetic technique involved here is that of "withheld meaning," a phrase that Shurr borrows from Lawrance Thompson. Shurr points out that "Writing here becomes a technique of concealment as much as communication and revelation, and the work produced is a quasi-gnostic document whose meaning is revealed only to the initiated" (244). But it may be added that, in his very late poetry, Melville often seems to be writing not even for the initiated but for some private audience that he, perhaps, has not completely identified. That audience may very well have considerable difficulties in penetrating the often bland surfaces of the poems to get to the dense, coiled, discordant centers of the poems. Some of these poems, like "The Marchioness of Brinvilliers," appear exceedingly hermetic, private and remote in their intimate language, the poems, in short, of an intellectual isolato.

Commenting upon "The Marchioness of Brinvilliers," William Bysshe Stein attacks the problems raised by the poem with the remark that "Western art for the most part is concerned with representing surface emotions, not eternal truths," and he goes on to add that the picture of the Marquise de Brinvilliers "captures none of her true qualities" (110). It is probably this paradox of the pictorial art that moves Melville to engage in this particular form of literary pictorialism. He seems attracted to the opportunities the visual artist has, ones denied to the artist in words, of using light, shade, pose, color, and attitude to reveal in a single, sweeping, holistic moment the entirety of a situation. This, for Melville, laboring over his word-pictures, is a clear exhibit of the superiority of the picture over the paragraph, or over the poem.

Melville's poem illustrates, in complex interplay, all the aspects of literary pictorialism named in Torgovnick's scheme. Decorative embellishment is there but hardly separable from the poem's deep structure. The pictorialism is biographical, for Melville is obviously moved, in a thoroughly personal way, by this story and the drawing of a beautiful female poisoner about to be executed for her crimes, in the same way that he found himself moved by a similar story and a portrait of Beatrice Cenci. What that personal commitment is, we are hardly privileged to say, but a guess might be hazarded that it is involved with the deaths of innocence, sometimes by violence, within the Melville family: that of the father; of Gansevoort, the wayward and successful brother; of Fly, the close friend who declined into a senseless, debilitating disease and pointless, innocent death; of Malcolm, the son, the beloved Mackie, insufficiently understood by a too lately repentant father, after his suicide; of Stanwix, the other son, promising but shiftless, self-condemned to an early death.

The ideological and interpretive elements in Torgovnick's plan are recognizable in the poem, but they tend to blend together. As Torgovnick points out, ideological use of the visual arts encompasses major themes in politics, society, history, or "reality," as well as a possible theory of fiction (19). Melville allows the pictorialism in his poem to offer a view of such a "reality" in the dubious feelings of the observing commentator, confounded by the painful anomaly of the mild portrait dedicated to sentient evil. And, finally, Melville seems to propound and practice a theory of poetry of a sort that is radical in its cloistered inwardness.

Melville seems to give much consideration to the effectiveness of literary pictorialism in working out the technical problems inherent in his poetic practice. His meditations upon the art analogy result in some troubling metaphors in "The Bench of Boors," an iconic poem that draws its initial impulse from the painting by David Teniers and then goes on to internalize the artistic debate between the boozy comforts of the lower, animal faculty and the aching necessities of intelligence and active creation. As the poem's speaker views the Teniers painting of a tavern scene, a fine example of the Dutch school of genre painting so admired by Melville and some of his contemporaries, he builds a little dramatic scene in which he is the chief actor. Unable to sleep, he considers the peasants portrayed by Teniers as unburdened by the labor of thought. This reflection should give him comfort, but, instead, he is left sleepless and uncomfortable by the workings of his own active imagination and has to conclude that "Thought's eager sight / Aches—overbright!" Wanting to reject the boozy restfulness of the boors, he is not satisfied with his own meditative capacities, burdened as they are with their concomitant restraints.

The literary pictorialism in the poem is exemplary and sophisticated, drawing upon a painterly vocabulary of considerable extent to describe the picture's chief points of interest. In what is, after all, a dark picture, the color patterns used by Teniers are strongly emphasized: the peasants are "embrowned," and the inn is a "hazy hovel," lit only by an "ember-mound." The lighting source for the picture is dim, and in the "pipe-bowl lights" the shapes tend to be part of the haze. The poet is interested, as well, in the disposition of the varied forms depicted, and in his description he attempts to evoke them for the reader, who is trying to imagine the appearance of the painting. The overall impression of the indoors structure is one of cramped vertical spaces; in a kind of refrain, on three separate occasions, the poem describes the scene as taking place "within low doors." Though frozen into their poses by the artist, the boors are depicted as if in sluggish action. They laze, yawn, and doze; they bask and "snugly hug the ember-mound"; they blink, their eyelids fall, and they take cat-naps. To the static overall effect of the painting, Melville attaches a dynamic sense of movement in slow motion.

Melville writes as an observant and experienced viewer of paintings, focusing his attention and the reader's upon the salient details that merge into the experience of understanding a work of visual art. The poems in *Timoleon* that consider architecture embody the essential characteristics of that art. What the poet sees in his descriptions of Greek buildings is the clarity of line and light. In "The Attic Landscape," he points out the "Pure outline pale, a linear charm" in which the "clear-cut hills" and temples will "share their sculptured grace." Following this notion of an art of clarity, he is able, in "The Parthenon," to describe the building from various vantage points: from afar, where it is "estranged in site"; from a nearer location, where details can be descried and described; and, finally, from a very near vantage point, where he is close enough to examine its frieze in close detail, with "eyes that do but revel" in the harmonious, artistically composed structure.

In his architectural poems, as Catherine Georgoudaki has demonstrated, Melville seems much concerned to elicit "the idea of unity between art and Nature"; as she points out, this view is contrary to the notes in his journal, which speak of a "strange contrast of rugged rock with polished temple" ("Melville's Artistic Use" 150–51). It seems likely that the poetic imagination, brooding for years upon its materials, its first opinions reshaped by further study, reading, and observation, has, like the imagination of the visual artist, engaged in "pentimento," a kind of "repenting" in which the artist paints a different picture over the original. In the Italian poems in the volume, softened shapes dominate the literary pictorialism. Such poems as "Pisa's Leaning Tower" and "Milan Cathedral" are examples. In the poem, "In a Church of Padua," the scrupulously detailed description allows the poet to visualize the vertical lines of the church vault and the door as a frame of darkness, suitable for the somberness of his theme. The dark shapes of the church itself encompass the equally dark shapes of the penitents who seek consolation in the confessional, which is portrayed as a "dread diving-bell" in which the priest descends into the sinner's soul as though he descends into the ocean's deeper darkness.

In bringing *Timoleon* to a close, Melville composed "L'Envoi," a poem that can seem somewhat puzzling. But, viewed in the light of the many art poems in the volume, it takes on an added point. The speaker is the Sire de Nesle, a seventeenth-century man, and, at the same time, an avatar, perhaps, of Melville himself. Transcripts of this much-revised poem indicate that Melville had considered placing it in the sixteenth century, possibly to make his protagonist a more clearly delineated Renaissance figure (Jarrard 286). His rovings, now coming to an end, have taken him through a morass of dead beliefs, or beliefs that cannot now be reanimated by faith, or possibly even by art. Like the woman in "After the Pleasure Party," he has discovered that "never passion peace shall bring, / Nor Art inanimate for long / Inspire." Instead, he has concluded that his "yearning infinite recoils, / For terrible is earth." The knowledge and the understanding, so laboriously acquired in his travels, seem to offer little of value or comfort, since "knowledge poured by pilgrimage / Overflows the banks of man." That he must find sole comfort in home and wife, after seeking so much elsewhere and so vigorously, appears to confirm a truth that he would as soon not know. He has found out precisely what the youthful Ishmael found out in the ninety-fourth chapter of *Moby-Dick,* "that in all cases man must eventually lower, or at least shift, his conceit of attainable felicity; not placing it anywhere in the intellect or the fancy; but in the wife, the heart, the bed, the table, the saddle, the fire-side, the country."

Although "L'Envoi" contains no specific allusion to the art analogy, it is clear that the poet means the poem as a true envoy, a summation of the themes of the volume, themes more often than not defined by the terms of literary pictorialism. To apprehend the world in the conceptions and language of the sister arts is to cast an unusual and reflective light upon one's poetic perceptions and to bring the reader into a subtle, far-ranging association with the poem. Here Melville's conspectus of failures and successes within the visual arts allows him to frame a whole range of his experiences and inspirations within a suitable mode of creative thinking.

Classical Iconography in
the Aesthetics of *Billy Budd, Sailor*

GAIL COFFLER

Some years ago, at the Jean Paul Getty museum in Malibu, I stood before an antique bust of an extraordinarily handsome young man—his head all curls, his mouth full and sensuous, his chest remarkably muscular (Fig. 1). The portrait's warm naturalism made the subject almost human, though the pensive cast of his eyes hinted of otherworldliness. Altogether, the effect was both captivating and disturbingly familiar, and I was struck with a thought: this is Billy Budd. The inscription read "Antinous." Three weeks later, at the back of Melville's *Journal of a Visit to London,* I found Eleanor Melville Metcalf's notation: her grandfather had, in his last years, kept a bust of Antinous.[1]

What did Antinous, the lover of a Roman emperor, signify to Melville? To him, the beauty of Antinous was "pre-eminently Greek," as he wrote beside a line of "Laodamia" in his book of Wordsworth's poems.[2] Like the god Apollo whom he resembles, Antinous symbolizes the Greek idea of perfect male beauty. Key icons in Melville's final work, both the *Apollo* and the *Antinous* are models for his hero and sources for his theme. More importantly, these ancient figures are a cynosure for Melville in his creation of a classic work of art.

What made the Handsome Sailor an object of reverence? The narrator tells us: "It was Strength and Beauty."[3] These essential attributes of the Handsome Sailor are elements of a dialectic that Melville associated with Rome and Greece; and these same attributes—Strength and Beauty—define the aesthetic of *Billy Budd, Sailor.*

Fig. 1. Bust of Antinous. Courtesy of the National Museum, Athens.

In Melville's age, the Greco-Roman heritage was the strongest cultural force in America, influencing both structure and image in government, law, education, architecture, and sculpture. Melville could hardly escape its effect, nor did he. In his youth he was active in the Ciceronian Debate Society and later became the outspoken president of the Philo Logos debating club. At the Albany Classical School he studied ancient history and Latin and returned after his graduation for an advanced course in Latin. Aside from schooltexts, where the number of references to the ancients equalled or surpassed those to the Bible, his exposure to classical history and myth was constant. The popular periodicals as well as the best literature continually compared America with Rome, and drew analogies between celebrated moderns and their ancient forebears. And in America, as in England, politicians aligned themselves either on the side of the "Romans" (conservatives, Whigs), who believed in the efficacy of institutions, or on the side of the "Greeks" (liberals, Democrats), who put their faith in humanity.[4]

The extensive allusions that enrich *Moby-Dick* and all his other works testify to Melville's continuous interest in classical history and myth. On the trip to Greece and Rome in 1856–57, he gained a firsthand education in ancient art. The immediate impact of classical sculpture on Melville's thought is documented in the journal of that trip and in the lecture "Statues in Rome," which he delivered in 16 cities the next year.[5] But the real contribution of classical models to his philosophy of art is revealed in both the form and the content of the important later works: *Battle-Pieces, Clarel, Timoleon,* and, especially, *Billy Budd, Sailor.*

Exactly where and when Melville obtained his sculptured *Antinous* is not known. Like the *Apollo Belvedere,* the icon was a fashionable objet d'art in the Victorian period; Hawthorne kept a bust of Antinous in the parlor of the little red house in Lenox, where Melville surely would have noticed it (Mellow 321). On his trip to Italy, Melville saw many original statues and portraits of Antinous, recording his impressions of some of these in his journal and in his lecture. Later still, the youth who gave up his life for Rome may well have reminded Melville of the young soldiers whose lives were cut short in the Civil War. By the time he came to write *Billy Budd,* in any case, the image of Antinous might have acquired deeper personal meaning for him: Antinous was that god worshiped by parents grieving for a son, and Melville had lost his own two sons—first Malcolm, called "Barney," who took his own life at 18, and then Stanwix, who died shortly before Melville began to write his narrative.[6] These several associations, along with the legendary beauty of the young man, may explain Melville's possession of the *Antinous.* Moreover, he was certain to have been attracted by the mysteries that permeate the Antinous myth as well as by the mythologizing process itself.

For centuries after his death, Antinous was famed throughout the Roman Empire as "Hadrian's Favorite." In the Western world his name is still synonymous with the love of man for man, and few figures in history have been the subject of as much moral controversy.[7] In the eyes of his devotees he was a god, oftentimes the avatar of a special deity—Dionysus, Osiris, Mithras, Hermes, or Apollo. He was likened to Memnon and, typifying the love in male friendship, to Achilles; for many he was the personification of Eros or of Ganymede, the boy-lover of Zeus; to the Christian fathers, outraged by comparisons of Christ with Antinous, he was the "odious catamite," the despicable god of pederasty (Lambert 60, 194). After Hadrian's death, the Antinous cult was suppressed, and then, with the rise of Christianity, the worship of Antinous was stamped out in the larger battle against paganism; the faith survived surreptitiously, however, and though most of his statues were destroyed, many remained hidden and preserved. In the late eighteenth century, renewed enthusiasm for the beauty of Antinous arose through the publication of Winckelmann's seminal work, *The History of Ancient Art,* and led to the nineteenth-century romanticization of the relationship between Antinous and Hadrian (Lambert 9, 195).

According to legend, Antinous was a native of Bithynia, a country in the region of Thrace, whose people claimed descent from the Arcadians (Lambert 41). On one of his travels, Hadrian saw the adolescent Antinous. An ardent Hellenophile, the emperor immediately fell in love with the boy's perfect beauty and brought him to Rome to be his companion. Several years later, Antinous was sailing with Hadrian in Egypt when an oracle proclaimed that the emperor would die unless someone dear to him was immolated for his preservation. Upon hearing this, by the official account, Antinous drowned himself in the Nile. By Hadrian's decree, his beloved friend was deified. Coins were stamped with his portrait, the city Antinoopolis was built in Egypt, a religious cult was established to worship the new god, and effigies of the beautiful Greek youth were erected across the Roman Empire.[8] Though he was a true lover of Hellenic ideals, Hadrian also followed the tradition of Augustus in using Greek art as propaganda. Because he died for his emperor, Antinous exemplified the loyalty of provincial subjects to Rome, so that his image could be used to strengthen the empire's unity. In particular, the Antinous icon symbolized the marriage of Rome to Greece and helped to accomplish Hadrian's personal aim—to safeguard and promote the cultural legacy of Hellas (Lambert 41).

Whether Antinous voluntarily gave his life or was sacrificed for political reasons remains an insoluble mystery. Whatever the true nature of the incident, Antinous was surely a victim of his remarkable personal beauty. Paradoxically, though the liaison with the emperor led to his early death, the union gave him immortality, for by the power of Rome

Hadrian perpetuated the Greek beauty of Antinous through all manner of "measured forms."

Called the "chameleon of ancient art," Antinous appeared in many manifestations—from the *Delphi Antinous* and the *Farnese Antinous,* (Fig. 2), naturalistic sculptures of his human likeness, to the highly idealized statues portraying him as a god. In the journal of his trip to Rome in 1856–57, Melville recorded his impression of the *Antinous* at the Capitoline Museum: "Antinous, beautiful.—Walked to the Pincian Hill. . . . Fashion and Rank—preposterous posturing within stone's throw of Antinous. How little influence has truth on the world!"[9]

In reference to his death and rebirth, Antinous was often assimilated to the fertility god Dionysus, or to his Egyptian counterpart—the underworld deity Osiris, god of the regenerative Nile. Indeed, the erotic, Dionysian impulse informs the identifying facial characteristics of Antinous: the full mouth with curved upper lip; the large, "melting" eyes; and the distinctive curls extending over his forehead.

In his journal, Melville described the *Antinous* at the Villa Albani: "—along the walls—Antinous . . . head like *moss-rose . . . with curls & buds*—[the] rest *all simplicity* . . . hand full of flowers & eyeing them" (107; emphasis mine). Billy Budd as a type of the Antinous is clearly adumbrated in that journal description. The rose bud iconography, identifying Antinous with the fertility god Dionysus, also links this journal passage with a Greek youth who anticipates Billy Budd: the gay Cypriote, whose image appears twice in Melville's poetry. All three figures (Antinous, the Cypriote[s], Billy Budd) are physically alluring and seductively dangerous, like the "rose" in Melville's "Naples in the Time of Bomba":

> And, lo again I saw the Rose,
> The red red ruddy and royal Rose!
> Expanded more from *bud* but late
> Sensuous it lured, and took the tone
> Of some light taunting *Cyprian gay*
> In shadow deep of college-wall. . . .
> (*Collected Poems* 350; emphasis mine)

While the rose of Venus connotes sensual love and beauty, in Melville's imagination it also signifies the "soft" aesthetic of the lyrical romance which, like Hautia's flowers, would lure the seeker from his philosophical quest and the artist from his truthful, more sublime purpose.[10] For Melville, the rose is an emblem of earthly beauty, a reminder that art based on beauty, without the strengthening fiber of transcendent truth, cannot last.

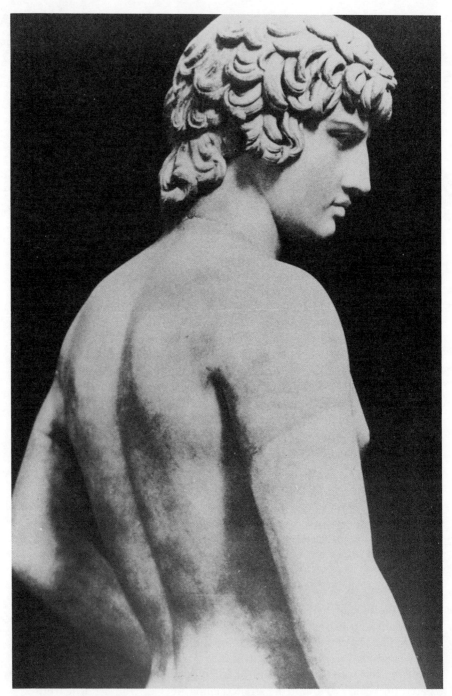

Fig. 2. The *Farnese Antinous*. Courtesy of the National Museum, Naples.

The lesson of the rose is further exemplified in the characterization of the gay Cypriote in *Clarel*. A false Apollo type, the handsome youth hails not from Apollo's Delos, as his good looks and his musicality led the pilgrims originally to think, but from Aphrodite's isle of Cyprus. The Cypriote, who retains the "gay Hellene lightheartedness" (289) of the pre-Christian Greek, typifies physical charm, as ephemeral as the rose of Venus. This "gold canary" pleases the company of pilgrims temporarily, but his song is soon forgotten: "Brief visitant, / It makes no lasting covenant; / It brings, but cannot leave, the ray" (291). The Cypriote's verse tells its own fate, which is the fate of all art that is merely beautiful:

"With a rose in thy mouth
  Through the world lightly *veer:*
Rose in the mouth
  Makes a rose of the year!
.   .   .   .
With the Prince of the South
  O'er the Styx bravely steer:
Rose in the mouth
  And a wreath on the bier!"
            (289–90; emphasis mine)

The lyrics sung by this young Greek recall the story of Antinous, with "moss-rose hair, curls and buds," sailing with the Emperor of Rome (Prince of the South), the sensuous, rosebud mouth of Antinous—his identifying trait—leading him to death in the Nile, and to the Styx in the Roman underworld (Fig. 3). At the same time, the Cypriote's song looks forward to the tale of Billy Budd, who sails with Vere and Claggart to his death. The word "veer" (to swerve) points to Captain Vere, whose name in Latin signifies "manliness" and "virtue" (*vir*) and also "truth" (*verus*), with all the contradictions that the terms imply. On another level, Vere's Latin name connects him with Hadrian and the Antonine emperors.

Shortly before his death, Hadrian arranged his succession, adopting Antoninus Pius on the condition that he, in turn, adopt as his sons and co-successors Marcus Aurelius and Lucius Verus, though the latter's reign was brief. By Gibbon's assessment, the age of Hadrian and the Antonines marked the high point of Western civilization. In a letter to John Hoadley, Melville said that his poem "The Age of the Antonines" was "suggested by a passage in Gibbon" (*Letters* 258). Despite the poem's underlying irony, Melville seems to agree in part with Gibbon and to admire what he called in his lecture "the fiery audaciousness of Roman power,"

Fig. 3. Close-up of the *Farnese Antinous*. Courtesy of the National Museum, Naples.

preferring it to the hypocritic idealism of modern demagogues: "We sham, we shuffle while faith declines— / They were frank in the Age of the Antonines" (*Collected Poems* 235).

In *Clarel*, Marcus Aurelius is praised by one of Melville's noblest characters. The Civil War veteran Ungar, whose sensibility Walter Bezanson describes as "very close to Melville's own," discusses the question of reform with Derwent, the meliorist Anglican clergyman.[11] Arguing against the feasibility of reform, the stoical military veteran chides the Anglican for his truth-skimming optimism and directs him to Roman history:

> "Go ask Aurelius Antonine,
> A Caesar wise, grave, just, benign,
> Lord of the world—why, in the calm
> Which through his reign the empire graced—
> Why he, that most considerate heart
> Superior, and at vantage placed,
> Contrived no secular reform,
> Though other he knew not, nor balm." (477)

The reign of Marcus Aurelius marked the furthest reach of the Roman Empire, geographically and culturally. By all historical accounts, the emperor himself was a modest man of great moral virtue. Warrior, writer, statesman, and stoic philosopher, this "Lord of the world" was also a man of contradictions. Though he was an Hellenophile like his adoptive grandfather Hadrian, Marcus Aurelius was unsympathetic to the devotees of Antinous; following the lead of Antoninus Pius, he ordered the eradication of the cult. Famed for his clemency, he was nevertheless the severe persecutor of Christians, whom he perceived as a serious threat to Roman authority. Where his own family was concerned, however, Marcus Aurelius was "erroneously indulgent" and "insensible" to defects. Tragically, he let his heart rule in choosing his successor—his natural son, a hero of the people, celebrated as the "Hercules" of Rome, for having in his youth killed countless opponents in the gladiator ring. In spite of the father's "unremitting" efforts, the son's dissolute character could not be reformed, and with the ascension of the brutal Commodus, the Roman Empire began its decline (Anthon 150–51).

Does Melville believe that reform is possible? "Go ask Aurelius Antonine," the veteran Ungar tells the pilgrims in *Clarel*. Following his directive, one finds on the title page of the *Meditations* the stoic emperor's original name: Marcus Aurelius *Verus* (emphasis mine).

Captain Vere, like virtually all of Melville's other officers and authority figures, is presented as a Roman, one "never to be scourged," a condition Melville associates with Roman citizenship.[12] Like Marcus Aurelius, Vere is of "stoical" exterior (115); the austere devotee of military duty, he speaks of the "imperial" conscience to which the private conscience should yield (111). Vere serves the Roman God of War, Mars (120), and the ship he commands has a Latin name—*Bellipotent,* meaning "strong in war," or, with a Melvillean twist, "beautiful and strong."

Finally, Vere's battle with the *Atheist* is the very meeting prophesied by Rolfe, the central figure of *Clarel* and the character whose view is most wholistic. Discussing revolution with the Anglican, Rolfe applauds Rome's "camp of tried instruction" and "her swordsmen of the priestly sword" (231). Whether in states or creeds, "men get tired at last of being free" (233), asserts Rolfe, as he predicts the sequel to rebellion:

> " . . . Who's gained by all the sacrifice
> Of Europe's revolutions? who?
> The Protestant? the Liberal?
> I do not think it—not at all:
> *Rome and the Atheist* have gained:
> *These two shall fight it out*—these two."
>
> (233; emphasis mine)

Destined to battle the *Atheist,* Vere is Rome—authority opposing anarchy; in keeping order he believes that "forms, measured forms, are everything" (128), just as Rome successfully used forms to unite and control the many disparate elements of her state and later of her church.

Impressed from the *Rights of Man* to serve the modern Empire, Billy is not a Roman, but "the good rustic out of his latitude in the Rome of the Caesars" (53). His barbaric beauty calls to mind the prized captives of Roman legions, "living trophies, made to march in the Roman triumph of Germanicus" (120), or the "British converts" brought to Rome, whom the Pope compared with the "angels" of the Hesperides, painted by Angelico (120–21).

Billy embodies the physical and moral attributes of a pagan or pre-Christian hero. He is compared to Adam before the fall, to the comely young David, and to Achilles being tutored by Chiron. Close-reefing top-sails, Billy is "Alexander curbing the fiery Bucephalus" (44), an image prefigured by the Cypriote in *Clarel,* as he rides into the pilgrims' view:

> How fair
> And light he leaned with easeful air
> Backward in saddle, so to frame
> A counterpoise as down he came.
> . . . .
> Young he was, and graced

> With fortunate aspect, such as draws
> Hearts to good will by natural laws.
> No furtive scrutiny he made,
> But frankly flung salute. (287)

The image above of the fair and frank young Cypriote, as he is first seen by the pilgrims of *Clarel,* is recalled in *Billy Budd,* when the man-of-war's crew first glimpses Billy, making farewell salute to the *Rights-of-Man:*

> if satire it was in effect, it was hardly so by intention, for Billy, though happily endowed with the gaiety of high health, youth, and a free heart, was yet by no means of a satirical turn. The will to it and the sinister dexterity were alike wanting. To deal in double meaning and insinuations of any sort was quite foreign to his nature. (49)

In accordance with the Greek belief that a man's exterior reflects his inner nature, Billy's moral goodness matches his outward beauty. He has the "humane look of reposeful good nature which the Greek sculptor in some instances gave to his heroic strong man, Hercules" (51). And, like the *Farnese Hercules* that Melville described in his lecture, Billy is characterized by "simplicity and bovine good nature," his strength being "reserved only for great occasions" ("Statues in Rome," *Piazza Tales and Other Prose* 406).

The unintellectual Hercules acted without calculation, and Billy is likewise characterized by simplicity of mind, a trait linking him again with Antinous, who was said by some to be only "partly lettered" and a mere "creature of the senses" (Lambert 63); his very name (anti-nous) in both Latin and Greek means "anti-mind" or "anti-intellectual." Similarly, Billy has "no sharpness of faculties or any trace of the wisdom of the serpent" (52); in the narrative's scheme, Billy's provincial innocence stands opposed to the urbane intelligence of the serpent Claggart.

Claggart's lie and Vere's insistence upon truth force the confrontation of Mind and Nature, of the intellectual and the sensual, of the rational and the spontaneous. When Billy's fist instinctively strikes Claggart's "intellectual brow," the opposing elements are imagistically joined, fused in the vision of Vere, who recognizes the divine archetype of beauty and knows he must serve as its executor: "Struck dead by the angel of God! Yet the angel must hang!" (101).

In *Billy Budd, Sailor,* archetypal participants enact Melville's theory of art in a dramatic analogue to John Ruskin's philosophy of art. Melville may have been familiar with *Six Lectures on Sculpture,* where Ruskin defined "Art wisdom" as "the knowledge of good and evil, and the love of good." He went on: "The true image-maker will idolise and force us also to idolise whatever is living and virtuous and victoriously right, opposing to it in some definite mode the image of the conquered evil."[13] Pertinently, Ruskin claimed that "*Verity* can only be known by our confession of the divine seal of *strength and beauty* upon the tempered frame and known in the fervent heart" (91; emphasis mine).

Vere's response to the scene before him illustrates the operation of the theoretic faculty, without which, according to Ruskin, there can be no *moral perception of beauty*. In *Modern Painters* (Sealts no. 431), Ruskin distinguishes between the "aesthetic" vision, which is the sensual perception of outward beauty, and *theoria,* which transcends both intellectual and sensual perception in its concern with the "idea" of beauty. When Vere recognizes Billy as the archetypal righteous angel, his moment of comprehension resembles what Ruskin calls the "exulting, reverent, and grateful perception" of Beauty as "something divine." This spiritual response, Ruskin argues, constitutes the only full contemplation of Beauty—as "a gift of God" that elevates the being of the beholder.[14]

The intellectual quality absent in the character of Billy Budd is undeniably present in *Billy Budd, Sailor,* the work of art, where moral intelligence is superimposed by the icon of Apollo, the god of art and the symbol of perfected manhood.

In Melville's theory of art, no icon is more important than the Apollo—the voice of prophecy, the bringer of light, the master of the muses, and the archer whose shafts bring sudden death to men. In the nineteenth century, as Edwin H. Miller has observed, Apollo-worship reached cult proportions, particularly among artists. The parlor of the Hawthornes' Berkshires home contained a cast of Apollo (as well as the one of Antinous), and, as Miller has noted, "Apollo" was Sophia's pet name for her own handsome husband (Miller 47, 51).[15] Long before he knew Hawthorne, however, Melville alluded to the beauty of Apollo, beginning with the first "Fragment from a Writing Desk," where the narrator refers to himself as being "beautiful as Apollo" (192). In *Typee,* the god-like Marnoo is the "Polynesian Apollo," whose back is tattooed with the graceful lines of the "Artu" tree. *Mardi's* Taji calls himself the god from the sun, while in *White-Jacket,* the maintop over which Jack Chase presides is a sort of "oracle at Delphi" (13).

By the time he came to write *Billy Budd, Sailor,* Melville was acquainted with many artistic renditions of Apollo, but the primary model for his aesthetic ideal was undoubtedly the *Apollo Belvedere,* celebrated in Melville's time as the most perfect work of art ever executed. The original Greek bronze, lost centuries ago, was a Hellenistic work of Alexander's time. The marble copy that survives, the *Apollo* that

Melville saw in the Vatican museum, is actually a Roman work, executed in the age of the Antonines (Fig. 4). In the lecture "Statues in Rome," Melville called the *Apollo Belvedere* the "crowning glory" of the Vatican: "How well in the Apollo is expressed the idea of the perfect man. Who could better it? Can art, not life, make the ideal?" (408).

His arm drawn back as he prepares to slay an adversary, the *Apollo Belvedere* portrays the god in the role of "Deliverer from Evil." An art critic of Melville's acquaintance described the statue, noting that the god is engaged in a violent act, yet his noble attitude expresses the "indomitable moral superiority and power" of the Apollonian being.[16] For Winckelmann, the *Apollo Belvedere* embodied "the highest ideal of art" (312), and Goethe praised it in his *Autobiography* (Sealts no. 228). According to *Anthon's Classical Dictionary,* a reference work Melville almost certainly used, the *Apollo Belvedere* represented "the perfection of united manly *strength and beauty,*"[17] the same qualities that Melville attributes to the Handsome Sailor in *Billy Budd* (44; emphasis mine).

In the *Analysis of Beauty,* William Hogarth distinguished between the loveliness of the *Antinous* and "the remarkable beauty in the *Apollo Belvedere;* which hath given it the preference even to the Antinous: I mean a super-addition of greatness." Comparing the two statues side by side, Hogarth wrote, "These two master-pieces of art are seen together in the same place at Rome, where the Antinous fills the spectator with admiration only, whilst the Apollo strikes him with surprise, and . . . an appearance of something *more than human*" (100).

The beauty of the *Apollo,* coolly austere as compared with the warmer realism of the *Antinous,* befits his Olympian stature. The son of the supreme god Zeus/Jupiter, Apollo was born of an earthly mother, and for a time he served King Admetus, disguised as an ordinary mortal— the shepherd to whom Melville alludes in describing the austere Vine, in *Clarel:*

> No trace
> Of passion's soil or lucre's stain . . .
>
> .   .   .   .
>
> Apollo slave in Mammon's mine?
> Better Admetus' shepherd lie. (94)

By slaying the Python that guarded the shrine at Delphi, Apollo became the god of prophecy, the ambiguous voice of the Delphic Oracle. The heroic act by which Apollo attained godhood was often portrayed in art; Melville himself owned an engraved print of Turner's famous *Apollo Killing the Python.*[18]

Fig. 4. The *Apollo Belvedere*. Courtesy of the Vatican Museum, Rome.

Several parallels exist between the tale of Billy Budd and the myth of Apollo. As Apollo was the simple shepherd of a king, Billy is a common sailor in the king's navy. Though an orphan of unknown origin, Billy is of "noble descent," and when asked who his father is, his enigmatic reply is "God knows." When Billy boards Vere's ship lugging his chest, the lieutenant remarks, "Here he comes, by Jove, Apollo with his portmanteau" (48). Apollo is the god of music; Billy is a "goldfinch" with a melodious singing voice and is sometimes "the composer of his own song" (52). Performing his foretop duties, Billy is "one of the lazy gods," brilliant against the blue sky—an aerial figure, suggestive of the golden-haired sun god.

In slaying Claggart, Billy enacts Apollo's role of the moral avenger, whose arm brings sudden death to man. Claggart's glance is one of "serpent fascination" (98), and, after being struck by Billy, he lies like a "dead snake" on the cabin floor (99). Apollo was transformed after slaying the python; Billy, after killing Claggart, is no longer the innocent "Baby" Budd, the "sweet and pleasant fellow." Through the closeting with Vere, Billy undergoes expiation and purification; he is transformed, the narrator tells us, "spiritualized now through late experiences so poignantly profound" (123). At Billy's hanging, the self-control exhibited in the "phenomenal" absence of body movement causes speculation among the witnesses. The purser wonders if Billy's death might have exemplified "will power" or even a "species of euthanasia." To this, the surgeon replies, "*Euthanasia,* Mr. Purser, is something like your *will power:* I doubt its authenticity as a scientific term—begging your pardon again. It is at once imaginative and metaphysical—in short, Greek" (125).

Melville's execution of *Billy Budd* is, to apply the surgeon's words quoted above, "imaginative and metaphysical—in short, Greek." The portrait of Billy is drawn from archetypes of beauty given form in Greek sculpture, forms that Melville repeatedly praised. Billy himself is a type of the Antinous—the Greek idea of male beauty incarnate in a living being, while *Billy Budd, Sailor* is an avatar of the Apollo, the divine archteype of Art. The first represents sensual, physical beauty that, like the rose, must die. The second is ideal, eternal beauty—informed essentially by moral and intellectual strength. The vision of combined "strength and beauty" (44) that underlies the tale's aesthetic derives from Melville's understanding of classical art.

Billy's simplicity, symbolizing his natural innocence, belies the complex moral truth of *Billy Budd, Sailor;* and this same contradiction, according to Ruskin, is art's legacy from the Greeks: "Greek art is the root of all simplicity, and, on the other side, of all complexity" (*Lectures* 174). In his lectures on the elements of sculpture, Ruskin referred to the

Greek ideal as the sceptre handed down by Apollo, "the first type of rightness," who "rules the arts to this day." It is "the work of the Greek," Ruskin continued, "to give health to what was diseased, and chastisement to what was untrue" (174–75).

Just as *Billy Budd, Sailor* is Greek in its delineation of physical beauty and metaphysical truth, it is Greek, too, in its transcendental idealism, arising from the wealth of allusions, classical and biblical, that comprise the archetype of the Handsome Sailor. The figure of Billy is idealized in the manner demonstrated by Winckelmann in *The History of Ancient Art* (Sealts no. 559). Because it is "almost impossible to find in nature a figure like that of the *Apollo* of the Vatican," said Winckelmann, "those wise artists, the ancients, sought to unite in one the beautiful parts of many beautiful bodies" (2: 314–15).

While the beauty of Billy Budd is Greek, the strength of Melville's tale is Roman, as personified in Vere, who expresses the typical Roman concern for the *res publica,* the welfare of the state, combined with an aspiration for power. Vere stands for law and authority, for structure and tradition, for the strength of all the "measured forms" that the Romans valued above ethereal beauty. Melville's admiration for Rome's power to preserve is revealed in the conclusion of his "Statues in Rome" lecture, where he draws a telling analogy: "As the Roman arch enters into and sustains our best architecture, does not the Roman spirit still animate and support whatever is soundest in societies and states? Or shall the scheme of Fourier supplant the code of Justinian?" (408). He then asks his audience to compare the fragile Crystal Palace with the durable Coliseum of Rome: "Will the glass of the one bide the hail storms of eighteen centuries as well as the travertine of the other?" (409).

Roman, too, is the element of realism in *Billy Budd, Sailor.* It was the Romans who brought verisimilitude into art by introducing character lines to their sculptured portraits. The face of the *Apollo Belvedere,* by way of contrast, is line-free and serene, typically idealized in the Greek manner. "A good *Greek* artist does not represent the agony of the contest," says Ruskin, who uses the *Apollo* as his precise example (*Lectures* 165; emphasis mine). At the critical moment, however, Melville violates the Greek rule. By showing Billy's agony in the contest with Claggart, he introduces (Roman) verism and gives the scene a powerful immediacy. Indeed, many details of the story were drawn from real life—from Melville's own sea experiences, from events in his personal history, and from other actual sources, such as the Somers mutiny and the life of Nelson.

This same subtle combining of idealism and realism distinguishes Roman art in the age of Hadrian and the Antonines, when "Augustan classicism and Republican verism" were equally valued by artists and kept in balance, with realism leaving the greater mark on successive generations (Erhart 9).[19] The union of idealism and verism accomplishes what Melville, in *The Confidence-Man,* declared that the art of fiction should do: "It is with fiction as with religion: it should present another world, and yet one to which we feel the tie," for the audience wants both novelty and nature, "but nature unfettered, exhilarated, in effect transformed" (183).[20]

In the creation of art, "unlike things must meet and mate," writes Melville in the poem "Art." For art to materialize from its evanescent "unbodied scheme," the abstract ideal must be infused with life and given intelligible form.

> In placid hours well-pleased we dream
> Of many a brave unbodied scheme.
> But form to lend, pulsed life create,
> What unlike things must meet and mate. . . .

Vere, then, represents the comprehensive vision the artist must possess in order to unite oppositions and execute his idea, which is to say, give it satisfactory form. In all three senses of the word "execute," he must paradoxically "annihilate" natural truth/beauty so that he might "carry out" the higher objective, which is to "create" truth/beauty in its ideal form.[21] In Melville's vision, this ideal form, or "divine" art, was represented by the *Apollo Belvedere* (Fig. 5). This statue, he said in his lecture,

> is not a mere work of art . . . for there is a kind of divinity in it, that lifts the imagination of the beholder above "things rank and gross in nature". . . .
> [It] gives a visible response to that class of human aspirations of beauty and perfection that . . . cannot be truly gratified except in another world. ("Statues in Rome," *Piazza Tales and Other Prose* 402)

Melville believed that the Apollo Belvedere had inspired Milton "to a great degree" and that the angel Zephon was "an exact counterpart of the *Apollo,*" which seemed "to embody the attributes, physical and intellectual, that Milton bestowed upon his angel" ("Statues in Rome," *Piazza Tales and Other Prose* 403).

In the creation of Billy Budd, his own "angel of God," Melville appears to have been similarly influenced by the statues in Rome. From them, he gained a deeper understanding of classic form, with its stress upon the integration of various parts in a unified and harmonious whole. In the decade following his trip and his lecture, he turned from the radically modern prose of *The Confidence-Man* to the measured lines of *Battle-Pieces.* The shattering reality of the Civil War, along with his own emotional fragmentation, may well have contributed to the new

Fig. 5. Close-up of the *Apollo Belvedere*. Courtesy of the Vatican Museum, Rome.

direction of his work, with its structural as well as thematic emphasis upon the maintenance of unity through form. Melville's poems, as Milton Stern has acutely observed, are "constant testimonials to the crucial importance of art as order" (Stern xvi). "The discipline of arms refines," concedes Melville, in "Commemorative of a Naval Victory." And in the poem "Dupont's Round Fight" he uses military order as a metaphor for both artistic discipline and cosmic law:

> In time and measure perfect moves
> All art whose aim is sure;
> Evolving rhyme and stars divine
> Have rules, and they endure.

This opening stanza shows Melville's conviction that without preservative form, there can be no lasting beauty, no enduring truth. At the end of the poem, the "rebel" is necessarily sacrificed to the law of unity: "A type was here / And victory of LAW." These final lines anticipate the judgment against Billy in Melville's last work, where the military imperative again signifies the law of art. Starry Vere assigns Billy to "holy oblivion." But precisely through the captain's (and Melville's) severe imposition of order, the beautiful sailor, "now spiritualized," assumes the "diviner magnanimity" of a mythic figure (115). Through Vere's act, Billy's story transcends romance and achieves the stature of tragedy.[22]

In Melville's symbolic vision, finally, Rome and Greece express a political and aesthetic dichotomy. He admires, on the one hand, the idealism associated with Greece—the independent, humanistic spirit of her democracy, the quest for ideal truth informing her philosophy, and the love of lyrical beauty, incarnated preeminently in Greek sculpture. On the other hand, he recognizes the necessity of material realism as a counterweight to ethereal idealism. After his visit to Greece, Rome, and the Levant, and after the fragmentation of the Civil War years, Melville developed an enlarged respect for the unifying and preservative powers encompassed in the idea of "Rome," as exhibited in Roman law, in Roman architecture, in the military order that solidified the Roman Empire, and in the assimilative catholicity of the Roman Church. The forms and themes of *Battle-Pieces* show Melville's new insistence upon structure, order, and tradition—"Roman" qualities that become more visible in the architectonics of *Clarel*.

Throughout his career, Melville experimented with form, achieving rare equilibrium in *Moby-Dick*, but failing in the matter of coherence in *Mardi* and *Pierre,* and falling short of lyrical expressiveness in much of the tightly structured poetry. At the end of his life, however, Melville balanced the strength of traditional form with the beauty of imaginative idea. Roman strength and Greek beauty: these attributes Melville revered, as testified by his execution of *Billy Budd, Sailor,* a work of art equal to its classical models in enduring resonance.

Appendix A

Books on the Visual Arts Owned or Borrowed
by Herman Melville

I am much indebted, for this listing, to Merton M. Sealts, Jr.'s *Melville's Reading.* Almost all of the following titles, and publication information and notes, are to be found there.

Anthon, Charles. *Anthon's Classical Dictionary.* New York: Harper, 1852.

The Bijou; or Annual of Literature and the Arts. London: Pickering, 1828.

Boaden, James. *An Inquiry into the Authenticity of Various Pictures and Prints, Which, from the Decease of the Poet to Our Own Times, Have Been Offered to the Public as Portraits of Shakespeare. . . .* London: Triphook, 1824.

Bohn, Henry George. *A Guide to the Knowledge of Pottery, Porcelain, and Other Objects of Vertu. Comprising an Illustrated Catalogue of the Bernal Collection . . . To Which Are Added an Introductory Essay on Pottery and Porcelain, and an Engraved List of Marks and Monograms. . . .* London: Bohn, 1857.

Braun, Emil. *Handbook of the Ruins and Museums of Rome. A Guide for Travellers, Artists and Lovers of Antiquity.* Brunswick: Frederick Vieweg; Rome: J. Spithöver, 1856.

Brock-Arnold, George Moss. *Gainsborough [and Constable].* New York: Scribner and Welford, 1881.

Burke, Edmund. *A Philosophical Inquiry into the Origin of Our Ideas of the Sublime and Beautiful with an Introductory Discourse concerning Taste. . . .* Philadelphia: Johnson, 1806.

Burnet, John. *A Treatise on Painting. . . .* London: Carpenter, 1834–37. 4[?]v. in 1.

Chambers, Ephraim. *Cyclopaedia: or, An Universal Dictionary of Arts and Sciences. . . .* London: Knapton [etc.], 1728. 2 vols.

Cundall, Frank. *The Landscape and Pastoral Painters of Holland: Ruisdael, Hobbema, Cuijp, Potter. . . .* New York: Scribner and Welford, 1891.

Dullea, Owen John. *Claude Gelée le Lorrain. . . .* New York: Scribner and Welford, 1887.

Duplessis, Georges. *The Wonders of Engraving . . . Illustrated with Ten Reproductions in Autotype; and Thirty-Four Wood Engravings, by P. Sellier.* London: Low and Marston, 1871.

Eastlake, Sir Charles L. *Contributions to the Literature of the Fine Arts. . . .* London: Murray, 1848.

———. *Materials for a History of Oil Painting. . . .* London: Longman [etc.], 1847.

Forsyth, Joseph. *Remarks on Antiquities, Arts, and Letters during an Excursion in Italy, in the Years 1802 and 1803....* 3rd ed. London: Murray, 1824. 2 vols.

Gilchrist, Alexander. *Life of William Blake, "Pictor Ignotus." With Selections from his Poems and Other Writings, by the Late Alexander Gilchrist ... Illustrated from Blake's Own Works, in Fascimilé by W. J. Linton, and in Photolithography; with a Few of Blake's Original Plates....* London: Macmillan, 1863. 2 vols.

Gower, Lord Ronald Charles Sutherland-. *The Figure Painters of Holland, by Lord Ronald Gower....* New York: Scribner and Welford, 1880.

Grimm, Jakob Ludwig Karl. *German Popular Stories, with Illustrations after the Original Designs of George Cruikshank.* Edited by Edgar Taylor, with Introduction by John Ruskin. London: Hotten, 1868.

Haydon, Benjamin Robert. *Life of Benjamin Robert Haydon, Historical Painter, from His Autobiography and Journals.* Edited and Compiled by Tom Taylor.... New York: Harper, 1853. 2 vols.

Haydon, Benjamin Robert, and William Hazlitt. *Painting and the Fine Arts: Being the Articles under Those Heads Contributed to the Seventh Edition of the Encyclopaedia Britannica, by B. R. Haydon ... and William Hazlitt....* Edinburgh: Black, 1838.

The Illustrated Magazine of Art: Containing Selections from the Various Departments of Painting, Sculpture, Architecture, History, Biography, Art-Industry, Manufactures, Scientific Inventions and Discoveries, Local and Domestic Scenes, Ornamental Works, etc., etc. New York: Montgomery, 1853–54. Vol. 1 (1853) only.

Jarves, James Jackson. *The Art-Idea: Part Second of Confessions of an Inquirer....* New York: Hurd and Houghton, 1864.

Jewitt, Llewellyn Frederick William. *The Ceramic Art of Great Britain from Pre-Historic Times down to the Present Day: Being a History of the Ancient and Modern Pottery and Porcelain Works of the Kingdom and of Their Productions of Every Class....* New York: Scribner, Welford, and Armstrong, 1878. 2 vols.

Keddie, Henrietta. *Childhood a Hundred Years Ago, by Sarah Tytler [pseud.] ... With Six Chromos after Paintings by Sir Joshua Reynolds.* London: Ward, 1877.

———. *Landseer's Dogs and Their Stories, by Sarah Tytler [pseud.]....* London: Ward, 1877.

King, Charles William. *The Handbook of Engraved Gems....* London: Bell and Daldy, 1866.

La Fontaine, Jean de. *Fables ... With Illustrations from Designs by J. J. Grandville.* Translated from the French by Elizur Wright, Jr. New York: Miller, [c. 1879].

Lanzi, Luigi Antonio. *The History of Painting in Italy, from the period of Revival of the Fine Arts to the End of the Eighteenth Century; Translated from the Italian ... By Thomas Roscoe....* New ed., revised. London: Bohn, 1847. 3 vols.

The Literary World. New York, [1847–53]. Melville's term of subscription: 1847[?]–Feb. 1852.

Loftie, William John. *Views in the English Lake District, from Original Drawings by T. L. Rowbotham ... with Descriptive Notes....* 2nd ed. London: Ward, 1875.

———. *Views in North Wales, from Original Drawings by T. L. Rowbotham ... with Descriptive Notes....* 2nd ed. London: Ward, 1875.

———. *Views in Scotland, from Original Drawings by T. L. Rowbotham ... with Descriptive Notes....* 2nd ed. London: Ward, 1875.

Macpherson, Robert. *Vatican Sculptures, Selected, and Arranged in the Order in Which They Are Found in the Galleries, Briefly Explained....* London: Chapman and Hall, 1863.

Mollet, John William. *Meissonier....* New York: Scribner and Welford, 1882.

————. *The Painters of Barbizon: Corot, Daubigny, Dupré.* . . . New York: Scribner and Welford, 1890.

————. *The Painters of Barbizon: Millet, Rousseau, Diaz.* . . . New York: Scribner and Welford, 1890.

————. *Rembrandt.* . . . New ed. London: Sampson Low, 1882.

————. *Sir David Wilkie.* . . . New York: Scribner and Welford, 1881.

Monkhouse, William Cosmo. *Turner.* . . . New York: Scribner and Welford, 1879.

Montalba, Anthony Reubens. *Fairy Tales from All Nations . . . With Twenty-Four Illustrations by Richard Doyle.* New York: Harper, 1850 [1849?].

Omar Khayyām. *Rubáiyát of Omar Khayyám, the Astonomer-Poet of Persia; Rendered into English Verse by Edward Fitzgerald, with an Accompaniment of Drawings by Elihu Vedder.* Boston: Houghton, Mifflin, [c. 1886].

Piles, Roger de. *The Art of Painting, with the Lives and Characters of above 300 of the Most Eminent Painters . . . Translated from the French . . . To Which is Added, An Essay towards an English School. The Third Edition: In Which Is Now First Inserted the Life of Sir Godfrey Kneller, by the Late B. Buckeridge . . . Who Wrote the Greatest Part of the English School.* London: Payne, [1754?].

Pulling, Frederick Sanders. *Sir Joshua Reynolds.* . . . London: Sampson Low, 1880.

Putnam's Magazine. Original Papers on Literature, Science, Art, and National Interests. New York, 1853–70. Melville's term of subscription uncertain.

Reynolds, Sir Joshua. *The Literary Works . . . To Which is Prefixed a Memoir of the Author; with Remarks on His Professional Character, Illustrative of His Principles and Practice. By Henry William Beechy . . . New and Improved Edition.* . . . London: Bohn, 1855. 2 vols.

Ruskin, John. *Modern Painters.* . . . London: Smith, Elder, 1846–60. 5 vols.

————. *Modern Painters . . . First American from the Third London Edition. Revised by the Author.* New York: Wiley, 1860–62. 5 vols.

Schiller, Johann Christoph Friedrich von. *Eight Sketches to Schiller's Fridolin, or The Message to the Forge. By Moritz Retzsch. With a Few Explanations, by C. A. Boettiger.* Stuttgart: Cotta, 1857.

————. *Schiller's Pegasus in the Yoke, with Explanations of the Illustrations. By Moritz Retzsch.* Stuttgart: Cotta, 1857.

Scott, Leader. *The Renaissance of Art in Italy: An Illustrated History.* New York: Scribner and Welford, 1883.

Scottish Art Review. Glasgow, 1888–89. Melville's holding: vol. 2 no. [?] (June–Dec. 1889), only.

Stephens, Frederic George. *A Memoir of George Cruikshank . . . and an Essay on the Genius of George Cruikshank by William Makepeace Thackeray.* New York: Scribner and Welford, 1891.

Valery, Antoine Claude Pasquin, known as. *Historical, Literary, and Artistical Travels in Italy, a Complete and Methodical Guide for Travellers and Artists . . . Translated with the Special Approbation of the Author, from the Second Corrected and Improved Edition by C. E. Clifton. With a Copious Index and a Road-Map of Italy.* Paris: Baudry, 1852.

Vasari, Giorgio. *Lives of the Most Eminent Painters, Sculptors, and Architects: Translated from the Italian . . . With Notes and Illustrations Chiefly Selected from Various Commentators. By Mrs. Jonathan Foster.* . . . London: Bohn, 1850–52. 5 vols. Borrowed by Melville: 4 [?] vols.

Walpole, Horace, Earl of Orford. *Anecdotes of Painting in England. Reprint of the Edition of 1786.* London: Alexander Murray, 1871.

Winckelmann, Johann Joachim. *The History of Ancient Art, Translated from the German . . . By G. Henry Lodge. . . .* Boston: Osgood, 1849–73. 4 vols.

Wordsworth, Christopher. *Greece: Pictorial, Descriptive, and Historical. . . .* 2nd ed. London: Orr, 1844.

The Works of Eminent Masters, in Painting, Sculpture, Architecture, and Decorative Art. . . . London: Cassell, 1854. 2 vols. in 1.

Yankee Doodle. New York, 1846–47.

Appendix B

Studies of Herman Melville and the Visual Arts: A Comprehensive Check-List

Adams, Karen Mary. "Black Images in Nineteenth-Century American Painting and Literature: An Iconological Study of Mount, Melville, Homer, and Mark Train." Diss. Emory U, 1977.

Adams, Timothy Dow. "Architectural Imagery in Melville's Short Fiction." *American Transcendental Quarterly* 44 (Fall 1979): 265–77.

Arvin, Newton. "Melville and the Gothic Novel." *New England Quarterly* 22 (March 1949): 33–48.

Birss, J. H. "Herman Melville and Blake." *Notes & Queries* 166, no. 18 (5 May 1934): 311.

Boudreau, Gordon V. "Of Pale Ushers and Gothic Piles: Melville's Architectural Symbology," *ESQ: A Journal of the American Renaissance* 18 (Second Quarter 1972): 67–82.

Carlson, Thomas C. "Melville as Art Critic: Double Metrical Irony in *Moby-Dick*," *Melville Society Extracts* 20 (Nov. 1974): 2–4.

Carothers, R. L. "Melville's 'Cenci': A Portrait of *Pierre*." *Ball State University Forum* 19 (1969): 53–59.

Coffler, Gail H. *Melville's Classical Allusions: A Comprehensive Index and Glossary.* Westport, CT: Greenwood, 1985.

———. "Melville, Dana, Allston: Analogues in *Lectures on Art*." *Melville Society Extracts* 44 (Nov. 1980): 1–6.

Cohen, Hennig, ed. *The Battle-Pieces of Herman Melville.* New York: Thomas Yoseloff, 1963.

———. "*Israel Potter:* Common Man as Hero." *A Companion to Melville Studies.* Ed. John Bryant. Westport, CT: Greenwood, 1986. 282.

———. "Melville's *Israel Potter* and Temple Church," *Melville Society Extracts* 76 (Feb. 1989): 9–13.

Cowen, Wilson Walker. "Melville's 'Discoveries': A Dialogue of the Mind with Itself." *The Recognition of Herman Melville: Selected Criticism since 1846.* Ed. Hershel Parker. Ann Arbor: U of Michigan P, 1967. 333–47.

———. "Melville's Marginalia." Diss. Harvard, 1965.

Dahl, Curtis. "The Architecture of Society and the Architecture of the Soul: Hawthorne's *The House of the Seven Gables* and Melville's *Pierre*." *University of Mississippi Studies in English* 5 (1984–87): 1–22.

———. "Arrowhead and the 'Razeed' Roof: An Architectural Speculation." *Melville Society Extracts* 55 (Sept. 1983): 5–7.

Dettlaff, Shirley M. "Ionian Form and Esau's Waste: Melville's View of Art in *Clarel*." *American Literature* 54 (May 1982): 212–28.

———. "Melville's Aesthetics." *A Companion to Melville Studies*. Ed. John Bryant. Westport, CT: Greenwood, 1986. 625–65; esp. "Fine Arts," 652–55, and "Works Cited," 658–65.

Eddy, D. Mathis. "Melville's Sicilian Moralist." *English Language Notes* 8 (March 1971): 191–200.

Frank, Stuart M. *Herman Melville's Picture Gallery*. Fairhaven, MA: Edward J. Lefkowicz, 1986.

Furrow, Sharon. "The Terrible Made Visible: Melville, Salvator Rosa, and Piranesi." *ESQ: A Journal of the American Renaissance* 19 (Fourth Quarter 1973): 237–53.

Garner, Stanton. "His (More Than) Fifty Years in Exile and Fanny's Toe." *Melville Society Extracts* 44 (Nov. 1980): 7–9.

———. "Melville and Sanford Gifford." *Melville Society Extracts* 48 (Nov. 1981): 10–12.

Georgoudaki, Catherine [Ekaterini]. "Ancient Greek and Roman Pieces of Art in Herman Melville's Iconography." *Scholarly Journal of the School of Philosophy of the Aristotelian University of Thessaloniki* 21 (1983): 84–95.

———. "*Battle-Pieces and Aspects of the War*: Melville's Poetic Quest for Meaning and Form in a Fallen World." *American Transcendental Quarterly*, New Series 1:1 (March 1987): 21–32.

———. *Melville's Artistic Use of His Journeys to Europe and the Near East*. Diss. Arizona State U, 1980.

Gilman, William H. *Melville's Early Life and Redburn*. New York: New York UP, 1951.

Glenn, Barbara. "Melville and the Sublime in *Moby-Dick*." *American Literature* 48 (May 1976): 165–82.

Gretchko, John M. J. "The Glassy-Eyed Hermit." *Melville Society Extracts* 48 (Nov. 1981): 14–15.

Heffernan, Thomas Farel. "Melville the Traveler." *A Companion to Melville Studies*. Ed. John Bryant. Westport, CT: Greenwood, 1986. 35–61.

Herbert, T. Walter, Jr. "The Osborne Collection." *Melville Society Extracts* 61 (Feb. 1985): 8–10. [Lists as "Personal Belongings of HM" two engravings from Melville's collection of art—(1) untitled open sailing boat in Harbor of New York by H. Feyner (?), 1879, and (2) bust of Napoleon by Joseph Longhi, 1806; and two J. M. W. Turner prints, *Abingdon, Berkshire* and *Brighton Chain Pier*.]

Hovanec, Carol P. "Melville as Artist of the Sublime: Design in 'The Tartarus of Maids.'" *Mid-Hudson Language Studies* 8 (1985): 41–51.

Howard, Leon. *Herman Melville: A Biography*. Berkeley: U of California P, 1951. 328–30.

Leyda, Jay. *The Melville Log: A Documentary Life of Herman Melville, 1819–1891*. 2 vols. 1951. Rpt. with a new supplement, New York: Gordian Press, 1969.

Litman, Vicki Halper. "The Cottage and the Temple: Melville's Symbolic Use of Architecture." *American Quarterly* 21 (Fall 1969): 630–38.

McCarthy, Paul. "Melville's Use of Painting in *Pierre*." *Discourse* 2 (1968): 490–505.

Mather, Frank Jewett, Jr. "Herman Melville." *The Review* 1 (Aug. 1919): 276–301. Rpt. in *The Recognition of Herman Melville*. Ed. Hershel Parker. Ann Arbor: U of Michigan P, 1967. 155–70.

Mathews, James W. "The Enigma of Beatrice Cenci: Shelley and Melville." *South Atlantic Review* 49, no. 2 (May 1984): 31–41.

Mazis, Glen A. "Modern Depths, Painting, and the Novel: Turner, Melville, and the Interstices." *Soundings: An Interdisciplinary Journal* 1–2 (Spring-Summer 1987): 121–44.

Moore, Richard S. *That Cunning Alphabet: Melville's Aesthetics of Nature.* Amsterdam: Rodopi, 1982.

———. "Piranesi, 'The Blanket,' and the 'Mathematical Sublime' in *Moby-Dick*." *Melville Society Extracts* 47 (Sept. 1981): 1–4.

Morsberger, Robert E. "Melville's 'The Bell-Tower' and Benvenuto Cellini." *American Literature* 44 (Nov. 1972): 459–62.

Planiscig, Leo. "Fasolato's Satan and Melville." *Art News* 50 (1952): 21.

Poenicke, Klaus. "A View from the Piazza: Herman Melville and the Legacy of the European Sublime." *Comparative Literature Studies* 4 (1967): 267–81.

Pommer, Henry F. *Milton and Melville.* Pittsburgh: U of Pittsburgh P, 1950. 31.

Reynolds, Larry J. "Melville's Catskill Eagle." *Melville Society Extracts* 64 (Nov. 1985): 11–12.

Robillard, Douglas. "Melville's *Clarel* and the Parallel of Poetry and Painting." *North Dakota Quarterly* 51 (Spring 1983): 107–20.

———. "The Visual Arts in Melville's *Redburn*." *Essays in Arts and Sciences* 12 (March 1983): 43–60.

Rowland, Beryl. "Grace Church and Melville's Story of 'The Two Temples.'" *Nineteenth-Century Fiction* 28 (Dec. 1973): 339–46.

Schless, Howard H. "Flaxman, Dante, and Melville's *Pierre*." *Bulletin of the New York Public Library* 64 (Feb. 1960): 65–82.

———. "Moby Dick and Dante: A Critique and Time Scheme." *Bulletin of the New York Public Library* 65 (May 1961): 289–312.

Scott, Sumner W. D. *The Whale in* Moby-Dick. Diss. U of Chicago, 1950.

Sealts, Merton M., Jr. *Melville as Lecturer.* Cambridge, MA: Harvard UP, 1957.

———. *Melville's Reading: A Checklist of Books Owned and Borrowed,* 1966. Rev. ed., Columbia: U of S Carolina P, 1988.

———. *Pursuing Melville, 1940–1980.* Madison: U of Wisconsin P, 1982.

Shurr, William. *The Mystery of Iniquity: Melville as Poet, 1857–1891.* Lexington: U of Kentucky P, 1972.

Stanton, Michael. "Blake, 'B.V.,' and *Billy Budd*." *Melville Society Extracts* 71 (Nov. 1987): 12–16.

Star, Morris. "Melville's Markings in Walpole's *Anecdotes of Painting in England*." *Papers of the Bibliographical Society of America* 66 (July-Sept. 1972), 321–27.

———. "Melville's Use of the Visual Arts." Diss. Northwestern U, 1964.

Stein, Roger B. *Seascape and the American Imagination.* New York: MOMA and Clarkson N. Potter, 1975.

Stein, William Bysshe. *The Poetry of Melville's Late Years: Time, History, Myth, and Religion.* Albany: State U of New York P, 1970.

Trimpi, Helen P. *Melville's Confidence Men and American Politics in the 1850s.* Hamden, CT: Archon Books, 1987.

Turnage, Maxine. "Melville's Concern with the Arts in *Billy Budd*." *Arizona Quarterly* 28 (1972): 74–82.

Vincent, Howard P. "Ishmael, Writer and Art Critic." *Themes and Directions in American Literature: Essays in Honor of Leon Howard.* Ed. Ray B. Browne and Donald Pizer. Lafayette, IN: Purdue U Studies, 1969. 69–79.

Wallace, Robert K. "Melville's Prints and Engravings at the Berkshire Athenaeum." *Essays in Arts and Sciences* 15 (June 1986): 59–90.

———. "New Evidence for Melville's Use of Turner in *Moby-Dick*." *Melville Society Extracts* 67 (Sept. 1986): 4–9. [Reprints condensed version of "'The Sultry Creator of Captain Ahab'" from *Turner Studies*.]

————. "'The Sultry Creator of Captain Ahab': Herman Melville and J. M. W. Turner." *Turner Studies* 5 (Winter 1985): 2–20.

————. "Teaching *Moby-Dick* in the Light of Turner." *Approaches to Teaching Melville's* Moby-Dick. Ed. Martin Bickman. New York: MLA, 1985. 135–39.

Wheelock, C. Webster. "Vere's Allusion to Ananais." *Melville Society Extracts* 15 (Sept. 1973): 9–10.

Wolf, Bryan. "When Is a Painting Most Like a Whale?: Ishmael, *Moby-Dick,* and the Sublime." *New Essays on* Moby-Dick. Ed. Richard H. Brodhead. Cambridge: Cambridge UP, 1986. 141–79.

Notes

Melville and the Visual Arts: An Overview

Page citations (unless otherwise noted) are to Eleanor Melville Metcalf's edition of Melville's *Journal of a Visit to London and the Continent* (cited here as *1849–50 Journal*); Howard C. Horsford's edition of Melville's *Journal of a Visit to Europe and the Levant* (cited here as *1856–57 Journal*); the Norton edition of *Moby-Dick;* and the Hayford-Sealts edition of *Billy Budd, Sailor.* Otherwise, references are to the following volumes of the North-western-Newberry Library edition of *The Writings of Herman Melville,* eds. Harrison Hayford, Hershel Parker, and G. Thomas Tanselle: *Typee, Omoo, Mardi, Redburn, White-Jacket, Pierre, Israel Potter, The Piazza Tales and Other Prose Pieces, 1839–1860,* and *The Confidence-Man.*

1. No authorized text or direct transcription of Melville's lecture, "Statues in Rome," has survived, but Merton M. Sealts, Jr., in *Melville as Lecturer,* has compiled a very close approximation from his study of existing newspaper reviews, and sometimes has managed even to reproduce Melville's own language.

2. Wallace's catalogue of Melville's prints and engravings at the Berkshire Athenaeum needs to be supplemented by the account of T. Walter Herbert, Jr., and Jon D. Swartz concerning the Osborne Collection of Melville Materials at Southwestern University, which includes four additional prints. In addition, Frank Jewett Mather, Jr., who visited Melville's New York home, reported that he owned prints after paintings by Claude and Rosa.

3. See Morris Star 148–50; also Howard Schless, "Flaxman, Dante, and Melville's *Pierre*" and "Moby Dick and Dante."

4. Berthold, in his essay for this volume, identifies this as an allusion to the work of Claude. However, Wallace (in "Melville's Prints," p. 64) suggests one or another earlier Dutch source.

5. See also Star 106–07.

6. Leyda, 1:261–62.

7. Schless, "Flaxman" 65.

8. Frank xvii. Melville was in Boston in March and November 1846, in March 1847, in July 1848, from early January through early April 1849, and on several other occasions thereafter.

9. It is especially noteworthy that in his copy of Thomas Beale's *Natural History of the Sperm Whale* Melville wrote on the frontispiece, "Turner's pictures of whalers were suggested by this book." (Wallace transcribes "whalers" where others have transcribed "whales"; see "'Sultry Creator'" 11.)

10. For another possible art source for *Moby-Dick,* one which is not explicitly mentioned, see Larry J. Reynolds's discussion of Asher Durand's *Kindred Spirits* (1849) in "Melville's Catskill Eagle."

11. *Pierre* contains several other portraits as well—one each of the boy's grandfathers, two of his father, and one of his mother. Similarly, in Melville's boyhood home, there were at least two portraits of Herman's father, Allan, both by American artists, John Reuben Smith and Ezra Ames. See Murray, ed., *Pierre* 454.

12. "The Architecture of Society and the Architecture of the Soul: Hawthorne's *The House of the Seven Gables* and Melville's *Pierre.*"

13. For details, see Dahl, "Architecture" 21, n. 4; also Litman 630, n. 3. Melville was acquainted with Downing's son, Alexander Jackson Davis, in the 1870s.

14. For evidence of the Wall Street architectural influence see Sealts, *Melville's Reading* 89; for "Temple First" see Rowland 344.

15. See Melville's 1849–50 *Journal* 26–27.

16. See Russell Lynes, "How a Few Artists . . ." 113.

17. In fact, Richard Moore's position is the more comprehensive one, arguing that in "The Piazza" Melville was also critiquing specifically the *American* faith in this same notion.

18. In Moore's view, "The Piazza" actually parodies all three of the ruling aesthetic notions of the eighteenth and nineteenth centuries—the beautiful and the sublime as well as the picturesque. See *That Cunning Alphabet* 1–58.

19. Novak, "Influences and Affinities," in *Shaping* 31.

20. For additional evidence of Melville's interest in political cartoons, in this instance in connection with his own early satirical sketches of Zachary Taylor for *Yankee Doodle,* Cornelius Mathews's weekly, see Leyda 250–51.

21. The Roman Forum had not yet been excavated to the point where tourists could visit it. Melville makes no mention of it or of the Pantheon in his journal, though he does speak of the latter in his lecture on "Statues in Rome" and again in *Clarel* 1:xii.

22. According to Sealts (*Melville as Lecturer* 27), in December 1857, in the midst of his lecture tour on Roman statuary, Melville also called on Erastus Dow Palmer, an American sculptor living in Albany, where Melville's uncle Peter Gansevoort also resided.

23. Sandford Robinson Gifford (1823–80), not Robert Swain Gifford (1840–1905), as some Melville scholars before Hennig Cohen have thought. See Star 220, n. 13. C. Georgoudaki, in "*Battle-Pieces and Aspects of the War:* Melville's Poetic Quest," argues that Melville's reference to Jane Jackson as a "sybil" suggests that he must have been familiar with Vedder's other Sybil figures, in either sculpture or painting, or both.

24. See Cohen, ed., *Battle-Pieces* 263; the 1963 edition of this work is one of the landmark studies of Melville's engagement with the visual arts. On Church, see Kelly 50–51.

25. See 1856–57 *Journal* 204 for a reference to Reni's ceiling fresco; as for the *Apollo Belvedere,* Cohen, *Battle-Pieces* 277, also points out that Robert Macpherson sent Melville a copy of his *Vatican Sculptures* (London, 1863) from Rome on May 4, 1866. Regarding Rosa's "battle-pieces," Cohen has argued that the collection is arranged like a series of pictures in a gallery, an idea which is further supported, he points out, by the rest of Melville's title, "and Aspects of the War" (14–15). Somewhat similarly, several of Melville's paired stories from the previous decade such as "Rich Man's Pudding and Poor Man's Crumbs" or "The Two Temples," appear to be based on the structural principle of the diptych, as Jay Leyda, in the introduction to *Complete Stories,* has said (xx).

26. Dettlaff, "Ionian Form and Esau's Waste: Melville's View of Art in *Clarel.*" Robillard, "Melville's *Clarel* and the Parallel of Poetry and Painting."

27. See Cohen, ed., *Selected Poems* 238–39, for a discussion of Le Brun's "Marchioness." Vincent *(Complete Poems)* and Star conclude that Teniers's *The Hour of Repose,* now at the Rijksmuseum in Amsterdam, served as the original for "The Bench of Boors," but Cohen and Berthold both argue for a more generalized source. See Berthold 241, 305–06n. 14 in this volume.

28. See Barbara Novak, "Influence and Affinities" 31–32.

29. For the *Farnese Hercules* see also *Moby-Dick* 315. Also, in connection with a memorable black version of the Handsome Sailor his narrator says he saw once in Liverpool, Melville speaks of the "grand sculptured Bull" of the Assyrian priests and the powerful, prostrating effect its image has on their followers. Clearly, as this example and the examples of Apollo and Antinous discussed by Coffler later in this volume suggest, sculpture—for the Melville who wrote *Billy Budd*—had the potential for generating a profound feeling of awe that was all but synonymous with religious feeling.

30. See in particular 315.

Melville's Reading in the Visual Arts

Page citations for this chapter are to the Northwestern-Newberry Library edition of Melville's *Journals.*

1. Wiley and Putnam published *Modern Painters* in 1846 and it was being advertised at the same time as *Typee.* Some typical articles in *The American Whig Review* include: "Something About Our Painters" (Aug. 1846), "Hints to Art Union Critics" (Dec. 1846), "Lectures on Art and Poems," a review of Allston's book (July 1850). Robillard, "The Metaphysics of Melville's Indian Hating," describes some of the reading Melville may have encountered in the *Review.* Typical articles in *The Democratic Review* are "American Works of Painting and Sculpture" (Jan. 1847), and "The American Art Union" (Oct. 1849).

2. In *The Literary World,* some exemplary pieces are "Exhibition at National Academy" (June 5, 1847); "What Can Be Done in Ten Weeks," a description of an art tour in Rome (Sept. 4, 11, 18, 1847); and a review of Lanzi's *History of Painting* (Feb. 10, 1849). Evert Duyckinck had a wide circle of acquaintances; on October 6, 1847, Melville went with him to the Art-Union and there met the American painter, William Sidney Mount (Yannella 241).

3. Wallace, "'The Sultry Creator of Captain Ahab,'" has an enlightening discussion of Melville's encounters with Samuel Rogers, Charles Robert Leslie, and others in London. Eleanor Metcalf's notes to Melville's 1849–50 *Journal* are also illuminating.

4. James McIntosh carefully analyzes Melville's varied responses to Goethe. Robson-Scott provides much information about Goethe's travels in the Italian art world (110–49).

5. Manfred Pütz discusses Ishmael as art critic responding to the painting of a whale in the Spouter-Inn (160–63). Howard H. Schless ("Flaxman, Dante" 65–82) deals with the Flaxman illustrations of Dante owned by Melville; see Wallace ("Melville's Prints" 73) for a description of the Flaxman plates.

6. Gibson tinted his statues and Melville remarks on his "Colored Venus." Melville also visited the American sculptors Edward Bartholomew and Hiram Powers (*Writings: Journals* 111, 116). The acquisition of Valery's *Historical, Literary, and Artistical Travels in Italy . . .* (1852), apparently while he was visiting Florence, gave him a useful source of information, and he marked passages on Domenichino, Guido Reni, and Michelangelo.

7. In *Melville as Lecturer,* Sealts has assembled a composite text of the lecture on statues (127–54).

8. Typical offerings in *The Democratic Review* included translations of Goethe's "Hermann and Dorothea" (Sept.–Dec. 1848) and "Iphigenia in Tauris" (May–Oct. 1849); Schiller's "The Diver" (May 1848); Lessing's "Emilia Galotti" (June–Dec. 1848) and "Minna von Barnhelm" (Feb.–July 1849).

9. Melville marked most of a chapter on Schiller and a long section on Goethe. A chapter, "Of Poetry," was heavily marked. In a marginal note he compares de Staël to Elizabeth Barrett Browning: "Mrs. B was a great woman, but Madam de S was a greater" (Cowen, "Melville's Marginalia" 11: 114).

10. James S. Malek (15–23) offers a useful account of Du Fresnoy's poem and Dryden's preface as well as an extended discussion of other eighteenth-century commentators. Wimsatt illustrates the uses that Johnson made, in his dictionary, of Dryden's aphorisms and precepts on art (26–39). Jean H. Hagstrum's *The Sister Arts* is a valuable examination of the comparison of the arts.

11. Here, as elsewhere, Walker Cowen's "Melville's Marginalia" is indispensable for any study of Melville's reading.

12. Roger B. Stein dates the American attacks on Ruskin from the late 1850s. Henry Greenough, James Eliot Cabot, and a number of others might have been part of Melville's reading. Cabot's "On the Relation of Art to Nature" appeared in the *Atlantic Monthly* Feb.–March 1864: 186–208.

13. "Tried to find A. Consul, Page, & Jarves. Failed in all" (*Writings: Journals* 106). Jarves begins *The Art-Idea* with "Some Preliminary Talk," a self-justifying preface that quotes Elizabeth Barrett Browning, discusses his own collection of Pre-Raphaelite art (which went, eventually, to Yale University), cites correspondence of Sir Charles Eastlake, and quotes a French article that calls his earlier book, *Confessions of an Inquirer*, "une espèce de roman psychologique" and likens it to Melville's writings. Steegmuller's biography gives a valuable picture of American responses to art in the nineteenth century.

14. Excellent analyses of the poem and its background are in Shurr (207–17) and William Bysshe Stein, *Poetry* (227–46).

15. As Wallace notes, however, "The collection at the Berkshire Athenaeum, in spite of its variety and range, is only indicative, not exhaustive, of Melville's interest in art" ("Melville's Prints and Engravings" 62). Wallace's catalogue of the extant collection convincingly illustrates Melville's taste and the range of his knowledge.

Bulkington, J. M. W. Turner, and "The Lee Shore"

Page citations for this chapter are to the Northwestern-Newberry Library edition of Melville's *Journals* and of *Typee, Omoo, Mardi, Redburn, White-Jacket*, and *Moby-Dick*.

1. Turner's oil paintings are customarily identified by using the catalogue numbers from the "Text" volume of Butlin and Joll's *The Paintings of J. M. W. Turner* (as in BJ 415 or BJ 398). References to written entries within this volume are customarily made by page number (as in Butlin and Joll, p. 245).

2. *Snow Storm—Steam-Boat* first arrived in the National Gallery in 1856—along with other works from the Turner Bequest that had been in Turner's private gallery at Queen Anne Street in the years preceding his death in 1851. The likely location of *The Whale Ship* in 1849 is, as Moore acknowledges, a much disputed issue. See my discussion in "'Sultry Creator'" 14–16.

3. Three of these works were in the Vernon Gallery when Melville visited it on December 17, 1849. *Venice—the Dogana* was installed in the nearby National Gallery, where it represented the entire Vernon Collection (Butlin and Joll 245). Later in life,

Melville, who first visited the National Gallery on November 8, 1849, acquired engravings of *Venice—the Dogana, The Golden Bough,* and *Prince of Orange, Landing at Torbay* (Wallace, "Prints" 81–82).

4. These "Lee-Shore" sketchbooks are part of the Turner Bequest now housed in the Clore Gallery of the Tate Gallery in London, where they are identified as T. B. LXVII and LXVIII.

5. A more peaceful side of Turner's powerful internalization of lee-shore strife is shown in other late unexhibited works, among them *Shore Scene with Waves and Break-water* (c. 1835, BJ 486) and *A Breaking Wave* (T. B. CCCLXIV–417).

6. Pp. 37–39. This unsigned review in the *Bulletin* was by far the most penetrating and admiring review of Turner's career to appear in America in the painter's lifetime. At a time when many critics who did admire Turner thought that he had done his best work before 1820, this critic affirmed with no hesitation that the late Turner was the great Turner. Evert Duyckinck, Melville's mentor and editor of *The Literary World,* was on the Board of Management for the *Bulletin.* Melville had followed this monthly art journal since 1848, when his brother Allan subscribed to it at the Fourth Avenue home where Herman and his wife Elizabeth were then living. In the Berkshires in the summer of 1851 he had access to this journal through his friend Nathaniel Hawthorne, who in April thanked Duyckinck for sending him the *Bulletin* (Metcalf, *Cycle* 103).

7. Leyda 1: 410–11. Opportunities remained for minor revisions in the text as late as September 1851, when the American proofs were sent to Bentley in London. Yet it seems unlikely that Melville would have added the Bulkington material, short as it is, after the early chapters had been set in type by mid-June or so (see Northwestern-Newberry ed. 629–33, 662–67).

8. Father Mapple's canvas is "a large painting representing a gallant ship beating against a terrible storm off lee coast of black rocks and snowy breakers." It resembles Turner's early lee-shore works in that "high above the flying scud and dark-rolling clouds, there floated a little isle of sunlight." It differs from them in the "angel's face" that "seemed to say, 'beat on, beat on, thou noble ship, and bear a hardy helm; for lo! the sun is breaking through; the clouds are rolling off—serenest azure is at hand'" (39–40). Such a painting, complete with "angel's face," hung in Boston's Seamen's Bethel, where Melville is likely to have seen it ("'Sultry Creator'" 10).

9. Fig. 9, "'Sultry Creator.'" Walker Cowen's mistranscription of "whales" for "whal-ers" in "Melville's Marginalia" (2: 275) has been followed by subsequent scholars.

10. Rogers owned a Bonington portrait entitled *The Turk.* Bonington's *The Columns of St. Mark, Venice* was illustrated in the Second Series of Hall's *The Vernon Gallery,* published in 1851, the year of *Moby-Dick.* Turner's two Venetian scenes in the Vernon Gallery had been published in Hall's First Series, in 1850.

Melville's Temples

Page citations for this chapter are to Eleanor Melville Metcalf's edition of Melville's *Journal of a Visit to London and the Continent* (cited here as *1849–50 Journal*); Howard C. Horsford's edition of Melville's *Journal of a Visit to Europe and the Levant* (cited here as *1856–57 Journal*); the Norton edition of *Moby-Dick;* and (unless otherwise noted) the Northwestern-Newberry Library edition of *Mardi, White-Jacket, Pierre,* and *The Piazza Tales and Other Prose Pieces.*

1. Melville's marked volumes of *Mosses* are in the Houghton Library, Harvard University.

2. "I love men who *dive*," Melville wrote in reference to Emerson and to "the whole corps of thought-divers that have been diving and coming up again with bloodshot eyes since the world began" (Melville to Duyckinck, March 3, 1849, *Letters* 79).

3. The church depicted appears to be a combination of Grace Church and Trinity Church, both consecrated within three months of each other early in 1846. See Dillingham 104–05; and Rowland.

4. Melville quotes from Milton's *Paradise Lost* 2.560.

5. 1856–57 *Journal* 118–19. Newton Arvin noted that "some of Melville's 'most profound intuitions . . . are embodied in metaphors of architectural or monumental grandeur,'" and Vincent Scully observed that Melville could "'perceive the reciprocal relationship' between the form and the site, the divine significance of a place in nature, and the representation of that place in form." Scully illustrates this point with Melville's quatrain "Greek Architecture." Both statements are cited by Boudreau 68.

6. Melville's admiration of such unity in art is perhaps best exemplified by his triplet "Greek Masonry":

Joints were none that mortar sealed:
Together, scarce with line revealed,
The blocks in symmetry congealed.
(*Collected Poems* 248)

7. This alleged account of the founding of Mar Saba was told to me at the monastery in June 1986 by Brother Chrysanthos, who was translating into English a historical pamphlet, *Iera Lavra Sabba tou Hagiasménou [The Holy Monastery of Saint Sabbas]* (Jerusalem: [n.p.] 1984), by Father Seraphim, the Archimandrite there. He gave me a copy of the original pamphlet, and I am grateful to my wife, Eleonora, who translated it for me from the formal modern Greek *(katharévousa).*

8. The illustrations have been drawn from four sources:

Figs. 1 and 2 are reproduced from William M. Thomson, *The Land and the Book; or, Biblical Illustrations . . . of the Holy Land: Southern Palestine and Jerusalem* (NY: Harper & Brothers, 1880).

Figs. 3, 4, and 5 appear in W. M. Thomson, *The Land and the Book; or, Biblical Illustrations . . . of the Holy Land* (NY: Harper & Brothers, 1858), vol. 2.

Figs. 6 and 7 are photographs I took during a visit to Mar Saba in June 1986.

Fig. 8 is a photograph of a watercolor by Peter Toft, *The Holy Palm of Mar Saba.* The original is in the Herman Melville Collection of the Berkshire Athenaeum, Pittsfield, MA; it has been reproduced here by permission, for which we are grateful, indeed, to Ms. Ruth T. Degenhardt, Department Head of Local History and Literature Services at the Athenaeum.

"Like bed of asparagus": Melville and Architecture

Research for this chapter was supported by a short-term fellowship at the Newberry Library and by the Northern Arizona University Organized Research Committee.

Page citations for this chapter are to Douglas Robillard's edition of Melville's *Poems* and the Northwestern-Newberry Library edition of *Typee, Mardi, Redburn, Moby-Dick, Pierre, Journals,* and *The Piazza Tales and Other Prose Pieces.*

Melville and John Vanderlyn:
Ruin and Historical Fate from "Bartleby" to *Israel Potter*

Page citations for this chapter are to the Northwestern-Newberry Library edition of *Redburn, Moby-Dick, Israel Potter, The Piazza Tales and Other Prose Pieces,* and *Journals.*

1. Vanderlyn kept the painting and exhibited it at various locations (Norfolk, VA, 1818; New York Rotunda, periodically, 1819–29; New Orleans, 1821; Charleston, SC, 1822; and in Havana, Cuba, 1829) until he sold it in 1834 to Leonard Kip. The painting was exhibited at the Albany Gallery of Fine Arts in 1848 before William Ingraham Kip took it to San Francisco in 1853–54. It was exhibited in San Francisco in 1872 and displayed by the M. H. De Young Memorial Museum in 1917–20, where it now remains (Lindsay 136, Kip 228–35). Jay Fliegelman first suggested to me the possible significance of this painting; but Stanton Garner and Hennig Cohen have seen the connection as well. I am grateful to both for their perceptive and helpful readings of this chapter.

2. Averill's is the most comprehensive biography of Vanderlyn. It includes the full, unpublished text of Robert Gosman, "Biographical Sketch of John Vanderlyn, Artist" 295–338. I have also relied on Lillian Miller, "John Vanderlyn and the Business of Art," *New York History* 36 (1951): 33–34; Salvatore Mondello, "John Vanderlyn," *New York Historical Society Quarterly Bulletin* 52 (1968): 161–83; and Marius Schoonmaker, *John Vanderlyn, Artist* (Kingston, NY: New York Senate House Association, 1950).

3. Rogin 56. Stanton Garner has provided me with the details of Clinton's appointments of Peter Gansevoort as private secretary to Clinton (1817–19) and as judge advocate general to the State of New York (1819–21). Stanton Garner's "The Picaresque Career of Thomas Melville, Junior," *Melville Society Extracts* 60 (Nov. 1984): 1–10; part 2, 62 (May 1985): 1, 4–10, offers another connection between Melville and Vanderlyn's painting.

4. Details on the American Art-Union and its members come from Mary Bartlett Cawdrey, *American Academy of Fine Arts and American Art Union* (New York: New York Historical Society, 1953); and *Transactions of the Apollo Association, 1842* (New York: Charles Vinten, 1842). Melville's relationships with New York luminaries are described in Perry Miller, *The Raven and the Whale: The War of Words and Wits in the Era of Poe and Melville* (New York: Harcourt Brace, 1956). Apparently Vanderlyn's ill temper was so well known that in S. B. H. Judah's *Gotham and the Gothamites* (New York, 1823) a friend of Vanderlyn's advised him to "imbibe daily a reasonable quantity of strong beer" (Lindsay 4). Melville's Turkey gives Bartleby the same advice.

5. Duyckinck's close relation with and intellectual influence over Melville are described in Leon Howard, *Herman Melville, a Biography;* Jay Leyda, *The Melville Log;* Perry Miller, *The Raven and the Whale;* and Donald and Kathleen Malone Yannella, "Evert A. Duyckinck's 'Diary: May 29–Nov. 8, 1847,'" *Studies in the American Renaissance: 1978* 207–58.

6. John Langhorne and William Langhorne, ed., *Plutarch's Lives* (New York: Harper and Brothers, 1846) 290–307. The famous Carthage incident, quoted almost verbatim in many accounts of Vanderlyn's life, reads as follows:

He [Marius] had just landed, with a few of his men, when an officer came and thus addressed him: "Marius, I come from the praetor Sextilius, to tell you, that he forbids you to set foot in Africa. If you obey not, he will support the senate's decree, and treat you as a public enemy." Marius, upon hearing this, was struck dumb with grief and indignation. He uttered not a word for some time, but stood regarding the officer with a menacing aspect. At length the officer asked him, what answer he should carry to the governor. "Go and tell him," said the unfortunate man with a sigh, "that

thou hast seen the exile Marius sitting on the ruins of Carthage." Thus in the happiest
manner in the world, he proposed the fate of that city and his own as warnings to
the praetor. (305)

Marius was also known as a rough-hewn plebeian who rose through the ranks to become
consul seven times, each reign bloodier than the last, until his rival Sulla brought about
his political and physical demise.

7. "Bartleby, the Scrivener" 27–28. Evert Duyckinck was reading *Dombey and Son*
enthusiastically in June 1847; in chapter 9, Marius appears in comic guise: "Mr. Brogley
himself was a moist-eyed, pink-complexioned, crisp-haired man, of a bulky figure and an
easy temper—for that class of Caius Marius who sits upon the ruins of other people's
Carthages, can keep up his spirits well enough." See Yannella and Yannella 222, and
Charles Dickens, *Dombey and Son*, ed. Alan Horsman (Oxford: Clarendon, 1974) 116.
Cf. Balzac's Madame Vauquer contemplating the departures of her boarders: "The old
landlady looked like Marius surveying the ruins of Carthage." Honoré de Balzac, *Père
Goriot*, trans. Henry Reed (New York: New American Library, 1962) 210. Melville uses
the same technique of diminution, but by making his Marius "innocent and transformed"
he removes the mockery of Dickens's and Balzac's allusions and gives Bartleby an ambiguous
dignity.

8. According to Lindsay, John Hamilton Mortimer painted *Caius Marius on the
Ruins of Carthage* in 1774, and in France, Schell (first name not cited), A. C. Caraffe,
and Jacques Taurel exhibited paintings on the same theme in 1793, 1795, and 1798.
Lindsay also notes the Benjamin West drawing (72). Morse's *Marius* was perhaps never
finished or was lost. He painted it in 1812 (Larkin 30). Averill mentions Allston's painting
and discusses the Allston/Vanderlyn relationship (71).

9. Averill (77) says that Napoleon had already given a medal to David and numerous
other artists, most of whom had painted portraits of Napoleon. He also distributed 16
"medals of encouragement," one of which went to Vanderlyn. The award was a great
coup for American art, however, and Napoleon was always linked with the painting in
further accounts of Vanderlyn's *Marius*. For an elaborate and fanciful version, see "Marius,"
The Democratic Review 475–512.

10. This poem is quoted in many of the contemporary biographies of Vanderlyn,
including those of Marius Schoonmaker and William Dunlap. It is also quoted in full by
Edgar Allan Poe as evidence of Lydia Maria Child's own genius in *The Literati of New
York City*, in *Edgar Allan Poe: Essays and Reviews*, ed. G. R. Thompson (New York:
Library Classics of the United States, 1984) 1198–99.

11. William Gilmore Simms, "Caius Marius," in *Poems, Descriptive, Dramatic, Legendary and Contemplative* (New York: Redfield, 1853) 2: 300–11. From the available
evidence, one can fairly certainly judge that Simms wrote this poem after Vanderlyn's
death and in recognition of the *Marius*. Another play based on Marius is Richard Penn
Smith, *Caius Marius*, ed. Neda McFadden Westlake (Philadelphia: U of Pennsylvania P,
1968), written in 1831. The ruin-among-ruins theme appears in an 1848 statement by
Lewis Cass that might have interested Melville: "I have seen the wandering Arab, the
descendant of Ishmael, sitting upon the ruins of Baalbek, himself a ruin" (Rogin 40).

12. "Marius" 475–512. Melville was in New York the month this issue appeared
(Dec. 1840) preparing to leave on a whaling cruise after Christmas.

13. The *Marius* engraving was executed by Steven Alonzo Schoff. In the same year
the American Art-Union purchased a copy of the *Marius* by Asher Durand, presumably
because Vanderlyn refused to sell his painting (Cawdrey 273, 287; *Transactions* 4; and
Lindsay 136–37). In a letter to Christopher Sten (April 28, 1988), John M. J. Gretchko

has provided the information that Schoff's engraving was also exhibited in 1844 by the National Academy of Design. Melville's visit to the American Art-Union is recorded in Leyda (261–62) and Yannella and Yannella (241).

14. In "His (More Than) Fifty Years in Exile and Fanny's Toe," *Melville Society Extracts* 44 (Nov. 1980): 7–9, Stanton Garner discusses the Bunker Hill Monument as ruinous masonry.

15. Gail Coffler, "Classical Elements in the Development of Melville's Aesthetic," diss. U of Wisconsin-Madison, 1981, discusses Melville's deepening classicism in aesthetic terms that apply as well, I think, to his sense of history.

The White Mountains, Thomas Cole, and "Tartarus": The Sublime, the Subliminal, and the Sublimated

Page citations for this chapter are to Eleanor Melville Metcalf's edition of Melville's *Journal of a Visit to London and the Continent* (cited here as 1849–50 *Journal*); Howard C. Horsford's edition of Melville's *Journal of a Visit to Europe and the Levant* (cited here as 1856–57 *Journal*); the Library of America edition of *Redburn, White-Jacket,* and *Moby-Dick;* and the Northwestern-Newberry Library edition of *The Piazza Tales and Other Prose Pieces.*

1. P. 73. Ballou (140) uses similar positioning words but in reference to other features.

2. Rosa did have a drawing of a hermit sitting in a hollow tree trunk with a cross, a skull, and books on the ground before him. As of this writing only my identification of Hieronymus Bosch's *Temptation of St. Anthony* fits Melville's prose painting; see "The Glassy-eyed Hermit," *Melville Society Extracts* 48 (Nov. 1981): 14. For the symbolic, sexual, and subliminal significance of this painting see Carl Linfert, *Hieronymus Bosch,* trans. Robert Erich Wolf (New York: Abrams, 1971) 132–34, and Wilson Bryan Key, *The Clam-plate Orgy: And Other Subliminal Techniques for Manipulating Your Behavior* (New York: Signet, 1981) 38–39. Curiously, Linfert's translator echoes Melville when he uses the words, "And that is the key to it all," in describing Bosch's *Anthony.*

3. P. 62. In chapter 81 of *Moby-Dick,* "The Pequod Meets the Virgin," a chapter heading appropriately corresponding to the "Tartarus" theme, Melville links the bleeding of a whale to a flowing river: "Yet so vast is the quantity of blood in him, and so distant and numerous its interior fountains, that he will keep thus bleeding and bleeding for a considerable period; even as in drought a river will flow, whose source is in the wellsprings of far-off and undiscernable hills" (1176). This represents an early association in Melville's mind between the concepts of the virgin, bleeding, and a flowing river.

4. In October 1828 Thomas Cole, in July 1832 Ralph Waldo Emerson, and in September 1832 Hawthorne stayed at the old Mount Washington House, then owned by Ethan Allen Crawford. Hawthorne records his trip through the Notch in his "Sketches from Memory," which appeared in *Mosses from an Old Manse* (1846).

5. For early depictions of the Notch, see Catherine Campbell, "The Gate of the Notch," *Historical New Hampshire* 33 (1978): 91–122; also Campbell, *New Hampshire Scenery* (212–14).

6. *Exhibition* 14. Cole's *A View in the Notch of the White Mountains of New Hampshire,* so named, then owned by Rufus L. Lord, is exhibit 40. In conjunction with this exhibition the New-York Gallery of the Fine Arts permitted Art-Union season ticket holders to view its 11 Coles as well.

7. Compare *Moby-Dick,* chapter 61: "The red tide now poured from all sides of the monster like brooks down a hill" (1098).

8. Thomas Doughty painted the Silver Cascade in 1835. Prints were widely distributed, even internationally, promoting this as a classic scene of Americana. In contrast, the painter in Hawthorne's "Prophetic Pictures" (1837), from *Twice-told Tales,* had gone "to the north to see the silver cascade of the Crystal Hills [an early name for the White Mountains], and to look over the vast round of cloud and forest from the summit of New England's loftiest mountain. But he did not profane that scene by the mockery of his art" (177).

9. P. 324. The Rhenish-Belgian Gallery at the National Academy of Design in 1853 featured the evocative *Winter Afternoon—Ruin Soneck, Near the Rhine* by Hermann Jaspers and *Dante and His Guide, Virgil, Passing the Styx* by Eugène Delacroix, in keeping with a subtheme in "Tartarus."

10. If Melville had toured the Düsseldorf Gallery in New York, he may have seen Carl Sohn's heralded *Diana and Her Nymphs Surprised at the Bath,* where several of the young ladies were turning Actaeon into a stag. Sohn painted a smaller version of this for the Picture Gallery in the Crystal Palace at the 1853–54 Exhibition of the Industry of All Nations in New York. This Gallery featured 654 principally modern European paintings— evidently the largest collection ever assembled in America at that time.

11. *Homes,* 2 vols., trans. Mary Howitt (New York: Harper, 1853), 2: 97. Michael Paul Rogin in *Subversive Genealogy: The Politics and Art of Herman Melville* (New York: Knopf, 1983) 204, suggests a possible source in Bremer, where Bremer relates how she "was most struck by the relationship between the human being and the machinery at [Lowell]," how the operatives "guarded [the machines] much as a mother would watch over and tend her children. The machinery was like an obedient child under the eye of an intelligent mother" (2: 210). Rogin asserts, "Bremer imposed the cult of domesticity on the factory; Melville inverted it" (204). Bremer also refers to a Green Mountain called "Le Lion couchant" (2: 589), and Melville writes of a rock "couchant like a lion" (325).

12. At about 60 miles from the Notch existed the Shaker colony of New Glouster, now Sabbathday Lake, Maine, which grew seeds for the Maine area. This is one candidate for the origin of the seedsman. Another Shaker colony at Canterbury, New Hampshire, was about 90 miles away.

13. Melville continues: "It's a Hyperborean winter scene.—It's the breaking-up of the ice-bound stream of Time." He may have taken these details from Chester Dewey's section 1 in David Dudley Field's *A History of the County of Berkshire, Massachusetts* (Pittsfield: printed by S. W. Bush, 1829) 30: "the Deerfield is a wild and mad stream. The ice frozen upon its rocks in winter, is very rarely broken up till spring. . . . The *breaking up of the river,* as it is familiarly called, is a sublime scene. . . . At this time the stream becomes a torrent." Melville's sense of the sublime, possibly tinged with sarcasm, seems casually borrowed from Field, whose book he owned and annotated.

Toning Down the Green: Melville's Picturesque

Page citations for John Bryant's essay are to the Northwestern-Newberry Library edition of *Mardi;* the Norton edition of *Moby-Dick;* and the Random House edition of *Selected Writings of Herman Melville.*

1. In her guide to the study of "Melville's Aesthetics," Shirley M. Dettlaff isolates various areas in the still-neglected field which require more systematic examination. The picturesque is one such area.

2. For a comprehensive philosophical assessment of the development of eighteenth-century British aesthetics, see Hipple.

3. The physiological metaphor is apposite to Melville's poetic placement of the self "on the marge" suspended between full tension (sea as doubt) and utter relaxation (land as repose). Here, too, are curiosity (a combination of wonder and doubt) and irregularity (improvisation) that typify Melville's style.

4. Taking the associational approach to the picturesque, certain critics show how Melville has adapted his prose to specific modes of painting, in particular the Dutch Genre School (Berthold) and Turner (Wallace).

5. How the notion of the picturesque was transmitted to America and used by our earlier writers is the subject of various critical works. Donald Ringe examines the influence of Scottish Common Sense thinkers on the "pictorial mode" in American writing, in particular the uses of light and shadow, precise detail and vastness to heighten mood and theme. Drawing upon E. H. Gombrich's theories and Hussey's overview, Blake Nevius shows how the picturesque was for Cooper a way of "seeing" that moved him toward a more Romantic vision. More recently Dennis Berthold has shown that the picturesque "mode of seeing" provided Charles Brockden Brown "an organized, cool aesthetic that restrained exaggerated emotion and framed one's view of rude nature with the artistic perspective of the landscape painter" (69). As with Brown, so it was with Melville.

6. Richard S. Moore's view that Melville "derides the passive state of aesthetic repose connected with the picturesque" (53) stresses the somnolence of repose without recognizing its inherent tensions. As we have seen in the poetry (which Moore does not discuss), Melville warns us away from soporific repose only so that he may embrace formal restraint more fully.

7. William Bysshe Stein attempts an ironic reading of this famous passage by observing that a tortoise when turned on its back (with bright side up) is therefore helpless ("Melville's Comedy" 323). Melville, however, does not press or even allude to this natural fact; hence, the irony, if one exists, does not seem intended nor is it strong enough to invert a straight reading of his message.

8. Sources for Melville's Marianna in Tennyson and Shakespeare have been recorded in Breinig (276) and Inge (34–36).

9. Scholars tend to read "The Piazza" as an ironic critique of faith (Stein, "Melville's Comedy"), the sublime (Poenicke), and the picturesque (Fisher 13–28; and Richard Moore 3–53). But as Poenicke aptly observes, the tale is "an inquiry into what such an experience [as the sublime] may do to human beings" (271), and like most valid inquiries, Melville's remains open. As I point out here, the speaker's disillusionment with sublimity is not as important as his return to the piazza, a symbolic vantage point of tense repose where dark vision may be brought to art.

10. The only critical (rather than textual) treatments available are Shurr's brief focus on the Puritan aspects in the poem and Stein's Jungian interpretation of Rip as Dionysus overcoming sexual impotence through his phallic lilac bush (*Poetry*).

11. The manuscript for "Rip Van Winkle's Lilac" is located in the Houghton Library at Harvard University, Box MS AM 188.369. The most accurate text for "Rip" and the basis for the forthcoming Northwestern-Newberry edition of the poem is Ryan's dissertation. Vincent's more accessible text, used here, is less accurate but generally reliable. Corrections of errors in the Vincent text have been inserted in brackets.

12. In addition, we find in the Houghton Library a 30-page pencil draft of a prose sketch entitled "The House of the Tragic Poet," apparently intended as an introduction to "At the Hostelry."

13. Since a fair copy of "Rip" has not been found, it seems certain that the heavily emended manuscript does not represent what might have been Melville's final text. If the author had lived to see the piece through publication, it may have been longer or shorter,

more or less structurally convoluted, better or worse. It is fruitless to speculate on where Melville was going with "Rip" except to say that a novella the size of *Billy Budd* is not out of the question. As it stands, the work exists in a kind of textual limbo as a collaborative effort begun by an author and completed by editors, and the best any textual editor can hope to achieve in bringing such a manuscript into print is as a verbal representation of a single, now frozen phase of a once fluid, creative process. But if "Rip" can never be taken as the author's final intention, its validity as a text lies squarely in our recognition that the glimpse it affords us of an evolving work of art reveals more of the artist's mind than does a final polished "whole."

**"Why talk of Jaffa?": Melville's *Israel Potter*,
Baron Gros, Zummo, and the Plague**

Page citations for this chapter are (unless otherwise noted) to Eleanor Melville Metcalf's edition of Melville's *Journal of a Visit to London and the Continent* (cited here as 1849–50 *Journal*); Howard C. Horsford's edition of Melville's *Journal of a Visit to Europe and the Levant* (cited here as 1856–57 *Journal*); and the Northwestern-Newberry Library edition of *Mardi, Redburn, Moby-Dick, Pierre,* and *The Piazza Tales and Other Prose Pieces.*

1. Ch. 3, p. 15. Page references are to the Northwestern-Newberry edition of the Writings of Herman Melville: *Israel Potter: His Fifty Years of Exile* (Evanston and Chicago, 1982), which includes "a photographic reproduction" of the first edition of *The Life and Remarkable Adventures of Israel R. Potter, . . .* (Providence: Henry Trumbull, 1824). The first edition is cited here as *Life and Adventures.*

2. Cf. the first paragraph of *Moby-Dick:* "whenever my hypos get such an upper hand of me, that it requires a strong moral principle to prevent me from . . . knocking people's hats off. . . ."

3. Nathalia Wright, "Biblical Allusion in Melville's Prose," *American Literature* 12 (May 1940): 186. Mansfield and Vincent note in their edition (New York, 1962) that in these chapters Melville draws on Bayle's *Dictionary* (Sealts, *Melville's Reading* no. 51), Sir Thomas Browne (Sealts, nos. 89 and 90), and John Kitto's *Cyclopedia of Biblical Literature* for the association of Joppa with Perseus and the sea monster. See also Vincent, *The Trying-Out of Moby-Dick* 280–86.

4. Ed. James Hastings (Edinburgh and New York, 1899).

5. Quoted in *Naval Documents of the American Revolution,* ed. William Bell Clark (Washington, 1968) 3: 522. This collection has information on the capture of the brig *Washington* in December 1775, on which the historical Israel Potter served, and the transport and treatment of the American prisoners. See especially 122–23, 483, 511, 514, 521–22.

6. [Raymond Escholier], *Gros: Ses Amis, Ses Élèves* (Paris, 1936) 59. It is still (in 1991) prominently displayed in the Louvre.

7. Yvonne Hibbott, "'Bonaparte Visiting the Plague-stricken at Jaffa' by Antoine Jean Gros . . . ," *British Medical Journal* 1 (Feb. 22, 1969): 501. For preliminary sketches, prints, reviews, verses, songs, and other evidence of the popularity of the Gros painting, see *Gros* exhibition catalogue, 58–60, and H. Mollaret and J. Brossollet, "Á propos 'Pestiférés de Jaffa' de A. J. Gros," *Jaarboek 1968* (Antwerp: Koninklijk Museum voor Schone Kunsten) 263–308.

8. *Gros* exhibition catalogue 58. Yet it is not entirely authentic. Gros, to extend the emotional appeal of the imperial and quasi-religious ambience of the Egyptian venture

to Napoleon himself, anachronistically costumes the soldiers in the resplendent uniforms of the Empire rather than the plainer campaign dress of the preceding revolutionary regimes. See William Vaughn, *Romantic Art* (London: Thames and Hudson, 1978) 63–66, and *French Painting, 1774–1830: The Age of Revolution* (Detroit: Wayne State UP, 1974) 466.

9. Anita Brookner, *Jacques-Louis David* 154.

10. James Matthew Thompson, *Napoleon Bonaparte* 130.

11. Walter Friedlaender, "Napoleon as 'Roi thaumaturge'" 139–40.

12. Brookner 161.

13. New York *Weekly Tribune* 26 June 1847. Published by Harper & Brothers, the book had 10 editions by 1851, the year of Stephens's death. His name does not appear on the title page, authorship being ascribed "to an American."

14. The two book-length studies—Merrell R. Davis, *Melville's* Mardi: *A Chartless Voyage,* and Maxine Moore, *That Lonely Game*—do not identify Napoleon or St. Helena nor, to my knowledge, is this done elsewhere in the scholarly literature.

15. Christopher Wright, *Poussin's Paintings* 148.

16. See Raymond Crawford, *Plague and Pestilence,* and Michele Mazzitelli, *La Pestilenza nell'Arte.*

17. Reproduced in Lois Marie Fink and Joshua C. Taylor, *Academy* 187. Abundant evidence of Melville's taste in the visual arts is to be found in his travel journals and print collection. This lifelong interest is summarized in the preface to Robert K. Wallace's checklist, "Melville's Prints." See my edition of Melville's *Battle-Pieces* (New York, 1963) 263, 267–68, 274.

18. Sealts no. 178.

19. *Holidays Abroad or Europe from the West* (New York: Baker and Scribner, 1849) 1: 239. Sealts no. 311. 1849–50 *Journal,* Oct. 14, 1849, 94.

20. Dec. 23, 1849, in the 1849–50 *Journal.* For his use of the *Penny Cyclopaedia* in *Israel Potter,* see Bezanson's "Historical Note," *Israel Potter* 197. For the article on Zummo, see *Penny Cyclopaedia* (London: Charles Knight & Co., 1843) 27: 822. Melville bought "a copy of Knight's London" (1849–50 *Journal,* Dec. 15, 1849; Sealts no. 312).

21. François Cagnetta, "La Vie et l'oeuvre de Gaetano Giulio Zummo," 489–500. For illustrations in color, bibliography, and evaluation of Zummo's scientific and artistic merit—"il maggior ceroplasta di tutti tempi"—see Benedetto Lanza, et al. 68–82.

22. Ronald W. Lightbrown, "Gaetano Giulio Zummo—I," 486–96.

23. D. Mathis Eddy documents "Melville's fascination with the facts of mortality" (193), as recorded in the 1856–57 *Journal* and evident elsewhere in his works. Eddy reprints Lightbrown's descriptions of the wax sculptures and accepts his reading of "their emphasis on human mutability" (193) and "the triumph of time" (200).

24. P. 155. For the "ancient" identification of "ditchers and gravemakers," see *Hamlet* 5.1.33.

25. Job (3.13–14) laments that he did not die at birth: "I should have slept: then had I been at rest, With kings and counsellors of the earth."

A curious permutation of this biblical passage occurs in Melville's pencil notes at the end of a blank page in his copy of *The Dramatic Works of William Shakespeare* (Boston, 1837), vol. 7; Sealts no. 460, purchased in 1849. Unusually provocative, they include another of his rhetorical questions: "Would you not rather be below with kings than above with fools?" The notes are transcribed and discussed fully in an appendix to the Northwestern-Newberry edition of *Moby-Dick* 955–70; see esp. 970. The question appears to be related to the "secret motto" of *Moby-Dick,* here given as "Ego non baptizo te in nominee Patris [sic] . . . ," and other references to diabolism and oppositions of Heaven and Hell contained in the annotation. The Northwestern-Newberry editors call attention to the relevance of the Shakespeare annotation to Melville's then recently completed *Mardi,* the work in which he first makes notable use of the Job passage.

26. Constantin François Chasseboeuf, Comte de Volney, *Volney's Ruins* 11. The title of a tourist guide he bought in Italy in 1857—Emil Braun, *Handbook of the Ruins of Rome . . .* (Rome, 1856), Sealts no. 86.1—shows the attraction for Melville and other tourists of ruins and antiquities. William B. Dillingham cites as a "likely source for Melville's image of Marius" a steel engraving of "The Ruins of Carthage" by A. L. Dick after an original by William Linton, presumably the English wood engraver and republican activist (31 n). The engraving was published in the *New York Mirror* of Jan. 2, 1841, and is reproduced without attribution as the dustjacket of Dillingham's book. More picturesque and poetic than the Vanderlyn painting, and regardless of whether Melville knew it, too, documents the continued popularity of the ruins motif. Beethoven's overture to "The Ruins of Athens," op. 113, written for a Kotzebue drama first performed in 1812, is musical evidence of the vogue.

27. In the religious discussions of *Clarel,* Volney is described as "A pilgrim deist from the Seine" (2.16.41).

28. The ruins of Petra, in Jordan, an opulent fortress city in biblical and classical times, were discovered in 1811 by John Lewis Burckhardt. His was one of the most important archeological finds of the century. Melville brooded on these ruins in "Of Petra," *Clarel* (2.30).

29. P. 121. Solomon built "Tadmor in the wilderness" (2 Chronicles 8.4), an oasis trading center in the Syrian desert, known to the Romans as Palmyra. Sacked and laid waste by Tamerlane, it is the initial setting of Volney's *Ruins* and the inspiration for his meditations.

30. Daniel G. Hoffman provides a statement pertinent to the limitations of the Jonah parallel, and by implication to that of the resurrection of Christ, in his "Moby-Dick: Jonah's Whale or Job's?": "Melville's God lies beyond even the Gospel truths. He is Job's God, not Jonah's prefiguration of Christ's rising" (217). Hence Israel has an additional reason to reject biblical resurrections but to accept resurrection in terms of nature.

31. For Longfellow see *Outre-Mer: A Pilgrimage Beyond the Sea* (1833–34). On Hawthorne, see *The French and Italian Notebooks* 308; Florence, June 11, 1858.

32. P. 169. I argue this point in "*Israel Potter:* Common Man as Hero"; see esp. 299–300, 307–08.

Melville knew Asher Durand and Frederic Church and admired their romantic landscape paintings. For such artists, blasted trees on the one hand were a mark of the sublime, the terror and wonder of the storm. But within the larger frame of nature, they merely marked a point in the cyclic process. Furthermore, like the sea-shattered cliffs along the British coast (*Israel Potter* 121), they are nature's counterpart to Volney's ruins of ancient civilizations.

Daumier's Robert Macaire and Melville's Confidence Man

Page citations for this chapter are to the Northwestern-Newberry Library edition of Melville's *The Confidence-Man.*

1. During the year prior to the publication of *The Confidence-Man* there were several performances of *Robert Macaire* or *Robert Macaire and Bertrand,* as follows: In August 1855, Gabriel Ravel and the Martinetti family appeared at the Broadway Theater in the Pantomime of *Robert Macaire* (*Times* 11 Aug. 1855). In September, the Broadway still had the "laughable Pantomime" of *Robert Macaire* with the Ravels (*Times* 13 Sept. 1855).

In February 1856 the Ravels, now at Niblo's Garden, were presenting the "comic Pantomime" of *Robert Macaire* with Antoine Ravel as Robert and François Ravel as Bertrand (*Times* and *Tribune* 13 Feb. 1856). In April the Ravels appeared again at Niblo's Garden in *Robert and Bertrand* (*Times, Herald,* and *Tribune* 2 April 1856), and in July, the two brothers in the same production (*Times* and *Herald* 7 July 1856). Then, still in July, John Brougham took over the evidently very popular vehicle for comic entertainment and put on at his Bowery Theater *Robert Macaire,* with C. Fisher as Robert (*Times* 16 July 1856). And, finally, Christy's Minstrels added their version (*Herald* 22 July 1856). That three different versions of the comic figure were presented on the New York stage during the summer of the 1856 election is suggestive of the possibilities for satire on current public events which the figure of Robert Macaire may have afforded.

2. The actual number of lithographs that feature Robert Macaire is uncertain. He appears in prints by Daumier and other artists in *Caricature* before 1836 and in *Charivari* after 1838. The figure of 100 is derived from the sequence of lithographs that appeared in *Charivari* from August 20, 1836, to November 25, 1838 (Delteil nos. 354–455). These were collected and issued in sets of 50 (1837), of 80 (1838), and of 100 (Dec. 1838) as *Caricaturana.* Later, Daumier took up the theme of Macaire again in a series of 20 prints in *Charivari* from October 1840 to November 1841 (Delteil nos. 866–85). Two early drawings of Macaire by Daumier in *Caricature* are "Petits! venez donc Dindons" (27 Nov. 1834; Delteil no. 97) in which King Louis Philippe, in Macaire garb, is pictured luring turkeys from a political turkey-roost by offering money as feed; and "Robert Macaire" (30 July 1835; Delteil no. 124), in which Adolphe Thiers, the king's minister, is caricatured as Macaire. The main sequence is illustrated in Delteil (nos. 354–455). They are more clearly illustrated in Adhémar (the legends are all legible), but in his edition the prints are grouped according to themes. Prints accompanying this essay as illustrations are reproduced courtesy of the Achenbach Foundation for Graphic Arts, California Palace of the Legion of Honor, Fine Arts Museums of San Francisco. For help received I wish to thank Maxine Rosston, Curator of Prints, Achenbach Foundation for Graphic Arts; Betsy G. Fryberger, Curator of Prints and Drawings, Stanford University Museum of Art; Ann Rosener, Occasional Works; Janet Lewis Winters, and Jeannette Ringold.

3. Symmons claims that the lithographs do not necessarily reflect Daumier's private views but were "editorial" only, produced by Daumier to make a living. She also suggests that there were other authors of the legends than Philipon (6–9).

4. For other accounts of the theatrical Robert Macaire see Champfleury 113–29; Osiakovski 388–92; Rey 20–22; Adhémar 11–13; and Coyle 19. For the most recent account of Daumier and his place in nineteenth-century French art see Eitner 232–36. Many of the historical persons of this interesting period, including Lemaître and Jean-Baptiste Gaspard Deburau, the famous Pierrot of the Théâtre des Funambules, are recreated in Marcel Carné's great film *Les enfants du paradis* (1945).

5. Pp. 70–78. Rey goes further in his claim that Robert Macaire is a "full portrayal of the important role of business and finance in nineteenth-century French life" and that Daumier's trickster is "the dominant symbol of the century" (20). Clark sees him as he "stalks" through Paris as "going through the poses of a whole corrupted civilization" (*Absolute Bourgeois* 179). Emphasizing Philipon's role, Passeron thinks he had an idea of publishing a series of prints on "la jobardise du public entrepris par un escroc aux multiples visages du monde de l'industrie" and that Macaire is a prototype "du filou, malin, rusé, attrape-gogo éternel sans morale et sans scrupules" in a "tableau complèt" of the actions of the world of the July Monarchy (115–18). Harper finds Daumier's art as a whole full of caricatures of politicians as theatrical and street performers. She comprehensively and suggestively explores all of his clowns, saltimbanques, acrobats, jugglers, mountebanks,

parade barkers, and other travelling entertainers in "Daumier's Clowns." Ramus finds the Macaire sequence somewhat "tedious because of the lengthy captions" (xv).

6. Cf. Henry James in *Daumier, Caricaturist* (1890), where he comments interestingly on the failure of great caricature to thrive in the United States, because "Irony, skepticism, pessimism are, in any particular soil, plants of gradual growth" (3) and caricature is essentially reactionary. Although he praises Daumier's art of caricature as sometimes "almost tragic," he finds it limited by the temporal nature of its occasions. For him Daumier "has no wide horizon; the absolute bourgeois hems him in and he is a bourgeois himself without poetic ironies, to whom a big cracked mirror has been given" (30). Cf. the very different estimate of Valéry (155–60).

7. "En vérité, en vérité!" (Delteil no. 389; Adhémar no. 9). The legend reads in full "En vérité, en vérité! Je te le dis, Bertrand, le temps de la commandite va passer, mais les badauds ne passeront pas. Occupons nous de ce qui est éternel. Si nous faisions une religion? Heim!"—[Bertrand:] "Diable! Diable! Une religion, ce n'est pas facile á faire!"—"T'es toujours bête, Bertrand! On se fait Pape, on loue une boutique, on emprunte des chaises et l'on fait des sermons sur la mort de Napoléon, la découverte de l'Amérique, sur Molière, sur n'importe quoi! V'là une religion, ce n'est pas plus difficile que ça." ("Verily, verily, I say unto you, Bertrand, the time of the joint-stock company is passing away, but the suckers do not pass away. Let us occupy ourselves with what is eternal. What if we were to found a religion? How about it?" [Bertrand:] "The devil! the Devil! A religion—that is not easy to do!" "You are always stupid, Bertrand! One makes oneself the Pope, one rents a shop, one borrows some chairs and one produces some sermons on the death of Napoleon, the discovery of America, on Molière, on it doesn't matter what! There's a religion for you. It's no more difficult than that.")

8. Thackeray is referring to "Robert-Macaire mendiant distingué" (Delteil no. 380; Adhémar no. 13). The conversation in the legend between Macaire and an older well-dressed gentleman walking his poodle reads: "Monsieur, est-ce bien á vous que j'ai l'honneur de parler?"—[Gentleman:] "A moi même, Monsieur."—"J'en suis charmé! Vous avez là un bien joli chien! En usez vous? . . . Parbleu! Monsieur, vous devez connaître ma famille, les *Macairbec?* Nous sortons tous de Brest, mon aïeul servait le Roi sur ses *galères,* mon père et moi *appartenons* aussi á la marine. Des malheurs *judiciaires,* des persécutions politiques nous ont plongé dans une affreuse décline et je n'hésite pas á vous demander un secours de dix francs."—"Monsieur, je ne donne pas aux personnes que je ne connais pas."—"C'est juste, c'est juste! Dans ce cas, *prêtez* moi dix francs." ("Sir, is it indeed yourself to whom I have the honor of speaking?" "To me, sir." "Charmed indeed. You have there a fine dog! Will you have some [snuff]? My word, Sir, you ought to know my family, the *Macairbec?* We are from Brest, my grandfather served the king in the *galleys,* my father and I *belonged* also to the navy. *Legal* misfortunes, some political persecution plunged us into a frightful decline and I do not hesitate to ask you for the assistance of ten francs." "Sir, I do not give to persons whom I do not know." "Very well, very well! In that case, *loan* me ten francs.")

9. See "A tous les coeurs biens nés que la patrie est chère!" (*Charivari* 28 Oct. 1838; Delteil no. 441; Adhémar no. 100); and "Piété filiale" (*Charivari* 25 Nov. 1838; Delteil no. 455; Adhémar no. 81).

10. Cf. Hogarth, about whose portrait caricatures Shesgreen notes that "the type exists in and through the individual"—many of whom are still identifiable today (xviii).

11. In Goya's prints, figures and concepts from demonology and witchcraft are important. See, for example, *Ensayos* ("Trials"), *Volaverunt* ("They have flown"), *Buen Viage* ("Bon Voyage"), and *Linda maestra!* ("Pretty teacher!"), and 60, 61, 64, and 68 in Goya. For discussion of figures and concepts conventional in the history of witchcraft and demon-

ology and of Melville's use of this lore in *Moby-Dick* see Trimpi, "Melville's Use." For *Los Disparates,* see Holo.

12. "Bertrand, j'adore l'industrie" (Delteil no. 354; Adhémar no. 2). "Bertrand, j'adore l'industrie. Si tu veux nous créons une banque, mais là, une vraie banque! Capital cent millions de millions, cent milliards de milliards d'actions. Nous enfonçons la banque de France, nous enfonçons les banquiers, les banquistes, nous enfonçons tout le monde!"—[Bertrand:] "Oui, mais les gendarmes?"—"Que tu es bête, Bertrand, est ce qu'on arrête un millionaire?" ("Bertrand, I love to be busy. If you like, we'll create a bank, but, then a real bank! Capital of a hundred million million, a hundred billion billion of shares. We'll sink the bank of France, we'll sink the bankers, the pseudo-bankers, we'll sink everyone!"—[Bertrand:] "Yes, but the police?"—"How stupid you are, Bertrand, does one arrest a millionaire?") For evidence that this print is based on Girardin, see Adhémar (233).

13. "Nous sommes actionnaires" (Delteil no. 370; Adhémar no. 3). "Nous sommes actionnaires de l'institut agricole et archi-colle de Goëtho, du Physiono-trappe, de feu la société sanitaire, des Mors-Lycos, du papier de sûreté pour les voleurs, de la *Blague,* journal très politique et d'une foule d'autres opérations philantropiques, nous venons de toucher nos dividendes et nous les mangeons en parties de plaisir. [To an awaiting gendarme:] Garçon, encore une sou de fromage!" ("We are shareholders in the Agricultural and [archi-colle?] Institute of Goëtho, in the Physiono Type, in the late Health Society, in the [Mors-Lycos?], in safety [toilet] paper for thieves, in the *Big Joke,* a newspaper that is very political and in a host of other charitable operations; we have drawn our dividends and we are feasting in pleasure parties. Waiter, another morsel of cheese!")

14. "Messieurs et Dames!" (Delteil no. 360; Adhémar no. 5). Macaire, standing on his vehicle, while Bertrand beats a large drum to call up the crowd: "Messieurs et Dames! Les mines d'argent, les mines d'or, les mines de diamant ne sont que de la pot-Bouille, de la ratatouille en comparaison de houille. Mais (que vous m'allez dire) tu vends alors les actions un million? Mes actions, Messieurs, je ne les vends pas, je les donne pour 200 misérables francs, j'en donne deux pour une, je donne une aiguille, un cure-oreille, un passe lacet, et je vous donne encore ma bénediction par dessus le marché. En avant la grosse caisse!" ("Gentlemen and ladies. Silver mines, gold mines, diamond mines are only scraps, lousy food in comparison with coal. But (you are going to say) you are selling a million shares [in coal]? My shares, Gentlemen, I do not sell; I *give* them for 200 miserable francs, I give two for one, I give a needle, an ear-pick, a bodkin [all free gifts], and I give you, besides, my blessing into the bargain. Move ahead to the large cashier's window!")

15. For a full reproduction of this series, see Vetrocq, pls. 1–39 and S1–S65. For commentary see the essay by Vetrocq and Adelheid M. Gealt's introduction to it.

Melville's Art: Overtures from the Journal of 1856–1857

Page citations for this chapter are (unless otherwise noted) to the Northwestern-Newberry Library edition of *Mardi, Moby-Dick, Pierre, The Piazza Tales and Other Prose Pieces,* and *The Confidence-Man;* and to the Hayford-Sealts edition of *Billy Budd, Sailor.*

1. Unless otherwise noted, all references to the 1856–57 journal are to the new Northwestern-Newberry *Journals* edited by Howard C. Horsford (with Lynn Horth). Horsford also edited the earlier text he entitled *Journal of a Visit to Europe and the Levant, October 11, 1856–May 6, 1857* (1955). Following Gilman's advice, I remove the misspellings or suspected misspellings and occasionally reinstate readings from the 1955 edition if substantiated by the new Textual Notes. It seems to me that Gilman's comments

on the 1955 edition, although adopted, are not fully acknowledged by the reference in the Northwestern-Newberry edition (235).

2. The few detailed accounts of this period are Sealts's, Finkelstein's, and Bezanson's introduction to *Clarel.*

3. Horsford, "Introduction," *Journal* (1955 ed.) 19 and Lebowitz 232; Pops 160. Lebowitz offers a "psychic biography" of an "obsessed" Melville whose art culminates in "willful silence" (ix). Baym's theory of Melville's "quarrel" with fiction sides with contemporary reviewers and imputes all sorts of transformations and insensitivities to Melville (e.g., he was an unkind friend to Hawthorne [914, 922]—even before they could have become acquaintances!). Dryden's earlier study of cynicism about fiction offers a more lasting approach based on the form and effect of Melville's fiction.

4. Pp. 58–59. Lebowitz (232) ends this quotation at "among," which coincides with a manuscript page-break in Horsford's 1955 edition.

5. Some are documented in Sealts's *Reading:* item numbers 97, 98, 169, 198, 199, 233, 262, 263, 291, 296, 320, 360–64, 403, 423, 430, 431, 534, 559, and 564.

6. Tobey discusses Downing's and Greenough's contributions.

7. Shepard 154; Auden 19, 23. Auden (15–42) provides an overview of the themes of desert and sea but tends (e.g., 28) to oversimplify Melville's distinctions.

8. Jones (177, 173), Horsford (7–8), Richard S. Moore (204–05; Hawthorne's "portrait" confirms Melville's "loss of faith in the imagination"), Lebowitz (214–15), and Hook (191–92) are some of the critics who have taken Hawthorne as a final authority on Melville. More evenhanded assessments are given by Stewart and Brodhead (197–204).

9. *Scarlet Letter* ch. 18, pp. 199–203. I cite chapter numbers for the novels to facilitate reference to other editions.

10. Curiously, in a postscript to the "Agatha" letter to Hawthorne, Melville writes: "If you find any *sand* in this letter, regard it as so many sands of my life, which run out as I was writing it" (162). There is no doubt the two authors shared some of the same iconographic vocabulary, to different effect. See Abel's study of how the natural picturesque is transferred to traits of moral picturesqueness in Hawthorne's characters.

11. Direct familiarity with Ruskin's first two volumes, 1843–46, is obvious in Downing (10–14) and in Melville (Cowen 8: 142–69; Sealts, no. 430), though later influence is also clear.

12. On associationism, see Hipple (esp. 90–97), and Ross on some of the eighteenth-century background.

13. Space prevents me from detailing these critical attempts. One example of interpretation is typical in general: Dettlaff (221) considers "Venetian tint" in *Clarel* an indication of "superficial color." But even its literal context in 2.30, apart from its identification with Vine, points to the essential life blood quality of the tint. Of what has been written, I find Wolf's essay most rewarding.

14. See Ruskin's discussion in *Stones* (*Works* 11: 159–60).

15. Writers on the grotesque (Harpham excepted) have relied unduly on "fearful" aspects of Ruskin's definition in *Stones* and neglected to consider *Modern Painters.* See O'Connor 4; Kayser 201; Thomson 19; Clayborough 14–15 and 36–42; Landow 31–32; Cook 544 and 548. Harpham's valuable study of the grotesque discusses the works of da Vinci, Poe, Brontë, Mann, Conrad, Lawrence, and others.

16. Inexplicably, Jonathan Scott (61), Wilton-Ely (73), and Harvey (9) place Piranesi in the context of Burke's *Enquiry,* using almost exactly the same words. Scott concedes, though, that "Piranesi's confusions [also] exist in the first states of the *Carceri* which antedate the *Enquiry.*"

17. On Melville, Conrad, and Faulkner, see Guetti. Harpham's study of the grotesque refers to da Vinci, Poe, Brontë, Mann, Conrad, Lawrence, and others.

18. Bell argues that Hawthorne adopts "a rather devious strategy for concealing or evading the more subversive implications of being a romancer, the implications Melville, to his peril, proclaimed openly" (41), the difference between their romances being entirely strategic—"irony" as against "defiance" (39).

19. This sentence derives from Robert Frost's "After Apple-Picking" (68) and from those "twisted, and contorted old trees . . . grotesque forms" in "Hawthorne and His Mosses" (*Piazza Tales* 241) to which the "grotesque contortions" of the olive trees are compared (*Journals* 89).

Melville and Dutch Genre Painting

Page citations for this chapter are (unless otherwise noted) to the Northwestern-Newberry Library edition of *Typee, Mardi, Redburn, White-Jacket, Moby-Dick, The Piazza Tales and Other Prose Pieces, Pierre,* and *Journals;* Warner Berthoff's edition of *Great Short Works of Herman Melville;* and the Hayford-Sealts edition of *Billy Budd, Sailor.*

1. Pp. 57, 63. In Discourse IV, Reynolds most fully developed his contrast between the "great" or "grand" style and the "lower," essentially a distinction based on his principle that painters should portray "general ideas" rather than "minute particularities." "Thus," he wrote,

> if a portrait-painter is desirous to raise and improve his subject, he has no other means than by approaching it to a general idea. He leaves out all the minute breaks and peculiarities in the face, and changes the dress from a temporary fashion to one more permanent, which has annexed to it no ideas of meanness from its being familiar to us. But if an exact resemblance of an individual be considered as the sole object to be aimed at, the portrait-painter will be apt to lose more than he gains by the acquired dignity taken from general nature. It is very difficult to ennoble the character of a countenance but at the expense of the likeness, which is what is most generally required by such as sit to the painter. (72)

Although he acknowledged the fine craftsmanship and technique of many Dutch painters, Reynolds believed that only works "built upon general nature" would "live for ever; while those which depend for their existence on particular customs and habits, a partial view of nature, or the fluctuation of fashion, can only be coeval with that which first raised them from obscurity" (73). Melville acquired Reynolds's *Literary Works* in 1870 and annotated them heavily, especially the *Discourses* (Cowen, "Melville's Marginalia," vol. 8).

2. Leyda 529. This critical tradition is represented well by Lawrance Thompson's *Melville's Quarrel With God* and continues in such current studies as T. Walter Herbert's and William P. Shurr's studies of Melville's Calvinism. But I am thinking here of any approach to Melville through his philosophical and theological ideas rather than his descriptive style, his immediate cultural and social milieu, and his artistic tastes.

3. Contemporary art critics recognize that Dutch genre painting goes far beyond the simple imitation of life and recording of actuality. It employs a symbolic iconography rich in psychological, political, even spiritual suggestiveness. Edward Snow's remarkable reading of Vermeer is only one among many such revaluations of seventeenth-century Dutch art that make it impossible to distinguish sharply between "ideal" and "realistic" schools of art. But for most earlier observers, certainly for nineteenth-century English and

American audiences, Dutch painting represented the polar extreme of a visual realism devoid of deep significations and ambiguities.

4. Ruskin, championing the cause of the innovative impressionist J. M. W. Turner, frequently condemned Dutch painting for its indelicate handling of vulgar subject matter. In *Modern Painters I* (1843) Ruskin declared that the effect of Dutch paintings "is so totally for evil, that though I do not deny the advantage an artist of real judgment may derive from the study of some of them, I conceive the best patronage that any monarch could possibly bestow upon the arts, would be to collect the whole body of them into one gallery and burn it to the ground" (*Works* 3: 188–89). Melville acquired *Modern Painters* in 1865 and annotated many passages, including one that Ruskin intended as a defense of Pre-Raphaelite painting but could also justify Dutch realism: "Finally, as it is to be remembered that all truths, as far as their being particular or general affects their value at all, are valuable in proportion as they are particular, and valueless in proportion as they are general; or to express the proposition in simpler terms, every truth is valuable in proportion as it is characteristic of the thing of which it is affirmed" (quoted from "Melville's Marginalia" 8: 151; see also Ruskin, *Works* 3: 154). In this regard, Ruskin has come a long way from Reynolds's position: "Peculiar marks, I hold to be, generally, if not always, defects; however difficult it may be wholly to escape them" (Discourse VI 102). Perhaps because of the vulgar subject matter of many Dutch paintings, this growing tolerance for visual realism failed to transfer into an increased official appreciation for Dutch art.

5. *Art Thoughts* 182. Melville probably would have paid close attention to Jarves's opinions. Jarves reviewed *Typee* and *Omoo* in the *Polynesian*, a journal he edited in Honolulu, and Melville twice tried unsuccessfully to visit him in Rome in 1857 (*Leyda* 265, 274, 556). In 1871 Melville acquired and annotated Jarves's *The Art-Idea* (1864), a comprehensive presentation of opinions Jarves had been expressing since his first volume of art criticism, *Art-Hints: Architecture, Sculpture, and Painting,* was published by Harper and Brothers in 1855.

6. Although the date of this poem is uncertain, Melville's acquisition of Jarves's *The Art-Idea* and numerous other art books about this time argues strongly for 1871 or even 1872, when he would have read through his new volumes. This corroborates Horsford's date of 1871 (*Journal of a Visit* 37 n) and suggests that, like *Moby-Dick,* the poem was more immediately inspired by reading than by earlier personal experiences.

7. The earliest American art historians denied the influence of Dutch painting in America, perhaps following the lead of Charles H. Caffin, who in 1907 claimed that American painting was too regional and diverse to admit of parallels with Dutch art (336). Similar views are expressed by E. P. Richardson (25–26) and Eliot Clark (53), both of whom stress the influence of the Düsseldorf school. But more recent critics, armed with better data about American collections and the significant presence of Dutch painting in early nineteenth-century America, have begun exploring the cultural, social, economic, as well as technical similarities between American and Dutch genre painting. See especially H. Nichols B. Clark's two essays.

8. According to Richard S. Moore, Duyckinck served on the board of the American Art-Union (121). *The Literary World* regularly ran commentary on local art exhibits and evidently maintained conservative tastes, for it condemned the Bingham painting as "a vulgar subject, vulgarly treated" (23 Oct. 1847: 277).

9. Hazlitt's views were available to Melville in *Criticisms on Art; and Sketches of the Picture Galleries of England* (1843), a book he acquired in May 1870. Melville annotated it heavily, especially the section referred to here, "Essay on the Fine Arts" ("Herman at Christie's"). Since this essay was originally published in 1824 and reprinted many times,

including the seventh edition of the *Encyclopedia Britannica* (1838), Melville might have known Hazlitt's views quite early. For example another Hazlitt volume, *Table-Talk* (2nd ed., 1824), was charged to Lemuel Shaw during July 1848 when Melville was visiting Boston. Its essay on "The Picturesque and Ideal" links both Rubens and Rembrandt with the picturesque, and another on "Why Distant Objects Please" mentions Wilkie's *The Blind Fiddler* in a note (228). Hazlitt was an early admirer of the Dutch, and Melville seems to have valued his opinions on the arts. He acquired *Table-Talk* in 1863 and made several notations in it, particularly in the essay "On the Pleasure of Painting" (Cowen 5: 499).

10. Pamela R. Matthews explores the significance of this term in "Four Old Smokers." Her analysis and comparison to *Walden* supports my notion that Melville uses the associations of the chimney and smoking to carve out a middle ground between the excesses of idealistic transcendentalism on the one hand and earthy materialism on the other, a balance implicit in much Dutch painting.

11. These figures are based on a careful review of the provenance of each painter's work as listed in Thiel's *All the Paintings of the Rijksmuseum in Amsterdam.*

12. A thorough discussion of the dates of these manuscripts appears in Merton M. Sealts, Jr., *Pursuing Melville* 78–90.

13. Perhaps as early as 1880, Melville began purchasing titles in Sampson and Low's series "Illustrated Biographies of the Great Artists," a list that ran to over 39 titles during Melville's lifetime. The books were simultaneously published in New York by Scribner and Welford, making them easily accessible. Melville eventually owned at least 12, including volumes on Reynolds, Wilkie, Turner, Cruikshank, Gainsborough and Constable, Rembrandt, Claude Lorrain, the Barbizon painters, Dutch figure painters, and the one quoted earlier, Frank Cundall's *The Landscape and Pastoral Painters of Holland: Ruisdael Hobbema Cuijp Potter* (1891). Insofar as this list is a reliable index of his mature taste, it indicates a strong interest in genre as opposed to the grand style, for the series included books on Titian, Tintoretto, Fra Angelico, and other Italian painters that Melville presumably passed over.

Just how far the Dutch had risen in esteem is shown in Ronald Gower's book in this series, *The Figure Painters of Holland* (1880). Gower quotes a famous passage from Reynolds often construed as a critique (for example in Burnet, 40 years earlier) and interprets it positively: "It is this almost universal power of painting nature, a nature animated by human actors, that makes the works of these old Dutch artists so precious to the collector and amateur, and so valuable to the student and artist, and it is that which elicited from our greatest artist, Joshua Reynolds, the opinion that 'painters should go to the Dutch school to learn the art of painting as they would go to a Grammar School to learn languages'" (2). In his copy of Gower's 1880 book Melville sidelined the quotation from Reynolds, a well-known statement he had undoubtedly read before. He must have taken some small pleasure in seeing it interpreted favorably (Cowen 5: 247).

14. Howard P. Vincent, in the Hendricks House *Collected Poems,* suggests that the source is Teniers's *The Hour of Repose* (229 and note). More judiciously, Hennig Cohen cites manuscript alterations to argue for a generalized source: Melville rejected the line "Suggested by a Flemish picture" as a subtitle and cancelled the comment that "A particular picture is here referred to" (235).

Vincent found the title and a description of the painting in a French catalogue of Teniers's works but apparently never saw the painting itself. The description, which Vincent quotes in French, unmistakably fits *Bricklayer Smoking a Pipe,* a painting Melville could have seen at the Trippenhuis in 1857 (now in the Rijksmuseum, Amsterdam). While some elements of this work parallel those in Melville's poem, the mood is too light and energetic. A much closer analogue is the Brouwer engraving (Fig. 8) and several other tavern scenes in Melville's copy of *The Works of Eminent Masters* (Ostade's *The Dutch Smoking-Room* 1: 217; Brouwer and Steen vignettes 1: 115 and 4). No painting I have seen duplicates precisely the iconography of the poem.

15. *Letters* 205. Melville may be echoing a critical commonplace regarding Street's poetry. In an 1841 article in *Arcturus,* Evert Duyckinck reviewed a volume of Street's verse and wrote, "Street studies nature as Van Huysum, the Dutch painter, painted his flower pieces" (1: 63). Melville borrowed this volume of *Arcturus* in 1850 (Leyda 376).

Wrestling with the Angel:
Melville's Use of the Visual Arts in *Timoleon*

Page citations for this chapter are to the Northwestern-Newberry Library edition of Melville's *Journals*.

1. Hagstrum's *The Sister Arts* is the best study of literary pictorialism; but see also Franklin R. Rogers's *Painting and Poetry,* Hugh Witemeyer's *George Eliot and the Visual Arts,* and Viola Hopkins Winner's *Henry James and the Visual Arts*.

2. I have not been able to ascertain whether copies of the Le Brun picture were ever made. The drawing is reproduced conveniently in *A Triptych of Poisoners* by Jean Plaidy (pseudonym of Christine Hibbert) with a popularized account of the Marquise's life and career (75–130).

3. An alternative title for the poem, canceled before printing, was "Portrait" (Jarrard 256).

Classical Iconography in the Aesthetics of *Billy Budd, Sailor*

Page citations for this chapter (unless otherwise noted) are to the Northwestern-Newberry Library edition of *The Piazza Tales and Other Prose Pieces, The Confidence-Man,* and *Journals;* the Hendricks House editions of *Clarel* and *Collected Poems;* and the Hayford-Sealts edition of *Billy Budd, Sailor*.

1. "A more than life-size bust of Antinous on a pedestal was among Melville's belongings. He must have seen the Antinous of the Louvre; but he makes no specific mention of one of his favorite pieces of sculpture till he saw the Vatican Antinous in 1857" (Metcalf 136). Frances Thomas Osborne, Melville's other granddaughter, also remembered the statue, which "stood on a tall white pedestal in the corner of the front parlor" and was draped to keep dust from "the beautiful features and curly hair of the young Roman" (Sealts, *Early Lives* 183). Although the bust has not been identified, it was more than likely a copy of either the head of the *Farnese Antinous* (Figs. 2 and 3) or the Athens head (Fig. 1), the versions most popularly reproduced. Others have observed the physical resemblance between Billy Budd and the *Antinous;* notable among them is Edwin Haviland Miller.

2. Sealts, *Melville's Reading* no. 563a. In his book of Wordsworth, Melville marked with an X and a Greek theta the line "Elysian beauty, melancholy grace," and wrote in the margin, "This line must have been suggested by the *Antinous*—or a cast [of it.] It is pre-eminently Greek, & could not have been spontaneous to the Northern imagination." See Heffernan, "Melville and Wordsworth" 341.

3. P. 44. Melville had earlier used the phrase "strength and beauty" to illustrate the youthful, naive idealism of Pierre, to whom his father's chair-portrait was "a glorious gospel framed and hung upon the wall, and declaring to all people, as from the Mount,

that man is a noble, god-like being, full of choicest juices; made up of *strength and beauty* (*Pierre* 30; emphasis mine).

4. The political formula was commonly understood; see Peterson 11.

5. Though the original manuscript of "Statues in Rome" is not extant, a reading text of the lecture has been reconstructed by Merton M. Sealts, Jr.

6. Baby Malcolm was called "Barney." See the October 16 entry in Melville's 1849– 50 *Journal* and Horsford's explanatory note (255).

7. Royston Lambert's documented study traces fully the evolution of the Antinous myth. Marguerite Yourcenar's fictionalized account, though supported by scholarly research, follows the romantic tradition. Both Lambert's and Yourcenar's books contain photographs of some of the best-known portraits of Antinous. A complete catalogue, with photographs and descriptions, is published in Christoph W. Clairmont's *Die Bildnisse des Antinous*. Melville alludes to Antinous in the lecture and journals; see Coffler.

8. The 1852 edition of *Anthon's Classical Dictionary* relates the legend and its aftermath, concluding that "the absurd and disgusting conduct of Hadrian needs no comment" (143).

9. *Journals* 106. In Horsford's discussions, the statue illustrated as the Antinous of the Capitoline Museum (464) is actually the Antinous-Dionysus (the *Braschi*) of the Vatican Museum (Lambert 233; Figs. 58 and 60). The Capitoline statue that Melville undoubtedly saw is still on view at that museum but is now called *Hermes*. It is illustrated in the *Guide to the Capitoline Museums* (1984) and described as "an eclectic creation that adheres to the dominating taste in the Hadrianic period" (47–48). This statue, a simple nude with Antinous-type curls, a muscular body, and a down-turned head, was found at Hadrian's villa; the attribution is still controversial (Lambert 237). The Capitoline statue very much resembles the *Farnese Antinous* (Figs. 2 and 3).

10. The lure of the rose is a recurring motif in Melville's work. In *Mardi*, Hautia's handmaiden throws Taji a moss-rose and a Venus-car. "Beware, beware the rose, / It's cankered at the heart," warns the poet Yoomy. In "Amoroso" and other poems in the rose cycle of Melville's *Weeds and Wildings, With a Rose or Two,* the rose and the moss-rose symbolize the romantic love and beauty associated with Aphrodite of Cyprus. The lines of "Naples in the Time of Bomba" link both Billy and the Cypriote with the corrupting sensual beauty that Cyprus and Venus have long signified. In Billy, however, "the rose had some ado visibly to flush through the tan" (50).

11. According to Bezanson's careful analysis of *Clarel,* Ungar ranks very high among the pilgrims in the poem. A "merciless critic of American democracy," he is "the symbol of Stoic Endurance in Defeat" (Bezanson, ed., *Clarel* 547–48). Ungar is a Confederate veteran, however, and therefore may represent an errored point of view. Melville connects Vere with Marcus Aurelius and Ungar, but also with Stonewall Jackson, of whom he writes (in two separate poems): "earnest in error, as we feel . . . Stonewall followed his star." All are military commanders—aristocrats of a sort—and all stoical veterans of life, of tragedy and, perhaps, of error. Melville did appreciate the aristocratic ideal, as well as the democratic, for his wholistic vision embraced the positive aspects—and perceived the faults—of both orders, all of which constitute a major theme of *Billy Budd.*

12. Authoritarians portrayed as Romans include the Captain of the *Dido,* the chief Mehevi and the entire cannibal tribe in *Typee;* Captain Riga in *Redburn;* the officers of the *Neversink* in *White-Jacket;* Ahab (Tarquin); Ungar and the Dominican priest in *Clarel.* "Nature's Roman, never to be scourged" is the concluding line of Melville's poem "The House-Top."

13. *Aratra Pentelici: Six Lectures on the Elements of Sculpture* 95–96. Ruskin began the work by addressing the connection between art and social duty: "These days only one

subject can seriously occupy your thoughts—the necessity, namely, of determining how it has come to pass, that in these recent days, *iniquity* the most reckless and monstrous can be committed unanimously, by men more generous than ever yet in the world's history were deceived into deeds of cruelty" (1–2; emphasis mine).

14. See Ruskin, *Modern Painters* 2: 9–15.

15. Miller's study, one of the first to explore the Apollo icon in Melville's work, suggests that Melville ultimately associated the figure with Hawthorne. See also Mellow 321. Melville's allusions to Apollo are enumerated in Coffler, *Melville's Classical Allusions.*

16. Robert Macpherson, *Vatican Sculptures,* pages unnumbered (Sealts no. 344). The book is inscribed: "Mr. Herman Melville from the author Rome May 4 1866." Of the *Apollo Belvedere,* Macpherson says: "According to Flaxman, the Python-slayer is here [in the *Apollo Belvedere*] represented in the character of the Deliverer from evil. . . . Despite some trifling defects of execution, the beholder never can or could look upon him as a mere man and hence the *indomitable* moral superiority and power acknowledged by us in its presence" (emphasis mine).

Another critic, A. S. Murray of the Department of Greek and Roman Antiquities at the British Museum, regretted that "the [*Apollo*] sculptor did not present this fairly elevated idea in a manner generally intelligible" (372). Following Winckelmann, Murray compares points of similarity between two celebrated statues of Praxiteles: the *Apollo Sauroktonos, or Lizard-Slayer,* which figures in Melville's story (see note 18), and the *Leaning Faun,* the central icon of Hawthorne's *The Marble Faun.*

17. *Anthon's Classical Dictionary* (1844 ed.). See Bercaw no. 16.

18. Melville's poem "On the Slain Collegians" refers to this event: "Apollo like in pride / Each would his Python slay." The allusion is of course ironic, since "Each [slain soldier] bloomed and died an unabated boy." Melville's engraved print of Turner's *Apollo Killing the Python* (no. A267) is in the Berkshire Athenaeum collection of Melville's prints and engravings, recently catalogued by Robert K. Wallace. At the Villa Albani, near the *Antinous* "with curls and buds," Melville saw the bronze Apollo—the *Apollo Sauroktonos, or Lizard-Slayer.* At the Villa Albani too, Melville saw the *Farnese Hercules.* All three sculptures contribute importantly to the iconography of *Billy Budd, Sailor.*

19. "A living, breathing quality is imparted [and] . . . becomes customary in the Antonine period and traditional henceforth" (Erhart 9). The original (bronze) *Apollo,* it will be remembered, was conceived in the Hellenistic age, but the (marble) *Apollo Belvedere* is a Hadrianic work. The *Antinous* sculptures, executed by Hadrian's decree, epitomized the union of Greek and Roman aesthetics.

20. The passage is quoted by Merton M. Sealts, Jr., *Melville as Lecturer* 14–16.

21. Like "aufheben," one of Hegel's characteristic keywords, the word "execute" can be used in three different contexts, meaning to annihilate, to carry out, to create. The paradoxical term illustrates the Hegelian system of dialectical synthesis. See also Barbara Johnson, "Melville's Fist: The Execution of *Billy Budd.*"

22. Vere's law is the law of Melville the artist, not of Melville the man. To be sure, the tale's other aspects—social, political, and religious, not to mention psychosexual and autobiographical—have implications that lead to different conclusions.

Works Cited

Abel, Darrel. *The Moral Picturesque: Studies in Hawthorne's Fiction*. West Lafayette, IN: Purdue UP, 1988.

Adams, Timothy Dow. "Architectural Imagery in Melville's Short Fiction." *American Transcendental Quarterly* 44 (Fall 1979): 265–77.

Adhémar, Jean. *Financial and Businessmen (Robert Macaire)*. Paris: Amiel, 1974.

Adler, Joyce Sparer. "The Imagination and Melville's Endless Probe for Relation." *American Transcendental Quarterly* 19 (1973): 37–42.

Aldington, Richard, ed. *Letters of Madame de Sévigné*. 2 vols. London: George Routledge and Sons, 1937.

Allston, Washington. *Lectures on Art*. Ed. Richard Henry Dana. 1850.

Alphabetical Index to the Astor Library. New York: R. Craighead, 1851.

Andrews, Edward D. *The Community Industries of the Shakers*. Albany: U of the State of New York P [c. 1932].

Anthon, Charles. *Anthon's Classical Dictionary*. New York: Harper, 1852.

Auden, W. H. *The Enchafèd Flood; or, The Romantic Iconography of the Sea*. New York: Vintage, 1950.

Averill, Louise Hunt. "John Vanderlyn, American Painter." Diss. Yale, 1949.

Bachrach, A. G. H. "Turner, Ruisdael, and the Dutch." *Turner Studies* 1 (Summer 1981): 19–30.

Ballou, Hosea, II. "The White Mountains." *The Universalist Quarterly and General Review* 3 (1846): 113–43.

Barbour, James. "Melville's Biography: A Life and the Lives." In Bryant, *A Companion* 3–34.

Bartlett, W. H. *Walks about the City and Environs of Jerusalem, Summer 1842*. 1844. Jerusalem: Canaan, 1974.

Baudelaire, Charles. *Selected Writings on Art and Artists*. Trans. P. E. Charvet. Harmondsworth: Penguin, 1972.

Baym, Nina. "Melville's Quarrel with Fiction." *PMLA* 94 (Oct. 1979): 909–23.

Beaver, Harold R. Commentary. *Moby-Dick*. By Herman Melville. London: Penguin, 1972.

Bell, Michael Davitt. "Arts of Deception: Hawthorne, 'Romance,' and *The Scarlet Letter*." In Colacurcio 29–56.

Bercaw, Mary K. *Melville's Sources*. Evanston: Northwestern UP, 1987.

Bergmann, Johannes D. "Melville's Tales." In Bryant, *A Companion* 241–78.

Berthoff, Warner. *The Example of Melville*. 1962. New York: Norton, 1972.

Berthold, Dennis. "Charles Brockden Brown, *Edgar Huntly,* and the Origins of the American Picturesque." *William and Mary Quarterly* 41 (Jan. 1984): 62–84.

Bezanson, Walter E., ed. Introduction and Notes. *Clarel: A Poem and Pilgrimage in the Holy Land.* By Herman Melville. New York: Hendricks House, 1960.

Bloom, Harold, ed. *Modern Critical Views: Herman Melville.* New Haven: Chelsea House, 1986.

———. *The Ringers in the Tower.* Chicago: U of Chicago P, 1971.

Boudreau, Gordon V. "Of Pale Ushers and Gothic Piles: Melville's Architectural Symbology." *ESQ: A Journal of the American Renaissance* 18 (Second Quarter 1972): 67–82.

Branch, Watson G., ed. *Melville: The Critical Heritage.* Boston: Routledge and Kegan Paul, 1974.

Breinig, Helmbrecht. "The Destruction of Fairyland: Melville's 'Piazza' in the Tradition of the American Imagination." *ELH* 35 (June 1968): 254–83.

Bremer, Frederika. *The Homes of the New World: Impressions of America.* Trans. Mary Howitt. 2 vols. New York: Harper, 1853.

Brodhead, Richard H. *Hawthorne, Melville, and the Novel.* Chicago: U of Chicago P, 1976.

———, ed. *New Essays on* Moby-Dick. Cambridge: Cambridge UP, 1986.

Brookner, Anita. *Jacques-Louis David.* London: Chatto and Windus, 1980.

Bryant, John, ed. *A Companion to Melville Studies.* New York: Greenwood, 1986.

———. "Melville's Comic Debate: Geniality and the Aesthetics of Repose." *American Literature* 55 (May 1983): 151–70.

Buchanan-Brown, John. *The Book Illustrations of George Cruikshank.* Rutland, VT: Charles E. Tuttle, 1980.

Burke, Edmund. *A Philosophical Enquiry into the Origin of Our Ideas of the Sublime and Beautiful.* Ed. J. T. Boulton. London: Routledge and Kegan Paul, 1958.

Burnet, John. *A Treatise on Painting. In Four Parts.* London: James Carpenter, 1837.

Butlin, Martin, and Evelyn Joll. *The Paintings of J. M. W. Turner.* 2 vols. Rev. ed. New Haven: Yale UP, 1984.

Caffin, Charles H. *The Story of American Painting: The Evolution of Painting in America.* 1907. Garden City, NJ: Garden City Publishing, 1937.

Cagnetta, Francois. "La Vie et L'oeuvre de Gaetano Giulio Zummo." In *Revista di Storia delle Scienze Mediche e Naturali* 20 (Florence: Leo S. Olschki Editore, 1977): 489–500. Atti del lo Congresso Internazionale sulla Ceroplastica nella Scienze e nell'Arte. . . 1975.

Campbell, Catherine H. *New Hampshire Scenery: A Dictionary of Nineteenth-Century Artists of New Hampshire Mountain Landscapes.* Canaan, NH: Phoenix, 1985.

Cannon, Agnes Dicken. "On Translating *Clarel.*" *Essays in Arts and Sciences* 5 (July 1976): 160–80.

Carlyle, Thomas. *Sartor Resartus: The Life and Opinions of Herr Teufelsdrockh.* 1836. New York: AMS Press, 1969.

Cawdrey, Mary Bartlett. *American Academy of Fine Arts and Art-Union, 1816–1852.* 2 vols. New York: New York Historical Society, 1953.

Champfleury [Fleury, Jules]. *Histoire de la caricature moderne.* Vol. 5. 3rd ed. Paris: Dentu, n.d.

Champney, Benjamin. *Sixty Years' Memories of Art and Artists.* Woburn, MA: Wallace and Andrews, 1899.

Chateaubriand, F. A. de. *Travels in Greece, Palestine, Egypt, and Barbary, . . . 1806 and 1807.* Trans. F. Shoberl. New York: Van Winkle and Wiley, 1814.

Clairmont, Christoph W. *Die Bildnisse des Antinous*. Die Schweiz: Schweizerisches Institut in Rom, 1966.

Clark, Eliot. *History of the National Academy of Design: 1825–1953*. New York: Columbia UP, 1954.

Clark, H. Nichols B. "A Fresh Look at the Art of Francis W. Edmonds: Dutch Sources and American Meanings." *American Art Journal* 14 (Summer 1982): 73–94.

——. "A Taste of the Netherlands: The Impact of Seventeenth-Century Dutch and Flemish Genre Painting on American Art 1800–1900." *The American Art Journal* 14 (Spring 1982): 23–38.

Clark, Kenneth. *Landscape into Art*. 2nd ed. New York: Harper and Row, 1976.

Clark, Thomas J. *The Absolute Bourgeois: Artists and Politics in France, 1848–1851*. Greenwich, CT: New York Graphic Society, 1973.

Clayborough, Arthur. *The Grotesque in English Literature*. Oxford: Oxford UP, 1965.

Coffler, Gail. *Melville's Classical Allusions*. Westport, CT: Greenwood, 1985.

Cohen, Hennig. "*Israel Potter*: Common Man as Hero." In Bryant, *A Companion* 279–313.

Colacurcio, Michael J. *New Essays on* The Scarlet Letter. Cambridge: Cambridge UP, 1985.

Cook, Richard M. "Evolving the Inscrutable: The Grotesque in Melville's Fiction." *American Literature* 49 (Jan. 1978): 544–59.

Cooper, James Fenimore. "American and European Scenery Compared." In *Home Book of the Picturesque* 51–69.

Cowan, Bainard. *Exiled Waters: Moby-Dick and the Crisis of Allegory*. Baton Rouge: Louisiana State UP, 1982.

Cowan, S. A. "In Praise of Self-Reliance: The Role of Bulkington in *Moby-Dick*." *American Literature* 38 (Jan. 1967): 547–56.

Cowen, Walker. "Melville's 'Discoveries': A Dialogue of the Mind with Itself." In *The Recognition of Herman Melville*. Ed. Hershel Parker. Ann Arbor: U of Michigan P, 1967. 333–46.

——. "Melville's Marginalia." 12 vols. Diss. Harvard, 1965.

Coyle, Susan. *The Human Comedy: Daumier and His Contemporaries*. Minneapolis: U of Minnesota Art Gallery, 1981.

Craven, Wayne. "The Grand Manner in Early Nineteenth-Century American Painting: Borrowings from Antiquity, the Renaissance, and the Baroque." *American Art Journal* 11 (1969): 4–43.

Crawfurd, Raymond. *Plague and Pestilence in Literature and Art*. Oxford: Clarendon, 1914.

Cummings, Thomas S. *Historic Annals of the National Academy of Design*. 1865. New York: Da Capo Press, 1969.

Cundall, Frank. *The Landscape and Pastoral Painters of Holland: Ruisdael Hobbema Cuijp Potter*. New York: Scribner and Welford, 1891.

Cunningham, Peter. "The Memoir." In *Turner and His Works*. By John Burnet. London: David Bogue, 1852.

Dahl, Curtis. "The Architecture of Society and the Architecture of the Soul: Hawthorne's *The House of the Seven Gables* and Melville's *Pierre*." *University of Mississippi Studies in English* 5 (1984–87): 1–22.

——. "Of Foul Weather and Bulkington." *Melville Society Extracts* 30 (May 1977): 10–11.

Davidson, Abraham A. *The Eccentrics and Other American Visionary Painters*. New York: Dutton, 1978.

Davidson, Jane P. *David Teniers the Younger.* Boulder: Westview Press, 1979.

Davis, Merrell R. *Melville's* Mardi: *A Chartless Voyage.* New Haven: Yale UP, 1952.

Davis, Merrell R., and William H. Gilman, eds. *The Letters of Herman Melville.* New Haven: Yale UP, 1960.

Delteil, Loys. *Le peintre-graveur illustré (XIXe XXe siècles). Honoré Daumier.* Vols. 20–29. Paris: Chez l'auteur, 1925–30.

Dettlaff, Shirley M. "Ionian Form and Esau's Waste: Melville's View of Art in *Clarel.*" *American Literature* 54 (May 1982): 212–28.

———. "Melville's Aesthetics." In Bryant, *A Companion* 625–65.

Dillingham, William B. *Melville's Short Fiction, 1853–1856.* Athens: U of Georgia P, 1977.

Downing, Andrew Jackson. *The Architecture of Country Houses.* 1850. New York: Da Capo Press, 1968.

Drake, Samuel Adams. *The Heart of the White Mountains: Their Legend and Scenery.* New York: Harper, 1882.

Dryden, Edgar A. *Melville's Thematics of Form: The Great Art of Telling the Truth.* Baltimore: Johns Hopkins UP, 1968.

Dubuisson, A. *Richard Parkes Bonington: His Life and Work.* London: John Lane, 1924.

Dunlap, William. *History of the Rise and Progress of the Arts of Design in the United States.* 3 vols. New York: Benjamin Blom, 1965.

Duyckinck, Evert. Rev. of *Nature,* by Alfred B. Street. *Arcturus* 1 (May 1841): 63.

[Dwight, Theodore]. *Sketches of Scenery and Manners in the United States.* New York: A. T. Goodrich, 1829.

Eastman, Samuel. *The White Mountain Guide Book.* 1858. Concord, NH: Lee and Shephard, 1869.

Eddy, D. Mathis. "Melville's Sicilian Moralist." *English Language Notes* 8 (March 1971): 191–200.

Eitner, Lorenz. *An Outline of Nineteenth-Century European Painting from David through Cezanne.* Vol. 1. New York: Harper, 1987.

Erhart, Patricia, Jiri Frel, and Sheldon Nodelman. *Roman Portraits: Aspects of Self and Society.* Los Angeles: U of California and the J. Paul Getty Museum, 1980.

[Escholier, Raymond]. *Gros: Ses Amis, Ses Élèves.* Paris, 1936. [Catalogue of an exhibition at the Petit Palais.]

Exhibition of the Paintings of the Late Thomas Cole. New York: Snowden and Prall, 1848.

Ferguson, Alfred R., ed. *The Journals and Miscellaneous Notebooks of Ralph Waldo Emerson, 1832–1834.* Vol 4. Cambridge: Harvard UP, 1964.

Finberg, A. J. *Turner's Sketches and Drawings.* London: Methuen, 1910.

Fink, Lois Marie, and Joshua C. Taylor. *Academy: The Academic Tradition in American Art.* Washington, DC: Smithsonian Institution Press, 1975. [Catalogue of an exhibition at the National Collection of Fine Arts, Washington.]

Finkelstein, Dorothee Metlitsky. *Melville's Orienda.* New Haven: Yale UP, 1961.

Fisher, Marvin. *Going Under: Melville's Short Fiction and the American 1850s.* Baton Rouge, LA: Louisiana State UP, 1977. 13–28.

Frank, Stuart M. *Herman Melville's Picture Gallery.* Fairhaven, MA: Edward J. Lefkowicz, 1986.

French Painting, 1774–1830: The Age of Revolution. Detroit: Wayne State UP, 1975. [Catalogue of an exhibition at the Grand Palais, Paris; Detroit Institute of Arts; and Metropolitan Museum of Art, New York.]

Friedlaender, Walter. "Napoleon as 'Roi thaumaturge.'" *Journal of the Warburg and Courtauld Institutes* 4 (1940–41): 139–41.

Frost, Robert. *The Poetry of Robert Frost.* Ed. Edward Connery Lathem. New York: Holt, Rinehart, 1969.

Georgoudaki, Catherine [Ekaterini]. "*Battle-Pieces and Aspects of the War:* Melville's Poetic Quest for Meaning and Form in a Fallen World." *American Transcendental Quarterly* 1:1 (March 1987): 21–32.

———. "Melville's Artistic Use of His Journeys to Europe and the Near East." Diss. Arizona State U, 1980.

Gilman, William H. Rev. of *Journal of a Visit to Europe and the Levant. . . . American Literature* 28 (March 1956): 82–93.

———. *Melville's Early Life and* Redburn. New York: New York UP, 1951.

———. "Melville's *Journal of a Voyage* [sic] *to Europe and the Levant:* A Reply to a Rejoinder." *American Literature* 28 (Jan. 1957): 523–34.

Glenn, Barbara. "Melville and the Sublime in *Moby-Dick.*" *American Literature* 48 (May 1976): 165–82.

Gower, Lord Ronald. *The Figure Painters of Holland.* New York: Scribner and Welford, 1880.

Goya y Lucientes, Francisco. *Los Caprichos.* Introduction by Philip Hofer. New York: Dover, 1969.

Greenough, Horatio. "American Architecture." In Small 51–68.

———. *The Travels, Observations, and Experience of a Yankee Stonecutter.* 1852. Gainesville, FL: Fascimiles and Reprints, 1958.

Gretchko, John M. J. "Melville and the New-York Gallery of the Fine Arts." *Melville Society Extracts* 82 (Sept. 1990): 7–8.

———. *Melvillean Ambiguities.* Cleveland: Falk and Bright, 1990.

Guetti, James. *The Limits of Metaphor: A Study of Melville, Conrad, and Faulkner.* Ithaca: Cornell UP, 1967.

Hagstrum, Jean H. *The Sister Arts: The Tradition of Literary Pictorialism and English Poetry from Dryden to Gray.* Chicago: U of Chicago P, 1958.

Hall, S. C. *The Vernon Gallery of British Art.* Four Series. London: George Virtue, 1850–54.

Harper, Paula Hays. "Daumier's Clowns: Les Saltimbanques et les Parades: New Biographical and Political Functions for a Nineteenth-Century Myth." Diss. Stanford, 1976.

Harper's New Monthly Magazine. Ed. Henry M. Alden. 56–63 (March 1878–July 1881).

Harpham, Geoffrey Galt. *On the Grotesque: Strategies of Contradiction in Art and Literature.* Princeton: Princeton UP, 1982.

Harvey, Miranda. *Piranesi: The Imaginary Views.* New York: Harmony Books, 1979.

Hawthorne, Nathaniel. *The English Notebooks.* Ed. Randall Stewart. New York: MLA, 1941.

———. *The French and Italian Notebooks.* Ed. Thomas Woodson. Columbus: Ohio State UP, 1963.

———. *The Marble Faun; or, The Romance of Monte Beni.* Columbus: Ohio State UP, 1968.

———. *Mosses from an Old Manse.* Columbus: Ohio State UP, 1974.

———. *The Scarlet Letter.* Columbus: Ohio State UP, 1962.

———. *Twice-told Tales.* Columbus: Ohio State UP, 1974.

Hayes, John. *Gainsborough: Paintings and Drawings.* London: Phaidon, 1975.

Hayford, Harrison. "Unnecessary Duplicates: A Key to the Writing of *Moby-Dick.*" In *New Perspectives on Melville.* Ed. Faith Pullin. Kent, OH: Kent State UP, 1978. 128–61.

Hazlitt, William. *Essays on the Fine Arts.* Ed. W. Carew Hazlitt. London: Reaves and Turner, 1873. [Contains the same essays as *Criticisms on Art,* 1843.]

Heffernan, Thomas Farel. "Melville and Wordsworth." *American Literature* 49 (Nov. 1977): 338–51.

———. "Melville the Traveler." In Bryant, *A Companion* 35–61.

Heimert, Alan. "*Moby-Dick* and American Political Symbolism." *American Quarterly* 15 (Winter 1963): 498–534.

Herbert, T. Walter, Jr. *Moby-Dick and Calvinism: A World Dismantled.* New Brunswick, NJ: Rutgers UP, 1977.

Herbert, T. Walter, Jr., and Jon D. Swartz. *The Osborne Collection of Melville Materials at Southwestern University.* Georgetown, TX: Cody Memorial Library, 1985. Rpt. in part in *Melville Society Extracts* 61 (Feb. 1985): 8–10.

"Herman at Christie's: On the Block—Again." *Melville Society Extracts* 63 (Sept. 1985): 10–12.

Herrmann, Luke. *Turner: Paintings, Watercolours, Prints & Drawings.* 2nd ed. Oxford: Phaidon, 1986.

Hibbott, Yvonne. "'Bonaparte Visiting the Plague-stricken at Jaffa' by Antoine Jean Gros (1771–1835)." *British Medical Journal* 1 (Feb. 22, 1969): 501–02.

Hillway, Tyrus, and Luther S. Mansfield, eds. Moby-Dick *Centennial Essays.* Dallas: Southern Methodist UP, 1953.

Hipple, Walter J., Jr. *The Beautiful, the Sublime, and the Picturesque in Eighteenth-Century British Aesthetic Theory.* Carbondale: Southern Illinois UP, 1957.

Hofer, Philip. Introduction. *The Prisons (Le Carceri): The Complete First and Second States.* By Battista Giovanni Piranesi. New York: Dover, 1973.

Hoffman, Daniel G. "Moby-Dick: Johah's Whale or Job's?" *Sewanee Review* 69 (Spring 1961): 205–24.

Hogarth, William. *Analysis of Beauty.* 1753. Oxford: Clarendon, 1955.

Holo, Selma. *Goya: Los Disparates.* Pullman: Washington State UP, 1976. [Catalogue of Exhibition at the J. Paul Getty Museum, June 8–Aug. 31, 1976.]

The Home Book of the Picturesque: American Scenery, Art, and Literature. 1852. Gainesville, FL: Scholars' Fascimile and Reprints, 1967.

Hook, Andrew. "Melville's Poetry." In Lee 176–98.

Horsford, Howard C. "Melville in the London Literary World." *Essays in Arts and Sciences* 13 (Sept. 1984): 23–42.

———. "Melville's *Journal of a Voyage* [sic] *to Europe and the Levant:* A Rejoinder to a Review." *American Literature* 28 (Jan. 1957): 520–23.

———, ed. Introduction and Notes. *Journal of a Visit to Europe and the Levant, October 11, 1856–May 6, 1857.* By Herman Melville. Princeton: Princeton UP, 1955.

Horsford, Howard C., and Lynn Horth, eds. Notes. *Journals.* Vol. 15 of *The Writings of Herman Melville.* Evanston: Northwestern-Newberry Library, 1989.

Hovanec, Carol P. "Melville as Artist of the Sublime: Design in 'The Tartarus of Maids.'" *Mid-Hudson Language Studies* 8 (1985): 241–51.

Howard, Leon. *Herman Melville: A Biography.* Berkeley: U of California P, 1951.

Howe, Winifred E. *A History of the Metropolitan Museum of Art.* 1913. New York: Arno, 1974.

Hunt, John Dixon. "Dickens and the Traditions of Graphic Satire." *Encounters: Essays on Literature and the Visual Arts.* Ed. John Dixon Hunt. New York: Norton, 1971. 124–55.

Huntress, Keith. "Melville, Henry Cheever, and 'The Lee Shore.'" *New England Quarterly* 44 (Sept. 1971): 468–75.

Hussey, Christopher. *The Picturesque: Studies in a Point of View.* New York: Putnam's, 1927.

The Illustrated Magazine of Art. 4 vols. New York: Alexander Montgomery, 1853–54.

Inge, M. Thomas, ed. *Bartleby the Inscrutable: A Collection of Commentary on Herman Melville's Tale "Bartleby the Scrivener."* Hamden, CT: Archon Press, 1979.

Irving, Washington. *Journals and Notebooks, Volume I, 1803–1806.* Ed. Nathalia Wright. Madison: U of Wisconsin P, 1969.

James, Henry. *Daumier, Caricaturist.* Emmaus, PA: Rodale, 1954.

Jarrard, Norman E. "Poems by Herman Melville: A Critical Edition of the Published Verse." Diss. U. of Texas, 1960.

Jarves, James Jackson. *Art-Hints: Architecture, Sculpture, and Painting.* New York: Harper and Brothers, 1855.

———. *The Art-Idea.* Ed. Benjamin Rowland, Jr. 1864. Cambridge, MA: Harvard UP, 1960.

———. *Art Thoughts: The Experiences and Observations of an American Amateur in Europe.* 1869. New York: Garland, 1976.

"John Vanderlyn." *Literary World* 11 (Oct. 2, 1852): 219.

Johnson, Barbara. "Melville's Fist: The Execution of *Billy Budd.*" *Studies in Romanticism* 18 (Winter 1979): 567–99.

Jones, Buford. "Some 'Mosses' from the *Literary World:* Critical and Bibliographical Survey of the Hawthorne-Melville Relationship." In Thompson and Lokke, *Ruined Eden* 173–204.

Kayser, Wolfgang. *The Grotesque in Art and Literature.* New York: McGraw-Hill, 1966. Trans. of 1957 German ed., Bloomington: Indiana UP, 1963.

Kelly, Franklin. *Frederic Edwin Church.* Washington, DC: National Gallery of Art, 1989.

King, Thomas Starr. *The White Hills: Their Legends, Landscape, and Poetry.* Boston: Woolworth and Amesworth, 1859.

Kip, William Ingraham. "Recollections of John Vanderlyn, the Artist." *Atlantic Monthly* 19 (Feb. 1867): 228–35.

Kirkland, Caroline Matilda. *Holidays Abroad or Europe from the West.* New York: Baker and Scribner, 1849.

Knight, Charles, ed. *London.* 6 vols. London: H. G. Bohn, 1851.

Kramer, Aaron. *Melville's Poetry: Toward the Enlarged Heart. A Thematic Study of Three Ignored Major Poems.* Rutherford, NJ: Fairleigh Dickinson UP, 1972.

Lambert, Royston. *Beloved and God: The Story of Hadrian and Antinous.* New York: Viking, 1984.

Landow, George P. *The Aesthetic and Critical Theories of John Ruskin.* Princeton: Princeton UP, 1971.

Langbaum, Robert. *The Poetry of Experience.* New York: Norton, 1963.

Langhorne, John, and William Langhorne, eds. *Plutarch's Lives.* New York: Harper & Brothers, 1846.

Lanza, Benedetto, et al. *Le Cere Anatomiche della Specola.* Florence: Arnaud Editore, 1979.

Larkin, Oliver W. *Samuel F. B. Morse and American Democratic Art.* Boston: Little, Brown, 1954.

Lebowitz, Alan. *Progress into Silence: A Study of Melville's Heroes.* Bloomington: Indiana UP, 1970.

Lee, A. Robert, ed. *Herman Melville: Reassessments.* London: Vision and Barnes and Noble, 1984.

Leslie, Charles Robert. *Autobiographical Recollections*. Ed. Tom Taylor. Boston: Ticknor and Fields, 1860.

Lessing, Gotthold. *Laocoön: An Essay on the Limits of Painting and Poetry.* 1766. Indianapolis: Bobbs-Merrill, 1962.

Lewis, R. W. B. *The American Adam.* Chicago: U of Chicago P, 1955.

Leyda, Jay. *The Melville Log: A Documentary Life of Herman Melville, 1819–1891.* 2 vols. 1951. Rpt. with a new supplement, New York: Gordian Press, 1969.

The Life and Remarkable Adventures of Israel R. Potter, . . . Providence: Henry Trumbull, 1824.

Lightbrown, Ronald W. "Gaetano Giulio Zummo—I: The Florentine Period." *Burlington Magazine* 106 (Nov. 1964): 486–96.

Lindsay, Kenneth. *The Works of John Vanderlyn, From Tammany to The Capital; A Loan Exhibition, October 11 to November 9, 1970.* Binghamton: University Art Gallery, [1970].

The Literary World. Ed. Charles Fenno Hoffman. Vol. 2, no. 38 (Oct. 23, 1847). New York: Osgood and Co., 1847–53.

Litman, Vicki Halper. "The Cottage and the Temple: Melville's Symbolic Use of Architecture." *American Quarterly* 21 (Fall 1969): 630–38.

Longfellow, Henry Wadsworth. "The Journey into Italy," in *Outre-Mer and Drift-Wood.* Boston and New York: Houghton Mifflin, 1886. 233–34.

Lynes, Russell. "How a Few Artists Wormed Their Way in the Course of a Century into the Confidence of a Small Percentage of Their Compatriots." *The Shaping of Art and Architecture in Nineteenth-Century America.* New York: Metropolitan Museum of Art, 1972. 104–16.

Lynton, Norbert. *The Story of Modern Art.* Oxford: Phaidon, 1980.

[McEntee, Jervis]. "John Vanderlyn." *Putnam's Monthly Magazine of American Literature, Science, and Art* 3 (June 1854): 593–95.

McIntosh, James. "Melville's Use and Abuse of Goethe: The Weaver-Gods in *Faust* and *Moby-Dick.*" *Amerikastudien* 25 (1980): 158–73.

Mackie, G. M. "Joppa," in *The Dictionary of the Bible, . . .* 5 vols. Ed. James Hastings. New York: C. Scribner's Sons, 1898–1904.

Macpherson, Robert. *Vatican Sculptures, Selected and Arranged in the Order in Which They are Found in the Galleries.* London: Chapman and Hall, 1863.

Malek, James S. *The Arts Compared: An Aspect of Eighteenth-Century British Aesthetics.* Detroit: Wayne State UP, 1974.

"Marius." *The United States Magazine and Democratic Review* 8 (1840): 475–512.

Mather, Frank Jewett, Jr. "Herman Melville." *The Review* 1 (Aug. 1919): 276–301. Rpt. in Hershel Parker, ed. *The Recognition of Herman Melville: Selected Criticism Since 1846.* Ann Arbor: U of Michigan P, 1967. 155–70.

Matthews, Pamela R. "Four Old Smokers: Melville, Thoreau, and Their Chimneys." *American Transcendental Quarterly* 51 (Summer 1981): 151–64.

Matthiessen, F. O. *American Renaissance: Art and Expression in the Age of Emerson and Whitman.* New York: Oxford UP, 1941.

Mazzitelli, Michele. *La Pestilenza nell'Arte.* Florence: Giuseppi Ciulli, 1952.

Mellow, James. *Nathaniel Hawthorne in His Times.* Boston: Houghton Mifflin, 1980.

Melville, Herman. *The Battle-Pieces of Herman Melville.* Ed. Hennig Cohen. New York: Thomas Yoseloff, 1963.

———. *Billy Budd, Sailor (An Inside Narrative).* Ed. Harrison Hayford and Merton M. Sealts, Jr. Chicago: U of Chicago P, 1962.

———. *Billy Budd, Sailor (An Inside Narrative)*. Ed. Milton Stern. Indianapolis: Bobbs-Merrill, 1975.

———. *Clarel: A Poem and Pilgrimage in the Holy Land*. Ed. Walter E. Bezanson. New York: Hendricks House, 1960.

———. *The Collected Poems of Herman Melville*. Ed. Howard P. Vincent. Chicago: Packard and Co./Hendricks House, 1947.

———. *The Complete Stories of Herman Melville*. Ed. Jay Leyda. New York: Random House, 1949.

———. *Great Short Works of Herman Melville*. Ed. Warner Berthoff. New York: Harper and Row, 1966.

———. "Hawthorne and His Mosses." Rpt. in *Moby-Dick*. Ed. Harrison Hayford and Hershel Parker. New York: Norton, 1967. 535–50.

———. *Herman Melville: Representative Selections*. Ed. Willard Thorp. New York: American Book, 1938.

———. *Journal of a Visit to Europe and the Levant, October 11, 1856–May 6, 1857*. Ed. Howard C. Horsford. Princeton: Princeton UP, 1955.

———. *Journal of a Visit to London and the Continent, by Herman Melville, 1849–1850*. Ed. Eleanor Melville Metcalf. Cambridge, MA: Harvard UP, 1948.

———. *The Letters of Herman Melville*. Ed. Merrell R. Davis and William H. Gilman. New Haven: Yale UP, 1960.

———. *Moby-Dick*. Ed. Harrison Hayford and Hershel Parker. New York: Norton, 1967.

———. *Moby-Dick*. Ed. Luther S. Mansfield and Howard P. Vincent. New York: Hendricks House, 1952.

———. *Pierre; or, The Ambiguities*. Ed. Henry A. Murray. New York: Hendricks House, 1949.

———. *Poems of Herman Melville*. Ed. Douglas Robillard. New Haven: College and UP, 1976.

———. *Redburn, White-Jacket, Moby-Dick*. New York: Library of America, 1983.

———. *Selected Poems of Herman Melville*. Ed. Hennig Cohen. Carbondale: Southern Illinois UP, 1964.

———. *Selected Writings of Herman Melville*. Ed. Jay Leyda. New York: Random House, 1952.

———. *Typee, Omoo, Mardi*. New York: Library of America, 1982.

———. "'Weeds and Wildings Chiefly: With a Rose or Two' By Herman Melville. Reading Text and Genetic Text, Edited from the Manuscript, with Introduction." Ed. Robert Charles Ryan. Diss. Northwestern U, 1967.

———. *The Writings of Herman Melville: The Northwestern-Newberry Edition*. Ed. Harrison Hayford, Hershel Parker, G. Thomas Tanselle, et al. 11 vols. Evanston: Northwestern UP, 1968–. [Volumes published so far are: *Typee* (1968), *Omoo* (1968), *Mardi* (1970), *Redburn* (1969), *White-Jacket* (1970), *Moby-Dick* (1988), *Pierre* (1971), *The Piazza Tales and Other Prose Pieces, 1839–1860* (1987), *Israel Potter* (1982), *The Confidence-Man* (1984), *Journals* (1989).]

Metcalf, Eleanor Melville. *Herman Melville: Cycle and Epicycle*. 1953. Westport, CT: Greenwood, 1970.

———, ed. Notes. *Journal of a Visit to London and the Continent, by Herman Melville, 1849–1850*. Cambridge, MA: Harvard UP, 1948.

Metropolitan Museum of Art. "John F. Kensett." In *American Paradise: The World of the Hudson River School*. New York: Metropolitan Museum of Art, 1987.

Milder, Robert. "*Nemo Contra Deum* . . . : Melville and Goethe's 'Demonic.'" In Thompson and Lokke, *Ruined Eden* 205–44.

Miller, Edwin Haviland. *Melville*. New York: Persea, 1975.

Moers, Ellen. "Mme de Staël and the Woman of Genius." *The American Scholar* 44 (Spring 1975): 225–41.

Mollaret, H., and J. Brossollet. "Á propos 'Pestiférés de Jaffa' de A. J. Gros." *Jaarboek 1968*. Koninklijk Museum voor Schone Kunsten, Antwerp.

Moore, Maxine. *That Lonely Game: Melville, Mardi, and the Almanac*. Columbia: U of Missouri P, 1975.

Moore, Richard S. *That Cunning Alphabet: Melville's Aesthetics of Nature*. Amsterdam: Rodopi, 1982.

Morgan, Lady. *The Life and Times of Salvator Rosa*. 2 vols. London: Colburn, 1824.

Murray, A. S. *A History of Greek Sculpture Under Pheidias and His Successors*. 2 vols. London: John Murray, 1883.

Naval Documents of the American Revolution. Ed. William Bell Clark. Washington: Naval History Center, Department of the Navy, 1964–.

Nevius, Blake. *Cooper's Landscapes: An Essay on the Picturesque Vision*. Berkeley: U of California P, 1976.

The New International Illustrated Encyclopedia of Art. New York: Greystone, 1970.

Noble, Louis Legrande. *The Course of Empire, Voyage of Life and Other Pictures of Thomas Cole, N. A. with Selections from His Letters and Miscellaneous Writings*. New York: Cornish, Lamport and Co., 1853.

Novak, Barbara. "Influences and Affinities: The Interplay between America and Europe in Landscape Painting before 1860." In *The Shaping of Art and Architecture in Nineteenth-Century America*. New York: Metropolitan Museum of Art, 1972.

——. *Nature and Culture: American Landscape and Painting, 1825–75*. New York: Oxford UP, 1980.

O'Connor, William Van. *The Grotesque: An American Genre and Other Essays*. Carbondale: Southern Illinois UP, 1962.

Osiakovski, Stanislav. "A History of Robert Macaire and Daumier's Place in It." *Burlington Magazine* (Nov. 1958): 388–92.

Passeron, Roger. *Daumier: Témoin de son temps*. Paris: Bib. des Arts, 1979.

Penny Cyclopaedia. 30 vols. London: Charles Knight and Co., 1833–58.

Peterson, Merrell D. *The Jefferson Image in the American Mind*. New York: Oxford, 1960.

Plaidy, Jean. *A Triptych of Poisoners*. London: Robert Hale and Co., 1970.

Poenicke, Klaus. "A View from the Piazza: Herman Melville and the Legacy of the European Sublime." *Comparative Literature Studies* 4 (1967): 267–81.

Pops, Leonard Martin. *The Melville Archetype*. Kent, OH: Kent State UP, 1970.

Powers, William. "Bulkington as Henry Chatillon." *Western American Literature* 3 (1968): 153–55.

Price, Martin. "The Picturesque Moment." *From Sensibility to Romanticism: Essays Presented to Frederick A. Pottle*. Ed. Frederick W. Hilles and Harold Bloom. New York: Oxford UP, 1965. 259–92.

Pütz, Manfred. "The Narrator as Audience: Ishmael as Reader and Critic in *Moby-Dick*." *Studies in the Novel* 19 (Summer 1987): 160–74.

Ramus, Charles F., ed. *Daumier: 120 Great Lithographs*. New York: Dover, 1978.

Rey, Robert. *Honoré Daumier*. Trans. Norbert Guterman. New York: Abrams, [1966].

Reynolds, David S. *Beneath the American Renaissance: The Subversive Imagination in the Age of Emerson and Melville*. New York: Knopf, 1988.

Reynolds, Sir Joshua. *Discourses on Art*. Ed. Robert R. Wark. 2nd ed. New Haven: Yale UP, 1975.

Reynolds, Larry J. "Melville's Catskill Eagle." *Melville Society Extracts* 64 (Nov. 1985): 11–12.

Richardson, E. P. *Painting in America: From 1502 to the Present.* New York: Thomas Y. Crowell, 1956.

[Richter], Jean Paul. "On the Ludicrous." Trans. George Adler. *The Literary World* 220 (April 19, 1851): 309.

Ringe, Donald A. *The Pictorial Mode: Space and Time in the Art of Bryant, Irving, and Cooper.* Lexington: U of Kentucky P, 1971.

Robillard, Douglas. "Melville's *Clarel* and the Parallel of Poetry and Painting." *North Dakota Quarterly* 51 (Spring 1983): 107–20.

———. "The Metaphysics of Melville's Indian Hating." *Essays in Arts and Sciences* 10 (May 1981): 51–58.

———, ed. *Poems of Herman Melville.* New Haven: College and UP, 1976.

———. "The Visual Arts in Melville's *Redburn*." *Essays in Arts and Sciences* 12 (March 1983): 43–60.

Robson-Scott, W. D. *The Younger Goethe and the Visual Arts.* Cambridge: Cambridge UP, 1981.

Rogers, Franklin R. *Painting and Poetry.* Lewisburg, PA: Bucknell UP, 1985.

Rogers, Nathaniel Peabody. *A Collection from the Newspaper Writings of Nathaniel Peabody Rogers.* Concord: J. R. French, 1847.

Rogin, Michael Paul. *Subversive Genealogy: The Politics and Art of Herman Melville.* New York: Knopf, 1983.

Rosenberry, Edward H. "Melville's Comedy and Tragedy." In Bryant, *A Companion* 603–24.

Ross, Stephanie. "The Picturesque: An Eighteenth-Century Debate." *Journal of Aesthetics and Art Criticism* 46 (1987): 271–79.

Rowland, Beryl. "Grace Church and Melville's Story of 'The Two Temples,'" *Nineteenth-Century Fiction* 28 (Dec. 1973): 339–46.

Ruskin, John. *Aratra Pentelici: Six Lectures on the Elements of Sculpture.* New York: John Wiley and Son, 1878.

———. *Modern Painters.* 5 vols. New York: John Wiley and Son, 1860–62; 1873.

———. *The Works of John Ruskin.* Ed. E. T. Cook and Alexander Wedderburn. 39 vols. London: George Allen, 1903–12.

Russell, H. Diane. *Claude Lorrain: 1600–1682.* New York: George Braziller, 1982.

Ryder, Frank G. Introduction. *George Ticknor's The Sorrows of Young Werther.* By Johann Wolfgang von Goethe. Chapel Hill: U of North Carolina P, 1952.

Schless, Howard H. "Flaxman, Dante, and Melville's *Pierre*." *Bulletin of the New York Public Library* 64 (Feb. 1960): 65–82.

———. "Moby Dick and Dante: A Critique and Time Scheme." *Bulletin of the New York Public Library* 65 (May 1961): 289–312.

Scott, Jonathan. *Piranesi.* New York: St. Martin's, 1875.

Scott, Sumner W. D. *The Whale in Moby-Dick.* Diss. U of Chicago, 1950.

Sealts, Merton M., Jr. *The Early Lives of Herman Melville.* Madison: U of Wisconsin P, 1974.

———. *Melville as Lecturer.* Cambridge, MA: Harvard UP, 1957.

———. *Melville's Reading: A Check-List of Books Owned and Borrowed.* 1966. Rev. ed. Columbia: U of South Carolina P, 1988.

———. *Pursuing Melville, 1940–1980.* Madison: U of Wisconsin P, 1982.

Shanes, Eric. *Turner's Rivers, Harbors, and Coasts.* London: Chatto and Windus, 1981.

The Shaping of Art and Architecture in Nineteenth-Century America. New York: Metropolitan Museum of Art, 1972.

Shepard, Paul. *Man in the Landscape: A Historic View of the Esthetics of Nature.* New York: Knopf, 1967.

Shesgreen, Sean, ed. *Engravings by Hogarth: 101 Prints.* New York: Dover, 1973.

Shneidman, Edwin S. "The Deaths of Herman Melville." *Melville and Hawthorne in the Berkshires: A Symposium.* Melville Annual 1966. Ed. Howard P. Vincent. Kent, OH: Kent State UP, 1968. 118–43.

Short, Bryan C. "Form as Vision in Herman Melville's *Clarel.*" *American Literature* 50 (Jan. 1979): 553–69.

———. "'Memory's Mint': Melville's Parable of the Imagination in *John Marr and Other Sailors.*" *Essays in Arts and Sciences* 15 (June 1986): 31–42.

Shurr, William H. *The Mystery of Iniquity: Melville as Poet, 1857–1891.* Lexington: U of Kentucky P, 1972.

Small, Harold A., ed. *Form and Function: Remarks on Art by Horatio Greenough.* Berkeley: U of California P, 1947.

Snow, Edward A. *A Study of Vermeer.* Berkeley: U of California P, 1979.

Spanos, William V. "The 'Nameless Horror': The Errant Art of Herman Melville and Charles Hewitt." *Boundary* 9 (1980): 127–39.

Spaulding, John H. *Historical Relics of the White Mountains.* Mt. Washington, NH: J. R. Hitchcock, 1855.

Stanley, Arthur Penrhyn. *Sinai and Palestine in Connection with Their History.* 2nd ed. London: John Murray, 1856.

Star, Morris. "Melville's Use of the Visual Arts." Diss. Northwestern U, 1964.

Steegmuller, Francis. *The Two Lives of James Jackson Jarves.* New Haven: Yale UP, 1951.

Stein, Roger B. *John Ruskin and Aesthetic Thought in America, 1840–1900.* Cambridge: Harvard UP, 1967.

Stein, William Bysshe. "Melville's Comedy of Faith." *ELH* 27 (Dec. 1960): 315–33.

———. *The Poetry of Melville's Late Years: Time, History, Myth, and Religion.* Albany: State U of New York P, 1970.

Stephens, James Lloyd. *Incidents of Travel in Egypt, Arabia Petrae, and the Holy Land.* New York: Harper & Brothers, 1837.

Stern, Milton R., ed. Introduction. *Billy Budd, Sailor: An Inside Narrative.* By Herman Melville. Indianapolis: Bobbs-Merrill, 1975.

Stewart, Randall. "Melville and Hawthorne." In Hillway and Mansfield 153–64.

Symmons, Sarah. *Daumier.* London: Oresko, 1979.

Thackeray, W. M. "Caricatures and Lithography in Paris." *The Paris Sketch Book, by Mr. Titmarsh.* By William Makepeace Thackeray. London: Dicks, 1840. 60–69.

Thiel, Pieter J. J. van, et al. *All the Paintings of the Rijksmuseum in Amsterdam: A Completely Illustrated Catalogue.* Amsterdam: The Museum, 1976.

Thompson, G. R. and V. L. Lokke, eds. *Ruined Eden of the Present: Hawthorne, Melville, and Poe: Critical Essays in Honor of Darrell Abel.* West Lafayette, IN: Purdue UP, 1981.

Thompson, James Matthew. *Napoleon Bonaparte: His Rise and Fall.* Oxford: Basil Blackwell, 1958.

Thompson, Lawrance. *Melville's Quarrel with God.* Princeton: Princeton UP, 1952.

Thomson, Philip. *The Grotesque.* London: Methuen, 1972.

Thomson, W[illiam]. M. *The Land and The Book; or, Biblical Illustrations . . . of the Holy Land.* 2 vols. New York: Harper & Brothers, 1858.

———. *The Land and The Book; or, Biblical Illustrations . . . of the Holy Land: Southern Palestine and Jerusalem.* New York: Harper & Brothers, 1880.

Thorp, Willard, ed. *Herman Melville: Representative Selections.* New York: American Book, 1938.

Tobey, G. B. *A History of Landscape Architecture: The Relationship of People to Environment.* New York: American Elsevier, 1973.

Torgovnick, Marianna. *The Visual Arts, Pictorialism, and the Novel.* Princeton: Princeton UP, 1985.

Transactions of the Apollo Association, 1842. New York: Charles Vinten, 1842.

Trimpi, Helen P. "Harlequin-Confidence Man: The Satirical Tradition of Commedia Dell'Arte and Pantomime in Melville's *The Confidence-Man.*" *Texas Studies in Literature and Language* 16.1 (1974): 147–93.

———. *Melville's Confidence Men and American Politics in the 1850s.* Transactions of the Connecticut Academy of Arts and Sciences. Vol 49: 1–339. Hamden, CT: Archon-Shoe String, 1987.

———. "Melville's Use of Witchcraft and Demonology in *Moby-Dick.*" *Journal of the History of Ideas,* 30.4 (1969): 543–62.

Valéry, Paul. *Degas, Manet, Morisot.* Bollingen Series 45. Vol. 12. *Collected Works of Paul Valéry.* Ed. Jackson Mathews. New York: Pantheon, 1960.

Vaughn, William. *Romantic Art.* London: Thames and Hudson, 1978.

Vetrocq, Marcia E. *Domenico Tiepolo's Punchinello Drawings.* Introduction by Adelheid M. Gealt. Bloomington: Indiana U Art Museum, 1979.

Vincent, Howard P. *Daumier and His World.* Evanston: Northwestern UP, 1968.

———. *The Trying-Out of Moby-Dick.* Boston: Houghton Mifflin, 1949.

Volney, Constantin François Chasseboeuf, Comte de. *Volney's Ruins; or, Meditation on the Revolutions of Empires.* Boston: Charles Gaylord, 1840.

Wallace, Robert K. "Melville's Prints and Engravings at the Berkshire Athenaeum." *Essays in Arts and Sciences* 15 (June 1986): 59–90.

———. "New Evidence for Melville's Use of Turner in *Moby-Dick.*" *Melville Society Extracts* 67 (Sept. 1986): 4–9. [Reprints condensed version of "'The Sultry Creator of Captain Ahab'" from *Turner Studies.*]

———. "'The Sultry Creator of Captain Ahab': Herman Melville and J. M. W. Turner." *Turner Studies* 5 (Winter 1985): 2–19.

Wenke, John. "'Ontological Heroics': Melville's Philosophical Art." In Bryant, *A Companion* 567–601.

Wheeler, Michael. *The Art of Allusion in Victorian Fiction.* New York: Barnes and Noble, 1979.

Willey, Benjamin. *Incidents in White Mountain History.* Boston: Nathaniel Noyes, 1856.

Wilton-Ely, John, cataloguer. *Piranesi.* London: Arts Council of Great Britain, 1978.

Wimsatt, William K., Jr. "Samuel Johnson and Dryden's *Du Fresnoy.*" *Studies in Philology* 48 (1951): 26–39.

Winckelmann, Johann Joachim. *The History of Ancient Art.* Trans. G. Henry Lodge. 2 vols. Boston: Munroe, 1849.

Winner, Viola Hopkins. *Henry James and the Visual Arts.* Charlottesville: U of Virginia P, 1970.

Witemeyer, Hugh. *George Eliot and the Visual Arts.* New Haven: Yale UP, 1979.

Wolf, Bryan. "When is a Painting Most Like a Whale?: Ishmael, *Moby-Dick,* and the Sublime." In Brodhead, *New Essays* 143–72.

The Works of Eminent Masters, in Painting, Sculpture, Architecture, and Decorative Art. 2 vols. London: John Cassell, 1854.

Wright, Christopher. *Poussin's Paintings: A Catalogue Raisonné.* London: Hippocrene Books, 1985.

Wright, Nathalia. "Biblical Allusion in Melville's Prose." *American Literature* 12 (May 1940): 185–99.

Yannella, Donald. "Writing the '*Other* Way': Melville, the Duyckinck Crowd, and Literature for the Masses." In Bryant, *A Companion* 63–81.

Yannella, Donald and Kathleen Malone Yannella. "Evert A. Duyckinck's Diary: May 29– Nov. 8, 1847." *Studies in the American Renaissance: 1978,* 207–58.

Yourcenar, Marguerite. *Memoirs of Hadrian.* New York: Modern Library, 1954; 1963; 1984.

Contributors

DENNIS BERTHOLD is professor of English at Texas A&M University where he currently directs the graduate program and teaches American literature. He is coauthor (with Alfred Weber and Beth L. Lueck) of *Hawthorne's American Travel Sketches* (1989) and has written articles on Melville, Hawthorne, C. B. Brown, and other American authors.

JOHN BRYANT is associate professor of English at Hofstra University. He has published several articles on Melville in such journals as *American Literature, Nineteenth-Century Fiction, Philological Quarterly,* and *The New England Quarterly.* He is the editor of and contributor to *A Companion to Melville Studies* and is currently working on a booklength study of Melville's comic sensibility, entitled *American Repose.* Professor Bryant is also the editor of the Melville Society *Extracts.*

GAIL COFFLER is associate professor of English at Suffolk University in Boston. Professor Coffler has also taught at the University of Kansas and, as a Fulbright Lecturer in American Literature, at Stuttgart University. She is the author of *Melville's Classical Allusions* (1985) and various published articles. A second reference book, *Melville's Allusions to Religion,* is forthcoming.

HENNIG COHEN is the John Welsh Centennial Professor in the History of Literature at the University of Pennsylvania. He has served as executive secretary of the American Studies Association and editor of its journal, *American Quarterly,* and as secretary and president of the Melville Society. He has a special interest in Melville's use of the visual arts and in his poetry. His annotated edition of *Israel Potter* is in press.

JOHN M. J. GRETCHKO is a literary detective and businessman who has contributed articles to *Essays in Arts and Sciences, Maladicta,* Melville Society *Extracts,* and *Studies in the American Renaissance.* He is the author of *Melvillean Ambiguities* (1990).

WYN KELLEY, currently a lecturer on the literature faculty at the Massachusetts Institute of Technology, has also taught at Stanford and Tufts. She has published essays on Melville and nineteenth-century culture, on colonial American literature, and on modern fiction in such journals as *American Literature, Partisan Review, RALS,* and *Essays in Arts and Sciences.* Currently she is writing a critical book entitled *Melville's City.*

323

SANFORD E. MAROVITZ is chair and professor of English at Kent State University. He has also taught at the University of Athens and at Shimane University in Japan. Coeditor of *Artful Thunder: Versions of the Romantic Tradition in American Literature in Honor of Howard P. Vincent* (1975) and cocompiler of *Bibliographical Guide to the Study of the Literature of the U.S.A.*, 5th ed. (1984), Professor Marovitz has published widely on nineteenth- and twentieth-century American literature. He holds special interests in Melville, the American Renaissance, American Jewish literature, and Western American writing.

BASEM L. RA'AD is an associate professor of English who has published in *ESQ, Literature East and West, American Speech, Modern Fiction Studies,* and elsewhere. His article, "'The Encantadas' and 'The Isle of the Cross': Melvillean Dubieties, 1856–57," appeared in the Spring 1991 issue of *American Literature.* Professor Ra'ad was involved in the research for *Bibliotheca Cisorientalis* and has a book in progress on Melville's landscape aesthetics.

DOUGLAS ROBILLARD is professor of English at the University of New Haven. He has edited a volume of Melville's poems and has published essays on a variety of American authors, including Melville, Hawthorne, Conrad Aiken, Mary Wilkins Freeman, and Edith Wharton. His edition of *The Kempton-Wace Letters,* by Jack London and Anna Strunsky, is forthcoming.

BRYAN C. SHORT has published articles on Melville, American literature, and rhetorical theory in *Texas Studies in Literature and Language, Arizona Quarterly, American Literature, Rhetoric Review,* and other journals and collections. His "Form as Vision in Herman Melville's *Clarel*" won the 1979 Norman Foerster Prize. Professor Short is also the author of a forthcoming book, *Cast by Means of Figures: Herman Melville's Rhetorical Development.* He is professor of English at Northern Arizona University.

CHRISTOPHER STEN is chair and professor of English at George Washington University, and has also served as Senior Fulbright Lecturer in American Literature at the University of Wurzburg. His articles on Melville and other American authors have appeared in *American Literature, Modern Language Quarterly, Studies in the Novel, Texas Studies in Literature and Language, Studies in American Fiction, American Studies International, On Melville: The Best from AMERICAN LITERATURE,* and elsewhere. He is currently completing a book on Melville's major-length fiction.

HELEN P. TRIMPI is an independent scholar and poet, who has taught most recently at the University of Alberta and at Michigan State University. Her book, *Melville's Confidence Men and American Politics in the 1850s,* appeared in 1987. She is currently completing a study to be titled, "Melville's Tragic Fiction," concerning the slavery controversy, and a study of poetic form, from the Greeks to the present, which will also include a series of poems on art. She lives in Palo Alto, California.

ROBERT K. WALLACE is Regents' Professor of Literature at Northern Kentucky University. His comparative works include *Jane Austen and Mozart* and *Emily Brontë and Beethoven.* His *Melville and Turner* is forthcoming.

Index

SAVAGE EYE

was composed in 10-point Sabon leaded two points
by Reporter Typographics, Inc.;
with display type set in Champion
by Dix Type Inc.;
printed by sheet-fed offset on 50-pound
Glatfelter Natural acid-free stock,
Smyth sewn and bound over 88-point binders boards
in ICG Arrestox B-grade cloth,
wrapped with dustjackets printed in two colors
on 80-pound enamel stock and film laminated
by BookCrafters, Inc.;
designed by Will Underwood;
and published by
THE KENT STATE UNIVERSITY PRESS
Kent, Ohio 44242